AF517930

Important Documents
on
Security and Diplomacy

Important Documents
on
Security and Diplomacy

Edited by

Arvind Gupta

Mukul Chaturvedi

and

Akshay Joshi

Published in collaboration with

National Security Council Secretariat

Manas Publications

New Delhi-110 002 (INDIA)

Manas Publications
(Publishers, Distributors, Importers & Exporters)
4858, Prahlad Street,
24, Ansari Road, Darya Ganj,
New Delhi - 110 002 (INDIA)
Ph.: 23260783, 23265523:, 23842660 (R)
Fax: 011-23272766
E-mail: manaspublications@vsnl.com

2005

ISBN 81-7049-248-3
Rs 995/-

Typeset at
Manas Publications

Printed in India at
Salasar Imaging Systems, Delhi
and Published by Mrs Suman Lata for
Manas Publications,
4858, Prahlad Street, 24,
Ansari Road, Darya Ganj,
New Delhi - 110 002 (INDIA)

Preface

The NSCS is happy to present the third yearly compilation of documents and speeches on security and diplomacy covering important developments in 2004.

The format of the compilation is similar to the one adopted in 2003. Part-1 (A&B) of the book deals with India's bilateral relations. It contains joint statements and speeches made by the Indian leaders. Part-2 (A&B) contains select international documents and speeches of international leaders. A short abstract has been added before each document. An exhaustive index at the end of the book will make referencing easier.

The year 2004 saw the general elections and change of government in India. On the foreign policy front, the Common Minimum Programme of the United Progressive Alliance (UPA) government announced on May 27, accorded highest priority to "building closer political, economic and other ties" with India's neighbours in South Asia and to strengthening SAARC. It also stated that "traditional ties with West Asia will be given a fresh thrust".

The leaders of India and Pakistan agreed to commence the process of the "composite dialogue" on January 6, 2004 after President Musharraf assured the Indian Prime Minister that "he will not permit any territory under Pakistan's control to be used to support terrorism in any manner". In a joint statement on September 8, the Foreign Ministers of the two countries reaffirmed their commitment to the principles of the UN and to implement the Simla Agreement "in letter and spirit". They agreed to implement the outcome of the August 2004 meeting of Defence Secretaries on Siachin and conduct a Joint Survey of the boundary pillars of the horizontal segment of the international border in Sir Creek area. Confidence Building Measures including the Srinagar-Muzzafarabad bus service and Munnabao-Khokhrapar rail link were also discussed.

In January 2004, the SAARC member states agreed to adopt necessary legal and administrative measures to suppress financing of terrorist acts and signed the framework agreement on SAFTA for broadening of economic cooperation. The Prime Minister conveyed India's willingness to make an initial contribution of US $ 100 million to a proposed SAARC poverty alleviation fund. At the BIMST-EC Summit in July 2004, he stressed the need for interconnectivity - physical, economic and technological - and identified the tri-lateral India-Myanmar-Thailand Highway and optical fibre telecommunication links as important projects.

India further strengthened its "strategic partnership" with Russia, the EU and the US. In December 2004, India and Russia expressed their determination to continue cooperation in the field of nuclear energy and development of new oil and gas fields. At the 5th India-EU Summit on November 8, India and the EU agreed to come up with a "comprehensive EU-India action plan for strategic partnership". On September 17, India and the US concluded Phase One of the Next Steps in Strategic Partnership (NSSP).

The Prime Minister expounded his vision for India from different platforms. In his address to the nation on June 24, The Prime Minister reiterated the government's commitment to giving a "new deal" to rural India and emphasized the need to adopt a comprehensive approach to national security through greater synergy between intelligence agencies and internal security structures, civil-military interface and the use of technology for national security management. In his Independence Day speech, he urged political leaders to take "a national and a holistic view" of managing water resources and pay special attention to governance in the North East and J&K. He identified agriculture, water, education, health care, employment, urban renewal and infrastructure as the seven priority sectors for focused attention.

India's views on nuclear issues, non-proliferation and disarmament were expressed at various fora. Addressing the UNGA on September 23, the Prime Minister stressed the need for evolving "a more cooperative and consensual international security order" which must differentiate between states whose actions strengthen non-proliferation and those that weaken them. In a speech at the Council on Foreign Relations in the US in September 2004, the PM emphasized that real partnership between India and the US "requires more than just a shared commitment to democracy". He believed that the time was ripe for US to seriously consider further enhancing the partnership on major international issues like nuclear non-proliferation and arms control by recognizing India's due place in global councils.

The threat posed by other non-conventional security threats like global warming, flu pandemic and India's approach to information security were also highlighted at different fora.

2004 was an important year for global non-proliferation. In a speech at the National Defence University in February 2004, President Bush made seven proposals to deal with proliferation of WMDs. In April 2004, the UN Security Council passed Resolution 1540 that called on states to refrain from providing support to non-state actors in the development, acquisition or use of weapons of mass destruction and their means of delivery. While supporting the passage of the resolution, India's Permanent Representative to the UN stated that "on our part, we shall not accept any interpretation of the resolution that imposes obligations arising from treaties that India has not signed or ratified...". The G-8 Action Plan on Non-Proliferation of June 2004, called for new actions to reduce the risk of proliferation while allowing the world to enjoy the benefits of peaceful nuclear technology.

The EU-3 continued to engage Iran in negotiations regarding its nuclear programme. Successive IAEA Resolutions called on Iran to take necessary steps to help resolve all outstanding questions. This finally led to Iran's "voluntary" suspension of all enrichment and reprocessing activities as a "non-legally binding confidence building measure" on 29 November, 2004.

China and Russia signed an agreement on October 14, to mark "the complete identification of the trend of the 4300 km long China-Russia border line". The UNSC passed resolution 1546 in June 2004 endorsing the formation of a "sovereign interim government of Iraq" by 30th June.

The high level panel on UN reform submitted its report to the UN Secretary General in November, 2004. The panel suggested two options, to increase the size of the Security Council from 15 to 24 members. Model A recommended inducting 6 new permanent members and 3 new non-permanent members and Model B recommended inducting 8 'semi-permanent' members with a renewable terms of four years and one new non-permanent member.

Since the texts of the documents have been taken from various open sources, the NSCS does not take the responsibility for the accuracy of the contents.

Thanks are due to Shri S.S. Paul, Senior Systems Analyst, for the assistance rendered in compiling the documents.

We hope that this book will prove useful to researchers, analysts, and students of international affairs.

Arvind Gupta
Mukul Chaturvedi
Akshay Joshi

Contents

India-UK

India-US

SAARC

Other

Part 1 B

Speeches delivered by Indian leaders

President of India

Prime Minister

External Affairs Minister

National Security Advisor

Foreign Secretary

Dy. to the National Security Advisor

India's Permanent Representative at the United Nations

Others

Part 2 A

Documents International

Part 2 B

Speeches delivered by International leaders

Part 1 A
Documents India

❮1❯

Joint Declaration on ASEAN-India Partnership for Peace, Progress and Shared Prosperity (30.11.2004)

> Realising that cooperation between ASEAN and India is essential for promoting peace, stability, development and prosperity in Asia and the world, both sides agreed to promote a long term cooperative partnership by adopting a Plan of Action to implement specific activities and projects.

We, the Heads of State/Government of Brunei Darussalam, the Kingdom of Cambodia (Cambodia), the Republic of Indonesia (Indonesia), the Lao People's Democratic Republic (Lao DPR), Malaysia, the Union of Myanmar (Myanmar), the Republic of the Philippines (the Philippines), the Republic of Singapore (Singapore), the Kingdom of Thailand (Thailand) and the Socialist Republic of Vietnam (Vietnam), Member Countries of the Association of Southeast Asian Nations (collectively, "ASEAN" or "ASEAN Member Countries", or individually, "ASEAN Member Country"), and the Republic of India (India) gathered in Vientiane, Lao PDR, on 30th November 2004 for the 3rd ASEAN-India Summit;

ADHERING to the principles and purposes of the Charter of the United Nations, the Five Principles of Peaceful Co-existence and other universally recognised principles of international law;

REAFFIRMING our faith in, and respect for, each other's independence, sovereignty, territorial integrity, non-interference in the internal affairs of other states, mutual respect and mutual benefit;

BOUND TOGETHER by our shared rich and valuable heritage of civilization, culture, and peaceful economic and social interaction and linkages extending over two millennia as well as by the pluralistic, multi-religious and culturally diverse nature of our respective societies;

NOTING with deep satisfaction that the close cooperative and multifaceted partnership, which our countries have fostered, encompassing the political, security, economic, scientific and technological, human resource development, social, cultural and other areas of mutual interest that provides a solid foundation for taking the ASEAN-India partnership to greater heights and new areas;

DETERMINED to optimally utilize our talented and youthful human and rich natural resources, and more competencies in many state-of-the-art technologies and knowledge-based industries;

CONVINCED that ASEAN-India cooperation serves the essential interests of their peoples and is essential for promoting peace, stability, development and prosperity in Asia and the world;

ASPIRING to play a more active role and to meet the political, economic, social and other challenges facing our region in the coming decades, and in helping to shape the world of the 21st century;

RECALLING the Joint Statement issued after the 1st ASEAN-India Summit Meeting in Phnom Penh in November 2002 and the agreements and understandings reached during the 2nd ASEAN-India Summit Meeting in Bali in October 2003; and

ATTACHING great significance to the Framework Agreement on Comprehensive Economic Cooperation between ASEAN and India signed in Bali for realizing the full potential of ASEAN-India Regional Trade and Investment Area (RTIA) and economic cooperation.

HEREBY commit ourselves to:

- Foster friendship, good neighbourliness, peaceful co-existence and prosperity in the region;
- Promote a long term co-operative partnership based on equality, shared ownership and mutual respect which will enable us to impart synergies to our respective strengths and complementarities to achieve our respective long-term national and regional development goals;
- Cooperate in a coordinated manner to accelerate and mutually reinforce sustainable growth and development of our economies towards shared prosperity, poverty alleviation and reduction of social disparities, to enable our people to enjoy unhindered access to opportunities for development;
- Co-operate in strengthening the UN system, including support for early reforms of the United Nations and the Bretton Woods institutions to make them more democratic and responsive to the priorities of its member states particularly, the developing countries;
- Co-operate in other multilateral fora, in particular the WTO, greater equity and greater benefits from globalization for the developing countries;
- Jointly address the common challenges to our comprehensive political and economic security, including food, human and energy security;
- Cooperate in combating the menace of international terrorism and other transnational crimes such as trafficking in drugs, arms smuggling, human trafficking particularly in women and children, cyber crimes,

international economic crimes, environmental crimes, sea piracy and money laundering, through effective institutional linkages and programmes of co-operation giving priority to information exchange and capacity building;

- Collaborate in areas of general and complete disarmament, and in the non-proliferation of weapons of mass destruction under strict and effective international control;
- Take full advantage of the geographical contiguity of Southeast Asia and India and synergise the strengths of these two significant economic regions to act as powerful engines of growth;
- Give high priority to development of regional infrastructure and road, rail, sea and air transportation links to increase physical connectivity that would facilitate greater movement of goods and people;
- Facilitate travel and tourism between ASEAN and India by developing links of tourist centres to enhance synergies of tourism destinations;
- Promote co-operation in science and technology, in particular information development and commercialization of new technologies;
- Work through both conventional and innovative trade and economic arrangements, and full implementation of the ASEAN-India free trade area by 2011 for ASEAN-5 and India, 2016 for the Philippines and India and by 2011 by India and 2016 by the 4 new ASEAN Members Countries, including the early implementation of the Early Harvest Programme, to achieve freer movement of goods, services, investment, and co-operation in other economic areas;

  Reiterate full support for the implementation of the Declaration of ASEAN Concord II, leading to the formation of a more integrated ASEAN Community comprising the ASEAN Security Community, the ASEAN Economic Community and the ASEAN Socio-Cultural Community;
- Co-operate to help bridge the development gap among various regions and countries, including through support to the Initiative for ASEAN Integration and sub-regional growth areas in ASEAN, and cooperation schemes between ASEAN Member Countries and India;
- Promote co-operation in human resource development, through capacity building, strengthening of institutions, training and entrepreneurship development focusing on small and medium enterprises;
- Promote people-to-people exchange involving, among others, parliamentarians, youth, artists, sportspersons and representatives from business, industry, media, academic and think-tank institutions; and
- Preserve our cultural heritage, and promote cultural co-operation for better understanding and friendship among our peoples.

Institutional and Funding arrangements for implementation:

To realize the objectives of the ASEAN-India Partnership, the following measures will be taken:

- ASEAN and India will implement specific activities and projects as contained in the attached Plan of Action;
- ASEAN and India will strengthen the existing funding mechanisms, including the ASEAN-India Co-operation Fund, for effective co-operation and implementation of the ASEAN-India Partnership and Plan of Action;
- ASEAN and India are committed to providing requisite resources and in accordance with their respective capacities, including mutually exploring effective and innovative external resource mobilization efforts, to accomplish the various strategies and measures outlined in the Plan of Action;
- The progress made in the implementation of the ASEAN-India Partnership and the Plan of Action will be reviewed by the Senior Officials and the Foreign Ministers of ASEAN and India under the ASEAN-India Dialogue Relations; and
- The Plan of Action will be reviewed periodically taking into consideration the dynamic developments in the region and the world.

Signed in Vientiane, Lao PDR this Thirtieth Day of November in the Year Two Thousand and Four in two originals in the English language.

❮2❯

New Delhi Declaration between India and Brazil (27.01.2004)

> **Both sides agreed to strengthen bilateral relations by undertaking mutually beneficial cooperation in various sectors like high technology, industrial areas, trade relations, tourism, efforts to protect environment etc. The two sides also agreed to extend mutual support to each other for a permanent seat in an expanded UN Security Council and to extend multi-polarity at the international level.**

1. At the invitation of the President of India, H. E. Dr. A.P.J. Abdul Kalam, the President of the Federative Republic of Brazil, H. E. Mr. Luiz Inácio Lula da Silva, paid a State Visit to India from January 25-28, 2004 and was the Chief Guest on the 55th Republic Day functions. Besides the First Lady, the President of Brazil was accompanied by the Minister of External Relations, Ambassador Celso Luiz Nunes Amorim, Minister of Development, Industry and Foreign Trade, Mr. Luis Fernando Furlan, Minister of Planning, Mr. Guido Mantega, Ministser of Tourism, Mr. Walfrido Mares Guia, the Chairman of the Brazil-India Parliamentary Friendship Group in the Brazilian Congress, Mr. Abelardo Lupion as well as other Congressmen and representatives of the private sector.
2. Within the framework of the visit, H. E. Mr. Luiz Inácio Lula da Silva held fruitful discussions with H.E. Dr. A.P.J. Abdul Kalam, the President of the Republic of India, H.E. Mr. A.B. Vajpayee, Prime Minister of India. Minister of External Affairs of India, Mr. Yashwant Sinha, Minister of Defence Mr. George Fernandes, Minister of Commerce and Industry, Mr. Arun Jaitley and the Leader of the Opposition in the Lok Sabha, Mrs. Sonia Gandhi, called on President Mr. Luiz Inácio Lula da Silva.
3. Brazil and India agreed that the visit to India of President Luiz Inácio Lula da Silva as Chief Guest on the occasion of the Republic Day signaled a new phase in bilateral relations given the common determination to fully utilize the substantial potential and opportunities for deepening mutually beneficial cooperation, to promote socio-economic development and prosperity of both India and Brazil, to strengthen multi-polarity at the international level and to enhance the positive factors of globalisation.

4. During the wide-ranging discussions held in a friendly and cordial atmosphere, both sides exchanged views on various bilateral, regional and international issues of mutual interest.
5. Both sides noted with satisfaction that India-Brazil relations, which have a strong historical basis, are marked by cordiality and a high degree of understanding and close proximity on current principal issues. Both sides reiterated their desire to strengthen bilateral relations based on the close ties between the two countries.
6. Both sides agreed that personnel exchanges and friendly contacts between Ministries, Parliament and political parties of the two countries should be further enhanced.
7. India noted the achievements of Brazil in contributing to the strengthening of Latin American regional organizations such as MERCOSUR and ALADI. Brazil noted India's contributions to strengthening regional and sub-regional organizations like SAARC and BIMST-EC and its increasing close cooperation with ASEAN. In this connection, both sides recognized that considerable potential exists for India and Brazil to undertake mutually beneficial cooperation with each other in various sectors.
8. Brazil and India are countries with rich untapped natural resources and emerging infrastructural requirements. Given their varied experience in high technology and industrial areas, they could, in a spirit of South-South cooperation, share expertise in areas such as railways, highways, waterways and aviation as well as in other priority areas identified by them.
9. Brazil and India expressed their satisfaction about the evolution of their bilateral trade, which over the last two years, reached a level higher than US$ 1 billion per annum. However, they also recognise that, in view of the size of the economies of both countries, there is a wide scope to enlarge bilateral exchanges and reciprocal investments, and that there is a vast potential for the integration of their production systems. In his meeting with Prime-Minister A. B. Vajpayee, President Luiz Inácio Lula da Silva praised advances made by the Indian pharmaceutical industry, which is participating as a supplier of medicines for HIV/AIDS treatment for the National Health Programme of the Brazilian Government. Prime Minister Vajpayee mentioned the competence of the Brazilian aeronautical industry, recalling the recent purchase of Brazilian aircrafts by the Indian Government. Both Parties considered that the success achieved by both countries in pharmaceutical and aeronautical fields will serve as a model for other high-tech industries to emulate and to join the flow of bilateral commerce. Hence, they expressed satisfaction at the support being extended by the Confederation

of Indian Industries, the Indian Federation of Chambers of Commerce & Industry and Brazil-India Chamber of Commerce in bringing businessmen from both countries closer.

10. The two Governments expressed their satisfaction with the signing of the Preferential Trade Agreement between MERCOSUR and India and reiterated their priority they attach to the expeditious conclusion of its annexes, which will constitute an important stimulus for trade relations between India, Brazil, Argentina, Paraguay and Uruguay.

11. Both Parties recalled the visit of the Brazilian Defence Minister, Ambassador Jose Viegas Filho to New Delhi in December 2003, and the signing of a Defence Co-operation Agreement between India and Brazil on that occasion. The two countries will continue to consult each other in identifying projects of mutual interest.

12. The visit provided an opportunity for the first meeting of the India-Brazil Common Agenda for Environment which lays emphasis on the need for close co-ordination of positions between the delegations of the countries in multilateral fora related to environment and sustainable development. They welcomed the holding of the India-Brazil Ministerial Meeting on Sustainable Development with participation of governmental experts, academics, the private sector and representatives of civil society, which provided a forum for discussing issues for future bilateral cooperation in the area of cleaner production technologies.

13. Both parties welcomed the proposal of India to organize the first ever "Weeks of Indian Culture" in Brazil in the first half of 2005, the principal highlight of which would be an exhibition of Indian Art in the city of Sao Paulo. The Brazilian Government offered to encourage state level and private sector support for the Indian cultural events.

14. The following agreements were signed during this State Visit:-

(i) Co-operation Agreement in the field of Tourism between the Government of the Federative Republic of Brazil and the Government of the Republic of India.

(ii) Framework Agreement between the Government of the Federal Republic of Brazil and the Government of the Republic of India on Co-operation in the Peaceful Uses of Outer Space.

(iii) Agreement between the Government of the Republic of India and the Government of the Federative Republic of Brazil on Exemption of visa requirement for holders of Diplomatic and Official/Service Passports.

(iv) Cultural Exchange Programme between the Government of the Republic of India and the Government of the Federative Republic of Brazil for the Years 2004-2005.

(v) Programme of Cooperation between the Indian Space Research Organisation and the Brazilian Space Agency for the year 2004.

(vi) Preferential Trade Agreement between MERCOSUR and the Republic of India.

15. The Agreement on Co-operation in the Peaceful Uses of Outer Space provides for co-operation in areas like receiving and collecting data from the Indian Remote Sensing satellite through ground automatic platforms and ground infrastructure in Brazil, possibility of launching of the Brazilian micro-satellite EQUARAS from India and also covers cooperation in other areas of mutual interest.

16. Both sides emphasized the need for creating better awareness of each other's strengths within the private sector of the two countries. Trade missions would be undertaken and participation in trade/commercial exhibitions in both countries would be encouraged. In keeping with these objectives, they welcomed the intention of the apex Indian industry association, CII (Confederation of Indian Industry) to establish an office in Brazil.

17. India and Brazil face special and similar challenges in their efforts to protect the environment while simultaneously forging ahead with rapid social and economic development of their countries. In this context, the two sides agreed to work together in a practical manner to cooperate on preserving the environment and ensuring sustainable development and to coordinate positions on climate change, bio-diversity and other issues in relevant multilateral fora.

18. Both countries expressed concern over the non-entry into force of the Kyoto Protocol and emphasized the importance of UN-centred multilateral cooperation to combat climate change based on the principle of common but differentiated responsibilities among countries. The development of clean technologies was also identified as one of the most relevant means to combat the increase of greenhouse gases into the atmosphere which lead to global warming.

19. Both countries highlighted the importance of negotiating an international regime to promote and safeguard the fair and equitable sharing of benefits under the Convention on Biological Diversity. This should ensure that the benefits arising out of the commercial use of genetic resources would accrue to the countries of origin. They also emphasized the need for a legally binding instrument for protecting intellectual property rights to traditional knowledge and folklore. United by their shared interest in fulfilling the objectives of the Group of Like-Minded Mega-diverse developing countries, Brazil and India agreed to strengthen co-ordination and co-operation particularly during the period of the Indian presidency of the group, with emphasis on multilateral negotiations and in fostering activities related to South-South Co-operation.

20. Both sides reaffirmed their commitment to promote the formation of an equitable multi-polar world order based on the principles of rule of law and equality, territorial integrity and non-interference in domestic affairs of States with a view to removing threats to stability and international security.

21. Brazil and India, being large democracies, and developing countries of continental size, have been playing a constructive rolé in international affairs and maintaining friendly relations with other countries. They are both committed towards a just and equitable international order. The two countries are unique in their respective regions and in the global sphere in view of their similarities and profile and potential. Considering these commonalities and convergences, the partnership between the two countries is natural.

22. Both sides strongly opposed unilateral use or the threat of use of force in violation of the UN Charter, as well as interference in internal affairs of other states.

23. The two sides acknowledged the vital importance of the role of the United Nations in world peace, stability and development. They are determined to continue their efforts in strengthening the UN system as the central mechanism for ensuring international peace and security as well as democratizing international relations. They reiterated their support for the need to reform the UN, particularly the expansion of the UN Security Council and reform of the Economic and Social Council. They stressed, in particular, the need for equitable balance in the expanded Security Council to provide a constructive voice to the aspirations of the developing countries. They believed that piecemeal and discriminatory approaches to such expansion will be inconsistent with the objectives of that world body. Both Governments share the understanding that the UNSC reform should result in the increase of its permanent as well as non-permanent membership, with greater participation of the developing countries in both categories. Considering that India and Brazil are large democracies and developing countries of continental size, that have been making contributions to the promotion of peace, the two countries extend mutual support to each other as appropriate, strong and deserving candidates for a permanent seat in an expanded UN Security Council.

24. India and Brazil, as two vibrant democracies, recognized the serious threat of terrorism confronting democracies and open societies. The two sides affirmed that international terrorism is a threat to peace and security, a grave violation of human rights and a crime against humanity. They affirmed that terrorism cannot be justified in any form, for any cause, on any political, ideological, philosophical, racial, ethnic, religious,

social or economic grounds. They agreed that the fight against terrorism by the international community has to be global, comprehensive and a sustained one, with the ultimate objective of eradication of terrorism in all regions. In this context, both Governments expressed their conviction that transnational organised crime, illegal traffic of weapons, narcotics and drugs and terrorism in all its forms and manifestations should be combated through the co-ordinated action of members of the international community, together with concerned international organisations, based on respect for national sovereignty and International Law.

25. The Brazilian side appreciated the evolving security concerns of India in the light of recent local, regional and global developments. It appreciated the initiatives taken by India to resume diplomatic relations with Pakistan. In this connection, the Brazilian side supported the peaceful resolution of differences between India and Pakistan through bilateral dialogue. The Brazilian side welcomes the recent Indo-Pak Joint Statement at Islamabad. In this context, Brazil supports the peaceful resolution of differences between India and Pakistan through a sustained and productive dialogue in an atmosphere free from terrorism, addressing all issues.

26. Both Governments reaffirmed their commitment to uphold the principles of the Doha Development Agenda of WTO and to their membership of the G-20. They viewed the results of the Ministerial meeting of the Group in December 2003 in Brasilia as an eloquent manifestation of the desire of G-20 members to continue to co-ordinate their positions that reflect the vital interests of the developing countries in the search for a just and equitable international trading system. Both Governments reiterated their commitment to multiateralism, and confidence in the success of the Doha Round of negotiations.

27. Brazil and India reiterated their commitment to making India-Brazil-South Africa (IBSA) Dialogue Forum a creative and operative forum. They expressed the hope that the First Meeting of the Trilateral Commission, in March 2004 in New Delhi will constitute an important landmark for launching concrete projects of trilateral co-operation in various areas of the Dialogue Forum. In this context, they also considered that the exchange of information and proposals made in New Delhi on January 6 was an important step for identifying concrete projects of trilateral cooperation for the benefit of the socially vulnerable populations of the three countries. They also highlighted the importance of the approval of IBSA Financial Fund under the UN Development Programme (UNDP) by the three countries, which will finance the implementation of successful social and economic programmes in other developing countries who want to repeat such experiences.

28. Brazil and India reiterated that efforts to eradicate hunger and poverty which still exists in some parts of the world is a multi-dimensional task that calls for coordinated action at national and international levels including through employment generation, access to education for all, food security, improved health standards and sustainable development for the benefit of their peoples as well as those of other developing countries. In this context, they emphasised their commitment to adopting policy measures in conformity with the goals set at UN Millennium Summit and for according priority to the promotion of social equity and inclusiveness, as mentioned in the Brasilia Declaration.
29. The President of Brazil, H.E. Mr. Luiz Inacio Lula da Silva extended invitations to the President of the Republic of India, H.E. Dr. A.P.J. Abdul Kalam, and to the Prime Minister of the Republic of India, H.E. Mr. A.B. Vajpayee, to visit Brazil at an early date. The invitations were accepted with pleasure. The dates of the visits would be finalized through diplomatic channels.
30. On behalf of the Government and the people of Brazil, H.E. President Mr. Luiz Inacio Lula da Silva expressed sincere thanks to the Government of the Republic of India for all the hospitality extended to him and his delegation and the excellent arrangements made for their visit to India.

❮3❯

Joint Press Statement for 5th India-EU Summit (08.11.2004)

> The two sides emphasized their commitment to democracy, pluralism and rule of law and to multilateralism in international relations. They agreed, inter alia, to come up with a "comprehensive EU-India Action Plan for a strategic partnership" and to work towards a mechanism to connect EU and Indian information network.

The 5th Summit between the EU and India was held in The Hague, The Netherlands, on 8 November 2004. The EU was represented by the President of the European Council, Dutch Prime Minister Dr. Jan Peter Balkenende, the President of the European Commission, Dr. Romano Prodi, the Secretary General/High Representative for Common Foreign and Security Policy Mr. Javier Solana, the Commissioner in charge of Trade Relations, Mr. Pascal Lamy, and the Netherlands Minister for Foreign Affairs, Dr. Bernard Bot. India was represented by the Prime Minister, Dr. Manmohan Singh, the External Affairs Minister, Mr. Natwar Singh, and the Commerce and Industry Minister, Mr. Kamal Nath.

The leaders sent the following message:

We express satisfaction with the excellent atmosphere of this Summit and the substantial results achieved over our agenda. This Summit has highlighted the considerable progress made in strengthening the EU-India relationship since our first Summit in 2000. We are particularly satisfied with the European Commission's Communication of June 2004 on an "EU-India Strategic Partnership", the Indian Response Paper of August 2004, the Conclusions of the Council of the EU on 11th October, 2004 and the Recommendation of the European Parliament of 28th October, 2004.

India and the EU representing the largest democracies in the world reiterate that their partnership is based on the sound foundation of shared values and beliefs. Our common commitment to democracy, pluralism and rule of law and to multilateralism in international relations, is a factor for global stability and peace. We recognise that our partnership has evolved over the years from economic and development cooperation, to acquire higher political and strategic dimensions, and that this should be further strengthened through more intensive dialogue.

1. We agree that in the immediate future we will take forward the implementation of key actions in the following areas, namely:
   - to jointly elaborate a comprehensive EU-India Action Plan for a strategic Partnership and a new Joint Political Declaration based on the Commission's Communication, the Council's Conclusions and India's response paper, for approval at the 6th Summit meeting;
   - to encourage the holding of regular, institutionalised parliamentary exchanges between the Indian Parliament and the European Parliament. We will also promote cooperation between political parties, trade unions, business associations, universities and civil societies;
   - to install a dialogue on disarmament and non-proliferation;
   - to consider regular exchange of views on possibilities for co-operation on themes like resolution of conflicts, peace operations and reconstruction;
   - to strengthen the flow of students and scholars between the EU and India through the funding of an India-specific scholarship programme under Erasmus Mundus;
   - to set up an Energy panel to coordinate joint efforts;
   - to organize joint workshops on automotive engineering, genomics and life sciences and nanotechnology.
   - to organize an EU-India environment forum to exchange views and information on issues of mutual interests, knowhow, technologies and on research and analyses of specific themes.
2. India welcomes the enlargement of the EU, the signing of the Treaty establishing a Constitution for Europe by the EU Heads of State and Government and the efforts to revitalise the Lisbon strategy to make Europe the world's most competitive economy by 2010. We affirm that deepening and widening of the EU should contribute to further strengthening of our relations.
3. The EU welcomes the policy initiatives the Indian Government made in the Common Minimum Programme and the abiding commitment of the Indian Government to economic reforms for stimulating growth, investment and employment.
4. We reviewed the developments since the last EU-India Summit in New Delhi on November 29, 2003. We express satisfaction on the progress made on the different elements mentioned in the Agenda for Action which was adopted at that Summit.
5. We agree to intensify co-operation and take action to facilitate and expand bilateral trade and investment flows, given the importance of realising the potential of the growing Indian and EU markets and the mutual benefits of increased economic interaction. We commit to pursue

issues key to increasing market access and creating an enabling economic environment.

6. We are encouraged by the holding of the first Steering Committee under the Science & Technology Agreement in March 2004 and the steps being taken to encourage greater co-operation in this domain vital to both communities.

7. We welcome the progress in the on-going discussion on the EU-India Draft Cooperation Agreement on the Galileo satellite navigation project. It will ensure India's equitable participation in Galileo space, ground and user segments and will guarantee the availability of highest quality signals over the Indian territory. Considering that India has well proven capabilities in space, satellite and navigation related activities, the agreement will provide an important positive impulse for Indian and European industrial co-operation in many high tech areas. We express our willingness to continue our discussions with a view to conclude the agreement in the near future.

   The EU and India both have very mature space programmes and a long history of working together through their respective space agencies ESA and ISRO in the peaceful exploration and use of outer space. The EU expresses its interest in the Indian unmanned lunar exploration mission Chandrayaan-1. We support and encourage the cooperation between ESA and ISRO.

8. We note the successful conclusion of the Customs Co-operation Agreement, and look forward to it being used to improve trade flows and fight against customs fraud.

9. We are pleased to note that the negotiations on the Maritime Agreement are progressing.

10. Our strategic dialogue on the Information Society continues to deliver outstanding results. We welcome the successful outcome of the 2004 Euro-India Cooperation Forum on the Information Society that was held in New Delhi on 24-26 March, 2004. We agree to work towards a mutually acceptable mechanism to connect EU and Indian Information networks in order to facilitate linkages in the area of research and technological development.

11. We commend the continued development of the Joint Initiative for Enhancing Trade and Investment through the launching of the Round Table of Business Leaders as well as the series of business seminars.

12. We recognise the special importance of strengthening the flow of students and scholars between the EU and India. We welcome the Scholarship initiative in conjunction with Erasmus Mundus (Euro 33 million) in supporting grants for Indian students in top quality European Master courses. We also encourage the setting up of chairs in designated universities in India and the EU.

13. We welcome the signing of the MOU between the two sides on the States Partnership Programme providing a framework for cooperation in the sectors of education, health and environment. We welcome the progress made in the implementation of the Disaster Management Preparedness Programme (Euro 10 million) and urge early operationalization of the States Partnership Programme (Euro 160 million) and Trade and Investment Development Programme (Euro 14 million).

14. We reaffirm our common belief in the equal importance of civil, political, economic, social and cultural rights and our commitment to their full realisation. We affirmed our willingness to continue discussing Human Rights in a comprehensive manner.

15. We stress the cultural dimension of our relationship. Based on our rich cultural heritage, we agree to encourage dialogue between European and Indian cultural actors and to promote exchanges, events and co-operation at all levels particularly to coincide with future EU-India Summits. The EU-India Joint Declaration on Cultural Relations sets out our objectives.

16. We unequivocally condemn all acts, methods and practices of terrorism and stress that solidarity and international co-operation are integral to combat terrorism. We emphasise that measures to combat terrorism should be comprehensive and sustained. We stress that further strengthening cooperation in combatting terrorism is a priority area for the EU-India Action Plan for a Strategic Partnership. We will in particular seek to

- deepen the international consensus and enhance international efforts to combat terrorism,
- reduce the access of terrorists to financial and other economic resources,
- protect the security of international transport and ensure effective systems of border control,
- address the issues which create an environment conducive to terrorism, including support for and recruitment into terrorism,
- explore ways to strengthen the counter-terrorism dialogue by covering, as appropriate, other security related issues.

We will continue to support the work of the United Nations to ensure universal adherence to, and full implementation of, all UN Security Council Resolutions, UN Conventions on Terrorism and related Protocols, including promoting an agreement on the draft Comprehensive Convention on International Terrorism. The fight against terrorism must be carried out in full respect of human rights, fundamental freedoms and the rule of law.

17. We confirm our strong support to the UN Framework Convention on Climate Change and emphasise the central role of its Kyoto Protocol. We welcome the ratification of the Kyoto Protocol by the Russian Federation and urge countries that have not yet ratified it to do so soon. We will work together for the post-2012 framework to guide global action in order to meet the objectives of the UNFCCC and increase the effectiveness of action in tackling climate change. We also intend to work together to implement the Johannesburg Plan of Implementation that was agreed upon at the WSSD.
18. We reiterate the importance of the implementation of the agenda formulated at the International Conference on Population and Development and the Declaration of Commitment on HIV/AIDS adopted by the General Assembly of the United Nations (2001). The need for community based and public oriented solutions to tackle communicable diseases, especially HIV/AIDS, was stressed. We underline the need for cooperation between our Research institutions, bio-technology sectors and the Governments in the research and development of preventive and therapeutic interventions including the development of vaccines against major diseases such as HIV/AIDS, Tuberculosis, Malaria.
19. India and the EU are partners in promoting global peace and security and remain committed to the goal of universal disarmament. In recognition of shared concerns of the international community regarding the danger posed by the proliferation of nuclear, chemical and biological weapons including acquisition by non state actors, we resolve to enhance collective action to fight the proliferation of WMD as well as the means of delivery. We believe that our response to proliferation challenges requires strengthened multilateral consultations and the pooling of all efforts and resources. Indian and EU experts shall meet to identify specific areas of co-operation. We agree that effective export control measures for dual use goods can play an important role in preventing proliferation, and at the same time, such measures should not hamper international co-operation in materials, equipment and technology for peaceful purposes.
20. We reiterate our commitment to strengthening the role of the UN. An effective multilateral system based on the principles of international law, with a strong United Nations at its center is essential for achieving peace and international security and meeting global threats and challenges. We recognize the need to make the multilateral system more responsive in bringing the objectives of the global agenda forward, including sustainable development and implementation of the Millennium Declaration. In this regard, we underlined our firm wish to make the UN Major Event 2005 a success, and agreed to support a comprehensive approach which would address the implementation of the Millennium

Declaration and of the Millennium Development Goals, as well as issues related to peace and security and UN reforms.

We stress the need for a negotiated outcome of the CSD-13 that expedites implementation of key actions to achieve agreed goals and targets in the field of water sanitation and human settlements.

21. We reiterate our support to the ongoing process of the reform of the UN and its principal organs, including the General Assembly and the Security Council with a view to strengthening and enhancing the representativeness, transparency and effectiveness of the UN System. We look forward to the report of the UN Secretary General's High Level Panel on Threats, Challenges and Change. We agree to exchange views on the report and the recommendations thereon.

22. We express our strong commitment to the re-construction and stabilisation of Afghanistan in partnership with the Afghan government. We welcome the process of democratization in Afghanistan and especially the presidential elections held on 9 October, when millions of Afghans cast their vote with great enthusiasm. However, we express concern at the continuing threats to stability and terrorist acts, particularly in South and South-East Afghanistan. The proliferation of poppy cultivation and drugs production is a major problem, and countering it is a priority issue. We, therefore, reaffirm our commitment to assist the Afghan authorities in their efforts in this regard.

23. We reviewed the situation in the Middle East and agree that Israeli intention to withdraw from all Gaza settlements and parts of the West Bank can constitute a step towards achieving the two State solution and had the possibility of restarting progress on the Roadmap, provided that it takes place in accordance with the relevant UNSC resolutions and in the context of the roadmap, that it is a step towards a two state solution, that it does not involve a transfer of settlement activity to the West Bank, that there is an organized and negotiated handover of responsibility to the Palestinian Authority, and that Israel facilitates rehabilitation and reconstruction in Gaza. The proposed withdrawal should be properly coordinated with the international community so as to ensure that an orderly situation in Gaza results, which would permit the maintenance of security as well as rehabilitation and reconstruction.

We reiterate our call to the parties to fulfill all their obligations under the Roadmap and to cooperate with the Quartet without delay. We reaffirm that a just, peaceful and lasting solution to the Middle East conflict can only be achieved through political negotiations between the parties with the active support of the international community. Such a comprehensive solution must also include Syria and Lebanon.

24. We welcome the restoration of full sovereignty to Iraq and the unanimous adoption of UNSCR 1546, which underlines the support of the international community to the Interim Government of Iraq as it guides the country towards elections. We note with particular satisfaction, the role accorded to the UN through UNSCR 1546. We underline our concern that the current campaign of terrorist violence is leading to significant loss of life, particularly among civilians. We condemn all violence and terrorist attacks, including the kidnappings and brutal murder of hostages, which impede the path to political progress and economic reconstruction in Iraq. We agree to continue our support to the emergence of a stable, secure, representative and democratic Iraq and to work together in the multilateral effort for Iraq's reconstruction for restoring peace and prosperity. We will encourage positive engagement and regional support from Iraq's neighbours for the political and reconstruction process in Iraq.
25. We welcome the commitment of the Government of Sri Lanka and the LTTE to a peaceful solution to the conflict and encourage the parties to resume peace talks without delay. We reiterate our common view that a peace settlement can only be sustained if it respects the legitimate rights and involvement of all ethnic groups, preserves the unity, sovereignty and territorial integrity of Sri Lanka and is based on the principles of democracy and human rights. We note that success will depend on the willingness of the parties to show political courage and flexibility in discussions towards a peaceful solution.
26. We share a common analysis of the situation in Nepal and welcome the formation of a multi party Government. We encourage the reopening of peace negotiations between the Government of Nepal and the Maoist insurgents. We support an early settlement of the crisis, based on multi-party democracy and constitutional monarchy. We call on all parties to respect international humanitarian law and Human Rights standards and commitments.
27. We discussed the situation in Burma/Myanmar. We agree that the National Convention should include all political parties and ethnic groups, and support the efforts of UN Special Envoy in facilitating political reconciliation. Both sides agree that progress towards democracy in Burma/Myanmar will contribute to both peace and prosperity in the country.
28. The EU welcomes the positive evolution of the relationship between India and Pakistan, and looks forward to its consolidation through the on-going "composite dialogue" in an atmosphere free from the menace of terrorism and violence, in accordance with the Joint Press Statement of January 6 and September 24, 2004. We share the view that improved

relations between India and Pakistan and closer regional integration in South Asia will be mutually reinforcing.

29. We welcome the successful SAARC Summit in Islamabad in January 2004 and the recent agreement on SAFTA which will promote economic integration in the region. We note EU's willingness to co-operate and to share its experience regarding regional cooperation with SAARC.
30. We note India's aspiration to become as early as possible a member of ASEM to complement its ASEAN Summit level dialogue status.
31. We reaffirm our commitment to further strengthening of the multilateral regime of WTO. We welcome the framework text adopted among WTO members in Geneva. While substantive work remains, the text reaffirms value and primacy of the multilateral trading system and the importance WTO Members attach to it. Both the EU and India played a pivotal role in the formulation and adoption of the text and worked closely and constructively together on key parts thereof. We reaffirm that the development dimension remains at the heart of the on-going negotiations. We will continue our working relationship throughout the remainder of the Round and thereby contribute to a successful conclusion of the Round.
32. We agree that the 6th EU-India Summit will be held in New Delhi end-2005, on dates to be mutually agreed.

❮4❯

Joint Press Statement on Eighth Round of Foreign Office Consultations (17.11.2004)

The two sides discussed ways to enhance bilateral relations in fields such as economy and commerce, agriculture, culture, science and technology and people to people contacts.

The 8th round of Foreign Office Consultations between India and Israel was held in New Delhi on 16th November 2004. The Indian delegation was headed by Mr. Rajiv Sikri Secretary (East). Ministry of External Affairs. Ambassador Amos Nadai, Deputy Director General (Asia & Pacific), Ministry of Foreign Affairs, led the Israeli delegation.

The two sides had a wide-ranging and constructive exchange of views in the spirit of friendship and mutual understanding. The discussions included a review of bilateral, regional and multilateral issues as well as ways to further enhance bilateral relations in diversified fields such as economy and commerce, agriculture, culture, science and technology and people to people contacts. Both sides exchanged views on steps needed to achieve peace in the West Asian region.

❮5❯

Joint Statement on the State Visit to India of the President of the Republic of Korea (6.10.2004)

While exchanging views on various aspects of bilateral relations and on regional and international issues of mutual interest, the two sides decided to establish a "Long-term Cooperative Partnership for Peace and Prosperity". The establishment of the India-ROK Foreign Policy and Security Dialogue and a Joint Study Group (JSG) to examine the feasibility of a comprehensive economic partnership agreement between India and ROK was also agreed upon.

1. H.E. Mr. Roh Moo-hyun, President of the Republic of Korea (ROK), paid a state visit to India from 4 to 6 October 2004, at the invitation of H. E. Dr. A.P.J. Abdul Kalam, President of the Republic of India. Accompanying H.E. President Roh Moo-hyun on his visit to India was a high-level delegation, including Minister of Foreign Affairs and Trade Mr. Ban Ki-moon, Minister of Commerce, Industry and Energy Mr. Lee Hee-beom, and Minister of Information and Communication Mr. Chin Dae-je, apart from leading representatives of business and industry from the Republic of Korea.
2. President Roh Moo-hyun met President Dr. A.P.J. Abdul Kalam. Vice President Mr. Bhairon Singh Shekhawat called on the President of the Republic of Korea. President Roh and Prime Minister of India Mr. Manmohan Singh held talks on a range of bilateral, international and regional issues. Chairperson of United Progressive Alliance Coordination Committee Mrs. Sonia Gandhi and External Affairs Minister Mr. K. Natwar Singh called on President Roh. The President of the Republic of Korea also delivered the keynote address at a joint FICCI-CII business meeting.
3. The wide-ranging deliberations between the two sides took place in a friendly and cordial atmosphere. Leaders of the two countries exchanged views on various aspects of bilateral relations as also on regional and international issues of mutual interest, including cooperation in international fora. They made a positive appraisal of the existing cooperation and exchanges while emphasizing the immense scope that exists for further enhancing these in diverse areas of interaction.

4. Both sides noted with satisfaction the steady development of friendly and cooperative relations between India and the ROK since the establishment of diplomatic relations in December 1973. The traditional friendship between the two countries has been developing on the strong foundations of commitment to democratic ideals and the shared desire to consolidate and diversify their exchanges. Close cooperation between India and the ROK will be a factor of stability in the politically and culturally diverse and rapidly transforming Asia.
5. The two sides resolved to take India-ROK relationship to a higher level in the 21st century. They have a mutual interest in the maintenance of peace, stability and prosperity in Asia and the world and share the desire to develop closer and more extensive understanding and cooperation in regional and international affairs. In this background, the two sides decided to establish a "Long-term Cooperative Partnership for Peace and Prosperity" with the aim of fully utilizing the substantial potential and opportunities for deepening mutually beneficial cooperation taking advantage of their economic complementarities and political convergences and also for pursuing peace and prosperity in the region and the world.
6. Both sides shared the view that high-level exchanges between governments, parliaments and political parties of the two countries play an important role in expanding overall bilateral cooperation between the two countries. They conveyed their determination to maintain the momentum of such exchanges in future and agreed on the need for regular meetings between their leaders alternately in respective capitals or elsewhere, including on the occasions of multilateral meetings, to review bilateral relations and consult on regional and international developments and issues. In this context, the two sides also reiterated the importance of the India-ROK Joint Commission co-chaired by the Foreign Ministers of the two countries and the Foreign Office Consultations. It was agreed that the third meeting of the Joint Commission will be held in Seoul at an early date. The two sides also confirmed their intention to promote regular ministerial-level exchanges, including between their Trade and Finance Ministers.
7. The two sides welcomed the establishment of the India-ROK Foreign Policy and Security Dialogue. The Dialogue will be broad-based and cover, inter alia, regional and international security issues, bilateral, defence and service-to-service exchanges and counter terrorism. It was also agreed that this dialogue will be held alternately in India and the ROK beginning from the year 2005.
8. Both sides noted the useful exchanges and interaction in the defence field and agreed to further promote such exchanges and interaction. They agreed on the need for cooperation in matters pertaining to safety and security of international maritime traffic. They also agreed to

promote cooperation between their navies, coast guards and related agencies in areas like anti-piracy and search and rescue operations.

9. Both sides shared the view that broadening and deepening of economic and trade cooperation between the two countries, based on the complementarities and growth potential of the two economies, will contribute to further promoting their common prosperity. They agreed to set a target of US$ 10 billion for bilateral trade by 2008 and emphasized the need to jointly work towards achieving it.

10. They agreed to continue policy dialogues in economic and trade area with a view to developing the bilateral relations into a more comprehensive and future-oriented one. As part of such an initiative, the two sides will establish a Joint Study Group (JSG), composed of government officials, economists and representatives of business community, to take a comprehensive view of bilateral economic linkages between the two countries, covering, among others, trade in goods and services, investment flows, and other areas of economic cooperation. The JSG will, inter alia, examine the feasibility of a comprehensive economic partnership agreement between India and ROK. The JSG will give concrete suggestions on ways and means to encourage closer economic engagement between the two countries based on the result of the study. It will start its work no later than in January 2005 and submit its report within one year.

11. Both sides expressed satisfaction with the steady increase in the volume of bilateral trade and investment in recent years. The Indian side welcomed investment from the ROK into India, including in the field of infrastructure, and manufacturing plants, and hoped that the inflow of such investment will significantly expand. The ROK side also welcomed Indian investment in the ROK. Both sides agreed to make further efforts to facilitate greater participation by the ROK companies in the development of infrastructure in India, including in highway construction, ports, etc.

12. In consideration of the importance of Mumbai as an economic and trade center in India, the ROK side conveyed to the Indian side that it planned to upgrade its office in Mumbai to a Consulate General at the earliest possible date in 2005. The Indian side welcomed the decision, noting that a Consulate General in Mumbai would contribute to the enhancement of cooperation in trade and investment between the two countries.

13. Both sides agreed to further strengthen the activities of India-Korea Joint Trade Committee and India-Korea Joint Committee on Investment Promotion—two major channels of consultation between the two governments in the fields of economy and trade. They agreed to facilitate broader and deeper economic and commercial relations, both in the

public and private sectors. Both sides agreed to conclude at the earliest an Agreement on Cooperation and Mutual Assistance in Customs Matters.

14. Noting the importance of air links in facilitating bilateral cooperation, the two sides agreed to enhance their air connectivity in order to facilitate enhanced trade, tourism and people-to-people exchanges. They also agreed to explore ways and means for improved shipping links between the two sides.

15. Both sides agreed to promote cooperation in various areas including among others, information and communication technology, infrastructure, textiles, petro-chemicals, oil and gas field development including third country collaborations, automobiles, shipbuilding and agriculture. They also agreed to strengthen cooperation in the field of iron and steel manufacturing, noting in this context the proposal by a Korean company POSCO for a large scale integrated iron and steel project in the State of Orissa.

16. In particular, they agreed to place special emphasis on cooperation in the IT sector to actively develop new cooperation projects, including in third country markets, combining ROK's competitive edge in hardware with India's advanced software. They also agreed to promote personnel exchanges, visits of business delegations and closer dialogue on IT, for sharing of experiences and technical know-how. The two sides agreed to encourage the establishment of an Indian software training center in the ROK. It was also agreed to encourage greater investment by the ROK companies in the IT hardware sector in India.

17. Both sides agreed to strengthen cooperation in international fora such as the UN and the WTO, and to continue to hold consultations on issues of common interest. They agreed to work together to preserve stability and growth in the global economy, reduce disparities in incomes and standards between developed and developing countries, and to join hands in an unrelenting battle against poverty in the world. They supported an open, fair, equitable and transparent rule-based multilateral trading system and decided to work together to strengthen it. In this context, they welcomed the Decision on the Doha Work Programme of August 1, 2004 and agreed to work together to achieve the objectives enshrined in the Doha mandate in the final outcome of the negotiations.

18. Both sides recognize the similar challenges they face in their efforts to protect the environment while simultaneously achieving robust economic growth. In this context, they agreed to make concerted efforts in addressing global environmental concerns such as adaptations to climate change and biodiversity conservation, and to strengthen their consultations and cooperation on sustainable development, environmentally sound technologies and other environmental issues in relevant international fora.

19. Both sides recognized the importance of science and technology cooperation and agreed to work together to exploit the enormous potential for cooperation in this field, including in the area of high-technology. In this context, they agreed to exchange visits by science and technology missions in 2005.
20. The Indian side drew the attention of the Korean side to their successful cooperation in the launch of KITSAT III in 1999, and proposed that both sides actively explore further cooperation in the field of space. The Korean side agreed to consider the proposal.
21. Both sides noted the importance of the Treaty on Extradition and the Treaty on Mutual Legal Assistance in Criminal Matters signed during the visit, and shared the view that the entry into force of the two Treaties will lay a foundation for the strengthening of cooperation between the two countries. In the light of expanding cooperation between the two countries, both sides agreed to conclude at the earliest an agreement on exemption of visa requirement for holders of diplomatic and official passports. They also agreed to enter into discussions for further simplification of visa procedures, including on issuance of multiple entry visas for the business community. They expressed hope that these will facilitate exchanges between the two sides and strengthen their friendly relations.
22. Both sides highly appreciated the various cultural events commemorating the 30th anniversary of their diplomatic relations organized by the two countries with the assistance of each other in India and the ROK during 2003 and 2004. They also noted with pleasure that the visit of President Roh Moo-hyun is taking place in the year marking the 30th anniversary of their diplomatic relations.
23. They noted that during the India-ROK Joint Cultural Commission held in New Delhi in May 2004, the two governments have agreed to the Cultural Exchange Programme which will be the framework for exchanges in this field until 2007. Both sides hoped that the Exchange Programme, will accelerate cultural exchanges between the two countries.
24. Both sides expressed satisfaction with recently strengthened exchanges in the areas of culture, education and films, and affirmed that mutual understanding and cultural exchanges will facilitate development of cooperation in other areas as well. Furthermore, the two sides highlighted the importance of youth exchange programmes for the long-term development of bilateral relations and agreed to expand such exchanges through bilateral consultations.
25. Both sides agreed to designate the third week of November 2004 as 'Korea Week' in India and a corresponding 'India Week' in the ROK

in September/October 2005. This will help raise the visibility of one country in the other, promote mutual awareness and highlight the cultural dimension of their relationship.

26. Both sides expressed their support for the efforts of the international community for a peaceful resolution of the issues of denuclearization of the Korean Peninsula. The Indian side also expressed support for all efforts to bring about peace, stability and reconciliation on the Korean Peninsula through dialogue and welcomed the recent developments in inter-Korean relations.
27. Recognizing that the ASEAN Regional Forum (ARF) is playing a positive role in confidence-building and security cooperation in the Asia-Pacific region, the two sides agreed to closely cooperate with each other in various areas of ARF activities such as exchanging views on security situation in the Asia-Pacific region, implementing confidence building measures and discussing the future direction of the ARF. Both sides also agreed that India and the ROK, Dialogue Partners of ASEAN, will closely cooperate with it for the development of the region.
28. The two sides reiterated their commitment to continue their fight against terrorism. They agreed that the fight against terrorism has to be a comprehensive and sustained effort. The two sides reaffirmed that terrorism cannot be justified wherever, whenever and for whatever reason and is to be condemned in all its forms and manifestations. They agreed to continue their consultations for expanding cooperation in the fight against international terrorism through various international and bilateral mechanisms.
29. The two sides acknowledged the vital importance of the role of the United Nations in promoting international peace, security and development. They agreed to strengthen bilateral cooperation in international affairs and to promote their dialogue and consultations on UN related issues, including on the reform of the UN. They also shared the understanding that it is crucial to make the UN Security Council more representative and effective, including through expanding its membership. They agreed to closely work together in this regard.
30. On behalf of the Government and the people of the Republic of Korea, H.E. President Roh Moo-hyun and his delegation thanked the Government and the people of India for the warm and friendly hospitality accorded to them. President Roh Moo-hyun extended cordial invitations to President A.P.J. Abdul Kalam and Prime Minister Manmohan Singh to visit the Republic of Korea at a mutually convenient time. The Indian side accepted the invitations with appreciation. The dates of the visits will be decided through diplomatic channels.

6

Joint Statement on the Visit of Minister of Foreign Affairs, State of Kuwait to India (26.08.2004)

> With a view to enhance economic, political and security cooperation, the two sides signed a Memorandum of Understanding for establishment of India-Kuwait Strategic Consultative Group. An extradition treaty and an Agreement on Mutual Legal Assistance in Criminal Matters were also signed.

H.E.Sheikh (Dr.) Mohammed Sabah Al-Salem Al-Sabah, Minister of Foreign Affairs of the State of Kuwait, paid an official visit to India from August 24-26, 2004, at the invitation of the Hon'ble Minister of External Affairs of India, Shri Natwar Singh. During the visit, the Foreign Minister of Kuwait held wide-ranging discussions with Minister of External Affairs and called on the Speaker of the Lok Sabha, the Prime Minister, and the President.

The two Ministers signed the following agreements:-

(i) Memorandum of Understanding for Establishment of India-Kuwait Strategic Consultative Group to facilitate periodic meetings between the Secretary, Ministry of External Affairs, Government of India and the Under Secretary, Ministry of Foreign Affairs of the State of Kuwait, to enhance economic, political, and security cooperation between the two countries, on a sustained and long-term basis.

(ii) Extradition Treaty;

(iii) Agreement on Mutual Legal Assistance in Criminal Matters;

The official level discussions were held in a friendly and cordial atmosphere. The two sides exchanged views on a wide range of bilateral, regional, and international issues of mutual interest. Both sides noted with satisfaction the enduring political, economic and cultural ties which have been enhanced by the consultations at the senior level. Both sides reiterated their desire to further strengthen bilateral relations based on a long tradition of mutual consultations and coordination on issues of vital importance to both countries and provide mutual support in various multilateral fora. Both sides recognized shared cultural affinities reinforced by institutional linkages and based on their commitment to a democratic polity and an open liberal society. Both sides agreed that the Indian community resident in Kuwait constituted valued link between the two countries, contributing to further strengthening the economic and cultural relations between the two countries. Both sides recognized a common interest in peace, security and stability of the Gulf and South Asian regions and agreed to periodic exchange of views and viewpoints in this regard, within the framework of the India-Kuwait Strategic Consultative Group. Both sides recognized Kuwait's role as a significant source of energy for India's rapidly growing economy and a factor in contributing to India's energy security.

Both sides emphasized the need for increased economic cooperation in four priority areas – trade, investment, industrial cooperation (including SME), and transfer of technology (including IT) – identified at the First India-GCC Industrial Conference. Both sides underlined the importance of building institutional linkages and direct investment in each other's economies. They also recognized India as a major source of technology and technical human resources. Both sides noted the new opportunities offered by the State of Kuwait through their revised foreign investment laws which would facilitate increased direct foreign investment. Both sides acknowledged the need for an early conclusion of negotiations on the Avoidance of Double Taxation Agreement.

Both sides exchanged views on their common concerns on the threat to open and democratic societies from terrorism and extremist violence. They called for effective international cooperation to combat terrorism and deny sanctuaries to terrorist outfits. They recognized the need for increased consultation and cooperation in this area.

Both sides underscored the importance of peace and stability in the Gulf region and the need to respect the sovereignty and territorial integrity of the countries in the region. Both sides welcomed the increased role for the United Nations in Iraq and noted with satisfaction that the process of political transition in Iraq, including restoration of its sovereignty, was underway.

Both sides underlined the need to revitalize the Middle East Peace Process, based on the relevant UN Resolutions, the Arab Initiative, and the Road Map, in order to achieve a just, lasting, and comprehensive peace in the region and the establishment of two states, Israel and Palestine, living side by side in peace and security. The Kuwaiti side recognized the positive efforts made by India to help secure peace and stability in the Middle East.

Both sides reaffirmed their commitment to the implementation of reforms within the United Nations, including the reform of the Security Council and expansion of both the Permanent and Non-Permanent Membership.

The Foreign Minister of Kuwait thanked the Government of India for the cordial welcome and hospitality extended to him and his delegation during their visit to India.

❮7❯

List of Agreements signed between India and Malaysia (20.12.2004)

The two sides signed a number of documents dealing with cooperation in various sectors like commercial satellite service including building and launching of "MEASAT-4 satellite", construction of Hyderabad International Airport, bioscience research and multimedia industry.

List of Agreements Signed in the Presence of Prime Ministers of India and Malaysia

1. Antrix Corporation Limited ("Antrix"), the commercial arm of the Indian Space Research Organisation ("ISRO"), and MEASAT Global Bhd. (BLOOM:MGB MK) ("MEASAT") signed an agreement today to form a Joint Venture Company ("JV Co") to pool their satellite capacities, in a major move to develop a satellite neighbourhood for millions of broadcasting and telecommunications customers across the wider Asia Pacific region.

   The Joint Venture, which will be equally owned by the two companies, represents a significant breakthrough and major step in the ongoing cooperation between the Indian and Malaysian satellite sectors.

   The JV Co will leverage capacity from both the high-powered Indian INSAT and Malaysian MEASAT satellite fleets to provide commercial satellite service across the wider Asia-Pacific region.

2. Letter of Intent by MEASAT Satellite Systems Sdn Bhd. of Malaysia o Antrix Corporation on procurement of MEASAT-4 Satellite.

   Within the overall framework of cooperation of Joint Venture, Antrix has proposed building and launching MEASAT-4 satellite. The technical and financial aspects have been mostly agreed upon and discussions are continuing over certain regulatory processes.

   Signed by Tun Hanif Bin Tun Omar, Director, MEASAT Satellite Systems from the Malaysian side and Shri K.R. Sridharmurthy, Executive Director, Antrix Corporation from the Indian side.

3. Concession Agreement for the Development, Construction, Operation and Maintenance of the Hyderabad International Airport between Ministry of Civil Aviation, Government of India and Hyderabad International Airport Limited

   The consortium of GMR Infrastructure Limited (GIL) and Malaysia Airports Holdings Berhad (MABH) has been selected by Government of Andhra Pradesh and Government of India following a competitive bidding to develop Greenfield international airport through Public Private Partnership (PPP) at Shamshabad near Hyderabad at about 20 kilometers from the existing airport at Begumpet. The consortium as majority partner, will be responsible for the design, finance, construction, operation, maintenance and management of Hyderabad International Airport Project, through a special purpose company viz. Hyderabad International Airport Limited (HIAL), in which Government of Andhra Pradesh and AAI together hold 26%. The approximate cost of the project is Rs. 1385 crores.

In addition, 12 Business to Business Agreements were signed at the Business luncheon meeting of H.E. Mr. Badawi, Prime Minister of Malaysia with Confederation of Indian Industries (CII)/Federation of Indian Chambers of Commerce and Industry(FICCI). The list is as follows:

1. CMC LIMITED(Tata group) and ARA TECHBIZ SDN. BHD. – IT cooperation
2. Institute of Bioinformaties and Applied Biotechnology(IBAB) and Inforvalley Life Sciences SDN. Bhd. (IVLS)
3. International Tractors Berhad (THB) and Tracoma Holdings Berhad
4. Antrix Corporation Limited and Binariang Satellite Systems Sdn. Bhd. – Operation of regional satellite network (MEASAT)
5. Indian Gas Ltd., India and Indofocus sdn Bhd
6. Bioscience Research Institute and SAL Group of Colleges
7. Hyderabad International Airport Ltd. and Malaysia Airports Holdings Bhd
8. Konkan Railway Corporation Limited and Sistem Kompakar Sdn bhd
9. XLR Technology India Pvt. Ltd. and SAL group of Companies
10. Learnet India Ltd. and Malaysia Institute of Integrative Media
11. Sun TV and Astro All Asia Networks PLC
12. NASSCOM and Association of Computer and Multimedia Industry of Malaysia

❮8❯

Joint Statement on the State Visit of Prime Minister of Mongolia, Mr. Nambariin Enkhbayar to India (16.01.2004)

While agreeing "to elevate their relations to a new level of partnership", the two sides signed documents on cooperation in the field of animal health and dairy, space science, technology and applications and in the field of biotechnology.

At the invitation of the Prime Minister of the Republic of India H.E. Shri Atal Bihari Vajpayee, the Prime Minister of Mongolia, H.E. Mr. Nambariin Enkhbayar, accompanied by his spouse, is presently on a State visit to India from January 14-19, 2004. During his visit, in addition to his talks with the Indian leadership, Prime Minister Enkhbayar will also be visiting Varanasi, Sarnath, Bodh Gaya, Calcutta and Hyderabad. During his visit to Varanasi, the Banaras Hindu University will be conferring on the Prime Minister D. Litt. (Honouris Causa) in recognition of his contributions to cementing the ties between India and Mongolia and his role in promoting democracy and Buddhism in his country.

2 The Prime Minister of Mongolia was accorded a ceremonial welcome at the Rashtrapati Bhawan on January 15, 2004. He called on the President of the Republic of India on the same day. Their discussions covered wide range of issues of bilateral relations and recent regional and international developments of mutual interest.

3 The Prime Minister of Mongolia also called on the Vice President of the Republic of India. The Minister of External Affairs, Rakṣha Mantri and Minister for Communications and Information Technology called on the Prime Minister of Mongolia.

4 The two Prime Ministers had a tête-à-tête followed by official talks. During these talks both the leaders exchanged views on further development of bilateral relations, regional and international issues of mutual interest, including the threat of terrorism. An official banquet was hosted by H.E. Shri Atal Bihari Vajpayee in honour of the visiting Prime Minister H.E. Mr. N. Enkhbayar.

5 Both sides reiterated the importance that they attach to the continuing relevance of the Treaty of Friendly Relations and Cooperation between the Republic of India and Mongolia of 1994. The Treaty has served

both countries well and has provided a solid foundation for further development of bilateral relations and cooperation on regional and international relations in the years ahead. In view of the rapidly developing close and cordial ties between the two countries, the two sides agreed to elevate their relations to a new level of partnership.

6 During the visit following documents were signed:

(i) Agreement on Cooperation in the Field of Animal Health and Dairy.

(ii) Agreement for Cooperation in Space Science, Technology and Applications.

(iii) Protocol of Cooperation in the Field of Biotechnology.

Both sides agreed that the new agreements would serve to further diversify and strengthen their bilateral relations and cooperation.

7 The two countries would complete 50 years of the establishment of their diplomatic relations in December 2005. In this context, the two Prime Ministers agreed that the 50th anniversary of the establishment of diplomatic relations would be observed in a befitting manner.

8 The two sides agreed to hold regular consultations at the functional level between the National Security Councils of India and Mongolia on issues of mutual concern.

9 The two sides agreed that the Joint Committee on Cooperation at Secretary/Deputy Foreign Minister level set up by the Agreement for the Establishment of a Joint Committee on Cooperation signed in 1994 should hold its meeting as soon as possible in order to further consolidate bilateral cooperation between the two countries. It was also agreed that as necessary functional Sub-Committees as provided in the Agreement would be set up at the level of Joint Secretary/Director.

10 The Government of India agreed to extend a soft loan to Mongolia amounting to US$ 10 million. Terms and conditions of the soft loan will be worked out through diplomatic channels.

11 The two sides also agreed to hold expert level discussions to identify specific projects for cooperation in areas like human resource development and IT, agriculture and livestock, mineral resources, hydrocarbon resources and infrastructure.

12 The Government of India agreed to undertake a pilot project for electrification of a Mongolian village using solar energy.

13 Recognizing the importance of education in the development of Mongolia and the contribution of India in this field, the Government of Mongolia requested an increase in scholarship slots to Mongolian students under the Cultural Exchange Programme and General Scholarship Schemes of the Indian Council for Cultural Relations. The Government of India agreed to increase the number of scholarship slots from 20 to 30 per year.

14 Noting that the programmes of education and training being undertaken with Indian assistance in Mongolia were both relevant and useful and in order to assist Mongolia in further development of its human resources, the Government of India agreed to enhance the total number of training slots for Mongolia under the Indian Technical and Economic Cooperation Programme.

15 The Government of Mongolia expressed its gratitude to the Government of India for setting up Atal Bihári Vajpayee Centre for Excellence in Information and Communication Technology (ABVCEICT) in Ulaanbaatar and community centres in five provinces. The Government of India agreed to the proposal to connect the five regional centres with the ABVCEICT through video conferencing to enable the Mongolian authorities to introduce a distance education programme in rural areas. Three experts would also be deputed to train local instructors.

16 Recognizing the need to strengthen their economic ties, the two sides considered the importance of setting up of joint ventures in the fields of IT, health and small and medium enterprises. These proposals would be followed up separately.

17 Both sides also agreed to organize an exclusive India Trade Exhibition in Ulaanbaatar in 2004 to promote development of commercial relations between the two countries.

18 The Mongolian side sought India's assistance in developing the existing India-Mongolia Friendship Farm into a Model Farm with Indian inputs of experts and seeds. The Indian side agreed to provide the necessary assistance.

19 The two sides agreed to further develop and strengthen defence cooperation within the framework of the Agreement on Cooperation in Defence Matters, including training of Mongolian military officers in India.

20 Considering the ancient and historic ties between India and Mongolia, the Government of India agreed to waive the payment for the plot of land allotted to Mongolia at Bodh Gaya for construction of a Mongolian monastery. The two sides also agreed to collaborate in digitisation of precious Buddhist manuscripts in Mongolia, so that this heritage of humanity could be preserved for eternity.

21 Mongolia and India recognize the importance of reforms and restructuring of the UN system including the need for expansion of the UN Security Council. Recognising India as a large democracy, an emerging economic power with significant scientific and technological advances and noting India's significant contribution to the promotion of international peace and security, Mongolia as a nation located in the same region as India and enjoying centuries old friendly ties with

India, would fully support India's candidature for permanent membership of the UN Security Council, when the expansion takes place. The Government of India expressed its appreciation to the Government of Mongolia for this expression of support.

22 Following their discussions on regional and international issues, the Prime Minister of India reiterated India's support for Mongolia's Nuclear Weapon Free Status, including at the United Nations.

23 The Prime Minister of India congratulated the Prime Minister of Mongolia for successful conclusion of the 5th International Conference of New or Restored Democracies held in Ulaanbaatar in September 2003. Two sides also agreed to work closely on the follow up action on the Ulaanbaatar Declaration and the Plan of Action adopted at the Conference. In this regard, Mongolia looks forward to India's role as a member of the Friends of the Chairman Group, in order to ensure an effective follow up to the Conference.

24 Both sides reiterated their readiness to enhance their cooperation on issues related to peace, stability, and development in the world at large and in the Asia-Pacific region in particular through enhanced interactions and exchange of views, bilaterally and in multilateral fora, including at the United Nations.

25 India and Mongolia support all efforts of the international community, including the six-party talks, for a peaceful settlement of the nuclear issue on the Korean Peninsula. They also welcome and support all efforts between the Republic of Korea and the Democratic People's Republic of Korea to bring about peace, stability, reconciliation and reunification on the Korean Peninsula.

26 Both India and Mongolia strongly condemned the menace of international terrorism and its devastating effect on democratic societies, development and on human civilization itself. The two countries affirmed that there could be no justification of terrorism: political, philosophical, ideological, religious, racial, or any other. The two sides expressed their full support for UNSC Resolution 1373 and strongly condemned States that aid, abet, and support cross-border and international terrorism or provide safe havens to terrorists. They reiterated their resolve to work towards strengthening the global consensus and legal regimes against terrorism, including early finalization of a Comprehensive Convention on International Terrorism.

27 While noting Mongolia's participation in the Iraqi reconstruction process, both sides highlighted the importance of transfer of sovereignty to the Iraqi people and the need for the international community's efforts to rebuild Iraq as a peaceful and democratic country and the important role of UN in this process.

28 India and Mongolia, as fellow members of the Non-Aligned Movement and the Group of 77, reiterated the importance of revitalising the role of the Movement. They stressed the need to develop action-oriented South-South cooperation and meaningful North-South partnership with a view to creating a more just and equitable world, free from fear and free from want.

29 The Prime Minister of India thanked the Prime Minister of Mongolia for his visit and stated that it has contributed immensely in strengthening the friendly ties between India and Mongolia and would provide a new dynamism for their further consolidation in the twenty-first century.

30 The Prime Minister of Mongolia expressed deep gratitude to the Prime Minister of the Republic of India for the warm hospitality extended to him and his delegation. He renewed earlier invitations to the President and the Prime Minister of the Republic of India to pay official visits to Mongolia at the earliest possible. Both the leaders accepted the invitations with gratitude. Dates of the visits would be finalized through the diplomatic channels.

❮9❯

Joint Statement on the State Visit of H.E. Senior General Than Shwe, Chairman of the State Peace and Development Council of the Union of Myanmar to India (29.10.2004)

The two sides agreed to expand bilateral interaction to the health, higher education and energy sectors. Agreements were also signed on cooperation in the field on non-traditional security, the Tamanthi Hydro-electric project, extending a line of credit of US $ 7 million for two telecom projects and a grant of $ 3 million for IT related projects.

At the invitation of H.E. Dr. A.P. J. Abdul Kalam, President of the Republic of India, H.E. Senior General Than Shwe, Chairman, State Peace and Development Council (SPDC) paid a State visit to India from October 25-29, 2004.

2. The Chairman of SPDC, H.E. Senior General Than Shwe was accompanied by a high level delegation including H.E. Lt.-Gen. Thein Sein, Secretary-I, SPDC; H.E. Lt-Gen. Thiha Thura Tin Aung Myint Oo, Member, SPDC; H.E. U Aung Thaung, Minister for Industry -I; H.E. U Nyan Win, Minister for Foreign Affairs; H.E. Brig.-Gen. Thein Zaw, Minister for Communication, Posts and Telegraphs; H.E. Brig.-Gen. Lun Thi, Minister for Energy; H.E. U Thaung, Minister for Science and Technology; H.E. Prof. Dr. Kyaw Myint, Minister for Health; H.E. Maj.-Gen. Aung Min, Minister for Rail Transportation; H.E. Brig-Gen. Thura Myint Maung, Minister for Religious Affairs; H.E. U Kyaw Thu, Deputy Foreign Minister, and other senior officials.
3. H.E. Senior General Than Shwe and Daw Kyaing Kyaing, and members of the Myanmar delegation were extended a warm and cordial welcome to India by H.E. Dr. A.P.J. Abdul Kalam and the Government and people of India. H.E. Senior General Than Shwe expressed his happiness at the opportunity to visit a close and friendly neighbour and conveyed his warm and sincere greetings to H.E. Dr. A.P.J. Abdul Kalam and to the Government and people of India.
4. In New Delhi, H.E. Senior General Than Shwe and Daw Kyaing Kyaing were accorded a ceremonial welcome by H.E. Dr. A.P.J. Abdul Kalam. H.E. Senior General Than Shwe and Daw Kyaing Kyaing

called on H.E. Dr. A.P.J. Abdul Kalam. H.E. Shri Bhairon Singh Shekhawat, Vice President of India, H.E. Shri K. Natwar Singh, Minister of External Affairs and Shri L.K. Advani, Leader of the Opposition (Lok Sabha) called on H.E. Senior General Than Shwe.

5. H.E. Senior General Than Shwe also held extensive discussions with H.E. Dr. Manmohan Singh, Prime Minister of India on bilateral, regional and international issues of mutual interest. The discussions enabled better understanding and appreciation of each other's concerns and perspectives and enhanced closer understanding at the political level. Both sides agreed to regular exchange of high-level visits in the future.

6. H.E. Senior General Than Shwe informed the Indian leadership about the implementation of country-wide all-round development tasks undertaken in Myanmar by SPDC. The Myanmar side reiterated its strong commitment to building a modern, democratic state suited to Myanmar's needs and conditions. The Myanmar side briefed the Indian leadership about the process of national reconciliation and reconvening of and deliberations in the National Convention in accordance with the seven-step Roadmap elaborated by the Government of the Union of Myanmar in August 2003.

7. The Indian side noted the resolve of the Myanmar leadership to build an enduring democratic system in Myanmar and expressed support for national reconciliation and early transition to democracy in Myanmar. The Indian side stressed that it wished to see a stable, peaceful, prosperous and democratic Myanmar and was ready to assist the Government and people of Myanmar on their path to further political and economic progress.

8. The two sides expressed satisfaction that bilateral cooperation was proceeding smoothly in a wide range of areas such as infrastructure, human resource development, industry, railways, oceanography, science & technology etc. and agreed to expand bilateral interaction to the health sector, the energy sector, ICT and higher education. While taking note of the steady expansion in the trade turnover between the two countries, they emphasised that the present bilateral trade level was not commensurate with existing potentialities. They agreed to direct their Ministers concerned to take appropriate measures in order to raise bilateral trade to US$ 1 billion by 2006 as proposed by the Joint Trade Committee. The two sides emphasised the role of the private sector and cross-border investment in strengthening bilateral economic and commercial cooperation and agreed to encourage efforts in this direction. The Myanmar side assured that it would welcome and actively facilitate private Indian investment in Myanmar.

9. The Indian side extended to the Government of the Union of Myanmar a Line of Credit of US$ 7 million for two telecom projects and announced a grant of US$ 3 million for implementation of IT-related projects. The Myanmar side expressed its deep gratitude for the Line of Credit and the grant. The Myanmar side also thanked warmly the Indian side for providing in July 2004 a special Line of Credit of US$ 56.358 million for upgradation of the Yangon-Mandalay trunk-line and allied facilities.
10. The two sides fully shared the view that economic development of the region along the India-Myanmar border required special focus. Noting that the Tamu-Kalemyo Road had greatly improved economic conditions in the area, the Myanmar side expressed appreciation for the maintenance of the road by the Indian side. Both sides expressed satisfaction that several other cross-border projects such as the Tamanthi Hydroelectric Project, the Rhi-Tiddim and Rhi-Falam roads and the Kaladan Multi-modal Transport Project were on the anvil. It was decided that, keeping in view the vital importance of these projects to the economic welfare of the peoples living in the border areas and to improving connectivity between the two countries, their implementation should be expedited. It was also decided that specific measures would be taken to encourage border trade.
11. At the same time, the two sides agreed that maintenance of peace and security along the border areas was an essential pre requisite to successful implementation of cross-border projects and to bringing about economic prosperity in the area. Both sides reiterated their firm determination to maintaining peace, stability and tranquillity along the entire length of their common border. The Myanmar side reiterated that it would not allow insurgent activities against India from its soil. The Indian side thanked the Myanmar side for the assurance. Both sides agreed to take necessary steps to prevent cross-border crimes, including drug trafficking and arms smuggling, and to upgrade substantially bilateral cooperation in this context.
12. Regular visits involving the three Services, Port Calls by Indian Naval Vessels, participation of Myanmar in 'Milan 2003' and 'DEFEXPO India 2004', performances by SKAT in Myanmar and visits by sports teams were reviewed with satisfaction and it was agreed to encourage such exchanges. The Myanmar side expressed appreciation with the training of Myanmar personnel in India. Both sides agreed that possibilities of expanding cooperation in the defence sphere would be examined.
13. The two sides recalled that they were bound by enduring cultural and spiritual links. They noted with satisfaction on-going bilateral

cooperation in the cultural sphere. The Myanmar side thanked the Indian side for extending facilities to pilgrims from Myanmar. Both sides underscored that tourism promotion would nurture age-old ties and contacts at the people to people level.

14. In discussing the international situation, the two sides reaffirmed the validity and relevance of the principles of Panchsheel to inter-State relations. They observed that an equitable world order alone would allow solutions to challenges emanating from processes of economic development and advancements in science and technology. They noted that growth of extremist ideologies and terrorism posed a serious threat to global peace and security. They declared that terrorism anywhere in the world and in any form and manifestation was completely unacceptable.

15. The two sides also agreed that the United Nations had an important role to play in dealing with present-day challenges and, therefore, restructuring and reform of the United Nations in line with global realities was necessary. They were of the view that an expanded UN Security Council would give it greater legitimacy and enhance its effectiveness. The Myanmar side conveyed full support for India's bid for Permanent Membership of the UNSC.

16. Both sides noted that India-Myanmar relations were an important factor in enabling regional cooperation. They expressed satisfaction that regional initiatives such as the India-ASEAN partnership and BIMST-EC had assumed concrete form and content. They agreed to work closely in promoting regional cooperation in its various dimensions. The Myanmar side thanked India for its assistance under the IAI of ASEAN.

17. While in New Delhi, H.E. Senior General Than Shwe laid a wreath at the memorial of Mahatma Gandhi. H.E. Senior General Than Shwe and Daw Kyaing Kyaing, and the Myanmar delegation will be visiting Agra, Bangalore, Bodh Gaya, Sarnath and Kolkata before returning to Yangon.

18. During the visit, the following documents were signed: (i) MoU on Cooperation in the field of Non-traditional Security Issues; (ii) MoU between the Ministry of External Affairs, Government of India and the Department of Hydropower, Government of the Union of Myanmar on the Tamanthi Hydro-electric Project; and, (iii) the Cultural Exchange Programme for the years 2004-2006. The Export-Import Bank of India and the Myanma Foreign Trade Bank signed an agreement on a special Line of Credit of USD 7 million for commissioning of CorDECT WLL based basic telephone and internet networks in Yangon and Mandalay and installation of an Optical Fibre Cable between the border towns of Moreh and Tamu. A comprehensive report on long-term

business linkages between India and Myanmar, prepared jointly by the Confederation of Indian Industry and the Union of Myanmar Federation of Chambers of Commerce and Industry, was also released.

19. Separately in New Delhi, bilateral discussions were held between India's External Affairs Minister H.E. Shri K. Natwar Singh and Myanmar's Minister of Foreign Affairs, H.E. U. Nyan Win; India's Commerce and Industry Minister, H.E. Shri Kamal Nath and Myanmar's Minister for Industry- I, H.E. U. Aung Thaung; India's Minister for Railways, H.E. Shri Laloo Prasad Yadav and Myanmar's Minister for Rail Transportation, H.E. Maj. Gen. Aung Min; India's Minister of Communications and Information Technology, H.E. Shri Dayanidhi Maran and Myanmar's Minister for Communications, Posts and Telegraphs, H.E. Brig.-Gen. Thein Zaw; India's Minister of State (Independent charge) for Science and Technology, H.E. Shri Kapil Sibal and Myanmar's Minister for Science and Technology, H.E. U. Thaung; and Myanmar's Minister for Energy, H.E. Brig.-Gen. Lun Thi and India's Secretary, Ministry of Petroleum and Natural Gas, Shri S.C. Tripathi.

20. H.E. Senior General Than Shwe invited H.E. Dr. A.P.J. Abdul Kalam to pay a State visit to Myanmar. The invitation was accepted with pleasure.

21. H.E. Senior General Than Shwe also invited H.E. Dr. Manmohan Singh to pay an official visit to Myanmar. H.E. Dr. Manmohan Singh conveyed an invitation to H.E. Lt Gen Soe Win, Prime Minister of the Union of Myanmar to visit India.

22. H.E. Senior General Than Shwe thanked H.E. Dr. A.P.J. Abdul Kalam and the Government and people of India for warm and friendly reception and gracious hospitality accorded to him and to the Myanmar delegation.

❮10❯

Joint Statement on the Visit of Minister of External Affairs Shri K. Natwar Singh to Muscat, Oman (26.12.2004)

The two sides signed an Extradition Treaty and reaffirmed the development of bilateral relations on issues like energy, information technology, trade and investment, labour relations and defence and security.

Minister of External Affairs His Excellency K. Natwar Singh visited Muscat from December 24-26 at the invitation of His Excellency Yousuf bin Alawi bin Abdullah, the Minister Responsible for Foreign Affairs. This has been an important visit, which has served to strengthen further the close bilateral relations between the Republic of India and the Sultanate of Oman at a strategic level.

During his visit External Affairs Minister Natwar Singh was received by His Majesty Sultan Qaboos bin Said, and handed a written message from the Prime Minister Dr. Manmohan Singh to His Majesty, concerning bilateral relations and ways and means of boosting ties between the two countries. In their meeting His Majesty and the External Affairs Minister reviewed aspects of Oman India bilateral relations and discussed a wide range of international and regional issues.

External Affairs Minister Natwar Singh also met the Minister Responsible for Foreign Affairs His Excellency Yousuf bin Alawi bin Abdullah to hold a round of official talks. The Ministers exchanged views on a number of political, international, and regional issues. There was a broad measure of agreement between them on these issues, in support of the need to make every effort to build peace and stability in the region and the world. In the same context, the two sides also agreed on the need to expand the UN Security Council and to coordinate their positions accordingly. The Sultanate of Oman supports India's candidature for a permanent seat in the expanded Security Council.

The Ministers also noted with satisfaction the steady development of bilateral relations between Oman and India, praised the work of the joint committee and the progress made by the Oman India Strategic Consultation group. They reaffirmed their commitment to support the continued development of bilateral relations on many fronts, including, among other issues, energy, information technology, trade and investment, labour relations, and defence and security.

The Ministers welcomed the constructive contribution of the Indian community in Oman towards economic development, and the further development of bilateral cooperation between the two countries.

During his visit External Affairs Minister K. Natwar Singh had the opportunity to meet His Highness Sayyid Haitham bin Tariq Al-Said the Minister of Heritage and Culture, His Excellency Sayyid Bader bin Saud bin Harub Al Busaidi the Minister Responsible for Defence Affairs, His Excellency Maqbool bin Ali bin Sultan Minister of Commerce and Industry and His Excellency Dr. Mohammed bin Hamad Al Rumhi Oil and Gas Minister. He was accompanied by a team of senior officials from Ministry of External Affairs in Delhi.

The visit concluded with the signing of an Extradition Treaty concerning the extradition of convicted and accused persons between Oman and India, and the signing of a Memorandum of Understanding between the State Audit Institution of the Sultanate of Oman and the Comptroller and Auditor General of India, for cooperation in audit matters.

<11>

Joint Press Statement issued after the SAARC Summit in Islamabad (06.01.2004)

> President Musharraf reassured Prime Minister Vajpayee that "he will not permit any territory under Pakistan's control to be used to support terrorism in any manner". To carry the process of normalisation forward, the two leaders agreed to commence the process of the "composite dialogue" in February 2004.

The President of Pakistan and the Prime Minister of India met during the SARRC summit in Islamabad.

The Indian Prime Minister while expressing satisfaction over the successful conclusion of the SAARC summit appreciated the excellent arrangements made by the host country.

Both leaders welcomed the recent steps towards normalisation of relations between the two countries and expressed the hope that the positive trends set by the CBMs would be consolidated.

Prime Minister Vajpayee said that in order to take forward and sustain the dialogue process, violence, hostility and terrorism must be prevented. President Musharraf reassured Prime Minister Vajpayee that he will not permit any territory under Pakistan's control to be used to support terrorism in any manner. President Musharraf emphasised that a sustained and productive dialogue addressing all issues would lead to positive results.

To carry the process of normalisation forward, the president of Pakistan and the Prime Minister of India agreed to commence the process of the composite dialogue in February 2004. The two leaders are confident that the resumption of the composite dialogue will lead to peaceful settlement of all bilateral issues, including Jammu and Kashmir, to the satisfaction of both sides.

The two leaders agreed that constructive dialogue would promote progress towards the common objective of peace, security and economic development for our peoples and for future generations.

❮12❯

Joint Statement on the Wullar Barrage/Tulbul Navigation Project (30.07.2004)

The discussions in Islamabad were a part of the "Composite Dialogue" in which both sides "reaffirmed their commitment" to the Indus Waters Treaty and agreed to continue the discussions in the next round.

The delegations of Pakistan and India met in Islamabad on 29-30 July 2004 for discussions on the Wullar Barrage/Tulbul Navigation Project as part of the Composite Dialogue. The Pakistan delegation was led by Mr. Ashfaq Mahmood, Secretary to the Government of Pakistan, Ministry of Water & Power and the Indian delegation was led by Mr. V.K. Duggal, Secretary to the Government of India, Ministry of Water Resources.

Mr. V.K. Duggal and the members of the Indian delegation called on Mr. Aftab Ahmad Khan Sherpao, Minister for Water & Power.

The talks were held in a cordial and constructive atmosphere. Both sides reaffirmed their commitment to the Indus Waters Treaty of 1960.

It was agreed that the discussions would continue at the next round of the dialogue process with a view to finding a solution to the issue consistent with the provisions of the Treaty.

❮13❯

Joint Statement on the status of the Composite Dialogue (08.09.2004)

While reviewing the status of the Composite Dialogue, the two sides reaffirmed their commitment to the principles of the UN and to implement the Simla Agreement "in letter and spirit". Some of the important confidence building measures discussed were : establishment of Committee of experts on issues related to trade; Srinagar-Muzzafarabad bus service; Munnabao-Khokhrapar rail link; etc. CBMs along the international boundary and LoC were also discussed.

External Affairs Minister of India, H.E. Shri. K. Natwar Singh and Foreign Minister of Pakistan, H.E. Mr. Khurshid M. Kasuri, met in New Delhi on September 5 and 6, 2004 to review status of the Composite Dialogue. Their meeting was preceded by a meeting between the Foreign Secretary of India Shri Shyam Saran and Foreign Secretary of Pakistan Mr. Riaz H. Khokhar on September 4, 2004. The talks were held in a cordial and constructive atmosphere.

2. They reiterated their commitment to the principles and purposes of the Charter of the United Nations, and their determination to implement the Simla Agreement in letter and spirit.
3. The Foreign Ministers expressed satisfaction at the progress made so far, and positively assessed the developments in bilateral relations over the past year.
4. Recalling the reassurance contained in the Joint Press Statement of January 6, 2004, they exchanged views on carrying the process forward in an atmosphere free from terrorism and violence.
5. The Ministers held detailed and substantive discussions and reiterated the confidence that the Composite Dialogue will lead to peaceful settlement of all bilateral issues, including Jammu and Kashmir, to the satisfaction of both sides. They agreed to continue with the serious and sustained dialogue to find a peaceful negotiated final settlement. They expressed their determination to take the process forward.
6. The wide ranging proposals on confidence building, promotion of friendly exchanges, and enhancing trade and economic cooperation,

made by both the sides, were examined and it was agreed that these would be discussed further.

7. The Ministers agreed on the following:
   (a) Expert level meetings on Conventional and Nuclear CBMs, inter alia, to discuss the draft agreement on advance notification of missile tests;
   (b) Meeting between railway authorities on the Munnabao - Khokhrapar rail link;
   (c) Biannual meeting between Indian Border Security Force (BSF) and Pakistan Rangers in October 2004;
   (d) Meeting between Narcotics Control Authorities, including for finalisation of an MoU in October/ November 2004;
   (e) Meeting between the Indian Coast Guards and the Pakistan Maritime Security Agency in November 2004 to, inter alia, discuss the Memorandum of Understanding for establishing communication link between them;
   (f) Establishment of Committee of Experts to consider issues related to trade;
   (g) On Siachen, the outcome of the August 2004 meeting of Defence Secretaries would be implemented;
   (h) Joint Survey of the boundary pillars in the horizontal segment (blue dotted line) of the international boundary in the Sir Creek area;
   (i) Meeting on all issues related to commencement of a bus service between Srinagar and Muzaffarabad;
   (j) Add a new category of Tourist Visa in the visa regime between the two countries, and to promote group tourism;
   (k) Set up a mechanism to deal with the issue of civilian prisoners and fishermen, effectively and speedily;
   (l) Further measures for facilitation of visits to religious shrines, and upkeep of historical sites;
   (m) Enhanced interaction and exchanges among the respective Foreign Offices, including study tours of young diplomats/probationers to each other's country.
8. They recognized the importance of availability and access to energy resources in the region around South Asia. The Ministers of Petroleum/ Gas could meet to discuss the issue in its multifarious dimensions.
9. The Foreign Minister of Pakistan met the National Security Adviser, Mr. J.N. Dixit, and also called on Prime Minister Dr. Manmohan Singh, during his stay in India.

10. The two sides agreed to the continuation of high level meetings and visits, including :
    (a) a meeting between President Musharraf and Prime Minister Dr. Manmohan Singh in New York on the margins of UNGA later in September 2004;
    (b) a visit by Pakistan's Prime Minister to India as Chairperson of SAARC;
    (c) a meeting between the Prime Minister of India and Pakistan's Prime Minister in Dhaka, in January 2005, on the margins of the SAARC Summit.
11. It was also agreed that the two Foreign Secretaries would meet in December 2004 to discuss overall progress, as well as subjects of Peace and Security including CBMs, and Jammu and Kashmir, in the Composite Dialogue. They would also work out the schedule of meetings on the other six subjects, i.e. Siachen; Wullar Barrage/ Tulbul Navigation Project; Sir Creek; Terrorism and Drug Trafficking; Economic and Commercial Cooperation; and Promotion of Friendly Exchanges in Various Fields, under the Composite Dialogue.
12. The Foreign Minister of Pakistan invited the External Affairs Minister of India to visit Pakistan. The invitation was accepted and the dates would be worked out through diplomatic channels.

❮14❯

Joint Statement on India-Pakistan Expert Level meeting on Conventional CBMs (15.12.2004)

The two sides discussed "the significance of and overall approaches to Conventional CBMs" and exchanged views on various proposals.

Pursuant to the agreement between the Foreign Ministers of Pakistan and India in September 2004, an Expert Level meeting on Conventional Confidence Building Measures was held in Islamabad on 15 December 2004. Mr. Tariq Osman Hyder, Additional Secretary (UN&EC), Ministry of Foreign Affairs, led the Pakistan delegation, and Mr. Arun Kumar Singh, Joint Secretary, Ministry of External Affairs, led the Indian side.

The talks between the two delegations were held in a cordial and constructive atmosphere.

The two sides held discussions on the significance of and overall approaches to Conventional CBMs, and exchanged views on various proposals. The results of the discussions will be reported to the respective Foreign Secretaries.

❮15❯

Joint Statement on Second Round of India-Pakistan Expert Level talks on Nuclear CBMs (15.12.2004)

The two sides had detailed consultations on the early operationalization of decisions taken earlier and the establishment of a "dedicated and secure hotline" between the two Foreign Secretaries. Both sides agreed to review and monitor the implementation of nuclear CBMs as called for by the Lahore MoU of 1999.

In accordance with the agreement between the Foreign Ministers of Pakistan and India in September 2004, the second round of the Expert Level talks on Nuclear Confidence Building Measures was held in Islamabad on 14-15 December 2004. The Indian delegation was led by Ms. Meera Shankar, Additional Secretary (UN), Ministry of External Affairs. The Pakistan delegation was led by Mr. Tariq Osman Hyder, Additional Secretary (UN&EC), Ministry of Foreign Affairs. The visiting Indian delegation called on the Foreign Minister of Pakistan Mr. Khurshid M. Kasuri.

2. The two sides held discussions in a cordial and constructive atmosphere, in the framework of the Lahore MoU of 1999 and the Joint Statement of 20 June 2004. Both sides reiterated their desire to keep working towards elaboration and implementation of Nuclear CBMs, within the agreed framework.

3. Detailed consultations were also held on the early operationalization of the decisions taken during the last round of Expert Level talks on Nuclear CBMs held in New Delhi on 19-20 June 2004, especially on the upgradation of the existing hotline between the DGMOs, and the establishment of a dedicated and secure hotline between the two Foreign Secretaries. These measures are, inter alia, intended to prevent misunderstanding and reduce risks relevant to nuclear issues.

4. Both sides agreed the future periodic Expert Level talks on Nuclear CBMs would discuss, review and monitor the implementation of Nuclear CBMs as called for by the Lahore MoU of 1999.

5. They also agreed to report the progress made in the present round of the talks to the respective Foreign Secretaries, who are scheduled to meet on 27-28 December 2004, and decide on the date and venue of the next Expert Level meeting on Nuclear CBMs.

❮16❯

Joint Statement on Meeting between Foreign Secretaries of India and Pakistan (28.12.2004)

> The Foreign Secretaries of India and Pakistan reviewed the progress made on Composite Dialogue, issues of peace and security including CBMs, and Jammu and Kashmir. Differences on the draft agreement on pre-notification of flight testing of ballistic missiles were also discussed, as were the issues related to apprehended fishermen, civilian prisoners and missing defence personnel.

The Foreign Secretaries of Pakistan and India met in Islamabad on 27 – 28 December 2004 to review overall progress, commence the next round of the Composite Dialogue and discuss the issues of Peace and Security including CBMs, and Jammu and Kashmir. Foreign Secretary of Pakistan Mr. Riaz H. Khokhar, led the Pakistan delegation while the Indian delegation was led by Foreign Secretary Mr. Shyam Saran. The talks were held in a frank, cordial and constructive atmosphere.

2. Recalling the solemn and categoric reassurance contained in the Joint Press Statement of 6th January, they expressed their determination to carry the process forward.
3. On the issue of Peace and Security including CBMs, the two Foreign Secretaries, inter-alia reviewed the progress made during the meetings of Experts on Nuclear and Conventional CBMs. Building upon the existing contacts between DG MOs, they agreed to promote regular contacts at local level at designated places and explore further CBMs along the international boundary and the LoC. They discussed and narrowed further their differences on the draft agreement on pre-notification of flight testing of ballistic missiles, and agreed to work towards its early finalization.
4. Both sides discussed the issue of Jammu and Kashmir and agreed to carry forward the process in the light of the Joint Statement issued after the meeting between President of Pakistan General Pervez Musharraf and Prime Minister of India Dr. Manmohan Singh in New York on September 24, 2004.
5. The meetings on the other six subjects under the Composite Dialogue, i.e. Siachen, Wullar Barrage/Tulbul Navigation Project, Sir Creek,

Terrorism & Drug Trafficking, Economic & Commercial Cooperation and Promotion of Friendly Exchanges in Various Fields would be held on mutually agreed dates between April and June 2005.

6. The two sides also agreed that technical meetings including the Joint Study Group on Trade matters headed by the Commerce Secretaries, Indian Coast Guards and Pakistan Maritime Agency, Pakistan Rangers and Border Security Force of India, Expert level dialogue on Nuclear and Conventional CBMs, technical level meeting on bus service between/through Amritsar and Lahore, meeting between the Narcotics Control Authorities would be held between January and June 2005.
7. They also discussed issues related to apprehended fishermen, civilian prisoners and missing defence personnel. It was inter-alia agreed that:
   (i) Immediate notification would be provided to the respective High Commissions through the Foreign Ministries of arrested Pakistani/Indian nationals;
   (ii) Consular access would be provided within three months of apprehension;
   (iii) Repatriation would be done immediately after completion of sentence and nationality verification;
   (iv) A mechanism would be introduced for early repatriation, without sentencing of inadvertent crossers;
   (v) A similar mechanism would be established for early release, without sentencing of those under 16 apprehended by either side.
8. The Foreign Secretaries of the two countries would meet in New Delhi to review the overall progress in the Composite Dialogue in July-August 2005.
9. The Foreign Ministers and the Prime Ministers of the two countries would meet during the SAARC Summit in Dhaka in January 2005. The External Affairs Minister of India Mr. K. Natwar Singh would visit Islamabad in February 2005 for bilateral discussions.
10. The Foreign Secretary of India called on Prime Minster Shaukat Aziz and Foreign Minister Khurshid M. Kasuri of Pakistan during the course of his visit to Islamabad.

❮17❯

Joint Declaration by the Russian Federation and the Republic of India (03.12.2004)

> The two sides, associated as they are in a strategic partnership, discussed a wide range of issues such as global terrorism, the situation in Central Asia, Iraq, the Arab-Israeli conflict, the reconstruction process in Afghanistan etc. They agreed to carry forward their bilateral relations in areas such as mutual investments in industries, cooperation in IT and banking and in the energy sector.

The Russian Federation and the Republic of India, hereinafter referred to as the Sides,

Guided by mutual trust and respect inherent in bilateral relations,

Drawing upon their wide ranging tradition of cooperation since the establishment of diplomatic relations in April 1947,

Recalling the Treaty on Friendship and Cooperation between the Republic of India and the Russian Federation of 28 January 1993,

Reaffirming the Declaration on Strategic Partnership between the Republic of India and the Russian Federation of 3 October 2000,

Convinced of the mutual desire to promote global peace and progress, and the need to counter challenges arising out of international terrorism,

Confirm their adherence to the common ideals of secularism, democracy, rule of law, cultural diversity and pluralism,

Affirm their commitment to develop further and enhance the strategic partnership based on nation-wide consensus in both the States,

Declare as follows;

I

India and Russia, as two of the largest democracies in the world, are deeply committed to the establishment of a more democratic world order, based on a multi-polar world, which takes into account the major changes that have taken place in the international political landscape over the past few decades. The two Sides note with satisfaction that the strategic partnership between them serves their long-term national interests, strengthens bilateral relations, deepens mutually beneficial cooperation and contributes to international peace and security.

The Sides agree to intensify exchanges in bilateral relations at the political and parliamentary levels, between the Security Councils and at official level. The significant degree of convergence in the overall perspective as well as interests of the two sides, have enabled Indo-Russian relations to withstand the test of time. Both sides recognize that their cooperation strengthens strategic stability in Asia and the world as a whole.

The Sides propose to continue consultations at all levels between the foreign ministries of the two countries, including those on disarmament as well as on the United Nations issues. Priority attention will be paid to coordination of efforts through the Joint Working Group on Combating Global Challenges and the Joint Working Group on Combating International Terrorism.

The Indian Side regards Russia as a major and fully active member of the international community, and as a country whose voice commands respect and attention on issues of global concern. In this context, the Indian Side strongly supports the earliest possible accession of Russia to the World Trade Organisation. The Sides regard this support as an important demonstration of Indo-Russian relations of strategic partnership, and express their desire to develop, after the accession of Russia to the WTO, cooperation within that Organisation, based on the principles of mutual respect, equality and mutual benefit.

The Sides are convinced that trade, culture and tourism promote economic cooperation, goodwill and people-to-people contact between nations. The Sides stress that the traditionally strong bilateral relations have rested on foundations of political, defence and economic exchanges of a substantial nature. In the current context, this process has to be carried forward and strengthened further. Mutual investments in industries, cooperation in IT and banking are some areas that offer a new scope.

Energy constitutes an important part of the bilateral relationship. Considering the expanding energy requirements of India, both Sides stress the need for employing resources that are environment-friendly and available in sufficient quantities. Nuclear power plants offer a pollution-free and substantial source of energy to provide for the sustainable development. Both Sides are determined to continue their cooperation in the field of nuclear energy, incorporating innovative technologies to ensure energy security, with due regard to their commitments to non-proliferation norms. The Sides also recognise the considerable scope for cooperation in the hydro-electric and thermal power sectors. Russia is a major exporter of oil and gas and India is emerging as a large consumer. The Sides affirm their desire to cooperate in development of new oil and gas fields and the means of their transportation in Russia, India and other countries. Both Sides agree to encourage and assist investments in the energy sector by Indian companies in Russia and those by Russian companies in this sector in India. The Sides view cooperation in energy as an area of priority attention in bilateral cooperation.

II

The Sides agree that the 21st century presents new challenges. In a globalised world, there are inherent inter-linkages not only between countries, but also between issues. Both Sides recognise the indivisibility between security and prosperity in the present-day world. They agree that the most effective way to address contemporary challenges is through multilateral approaches based on the widest possible international support. Multi-lateralism is an instrument to work towards the objective of a multi-polar world.

The UN system is at the centre of multi-lateralism. Both Sides agree to cooperate closely at the UN and in other international organizations. In 2005 the UN will be 60 years old. Both Sides emphasise the necessity of comprehensive reforms in the UN system so as to reflect both the enlarged membership in the UN and the contemporary realities. India and Russia emphasise that the expansion of the UN Security Council is an urgent imperative to make the Security Council more representative and effective. In this framework, the Russian Federation reiterates once again that it regards India as an influential and major member of the international community. The Russian Federation reaffirms its support to India as a deserving and strong candidate for the permanent membership in an expanded UN Security Council.

III

India and the Russian Federation reiterate their common resolve to fight terrorism. They reaffirm that global terrorism in all its forms and manifestations constitutes one of the most serious threats to international peace and security, and condemn in the strongest terms all acts of terrorism irrespective of their motivation, whenever and by whomsoever committed. They underscore that there can be no justification for terrorism on any grounds, including ideological, religious, racial, ethnic or any other. They believe that the fight against terrorism has to be long-term, sustained and comprehensive. In this regard they emphasise the need for giving substance and credibility to the global fight against terrorism and avoid selective approaches and political expediency. With the recent targeting of open societies around the world, India and the Russian Federation as two large and influential democracies, have reasons to be concerned about the vulnerability of democracies to terrorist attacks, because terrorism exploits the strengths of democracies such as, the protection of human rights, freedom of expression and movement.

Both countries welcome the unanimous adoption of the UN Security Council resolution 1566 [piloted by the Russian Federation]. Noting that it seeks to consider action against terrorists including sanctions and judicial action and aims at making the Counter Terrorism Committee more action-oriented, both countries decided to actively cooperate with each other in counter-terrorism efforts.

India and the Russian Federation re-emphasise the need for an early adoption by the General Assembly of the Comprehensive Convention on International Terrorism and the International Convention for the Suppression of Acts of Nuclear Terrorism.

IV

Both Sides reaffirm that proliferation of weapons of mass destruction (WMD), their means of delivery and related materials, particularly the risk of their falling into the hands of terrorists constitutes a threat to international peace and security. They highlighted the need to prevent terrorists or those who harbour them from acquiring or developing WMD, their means of delivery and related materials. Both sides emphasised the necessity to further address this threat on national basis as well as through forward looking multilateral long term efforts by all partners against proliferation with the central role of the United Nations. As strategic partners India and Russia affirmed their commitment to cooperate bilaterally as well as through appropriate multilateral forum towards contributing to this objective.

Both Sides also reaffirm their commitment to support efforts to prevent the deployment of weapons in outer space while preserving it for peaceful and cooperative activities aimed at developmental benefits.

V

The Sides note with satisfaction that the Trilateral Meetings at the Foreign Ministers level of India, China and Russia have been taking place regularly. These meetings have been useful in promoting understanding and exploring areas of possible cooperation at a trilateral and at an international level. The Trilateral Meetings have also reflected a strong concern against terrorism anywhere and in any form. The Sides express their conviction in favour of progressive increase in the trilateral cooperation, which could also result in social and economic development amongst the three countries.

VI

The Sides considered the situation in Central Asia and note that security and stability in that region coincides with the priorities of India and Russia for the region. Greater economic growth and democratic progress of the Central Asian States demand the respect for their freedom to choose the models of development and implementation of reforms.

VII

The Sides express concern over continuing violence in Iraq and stress the need for an intra-Iraqi dialogue aimed at building national consensus on a new constitution and on restoring stability and security in the country. The

Sides advocate strict compliance of the UN Security Council resolution 1546, particularly with regard to the interim timetable of political process stipulated by it with a view to facilitating the formation of a new, democratic Iraq.

The Sides affirm their continuing interest in contributing to the reconstruction efforts in Iraq and urged a wider degree of international consultation in the ongoing peace efforts. The Sides believe that it would be in the interest of the international community to restore the efficacy of multilateral approaches in addressing situations such as the war in Iraq.

VIII

The Sides support the objective of a lasting, just and comprehensive settlement of the Arab Israeli conflict, based on relevant resolutions of the UN Security Council. The sides encourage the resumption of peaceful negotiations as soon as possible in accordance with the Road Map worked out by the Quartet of international intermediaries and approved by the UN Security Council in its resolution 1515.

IX

The Sides welcome the successful conclusion of the Presidential elections in Afghanistan and underline the importance of efforts at national reconciliation and unity. The Sides also look forward to conduct of the parliamentary elections as scheduled in April/May 2005. They express support for a strong, united, sovereign and independent Afghanistan and underline the importance of empowering the Central authority with indigenous security institutions.

The Sides reiterate their support for the reconstruction process in Afghanistan. The Sides express their concern at the continuing threat to security, especially in the South and Southeastern provinces and also over the continued increase in the cultivation, production and trafficking of narcotic drugs in Afghanistan and underline the need for effective steps to counteract the drug and terrorist threats.

X

The Russian Federation and the Republic of India are convinced that their bilateral cooperation in all forms, and their strategic partnership, contributes to the strengthening of the regional and global goodwill and cooperation. They are determined to further enhance in every possible way the relations of partnership and closely interact on a bilateral and multilateral basis, with other states, regional and international forums.

❮18❯

Joint Press Statement on State Visit of Prime Minister of Singapore to India (10.07.2004)

> The two sides agreed that their strategic and economic interests are convergent. The progress made towards the conclusion of a Comprehensive Economic Cooperation Agreement (CECA) was reviewed. The initiative taken by the Prime Minister of Singapore to set up the Singapore-India Partnership Foundation for further promoting the development of Singapore-India bilateral relations was welcomed by both sides.

His Excellency Mr. Goh Chok Tong, Prime Minister of Singapore paid a State Visit to India from 8th to 11th July, 2004 at the invitation of Prime Minister Manmohan Singh. He was accompanied by Minister of Foreign Affairs and Law, Prof. S. Jayakumar; Minister of Trade and Industry Mr. George Yeo Yong-boon and senior officials from the Government of Singapore.

During the visit, Prime Minister Goh called on the President and Vice President of India. He also had a restricted meeting as well as delegation-level talks with the Prime Minister, who also hosted a banquet in honour of the visiting dignitary. President of Congress Party and Chairman of the United Progressive Alliance Coordination Committee; Minister of External Affairs; Minister of Commerce and Industry; and Leader of the Opposition in the Lok Sabha called on Prime Minister Goh Chok Tong. Prime Minister Goh also had a meeting with Shri Atal Bihari Vajpayee, former Prime Minister.

The President of India presented the Jawaharlal Nehru Award for International Understanding 2003 to His Excellency Prime Minister Goh Chok Tong. Prime Minister Goh paid a glowing tribute to Pt. Jawaharlal Nehru, whom he described as "an inspiration to the generation that had fought to free themselves from colonial rule".

The two Prime Ministers led their delegations at the bilateral talks. Both sides agreed that their strategic and economic interests are convergent. India expressed appreciation for Singapore's very positive and constructive role in enhancing India's interaction with ASEAN. They expressed great satisfaction at the strengthening and diversification of their bilateral relations and resolved to take them to even greater heights in a variety of areas.

In that context, the two Prime Ministers noted their common concerns and the identity of their views on the threat to open and democratic societies from terrorism and extremist violence. They called for effective international cooperation to combat terrorism and deny sanctuaries to terrorist outfits. They expressed satisfaction at their growing consultation and cooperation in this area. They welcomed the institutionalisation of the bilateral Joint Working Group on Intellligence Cooperation on Combatting Terrorism and Transnational Organised Crime and the finalisation of the bilateral Mutual Legal Assistance Treaty on Criminal Matters. They hoped that the Treaty would come into effect shortly and further enhance bilateral cooperation in the area of law enforcement.

The two sides noted the signing of the Defence Cooperation Agreement in October 2003 and the establishment of the Defence Policy Dialogue under its auspices. Bilateral interactions between the Armed Forces of the two countries have increased in depth and scope. Both sides positively assessed the potential and scope for defence cooperation between the two countries covering bilateral exercises, training arrangements, professional and high level exchanges and visits and collaboration in defence technology research. They saw the consolidation of defence ties as a natural evolution of their excellent political understanding. These ties would be a factor for peace and stability in the region.

The Prime Ministers reviewed the progress of negotiations for the conclusion of a Comprehensive Economic Cooperation Agreement (CECA). Both Sides attached importance to the Agreement, recognizing its potential for further cementing their growing economic and commercial ties. The Prime Ministers commended the progress so far and directed their officials to work purposefully towards concluding the negotiations early.

Both sides welcomed the initiative of the Prime Minister of Singapore, with the support of the Singapore Business Federation and the Confederation of Indian Industry to set up the Singapore-India Partnership Foundation to promote exchanges between the two countries. They expressed hope that this Foundation would play an important catalytic role in promoting the further development of Singapore-India bilateral relations.

‹19›

Joint Press Release on the Visit to India of President of Sri Lanka Mrs. Chandrika Bandaranaike Kumaratunga (07.11.2004)

> The two sides reaffirmed a convergence of views on a range of international issues and resolved to expedite negotiations on the Comprehensive Economic Partnership Agreement (CEPA). They also discussed the utilisation of $ 100 million credit line offered by India for the development of rural infrastructure projects in Sri Lanka and a credit line of US $ 150 million for the purchase of petroleum products.

H.E. Mrs. Chandrika Bandaranaike Kumaratunga, President of Sri Lanka, visited India from November 3-7, 2004 at the invitation of the President of India, H.E. Dr. A.P.J. Abdul Kalam. She was accompanied by Hon'ble Lakshman Kadirgamar, Minister of Foreign Affairs; Hon'ble A.D. Susil Premajayantha, Minister of Power and Energy; and senior officials.

2. The President of Sri Lanka held wide-ranging discussions with President Dr. A.P.J. Abdul Kalam, Prime Minister Dr. Manmohan Singh, External Affairs Minister Shri K. Natwar Singh, and Defence Minister Shri Pranab Mukherjee. The discussions were detailed and substantive in consonance with the close and friendly ties that exist between the two countries.

3. Smt. Sonia Gandhi, Chairperson of the United Progressive Alliance, called on President Kumaratunga.

4. The President of Sri Lanka also met former Prime Minister Shri Atal Bihari Vajpayee.

5. The discussions reaffirmed the traditional convergence of views between the two countries on a range of international issues. Both sides remain deeply committed to opposing terrorism in all its forms and manifestations. They agreed that there could be no justification for terrorism, be it political, religious or ideological. There was also a meeting of minds on the need for urgent reform of the UN system to meet global challenges, including the expansion of the permanent membership of the Security Council. India expressed its sincere appreciation of Sri Lanka's endorsement of India's candidature for the

permanent membership of the UN Security Council. They also agreed to cooperate in other forums, including the WTO.

6. Both sides expressed deep satisfaction at the dynamism and energy in bilateral economic ties since the entry into force of the India-Sri Lanka Free Trade Agreement (ISLFTA) in March 2000. Both sides expressed happiness that bilateral trade has exceeded US$ 1.5 billion in 2003-04. Consideration will be given to establish a Joint Working Group to keep under review any practical problems arising out of the implementation of the FTA. They resolved to inject impetus to the process of further economic integration of the two economies by expediting negotiations on the Comprehensive Economic Partnership Agreement (CEPA) between the two countries.

7. It was noted that India is the second highest tourism generating country in Sri Lanka and the number of Sri Lankan Airline flights into various cities in India has reached 77 per week, which is the highest number of flights to India by any airline. The relatively new destinations introduced are Bangalore, Hyderabad and Bodh Gaya.

8. The President of Sri Lanka and the Prime Minister of India agreed that the US$ 100 million credit line offered by India for the development of Rural Infrastructure projects in Sri Lanka would be used for setting up of vocational training institutes in various parts of the country ranging from the south to the north-east, rural feeder roads, water supply development schemes, community development projects, rural telephony and refurbishing of the road between Anuradhapura and Trincomalee, which is to be named the Rajiv Gandhi Amity Highway. The credit line is aimed at creating durable infrastructure and providing training and employment opportunities to people in rural areas.

9. The utilization of the credit line for US$ 150 million for the purchase of petroleum products, signed on 15th October 2004 was also discussed.

10. The two sides agreed to explore the possibilities of intensification of cooperation in the power sector.

11. The two sides decided to expedite the signing of a Memorandum of Understanding on Fisheries, presently under consideration. While agreeing to continue with the existing understandings on the humane treatment and early release of apprehended fishermen, it was decided to constitute a Joint Working Group which could meet frequently to deal with issues relating to straying fishermen, work out modalities for prevention of use of force against them and the early release of confiscated boats, and explore possibilities of working towards bilateral arrangements for licensed fishing.

12. The two sides noted that cultural exchanges is an area, which has great scope in bringing the two peoples together. There have always been an interest in each other's cultures due to the synergies and diversities, which offer many opportunities for fruitful cooperation. Both sides agreed that the Cultural Exchange Programme, which was signed in October 2003, needs to be actively implemented.
13. The Sri Lankan side proposed that a lecture titled "Rajiv Gandhi Memorial Oration" should be jointly organized annually by the Bandaranaike Centre for International Studies (BCIS) and the Rajiv Gandhi Foundation. The first lecture would be delivered by President Kumaratunga. It was also suggested that a unit be set up in the BCIS titled "Centre for India Sri Lanka Studies". The Indian side welcomed the proposals.
14. With regard to activities relating to Buddhism, the Sri Lankan side took up with the Indian side the possibilities of obtaining concessions on the entrance fees to Buddhist pilgrim sites in India and exemption of visa fees for Buddhist pilgrims. Sri Lanka expressed appreciation for the Indian assistance to repair the Mulkirigala Temple at Hambantota and Thiruketheeswaram Temple complex in Mannar.
15. It was noted with satisfaction that the Indian offer of a grant of US$ 7.5 million to build a state-of-the-art Cancer Hospital in Sri Lanka would be expedited by the visit of an Indian technical team in Sri Lanka next week.
16. During discussions on the Defence Cooperation Agreement, it was resolved that a bilateral Defence Cooperation Agreement and the MoU on the Rehabilitation of the Airfield in Palaly would be signed between the two Governments on mutually convenient dates. The Indian side also agreed to carry out the refit of the Sri Lankan Naval Ship "Sayura" and underwrite the costs.
17. On the question of the Sethusamudram Canal Project, it was agreed that an exchange of views on the economic and environmental aspects in relation to Sri Lanka would be arranged between the technical experts of India and Sri Lanka.
18. The President of Sri Lanka apprised the Indian leadership of the current status of the peace process in Sri Lanka and the steps she has taken to advance it further. India, for its part, reiterated its support for the process of seeking a comprehensive, negotiated settlement acceptable to all communities of Sri Lanka, and reflecting the pluralistic nature of Sri Lankan society, within the framework of a united Sri Lanka and consistent with democracy and respect for individual rights. India maintains an abiding interest in the security of Sri Lanka and remains committed to its unity, sovereignty and territorial integrity. India favours the early resumption of negotiations pertaining to the

peace process. Any interim arrangement on administration should be an integral part of an enduring final settlement that maintains the unity and territorial integrity of Sri Lanka and ensures the safety, well-being and prosperity of the people.

19. The discussions during the visit served to underline the excellent state of bilateral ties and the growing partnership for economic cooperation between the two countries. Both sides resolved to further strengthen their high-level interaction through sustained dialogue in order to expand their cooperation in areas of mutual benefit to their peoples.

20. The President also addressed the Hindustan Times Leadership Initiative and made a Keynote Speech on the topic "Unity and Diversity – Keeping South Asia together".

21. The President of Sri Lanka will visit Bodh Gaya.

❮20❯

India-UK Joint Declaration (20.09.2004)

> The two sides agreed to step up their bilateral cooperation on terrorism, poverty, HIV/AIDS, environmental degradation, climate change, drugs, international crime, illegal migration and trafficking in people. It was decided to establish an Indo-British Economic and Financial Dialogue on bilateral and global issues, on financial systems, and to enhance economic and financial cooperation. It was also decided to establish a Joint Economic and Trade Committee.

We, the Prime Ministers of India and the UK, believe that the relationship between our two countries is now the strongest it has ever been. Building on the achievements of the 2002 New Delhi Declaration, we commit ourselves and our Governments to strengthening and deepening the comprehensive partnership that exists between our countries – to benefit our peoples, and to create a safer and more prosperous world.

People are at the heart of our relationship. Almost 1.5 million people of Indian origin live in Britain today. Their cultural values contribute significantly towards making Britain the vibrant, dynamic society that it is today. They are a vital bond between our countries.

Both our societies value, and encourage, cultural and ethnic diversity.

Both our countries have a long and proud historical tradition, and yet are countries looking forward, adapting to the challenges, and trying to shape the outcome of the 21st century.

The flow of people between our countries is huge. 500,000 Indians visit Britain each year. 400,000 Britons visit India. These people-to-people links flourish in many areas—education, health, development, science and technology, including in the frontier technologies, investment, trade and tourism.

India and the UK are natural economic partners. As India emerges as a global power, trade and investment relations are becoming more diverse. Bilateral trade grew by over 20% last year. We want this rapid growth to continue. But the real partnership lies in the strength of investment in both directions. The UK is the second largest investor into India. India was the 8th largest investor in the UK in 2003. It is one of the fastest growing, investing in the UK's knowledge economy. The UK provides an important bridge into the European market, attracting over 60% of India's investment in Europe.

Shared democratic values and a commitment to human rights, justice and the rule of law underpin our relationship. We share a global vision of peace, security and shared prosperity, based on sustainable development. We have shared interests in combating key global challenges—terrorism, poverty, HIV/AIDS, environmental degradation, climate change, drugs, international crime, illegal migration and trafficking in people. We will step up our bilateral co-operation on these issues.

However, we must also urgently strengthen the multilateral system to meet these global challenges. We will co-operate closely on this and the UK will continue to work for India's Permanent Membership of the UN Security Council.

We can achieve even more together than we already do. We now intend to take our relationship to a new level. We see the relationship between our two countries as among our top international priorities. As Heads of Government, we will work for a long-term comprehensive strategic partnership for the 21st century of shared values and interests. In particular we will strengthen our links in the following areas.

Foreign and Defence Policy

Heads of Government and foreign ministers will exchange visits annually to reinforce and extend our bilateral co-operation in the fields we have identified for joint action.

We will reinforce our strategic partnership, and enhance our defence co-operation, in the pursuit of a more peaceful and secure world. We will build upon, and expand, programmes of joint military training and exercises. We will explore the co-production of defence equipment. We will work towards the objective of non-proliferation of weapons of mass destruction and the means of their delivery.

Security Challenges

Both our countries are deeply committed to combating terrorism in all its forms and manifestations. We will work together to try to ensure that the global norms against terrorism are upheld by all countries. We will share our experience and augment our co-operation, including operational co-operation between police, law enforcement agencies and others in our criminal justice system. We will enhance our co-operation to counter moneylaundering and terrorist financing.

The UK will support India to join the Financial Action Task Force. We will identify specific needs and share best practice in the areas of justice, judicial co-operation and mutual legal assistance. We will co-operate in the light against international, organised and serious crime and new forms of criminality, including illegal migration, drugs trafficking and trafficking in people.

Economic and Trade Issues

Our economic ties will continue to expand. We will establish a Ministerially-led Joint Economic and Trade Committee to further develop a strategic economic relationship, and develop business-led vehicles to enhance bilateral trade and investment in specific sectors including services and knowledge-based industries. We will enhance our dialogue on international trade and investment issues.

We will also establish an Indo-British Economic and Financial Dialogue on bilateral and global issues, on financial systems, and to enhance economic and financial co-operation.

At this important time in the development of the international trade regime, we will work closely together for a successful conclusion to the WTO's Doha Round of multilateral trade negotiations.

The UK and India agree to expand co-operation in the fields of civilian nuclear activities, civilian space programmes, and high technology trade, in accordance with their international obligations.

Science and Technology

The UK and India already co-operate closely on science and technology. We have established a Joint Committee on Science and Technology and a networking scheme that enables scientists to meet each other, exchange research ideas and establish links. We will now enhance existing collaboration and identify new areas for co-operation in fields such as: climate change, alternative and clean energy technologies, environmental science, commercial applications of high technology like biotech and bio-informatics, nano-technology, agriculture, and health research and development. We will encourage collaborative opportunities in these areas.

Development Partnership

We have an important development partnership. The UK is recognised as a leader in international development. India has made great development progress over the last two decades and is now establishing itself as a development partner for other developing countries. Our shared commitment to the UN Millennium Development Goals provides an opportunity to exchange experience on aid effectiveness and development practices. Working together, we can accelerate development and make progress globally towards the Millennium Goals.

Sustainable Development

Both our countries recognize that co-operation is essential to deliver the progressive global agenda set by the Johannesburg World Summit on

Sustainable Development and the Millennium Declaration. We will initiate regular high-level dialogue to share experiences on how we can overcome social, economic and environmental challenges, and bring real quality of life improvements for people in both our countries and around the world.

Climate change and broader issues of sustainable energy security are high on our respective agendas. Climate change will be a central theme of the UK's Presidencies of the G8 and EU next year. We will promote effective co-operation in our responses to climate change, including by building on the successful joint work that has already been carried out by the UK and India on climate change impacts and modelling. To this end, we will establish a structured dialogue to exchange views and information and take forward any bilateral co-operation projects.

Education and Culture

There are strong and vibrant academic links between the UK and India. By 2008, we expect that 25,000 students from the UK and India will be studying in each other's academic institutions. We will explore ways to help educational establishments in our countries to establish lasting partnerships.

The cultural influence of the UK, not least through the use of English, has added to the richness of Indian culture, and Indian writers have enriched English literature. Now, through the community of Indian origin in the UK, and directly, Indian culture is becoming an important component of multi-ethnic Britain. We welcome this and will work to strengthen cultural linkages between our countries, including in areas like publishing and film production.

Conclusion

On this historic occasion we reaffirm our commitment to strengthen our comprehensive strategic partnership for the benefit of both our peoples and the international community based on universal values of democracy and respect for the rule of law, human rights and fundamental freedoms. We stress our commitment to work towards promoting international peace, stability and security and the eradication of poverty. We recognize that a strengthened multilateral system, including a reformed Security Council that would reflect the changing aspirations of the 21st century, is an important element of this process. In recognition of our comprehensive strategic partnership we will hold annual summit meetings alternating in our capitals and will continue the high level dialogue established through our Personal Envoys.

(Signed by Prime Ministers Manmohan Singh and Tony Blair)

❮21❯

Indo-US Joint Statement on Next Steps in Strategic Partnership (NSSP) (17.09.2004)

Under the NSSP initiative, US and India agreed to expand cooperation in civilian nuclear activities, civilian space programmes and high technology trade and to "expand the dialogue" on missile defence. In Phase One of the NSSP, US made modifications to US export licensing policies and removed ISRO headquarters from the Department of Commerce Entity List.

The United States and India announced today major progress in the Next Steps in Strategic Partnership (NSSP) initiative. Implementation of the NSSP will lead to significant economic benefits for both countries and improve regional and global security.

In January 2004, the United States and India agreed to expand cooperation in three specific areas: civilian nuclear activities, civilian space programs, and high-technology trade. In addition, the two countries agreed to expand our dialogue on missile defense. These areas of cooperation are designed to progress through a series of reciprocal steps that build on each other.

Since January, the two governments have worked closely together to conclude Phase One of the NSSP. This has included implementation of measures to address proliferation concerns and ensure compliance with U.S. export controls.

These efforts have enabled the United States to make modifications to U.S. export licensing policies that will foster cooperation in commercial space programs and permit certain exports to power plants at safeguarded nuclear facilities. These modifications, including removing the Indian Space Research Organization (ISRO) Headquarters from the Department of Commerce Entity List, are fully consistent with U.S. Government nonproliferation laws, obligations, and objectives.

The United States and India will continue to move forward under the NSSP, and have a joint implementation group for this purpose. The progress announced today is only the first phase in this important effort, which is a significant part of transforming our strategic relationship.

❮22❯

Press Release at the conclusion of second meeting of the US-India Cyber Security Forum (10.11.2004)

> The Government and industry representatives from both countries identified areas for collaboration in combating cyber crime, cyber security research and development, information assurance and defence cooperation, standards and software assurance, and cyber incident management and response. They also established five joint working groups and identified action plans for each.

On November 9-10, the United States hosted the second meeting of the U.S.-India Cyber Security Forum, convening both government and industry representatives from each country to identify areas for collaboration in combating cyber-crime, cyber security research and development, information assurance and defense cooperation, standards and software assurance, and cyber incident management and response.

Under Secretary of State for Political Affairs Marc Grossman, in prepared remarks, stated that the U.S.-India Cyber Security Forum "holds great promise for future cooperation." Indian Head of Delegation, National Security Council Secretariat Joint Secretary Arvind Gupta, delivering a statement to the Forum on behalf of J.N. Dixit, India's National Security Advisor stating that "Security cyberspace will remain one of the biggest challenges facing the international community for years to come and this Cyber Security Forum has emerged as an important bilateral mechanism to address such issues".

The first meeting of the U.S.-India Cyber Security Forum was held in New Delhi in April 2002 in recognition of the increasing interdependency between India and the United States in the information technology arena. Cooperation between the United States and India is of growing importance as U.S. government and corporations utilize information technology companies in India at a rate of about $9 billion annually. "As this trend increases, it is crucial that our governments and private industry work together to ensure an environment for secure transactions, networks, and software development," said U.S. State Department Assistant Secretary for Political-Military Affairs Lincoln P. Bloomfield, Jr., the U.S. Head of Delegation.

During the conference the United States and India reaffirmed their commitment to cooperation on securing cyberspace by establishing five joint working groups and identifying action plans for each. Future efforts will include workshops in New Delhi and Washington and scientific exchanges. Representatives of private industry similarly identified areas to strengthen cooperation.

❮23❯

Islamabad (SAARC) Declaration (06.01.2004)

The document covers a wide range of issues such as regional cooperation, poverty alleviation, science and technology, environment, combating terrorism, information and communication etc. The signing of the Frame- work Agreement on SAFTA (for broadening of economic cooperation and to ensure equitable distribution of benefits of trade) and the SAARC Social Charter; the approval of a Plan of Action of Poverty Alleviation; and the decision to set up a SAARC Health Surveillance Center and Rapid Deployment Health Response system were some of the highlights of the Islamabad Declaration.

"We, the Prime Minister of the people's republic of Bangladesh, Begum Khaleda Zia, the Prime Minister of the Kingdom of Bhutan, Lyonpo Jigmi Yoezer Thinley, the Prime Minister of the Republic of India, Atal Behari Vajpayee, the President of the Republic of Maldives, Maumoon Abdul Gayoom, the Prime Minister of the Kingdom of Nepal, Surya Bahadur Thapa, the Prime Minister of the Islamic Republic of Pakistan, Mir Zafarullah Khan Jamali and the President of the Democratic Socialist Republic of Sri Lanka, Chandrika Bandaranaike Kumaratunga:

Having met at the Twelfth Summit meeting of the South Asian Association for Regional cooperation (SAARC) in Islamabad, Pakistan on 4-6 January 2004;

Guided by the vision of a peaceful and prosperous South Asia and proud of its rich culture and traditions;

Deeply conscious of the growing interdependence within and amongst nations and regions in an increasingly globalising world;

Desirous of promoting peace, stability, amity and progress in the region through strict adherence to the principles of the United Nations Charter and Non-Alignment, particularly respect for the principles of sovereign equality, territorial integrity, national independence, non-use of force and non-interference in the internal affairs of the states and peaceful settlement of all disputes;

Reaffirming the centrality of SAARC for promoting regional cooperation and emphasizing the need to enhance its efficacy;

Strongly reaffirming our commitment to the objectives, principles and provisions of the Charter of the South Asian Association for Regional Cooperation (SAARC);

Declare that:

Regional Cooperation

Economic

1. We renew our commitment to the objectives and principles of SAARC and pledge to reinvigorate cooperation to realize peace amity, progress and prosperity of all peoples of South Asia.
2. We affirm our determination to create an inclusive, just and equitable partnership for peace, development and prosperity. Satisfactory progress has been made in SAPTA. The signing of the Framework Agreement on SAFTA is a major milestone. It is important to maintain this momentum and move towards further broadening of economic cooperation and to ensure equitable distribution of benefits of trade and cater to the special needs of the small and LDC Member States by providing them special and differential treatment.
3. We reiterate our commitment made at the 11th SAARC Summit at Kathmandu in January 2002 for the creation of a South Asian Economic Union. In this context, we underline that creation of a suitable political and economic environment would be conducive to the realization of this objective.
4. A study on creating a South Asian Energy Cooperation including the concept of an Energy Ring should be undertaken by the Working Group on Energy.
5. For accelerated and balanced economic growth it is essential to strengthen transportation, transit and communication links across the region.
6. Public and private sector cooperation, particularly joint ventures holds great promise. It is important to move towards Project cooperation under SAARC. Prospects for setting up of a South Asian Development Bank should be examined by the SAARCFINANCE through the Council of Ministers.
7. Priority attention should also be given to the need for harmonization of standards, simplification of custom procedures, as well as cooperation among the central banks.
8. Development of tourism within South Asia could bring economic, social and cultural dividends. There is a need for increasing cooperation to jointly promote tourism within South Asia as well as to promote South Asia as tourism destination inter alia by improved air links. To achieve this and to commemorate the twentieth year of the establishment of SAARC, the year 2005 is designated as "South Asia Tourism Year", for the success of which, each member would individually and jointly organize special events.
9. SAARC members should continue to safeguard their collective interests in multilateral forums by discussing, coordinating and exchanging information with a view to adopting common positions, where appropriate on various issues.

Poverty Alleviation

10. We recognize poverty alleviation as the greatest challenge facing the peoples of South Asia and declare poverty alleviation as the overarching goal of all SAARC activities. It is, imperative to relate regional co-operation to the actual needs of the people.
11. Provision of basic needs, promotion of literacy, and better healthcare are a regional priority. It is important to undertake effective and sustained poverty reduction programmes through pro-poor growth strategies and other policy interventions with specific sectoral targets.
12. The Plan of Action of Poverty Alleviation, prepared by the meeting of Finance and Planning Ministers in Islamabad in 2002, is hereby approved.
13. The reconstituted Independent South Asian Commission for Poverty Alleviation (ISACPA) has done commendable work. An effective strategy should be devised to implement suggestions made in its report "Our Future Our Responsibility". In this context, ISACPA should continue its advocacy role. It should prepare and submit to the next SAARC Summit a comprehensive and realistic blue-print setting out SAARC Development Goals for the next five years in the areas of poverty alleviation, education, health and environment giving due regard, among others, to the suggestions made in ISACPA report.
14. The SAARC Secretariat should periodically update and submit regional poverty Profiles.
15. SAARC should continue to collaborate with international organizations and UN agencies in the field of Poverty Alleviation. Arrangements for SAARC Food Security Reserves should be made more effective. We also recommend the establishment of a Regional Food Bank for which a concept paper should be prepared.
16. Investment in human resources is critical for future development of South Asia. It is, therefore, essential to establish a network of centres of higher learning, training and Skill Development Institutes (SDI's) across South Asia. In this context, the role of the SAARC Human Resource Development Centre (SHRDC) is important.

Science and Technology

17. Strengthening of scientific and technological co-operation across the region is fundamental to accelerating the pace of economic and social development. Sharing of scientific and technological expertise, joint research and development and industrial application of higher technology should be encouraged and facilitated.

Social

18. We hail the signing of the SAARC Social Charter as a historic development, which would have a far reaching impact on the lives of

millions of South Asians. Issues covered under the Charter such as poverty alleviation, population stabilization, empowerment of women, youth mobilization, human resource development, promotion of health and nutrition and protection of children are key to the welfare and well being of all South Asians.

19. Progress has been made in the constitution of SAARC Autonomous Advocacy Group of Prominent Women Personalities (SAWAG). To enable women to contribute to the socio-economic development, there is a need for SAARC to encourage women entrepreneurs in the region.
20. Member states should move towards an early ratification of the two Conventions on Child Welfare and Trafficking in Women and Children for Prostitution.
21. Easy and affordable healthcare, prevention and treatment of HIV/AIDS, Tuberculosis and other serious communicable diseases are priorities. The year 2004 is declared as the "SAARC Awareness Year". The SAARC Secretariat should effectively implement the proposed programmes on the observation of the SAARC Awareness year and develop a regional strategy through a consultative process and collaborate closely with the Joint UN Programme on HIV/AIDS (UNAIDS) and other international organizations and civil society.
22. The important initiative taken by Maldives in hosting the Emergency Meeting of the SAARC Health Ministers on SARS epidemic in Male on 29 April 2003 was a welcome development.
23. As agreed by the SAARC Health Ministers' Conference held recently in New Delhi, a SAARC Health Surveillance Center and Rapid Deployment Health Response System should be set up to deal with the emerging and re-emerging diseases as well as to establish a network between various institutions dealing with malaria and other vector borne diseases in the Member States. Also, documentation of traditional knowledge to safeguard Intellectual Property Rights (IPRS) in medicine needs attention.
24. The importance of cooperation in medical expertise and pharmaceuticals as well as in the field of traditional medicine requires elaboration of a SAARC Plan of Action that should be developed in the shortest possible time.
25. We take pride in the rich cultural mosaic of the peoples of South Asia and underline the need for preservation of traditional skills and crafts and promotion of cultural exchanges between nations.
26. We welcome the establishment of a SAARC Cultural Centre in Kandy, which will serve as symbol of South Asian shared cultural heritage.

Environment

27. It is important to undertake and reinforce regional cooperation in the conservation of our water resources, environment, pollution prevention

and control as well as our preparedness to deal with natural calamities. We welcome the early establishment of the Coast Zone Management Centre in the Maldives.

28. The early and effective implementation of the SAARC Environment Plan of Action is important. We further stressed the early submission of the State of the Environment reports to expedite the preparation of SAARC State of Environment report and the commissioning of the work on drafting a Regional Environment Treaty.

Combating Terrorism

29. We condemn terrorist violence in all its forms and manifestations and note that people of South Asia continue to face a serious threat from terrorism.

30. We are convinced that terrorism, in all its forms and manifestations, is a challenge to all states and to all of humanity, and cannot be justified on any ground, whatsoever. Terrorism violates the fundamental values of the United Nations and the SAARC Charter and constitutes one of the most serious threats to international peace and security. We agree to fully implement the relevant international conventions to which we are parties.

31. We reaffirm our commitment to SAARC Regional Convention on Suppression of terrorism, which, among others, recognizes the seriousness of the problem of terrorism as it affects the security, stability, and development of the region.

32. The signing of the Additional Protocol to the SAARC Regional Convention on Combating Terrorism to deal effectively with financing of terrorism is a further manifestation of our determination to eliminate all forms and manifestations of terrorism from South Asia.

SAARC Award

33. We welcome the institution of the SAARC Award on the basis of a concept paper drawn up by His Majesty's Government of Nepal and decide to present the Award during the Summits in future. The Award will honour and encourage outstanding individuals and organizations within the region in the fields of peace, development, poverty alleviation, and in other areas of regional cooperation.

Information and Communications

34. We recognize the vital role that information and media can play in the promotion of peace, progress and harmony in South Asia. In this context, the initiatives for introducing regular 'SAARC Roundup' and 'SAARC News' programmes for telecast and broadcast on National TV and Radio channels, respectively in Member Countries is a welcome development. We agree to the establishment of a SAARC Information Centre in Kathmandu.

35. SAARC should endeavour to bring the benefits of information and communications technology to all peoples of the region, bridging the digital divide and assist in the development of knowledge based societies.

SAARC Integrated Programme of Action (SIPA)

36. We note with satisfaction the progress achieved in regional cooperation through SIPA. The commitment to SIPA must be matched by a corresponding allocation of resources for it.

Sub-Regional Cooperation

37. We encourage the development of specific projects relevant to the individual needs of three or more Member states under the provisions articles VII and X of the SAARC Charter.

Inter-Regional Cooperation

38. We express our determination to develop mutually beneficial links between SAARC and other regional and international organizations, bodies and entities and agree to establish dialogue partnership with other regional bodies and with states outside the region, interested in SAARC activities.

Enhancing Political Cooperation

39. We envision South Asia to be a peaceful and stable region where each nation is at peace with itself and its neighbours and where conflicts, differences and disputes are addressed through peaceful means and dialogue.

40. Reaffirm our pledge to promote good neighbourly relations on the basis of the principles of sovereign equality, territorial integrity and national independence, non-use of force, non-intervention and non-interference and peaceful settlement of disputes and recognize the importance of informal political consultations in promoting mutual understanding and reinforcing confidence building process among Member states.

Security of Small States

41. We are particularly mindful of the security concerns of small states that arise, inter alia, from their particular vulnerabilities, which should be firmly addressed by scrupulous adherence to the UN Charter, rules of international law and strict adherence to the universally accepted principles and norms related to sovereign rights and territorial integrity of all states. This should be ensured by all, both severally and collectively, through appropriate actions.

42. We endorse the recommendations made by the Council of Ministers at its Twenty-third and Twenty-fourth sessions.

Thirteenth SAARC Summit

43. We appreciate the offer the People's Republic of Bangladesh to host the Thirteenth SAARC Summit in January 2005."

❮24❯

Additional Protocol to the SAARC Regional Convention on Suppression of Terrorism (06.01.2004)

SAARC member states agreed to adopt necessary legal and administrative measures to strengthen cooperation among them with a view to prevent and suppress the financing of terrorist acts by "criminalizing the provision, collection or acquisition of funds for the purpose of committing terrorist acts".

The Member States of the South Asian Association for Regional Cooperation (SAARC)

Mindful of the purposes and the principles of cooperation enshrined in the SAARC Charter and the Charter of the United Nations;

Recalling the declaration of the Eleventh SAARC Summit adopted at Kathmandu on 6th January 2002;

Further Recalling that, at the Eleventh SAARC summit, the Heads of State or Government, reiterated their support to the United Nations Security Council Resolution 1373 of September 28, 2001 and affirmed their determination to re-double efforts collectively as well as individually, to prevent and suppress terrorism in all its forms and manifestations, including, by increased co-operation and full implementation of the relevant international conventions relating to terrorism to which they are parties and called on all Member States, inter-alia, to prevent and suppress the financing of terrorist acts by criminalizing the provision, acquisition and collection of funds for such acts;

Bearing in Mind the decision of the SAARC Council of Ministers at its Twenty Third session in Kathmandu on 22nd August, 2002, wherein the Council mandated the preparation of an Additional Protocol to the SAARC Regional Convention on Suppression of Terrorism, recognizing the importance of updating the Convention, in order to meet the obligations devolving in terms of Security Council Resolution 1373 (2001);

Have Agreed as follows:

Article 1
Objectives and Purposes

The purpose of this Additional Protocol is to strengthen the SAARC Regional Convention on Suppression of Terrorism, particularly by criminalizing the provision, collection or acquisition of funds for the purpose of committing terrorist acts and taking further measures to prevent and suppress financing of such acts. Towards this end, State Parties agree to adopt necessary measures to strengthen co-operation among them, in accordance with the terms of this Additional Protocol.

Article 2

Relationship to SAARC Convention

This Additional Protocol supplements the SAARC Regional Convention on Suppression of Terrorism, done at Kathmandu on 4th November, 1987 (hereinafter referred to as the "1987 SAARC Convention"). The 1987 SAARC Convention and this Additional Protocol shall be read and interpreted together as a single instrument.

Article 3

Definitions

1. "Funds" mean assets of every kind, whether tangible or intangible, movable or immovable, however acquired, and legal documents or instruments in any form, including electronic or digital, evidencing title to, or interest in, such assets, including, but not limited to, bank credits, travellers cheques, bank cheques, money orders, shares, securities, bonds, drafts and letters of credit.
2. "Proceeds" mean any funds derived from or obtained, directly or indirectly, through the commission of an offence set forth in Article 4.

Article 4

Offences

1. Any person commits an offence within the meaning of this additional protocol if that person by any means, directly or indirectly, unlawfully and willfully, provides or collects funds with the intention that they should be used or in the knowledge that they are to be used, in full or in part, in order to carry out:
   a) An act which constitutes an offence within the scope of and as defined in one of the treaties listed in the Annex to this Protocol: or
   b) Any other act intended to cause death or serious bodily injury to a civilian, when the purpose of such act, by its nature or context, is to intimidate a population, or to compel a Government or an international organization to do or to abstain from doing any act; or
   c) An offence within the scope of any Convention to which SAARC Member States concerned are parties and which obliges the parties to prosecute or grant extradition.

2 (a) On depositing its instrument of ratification, acceptance, approval or accession, a State Party which is not a party to a treaty listed in the annex may declare that, in the application of this Convention

to the state party, the treaty shall be deemed not to be included in the annex referred to in paragraph 1, subparagraph (a). The declaration shall cease to have effect as soon as the treaty enters into force for the State Party, which shall notify the depository of this fact;

(b) When a State Party ceases to be a party to a treaty listed in the annex, it may make a declaration as provided for in this article, with respect to that treaty.

3. For an act to constitute an offence set forth in paragraph 1, it shall not be necessary that the funds were actually used to carry out an offence referred to in paragraph 1, subparagraph (a) or (b).
4. Any person also commits an offence if that person attempts to commit an offence as set forth in paragraph 1 of this article.
5. Any person also commits an offence if that person:
   (a) Participates as an accomplice in an office as set forth in paragraph 1 or 4 of this article;
   (b) Organizes or directs others to commit an offence as set forth in paragraph 1 or 4 of this article;
   (c) Contributes to the commission of one or more offences as set forth in paragraph 1 or 4 of this article by a group of persons acting with a common purpose. Such contribution shall be intentional and shall either:
   i) be made with the aim of furthering the criminal activity or criminal purpose of the group, where such activity or purpose involves the commission of an offence as set forth in paragraph 1 of this article; or
   ii) be made in the knowledge of the intention of the group to commit an offence as set forth in paragraph 1 of this article.

Article 5
Domestic Measures

States Parties, in accordance with the provisions of their respective Constitutions, shall endeavour to become Parties to the international instruments listed in the Annex to which they are not yet a Party.

Article 6
Liability of legal entities

1. Each State Party, in accordance with its domestic legal principles, shall take the necessary measures to enable a legal entity located in its territory or organized under its laws to be held liable when a persons responsible for the management or control of that legal entity has, in that capacity, committed an offence as set forth in Article 4. Such liability may be criminal, civil or administrative.

2. Such liability is incurred without prejudice to the criminal liability of an individual or individuals who have committed the offences.
3. Each State Party shall ensure, in particular, that legal entities liable in accordance with paragraph 1 above are subject to effective, proportionate and dissuasive criminal, civil or administrative sanctions. Such sanctions may include monetary sanctions.

Article 7

Measures to prevent, suppress and eradicate the financing of terrorism

1. State parties shall consider and take all practical measures at the national level, inter-alia by adapting their domestic legislation to prevent, suppress and eradicate the financing of terrorism, and for effective international cooperation with respect thereto including:
   a) A comprehensive domestic regulatory and supervisory regime for banks, other financial institutions and other entities deemed particularly susceptible to being used for the financing of terrorist activities. This regime shall require banks and other financial institutions and other entities to utilize effective measures for the identification of customers, paying special attention to unusual or suspicious transactions and to report promptly to the Competent Authorities, all complex, unusual large transactions and unusual patterns of transactions, which have no apparent economic or obviously lawful purpose;
   b) Measures to detect and monitor movements across national borders, of cash, bearer negotiable instruments and other appropriate movements of value. These measures shall be subject to safeguards to ensure proper use of information and should not impede legitimate capital movements;
   c) Measures of assistance in connection with criminal investigations or criminal proceedings relating to the financing or support of any act constituting an offence within the scope of the international instruments listed in Article 4 of this Additional Protocol, including assistance in obtaining evidence in their possession, necessary for the proceedings; and
   d) Establishing and monitoring channels of communication between their competent agencies and services to facilities the secure and rapid exchange of information concerning all aspects of offences set forth in Article 4, within the conditions prescribed by domestic law.
2. Towards facilitating the above, each State Party shall consider measures to establish and maintain a financial intelligence unit to serve as a national center for the collection, analysis and dissemination of pertinent money laundering and terrorist financing information.

Article 8

Seizure and confiscation of funds or other assets

1. Each State Party shall take appropriate measures, in accordance with its domestic legal principles, for the identification, detection and freezing or seizure of any funds used or allocated for the purpose of committing the offences set forth in Article 4 as well as the proceeds derived from such offences, for purposes of possible forfeiture.
2. Each State Party shall take appropriate measures, in accordance with its domestic legal principles, for the forfeiture of funds used or allocated for the purpose of committing the offences set forth in Article 4 and the proceeds derived from such offences.
3. Each State Party concerned may give consideration to concluding agreements on the sharing with other State Parties, on a regular or case-by-case basis, of the funds derived from the forfeiture referred to in this article.
4. The provisions of this Article shall be implemented without prejudice to the rights of third parties acting in good faith.
5. The measures referred to in paragraph 1 shall apply with respect to offences committed both within and outside the jurisdiction of a State Party.

Article 9

Predicate offences to money laundering

1. State Parties shall take the necessary measures to ensure that its domestic money laundering legislation also includes as predicate offences those offences set forth in Article 4 of this Additional Protocol.
2. Money laundering predicate offences referred to in paragraph 1, shall include those committed both within and outside the jurisdiction of a State Party.

Article 10

Cooperation on immigration and customs controls

1. State Parties, consistent with their respective domestic legal and administrative regimes, shall promote co-operation and the exchange of information in order to improve immigration and customs control measures to detect and prevent the international movement of terrorists and their accomplices and trafficking in arms, narcotics and psychotropic substances or other materialist intended to support terrorist activities.
2. To this end, they shall promote co-operation and the exchange of information to improve their controls on the issuance of travel and identify documents and to prevent their counterfeiting, forgery, or fraudulent use.

3. Such co-operation shall be carried out without prejudice to applicable international commitments in relation to the free movement of people and the facilitation of commerce.

Article 11

Cooperation among law enforcement authorities

State parties shall work closely with one another, consistent with the respective domestic legal and administrative systems, to enhance the effectiveness of law enforcement action for the prevention, suppression and prosecution of the offences set forth in Article 4.

Article 12

Mutual legal assistance

The provisions of Article VIII of the 1987 SAARC Convention relating the Mutual Legal Assistance shall apply, mutatis mutandis, in respect of the offences set forth in Article 4 of this Additional Protocol.

Article 13

Extradition

The provisions of Article III of the 1987 SAARC Convention shall apply, mutatis mutandis, in respect of the offences set forth in Article 4 of this Additional Protocol.

2. The provisions of Article IV of the 1987 SAARC Convention relating to the duty to extradite or prosecute shall apply, mutatis mutandis, in respect of the offences set forth in Article 4 of this Additional Protocol.

Article 14

Exclusion of Fiscal Offence exception

None of the offences set forth in Article 4 shall be regarded, for the purpose of extradition or mutual legal assistance, as a fiscal offence. Accordingly, State Parties may not refuse a request for extradition or for mutual legal assistance on the sole ground that it concerns a fiscal offence.

Article 15

Exclusion of political offence exception

For the purpose of extradition or mutual legal assistance, none of the offences established in the international instruments set forth in Article 4, shall be regarded as a political offence or an offence connected with a political offence or an offence inspired by political motives. Accordingly, a request for extradition or mutual assistance may not be refused on the sole ground that it concerns a political offence or an offence connected with a political offence or an offence inspired by political motives.

Article 16

Denial of refugee status

Each State Party shall take appropriate measures, consistent with the relevant provisions of national and international law, for the purpose of ensuring that refugee status is not granted to any person in respect of whom there are serious reasons for considering that he or she has committed an offence set forth in Article 4 of this Additional Protocol.

Article 17

Non-discrimination

None of the provisions of this Additional Protocol shall be interpreted as imposing an obligation to extradite or to provide mutual legal assistance, if the requested State Party has substantial grounds to believe that the request to extradite or to provide mutual legal assistance, has been made for the purpose of prosecuting or punishing a person on account of that person's race, religion, nationality, ethnic origin or political opinion, or that compliance with the request would cause prejudice to that person's position for any of these reasons.

Article 18

Principles of Sovereign Equality and Territorial Integrity

1. State Parties shall carry out their obligations under this additional protocol in a manner consistent with the principles of sovereign equality and territorial integrity of states and that of non-intervention in the domestic affairs of other states.
2. Nothing in this Additional Protocol entitles a State Party to undertake in the territory of another State Party exercise of jurisdiction or performance of functions that are exclusively reserved for the authorities of that other State Party by its domestic law.

Article 19

Rights and Obligations under International Law

Nothing in this Additional Protocol shall be interpreted as affecting other rights and obligations and responsibilities of states and individuals under international law, in particular, the purposes and principles of the Charter of the United Nations, international humanitarian law, and international human rights law.

Article 20

Technical Cooperation

State Parties shall promote, where appropriate, technical co-operation and training programmes with other regional and international organizations conducting activities related to the objectives and purposes of this Additional Protocol.

Article 21

Consultations

State parties shall hold periodic consultations, as appropriate, with a view to facilitating:

a) The effective implementation of this Additional Protocol; and

b) The exchange of information and experiences on effective means and methods to prevent, detect, investigate and punish offences within the scope of the Additional Protocol.

Article 22

Signature and ratification

This Additional Protocol is open for signature by all Member States of SAARC at the SAARC Secretariat in Kathmandu. It shall be subject to ratification. Instruments of Ratification shall be deposited with the Secretary-General of SAARC.

Article 23

Entry into Force

The Additional Protocol shall enter into force on the thirtieth day following the date of deposit of the seventh Instrument of Ratification with the Secretary-General of SAARC.

Article 24

Depositary

The Secretary-General of SAARC shall be the depositary of this additional protocol and shall notify Member States of signatures to this additional protocol and all deposits of Instruments of Ratification. The Secretary-General shall transmit certified copies of such instruments to each Member State. The Secretary-General shall also inform Member States of the date on which this Additional Protocol will have entered into force in accordance with Article 23.

In Witness Whereof the undersigned, being duly authorized thereto by their respective Governments have signed this Additional Protocol.

Done in ISLAMABAD, PAKISTAN, On This the Sixth Day of January Of the Year Two Thousand Four, In Nine Originals, In The English Language, All Texts Being Equally Authentic.

M. Morshed Khan
Minister for Foreign Affairs
People's Republic of Bangladesh

Nado Rinchhen
Officiating Minister for Foreign Affairs
Kingdom of Bhutan

Yashwant Sinha
Minister of External Affairs
Republic of India

Fathulla Jamell
Minister of Foreign Affairs
Republic of Malives

Dr Bhekh B Thapa
Ambassador-at-large for Foreign Affairs
His Majesty's Government of Nepal

Khurshid M Kasuri
Minister of Foreign Affairs
Islamic Republic of Pakistan

Tyronne Fernando
Minister of Foreign Affairs
Democratic Socialist Republic of Sri Lanka

ANNEX

a) Convention for the Suppression of Unlawful Seizure of Aircraft, signed at the Hague on 16 December 1970.

b) Convention for the Suppression of Unlawful Acts against the Safety of Civil Aviation, signed at Montreal on 23 September1971.

c) Convention on the Prevention and Punishment of Crimes against Internationally Protected Persons, including Diplomatic Agents, approved by the General Assembly of the United Nations on 14 December 1973.

d) International Convention against the Taking of Hostages, adopted by the General Assembly of the United Nations on 17 December 1979.

e) Convention on the Physical Protection of Nuclear Material, signed at Vienna on 3 March 1980.

f) Protocol for the Suppression of Unlawful Acts of Violence at Airports Serving International Civil Aviation, supplementary to the Convention for the Suppression of Unlawful Acts against the Safety of Civil Aviation, signed at Montreal on 24 February 1988.

g) Convention for the Suppression of Unlawful Acts against the Safety of Maritime Navigation, done at Rome on 10 March 1988.

h) Protocol for the Suppression of Unlawful Acts against the Safety of Fixed Platforms located on the Continental Shelf, done at Rome on 10 March 1988.

i) International Convention for the Suppression of Terrorist Bombings, approved by the General Assembly of the United Nations on 15 December 1997.

j) International Convention for the Suppression of the Financing of Terrorism, approved by the General Assembly of the United Nations on 9 December 1999.

❮25❯

Agreement on South Asian Free Trade Area (SAFTA) (06.01.2004)

The member states agreed to establish South Asian Free Trade Area (SAFTA) to promote and enhance mutual trade and economic cooperation with effect from 1st January 2006. The States agreed on timeframes for tariff reduction by "Least Developed States" and "Non-Least Developed States" respectively (that may not apply to the tariff lines included in the "Sensitive Lists"). They also agreed on "additional measures" like simplification of customs procedures, banking and import financing and development of communication and transport infrastructure.

The Governments of the SAARC (South Asian Association for Regional Cooperation) Member States comprising the People's Republic of Bangladesh, the Kingdom of Bhutan, the Republic of India, the Republic of Maldives, the Kingdom of Nepal, the Islamic Republic of Pakistan and the Democratic Socialist Republic of Sri Lanka hereinafter referred to as "Contracting States".

Motivated by the commitment to strengthen intra-SAARC economic cooperation to maximise the realisation of the region's potential for trade and development for the benefit of their people, in a spirit of mutual accommodation, with full respect for the principles of sovereign equality, independence and territorial integrity of all States;

Noting that the Agreement on SAARC Preferential Trading Arrangement (SAPTA) signed in Dhaka on the 11th of April 1993 provides for the adoption of various instruments of trade liberalisation on a preferential basis;

Convinced that preferential trading arrangements among SAARC Member States will act as a stimulus to the strengthening of national and SAARC economic resilience, and the development of the national economies of the Contracting States by expanding investment and production opportunities, trade, and foreign exchange earnings as well as the development of economic and technological cooperation;

Aware that a number of regions are entering into such arrangements to enhance trade through the free movement of goods;

Recognising that least developed countries in the region need to be accorded special and differential treatment commensurate with their development needs; and

Recognising that it is necessary to progress beyond a Preferential Trading Arrangement to move towards higher levels of trade and economic cooperation in the region by removing barriers to cross-border flow of goods;

Have agreed as follows:

Article 1
Definitions

For the purposes of this Agreement:

1. **Concessions** mean tariff, para-tariff and non-tariff concessions agreed under the Trade Liberalisation Programme;
2. **Direct Trade Measures** mean measures conducive to promoting mutual trade of Contracting States such as long and medium-term contracts containing import and supply commitments in respect of specific products, buy-back arrangements, state trading operations, and government and public procurement,
3. **Least Developed Contracting State** refers to a Contracting State which is designated as a "Least Developed Country" by the United Nations;
4. **Margin of Preference** means percentage of tariff by which tariffs are reduced on products imported from one Contracting State to another as a result of preferential treatment,
5. **Non-Tariff Measures** include any measure, regulation, or practice, other than "tariffs" and "paratariffs".
6. **Para-Tariffs** mean border charges and fees, other than "tariffs", on foreign trade transactions of a tariff-like effect which are levied solely on imports, but not those indirect taxes and charges, which are levied in the same manner on like domestic products. Import charges corresponding to specific services rendered are not considered para-tariff measures;
7. **Products** mean all products including manufactures and commodities in their raw, semi-processed and processed forms;
8. **SAPTA** means Agreement on SAARC Preferential Trading Arrangement signed in Dhaka on the 11th of April 1993;
9. **Serious injury** means a significant impairment of the domestic industry of like or directly competitive products due to a surge in preferential imports causing substantial losses in terms of earnings, production or employment unsustainable in the short term;

10. **Tariffs** mean customs duties included in the national tariff schedules of the Contracting States;
11. **Threat of serious injury** means a situation in which a substantial increase of preferential imports is of a nature to cause "serious injury" to domestic producers, and that such injury, although not yet existing, is clearly imminent. A determination of threat of serious injury shall be based on facts and not on mere allegation, conjecture, or remote or hypothetical possibility.

Article 2
Establishment

The Contracting States hereby establish the South Asian Free Trade Area (SAFTA) to promote and enhance mutual trade and economic cooperation among the Contracting States, through exchanging concessions in accordance with this Agreement.

Article 3
Objectives and Principles

1. The Objectives of this Agreement are to promote and enhance mutual trade and economic cooperation among Contracting States by, inter-alia:
   a) eliminating barriers to trade in, and facilitating the cross-border movement of goods between the territories of the Contracting States;
   b) Promoting conditions of fair competition in the free trade area, and ensuring equitable benefits to all Contracting States, taking into account their respective levels and pattern of economic development;
   c) Creating effective mechanism for the implementation and application of this Agreement, for its joint administration and for the resolution of disputes; and
   d) Establishing a framework for further regional cooperation to expand and enhance the mutual benefits of this Agreement.
2. SAFTA shall be governed in accordance with the following principles:
   a) SAFTA will be governed by the provisions of this Agreement and also by the rules, regulations, decisions, understandings and protocols to be agreed upon within its framework by the Contracting States;
   b) The Contracting States affirm their existing rights and obligations with respect to each other under Marrakesh Agreement Establishing the World Trade Organisation and other Treaties/Agreements to which such Contracting States are signatories;

c) SAFTA shall be based and applied on the principles of overall reciprocity and mutuality of advantages in such a way as to benefit equitably all Contracting States, taking into account their respective levels of economic and industrial development, the pattern of their external trade and tariff policies and systems;

d) SAFTA shall involve the free movement of goods, between countries through, inter alia, the elimination of tariffs, para tariffs and non-tariff restrictions on the movement of goods, and any other equivalent measures;

e) SAFTA shall entail adoption of trade facilitation and other measures, and the progressive harmonisation of legislations by the Contracting States in the relevant areas; and

f) The special needs of the Least Developed Contracting States shall be clearly recognised by adopting concrete preferential measures in their favour on a non-reciprocal basis.

Article 4

Instruments The SAFTA Agreement will be implemented through the following instruments:

1. Trade Liberalisation Programme
2. Rules of Origin
3. Institutional Arrangements
4. Consultations and Dispute Settlement Procedures
5. Safeguard Measures
6. Any other instrument that may be agreed upon.

Article 5
National Treatment

Each Contracting State shall accord national treatment to the products of other Contracting States in accordance with the provisions of Article III of GATT 1994.

Article 6
Components

SAFTA may, inter-alia, consist of arrangements relating to:

a) tariffs;

b) para-tariffs;

c) non-tariff measures;

d) direct trade measures.

Article 7
Trade Liberalisation Programme

1. Contracting States agree to the following schedule of tariff reductions:

   a) The tariff reduction by the Non-Least Developed Contracting States from existing tariff rates to 20% shall be done within a time frame of 2 years, from the date of coming into force of the Agreement. Contracting States are encouraged to adopt reductions in equal annual installments. If actual tariff rates after the coming into force of the Agreement are below 20%, there shall be an annual reduction on a Margin of Preference basis of 10% on actual tariff rates for each of the two years.

b) The tariff reduction by the Least Developed Contracting States from existing tariff rates will be to 30% within the time frame of 2 years from the date of coming into force of the Agreement If actual tariff rates on the date of coming into force of the Agreement are below 30%, there will be an annual reduction on a Margin of Preference basis of 5% on actual tariff rates for each of the two years.

c) The subsequent tariff reduction by Non-Least Developed Contracting States from 20% or below to 0-5% shall be done within a second time frame of 5 years, beginning from the third year from the date of coming into force of the Agreement. However, the period of subsequent tariff reduction by Sri Lanka shall be six years. Contracting States are encouraged to adopt reductions in equal annual installments, but not less than 15% annually.

d) The subsequent tariff reduction by the Least Developed Contracting States from 30% or below to 0-5% shall be done within a second time frame of 8 years beginning from the third year from the date of coming into force of the Agreement. The Least Developed Contracting States are encouraged to adopt reductions in equal annual installments, not less than 10% annually.

2. The above schedules of tariff reductions will not prevent Contracting States from immediately reducing their tariffs to 0-5% or from following an accelerated schedule of tariff reduction.

3. a) Contracting States may not apply the Trade Liberalisation Programme as in paragraph 1 above, to the tariff lines included in the Sensitive Lists which shall be negotiated by the Contracting States (for LDCs and Non-LDCs) and incorporated in this Agreement as an integral part. The number of products in the Sensitive Lists shall be subject to maximum ceiling to be mutually agreed among the Contracting States with flexibility to Least Developed Contracting States to seek derogation in respect of the products of their export interest; and

b) The Sensitive List shall be reviewed after every four years or earlier as may be decided by SAFTA Ministerial Council (SMC), established under Article 10, with a view to reducing the number of items in the Sensitive List.

4. The Contracting States shall notify the SAARC Secretariat all non-tariff and para-tariff measures to their trade on an annual basis. The notified measures shall be reviewed by the Committee of Experts, established under Article 10, in its regular meetings to examine their compatibility with relevant WTO provisions. The Committee of Experts shall recommend the elimination or implementation of the measure in the least trade restrictive manner in order to facilitate intra SAARC trade.
5. Contracting Parties shall eliminate all quantitative restrictions, except otherwise permitted under GATT 1994, in respect of products included in the Trade Liberalisation Programme.
6. Notwithstanding the provisions contained in paragraph 1 of this Article, the Non-Least Developed Contracting States shall reduce their tariff to 0-5% for the products of Least Developed Contracting States within a time frame of three years beginning from the date of coming into force of the Agreement.

Article 8
Additional Measures

Contracting States agree to consider, in addition to the measures set out in Article 7, the adoption of trade facilitation and other measures to support and complement SAFTA for mutual benefit. These may include, among others:

a) harmonisation of standards, reciprocal recognition of tests and accreditation of testing laboratories of Contracting States and certification of products;
b) simplification and harmonisation of customs clearance procedure;
c) harmonisation of national customs classification based on HS coding system;
d) Customs cooperation to resolve dispute at customs entry points;
e) simplification and harmonisation of import licensing and registration procedures;
f) simplification of banking procedures for import financing;
g) transit facilities for efficient intra-SAARC trade, especially for the land-locked Contracting States;
h) removal of barriers to intra-SAARC investments;
i) macroeconomic consultations;
j) rules for fair competition and the promotion of venture capital;
k) development of communication systems and transport infrastructure;
l) making exceptions to their foreign exchange restrictions, if any, relating to payments for products under the SAFTA scheme, as well as repatriation of such payments without prejudice to their rights under Article XVIII of the General Agreement on Tariffs and Trade (GATT) and the relevant provisions of Articles of Treaty of the International Monetary Fund (IMF); and
m) Simplification of procedures for business visas.

Article 9
Extension of Negotiated Concessions

Concessions agreed to, other than those made exclusively to the Least Developed Contracting States, shall be extended unconditionally to all Contracting States.

The initial notification shall be made within three months from the date of coming into force of the Agreement and the COE shall review the notification in its first meeting and take appropriate decisions.

Article 10
Institutional Arrangements

1. The Contracting States hereby establish the SAFTA Ministerial Council (hereinafter referred to as SMC).
2. The SMC shall be the highest decision-making body of SAFTA and shall be responsible for the administration and implementation of this Agreement and all decisions and arrangements made within its legal framework.
3. The SMC shall consist of the Ministers of Commerce / Trade of the Contracting States.
4. The SMC shall meet at least once every year or more often as and when considered necessary by the Contracting States. Each Contracting State shall chair the SMC for a period of one year on rotational basis in alphabetical order.
5. The SMC shall be supported by a Committee of Experts (hereinafter referred to as COE), with one nominee from each Contracting State at the level of a Senior Economic Official, with expertise in trade matters.
6. The COE shall monitor, review and facilitate implementation of the provisions of this Agreement and undertake any task assigned to it by the SMC. The COE shall submit its report to SMC every six months.
7. The COE will also act as Dispute Settlement Body under this Agreement.
8. The COE shall meet at least once every six months or more often as and when considered necessary by the Contracting States. Each Contracting State shall chair the COE for a period of one year on rotational basis in alphabetical order.
9. The SAARC Secretariat shall provide secretarial support to the SMC and COE in the discharge of their functions.
10. The SMC and COE will adopt their own rules of procedure.

Article 11
Special and Differential Treatment for the Least Developed Contracting States

In addition to other provisions of this Agreement, all Contracting States shall provide special and more favourable treatment exclusively to the Least Developed Contracting States as set out in the following sub-paragraphs:

a) The Contracting States shall give special regard to the situation of the Least Developed Contracting States when considering the application of anti-dumping and/or countervailing measures. In this regard, the Contracting States shall provide an opportunity to Least Developed Contracting States for consultations. The Contracting States shall, to the extent practical, favourably consider accepting price undertakings offered by exporters from Least Developed Contracting States. These constructive remedies shall be available until the trade liberalisation programme has been completed by all Contracting States.

b) Greater flexibility in continuation of quantitative or other restrictions provisionally and without discrimination in critical circumstances by the Least Developed Contracting States on imports from other Contracting States.

c) Contracting States shall also consider, where practical, taking direct trade measures with a view to enhancing sustainable exports from Least Developed Contracting States, such as long and medium-term contracts containing import and supply commitments in respect of specific products, buy-back arrangements, state trading operations, and government and public procurement.

d) Special consideration shall be given by Contracting States to requests from Least Developed Contracting States for technical assistance and cooperation arrangements designed to assist them in expanding their trade with other Contracting States and in taking advantage of the potential benefits of SAFTA. A list of possible areas for such technical assistance shall be negotiated by the Contracting States and incorporated in this Agreement as an integral part.

e) The Contracting States recognise that the Least Developed Contracting States may face loss of customs revenue due to the implementation of the Trade Liberalisation Programme under this Agreement. Until alternative domestic arrangements are formulated to address this situation, the Contracting States agree to establish an appropriate mechanism to compensate the Least Developed Contracting States for their loss of customs revenue. This mechanism and its rules and regulations shall be established prior to the commencement of the Trade Liberalisation Programme (TLP).

Article 12

Special Provision for Maldives

Notwithstanding the potential or actual graduation of Maldives from the status of a Least Developed Country, it shall be accorded in this Agreement and in any subsequent contractual undertakings thereof treatment no less favourable than that provided for the Least Developed Contracting States.

Article 13
Non-application

Notwithstanding the measures as set out in this Agreement its provisions shall not apply in relation to preferences already granted or to be granted by any Contracting State to other Contracting States outside the framework of this Agreement, and to third countries through bilateral, plurilateral and multilateral trade agreements and similar arrangements.

Article 14
General Exceptions

a) Nothing in this Agreement shall be construed to prevent any Contracting State from taking action and adopting measures which it considers necessary for the protection of its national security.

b) Subject to the requirement that such measures are not applied in a manner which would constitute a means of arbitrary or unjustifiable discrimination between countries where the similar conditions prevail, or a disguised restriction on intra-regional trade, nothing in this Agreement shall be construed to prevent any Contracting State from taking action and adopting measures which it considers necessary for the protection of:

   (i) public morals;

   (ii) human, animal or plant life and health; and

   (iii) articles of artistic, historic and archaeological value.

Article 15
Balance of Payments Measures

1. Notwithstanding the provisions of this Agreement, any Contracting State facing serious balance of payments difficulties may suspend provisionally the concessions extended under this Agreement.
2. Any such measure taken pursuant to paragraph 1 of this Article shall be immediately notified to the Committee of Experts.
3. The Committee of Experts shall periodically review the measures taken pursuant to paragraph 1 of this Article.
4. Any Contracting State which takes action pursuant to paragraph 1 of this Article shall afford, upon request from any other Contracting State, adequate opportunities for consultations with a view to preserving the stability of concessions under SAFTA.
5. If no satisfactory adjustment is effected between the Contracting States concerned within 30 days of the beginning of such consultations, to be extended by another 30 days through mutual consent, the matter may be referred to the Committee of Experts.

6. Any such measures taken pursuant to paragraph 1 of this Article shall be phased out soon after the Committee of Experts comes to the conclusion that the balance of payments situation of the Contracting State concerned has improved.

Article 16

Safeguard Measures

1. If any product, which is the subject of a concession under this Agreement, is imported into the territory of a Contracting State in such a manner or in such quantities as to cause, or threaten to cause, serious injury to producers of like or directly competitive products in the importing Contracting State, the importing Contracting State may, pursuant to an investigation by the competent authorities of that Contracting State conducted in accordance with the provisions set out in this Article, suspend temporarily the concessions granted under the provisions of this Agreement. The examination of the impact on the domestic industry concerned shall include an evaluation of all other relevant economic factors and indices having a bearing on the state of the domestic industry of the product and a causal relationship must be clearly established between "serious injury" and imports from within the SAARC region, to the exclusion of all such other factors.
2. Such suspension shall only be for such time and to the extent as may be necessary to prevent or remedy such injury and in no case, will such suspension be for duration of more than 3 years.
3. No safeguard masure shall be applied again by a Contracting State to the import of a product which has been subject to such a measure during the period of implementation of Trade Liberalisation Programme by the Contracting States, for a period of time equal to that during which such measure had been previously applied, provided that the period of non-application is at least two years.
4. All investigation procedures for resorting to safeguard measures under this Article shall be consistent with Article XIX of GATT 1994 and WTO Agreement on Safeguards.
5. Safeguard action under this Article shall be non-discriminatory and applicable to the product imported from all other Contracting States subject to the provisions of paragraph 8 of this Article.
6. When safeguard provisions are used in accordance with this Article, the Contracting State invoking such measures shall immediately notify the exporting Contracting State(s) and the Committee of Experts.
7. In critical circumstances where delay would cause damage which it would be difficult to repair, a Contracting State may take a provisional safeguard measure pursuant to a preliminary determination that there is clear evidence that increased imports have caused or are threatening

to cause serious injury. The duration of the provisional measure shall not exceed 200 days, during this period the pertinent requirements of this Article shall be met.

8. Notwithstanding any of the provisions of this Article, safeguard measures under this article shall not be applied against a product originating in a Least Developed Contracting State as long as its share of imports of the product concerned in the importing Contracting State does not exceed 5 percent, provided Least Developed Contracting States with less than 5% import share collectively account for not more than 15% of total imports of the product concerned.

Article 17
Maintenance of the Value of Concessions

Any of the concessions agreed upon under this Agreement shall not be diminished or nullified, by the application of any measures restricting trade by the Contracting States, except under the provisions of other articles of this Agreement.

Article 18
Rules of Origin

Rules of Origin shall be negotiated by the Contracting States and incorporated in this Agreement as an integral part.

Article 19
Consultations

1. Each Contracting State shall accord sympathetic consideration to and will afford adequate opportunity for consultations regarding representations made by another Contracting State with respect to any matter affecting the operation of this Agreement.
2. The Committee of Experts may, at the request of a Contracting State, consult with any Contracting State in respect of any matter for which it has not been possible to find a satisfactory solution through consultations under paragraph 1.

Article 20
Dispute Settlement Mechanism

1. Any dispute that may arise among the Contracting States regarding the interpretation and application of the provisions of this Agreement or any instrument adopted within its framework concerning the rights and obligations of the Contracting States will be amicably settled among the parties concerned through a process initiated by a request for bilateral consultations.
2. Any Contracting State may request consultations in accordance with paragraph 1 of this Article with other Contracting State in writing stating the reasons for the request including identification of the

measures at issue. All such requests should be notified to the Committee of Experts, through the SAARC Secretariat with an indication of the legal basis for the complaint.

3. If a request for consultations is made pursuant to this Article, the Contracting State to which the request is made shall, unless otherwise mutually agreed, reply to the request within 15 days after the date of its receipt and shall enter into consultations in good faith within a period of no more than 30 days after the date of receipt of the request, with a view to reaching a mutually satisfactory solution.
4. If the Contracting State does not respond within 15 days after the date of receipt of the request, or does not enter into consultations within a period of no more than 30 days, or a period otherwise mutually agreed, after the date of receipt of the request, then the Contracting State that requested the holding of consultations may proceed to request the Committee of Experts to settle the dispute in accordance with working procedures to be drawn up by the Committee.
5. Consultations shall be confidential, and without prejudice to the rights of any Contracting State in any further proceedings.
6. If the consultations fail to settle a dispute within 30 days after the date of receipt of the request for consultations, to be extended by a further period of 30 days through mutual consent, the complaining Contracting State may request the Committee of Experts to settle the dispute. The complaining Contracting State may request the Committee of Experts to settle the dispute during the 60-day period if the consulting Contracting States jointly consider that consultations have failed to settle the dispute.
7. The Committee of Experts shall promptly investigate the matter referred to it and make recommendations on the matter within a period of 60 days from the date of referral.
8. The Committee of Experts may request a specialist from a Contracting State not party to the dispute selected from a panel of specialists to be established by the Committee within one year from the date of entry into force of the Agreement for peer review of the matter referred to it. Such review shall be submitted to the Committee within a period of 30 days from the date of referral of the matter to the specialist.
9. Any Contracting State, which is a party to the dispute, may appeal the recommendations of the Committee of Experts to the SMC. The SMC shall review the matter within the period of 60 days from date of submission of request for appeal. The SMC may uphold, modify or reverse the recommendations of the Committee of Experts.

10. Where the Committee of Experts or SMC concludes that the measure subject to dispute is inconsistent with any of the provisions of this Agreement, it shall recommend that the Contracting State concerned bring the measure into conformity with this Agreement. In addition to its recommendations, the Committee of Experts or SMC may suggest ways in which the Contracting State concerned could implement the recommendations.
11. The Contracting State to which the Committee's or SMC's recommendations are addressed shall within 30 days from the date of adoption of the recommendations by the Committee or SMC, inform the Committee of Experts of its intentions regarding implementation of the recommendations. Should the said Contracting State fail to implement the recommendations within 90 days from the date of adoption of the recommendations by the Committee, the Committee of Experts may authorise other interested Contracting States to withdraw concessions having trade effects equivalent to those of the measure in dispute.

Article 21

Withdrawal

1. Any Contracting State may withdraw from this Agreement at any time after its entry into force. Such withdrawal shall be effective on expiry of six months from the date on which a written notice thereof is received by the Secretary-General of SAARC, the depository of this Agreement. That Contracting State shall simultaneously inform the Committee of Experts of the action it has taken.
2. The rights and obligations of a Contracting State which has withdrawn from this Agreement shall cease to apply as of that effective date.
3. Following the withdrawal by any Contracting State, the Committee shall meet within 30 days to consider action subsequent to withdrawal.

Article 22

Entry into Force

1. This Agreement shall enter into force on 1st January 2006 upon completion of formalities, including ratification by all Contracting States and issuance of a notification thereof by the SAARC Secretariat. This Agreement shall supersede the Agreement on SAARC Preferential Trading Arrangement (SAPTA).
2. Notwithstanding the supersession of SAPTA by this Agreement, the concessions granted under the SAPTA Framework shall remain available to the Contracting States until the completion of the Trade Liberalisation Programme.

Article 23
Reservations

This Agreement shall not be signed with reservations, nor will reservations be admitted at the time of notification to the SAARC Secretariat of the completion of formalities.

Article 24
Amendments

This Agreement may be amended by consensus in the SAFTA Ministerial Council. Any such amendment will become effective upon the deposit of instruments of acceptance with the Secretary General of SAARC by all Contracting States.

Article 25
Depository

This Agreement will be deposited with the Secretary General of SAARC, who will promptly furnish a certified copy thereof to each Contracting State.

In witness whereof the undersigned being duly authorised thereto by their respective Governments have signed this Agreement.

Done In Islamabad, Pakistan, On This The Sixth Day Of the Year Two Thousand Four, In Nine Originals In The English Language All Texts Being Equally Authentic.

‹26›

Joint Statement on Ministerial Meeting of TEAM-9 Countries (01.03.2004)

> The participants (representing eight countries in West Africa and India) agreed upon identification, implementation of priority projects and corporate schemes in sectors critical for employment and growth such as agriculture, small scale industries and rural development, pharmaceuticals and health care, information technology and telecommunications, transport energy etc. Under this regional cooperation mechanism, India would provide concessional credit facilities of US $ 500 million.

The First Ministerial Meeting of TEAM-9 countries was held in New Delhi on March 1, 2004 at Vigyan Bhawan. Eight countries in West Africa (Burkina Faso, Chad, Cote d'Ivoire, Equatorial Guinea, Ghana, Guinea Bissau, Mali, Senegal) attended the meeting.

The Ministers held wide-ranging discussions in a friendly and cordial atmosphere, and exchanged views on various issues of mutual interest. They noted with satisfaction that the close relations existing between Africa and India, which have a strong cultural and historical basis, are marked by cordiality and a deep mutual understanding as well as converging interests on major issues. All of them reiterated their desire to further strengthen the excellent cooperation and close ties between the two peoples. It was agreed that TEAM-9 is the right step in this direction.

It was decided that the TEAM-9 cooperation mechanism will operate at Government, institutional and private sector levels, sharing various types of expertise, intellectual and physical resources as well as economic opportunities for promoting welfare, growth and prosperity of the people. It would thus involve providing opportunities for education and training in crucial sectors. It would enable transfer of critical technologies. It would imply undertaking specific projects in individual TEAM-9 countries, which would have region-wide beneficial impact in the sectors critical for employment and growth such as agriculture, small scale industries and rural development, pharmaceuticals and healthcare, information technology and telecommunications, transport, energy etc. The cooperation would derive synergy based on the diverse capacities, capabilities of the member countries.

The Ministers agreed to undertake the following steps:

1.Identification, implementation of priority projects and corporate schemes in the sectors and to set up a Business Council for facilitating identification, entrepreneurship and implementation of specific projects.

2.The Government of India would provide concessional credit facilities of US$ 500 million for financial assistance for the various projects and schemes identified for implementation under this regional cooperation mechanism. The Government of India also offered access to training resources in India and facilitate deputation of Indian scientists, technologists and other experts.

All participants also agreed upon a decision-making structure to formulate policies of cooperation, to review progress as well as for overall monitoring and coordination.

They affirmed their commitment to making the TEAM-9 organisation a success.

❮27❯

Excerpts on Foreign Policy from the Common Minimum Programme of the United Progressive Alliance (27.05.2004)

On all regional and global issues, the UPA Government will pursue an independent foreign policy and will seek to promote multi-polarity in world relations. The highest priority will be given to "building closer political, economic and other ties" with India's neighbours

The UPA Government will pursue an independent foreign policy, keeping in mind its past traditions. This policy will seek to promote multi-polarity in world relations and oppose all attempts at unilateralism.

The UPA Government will give the highest priority to building closer political, economic and other ties with its neighbours in South Asia and to strengthen SAARC. Particular attention will be paid to regional projects in the area of water resources, power and ecological conservation. Dialogue with Pakistan on all issues will be pursued systematically and on a sustained basis.

The UPA will support peace talks in Sri Lanka that fulfil the legitimate aspirations of Tamils and religious minorities within the territorial integrity and solidarity of Sri Lanka. Outstanding issues with Bangladesh will be resolved. Intensive dialogue will be initiated with Nepal for developing water resources to mutual advantage.

Trade and investment with China will be expanded further and talks on the border issue pursued seriously. Relationships with East Asian countries will be intensified. Traditional ties with West Asia will be given a fresh thrust. The UPA Government reiterates India's decades-old commitment to the cause of the Palestinian people for a homeland of their own. Steps will be taken to withdraw Indian mercenaries from Iraq, while further recruitment for this purpose will be banned.

Even as it pursues closer engagements and relations with the USA, the UPA Government will maintain the independence of India's foreign policy position on all regional and global issues. The UPA is committed to deepening ties with Russia and Europe as well.

In keeping with the stance adopted by the late Shri Murasoli Maran at Doha, the UPA Government will fully protect the national interest, particularly of farmers, in all WTO negotiations. Commitment made earlier will be adhered to even as efforts are mounted to ensure that all agreements reflect our concerns fully, particularly in the area of intellectual property and agriculture. The UPA Government will use the flexibility afforded in existing WTO agreements to fully protect Indian agriculture and industry. The UPA Government will play a proactive role in strengthening the emerging solidarity of developing countries in the shape of G-20 in the WTO.

Part 1 B

Speeches delivered by Indian leaders

<28>

Address to the Nation by President, Dr. A.P.J. Abdul Kalam on the Eve of 58th Independence Day (14.08.2004)

The President emphasized the role of the education system in creating an "enlightened, dynamic and prosperous society utilizing the advancement of science and technology". He also recommended the construction of layered wells at entry points of Kosi River flowing from Nepal and Brahamputra River flowing from Tibet to control the intensity of damage from flood waters in low lying areas.

Education For Dignity Of Human Life

My Dear Citizens of India,

On the eve of the 58th Independence Day, I extend to you my best wishes for your happiness and prosperity. My greetings to all of you at home and abroad. Let us, on this occasion, remember with gratitude, the selfless and devoted services of our Armed Forces and those of the Paramilitary Forces, who are guarding our frontiers on the land, at sea, and in the air. I take this opportunity on this Independence Day to convey the best wishes of the people of India, to our men and women participating in the Olympic Games in Athens.

I met 200 freedom fighters from different parts of the country on 9th August 2004. I saw in their ripe age, their enthusiasm to bring back nationalism as a living movement. I salute all our freedom fighters on this occasion. Let me dedicate this Independence Day broadcast to those great souls who pioneered our Independence Movement. We remember them with reverence and gratitude for liberating us from centuries of foreign rule. Their saga of sacrifice has led to the realization of the singular and noble vision of heralding an independent nation.

Dear citizens, we must realise, the significance and the value of our freedom movement. Fortunately after our independence in 1947, we have come a long way in the field of education and have moved towards a knowledge society, as a result of the vision of our educationalists and the policies and actions of successive governments. Many of our educational institutions have excelled in the world. In order to revitalise our self-esteem and culture, it is vital to emphasise the role of the education system in creating an enlightened, dynamic and prosperous society utilising the advancement of science and technology. I therefore propose to discuss the education system in some detail in the later part of my address.

General Elections

The nation is happy that the conduct of the recent general elections and transition to a new government has taken place in a peaceful and orderly manner. In an increasingly complex world environment, this significant achievement emerging from India is yet another valuable contribution to world peace and stability. Now that the government is in place, we all have to get on with the work of building the nation.

External Relations

We are steadily strengthening our presence in regional and international institutions including the United Nations. We also realize that it is essential to strengthen and restructure the United Nations to make it more purposeful. We cherish and advocate multi-polarity in the world order that respects the principles of sovereignty, non-intervention, freedom and democracy. While not forgetting the painful lessons of history, our foreign policy is aimed at a vision that seeks to establish India, the largest democracy in the world as a developed country with its rightful place in the international fora.

Defence and Security

With the rapidly changing global security environment, our nation's domains of security concerns have greatly expanded from what they were after Independence. Another measure of our nation's strength is the effective, firm and fair handling of a series of internal low intensity conflicts and the proxy war. I note with satisfaction our continuing efforts towards good neighbourly relations, particularly the sustained progress of the peace process between India and Pakistan.

Economy

Our economy has yielded a growth rate of the Gross Domestic Product by over 8 percent, driven by broad based accelerated growth in agriculture, infrastructure, manufacturing and services. Sustaining our growth, containing the annual inflation rate, containing the revenue deficit through prudent revenue enhancement and expenditure management are other challenges for the Centre and the States. The root cause of poverty lies in illiteracy, unemployment and lack of basic healthcare and there is a need to sharply increase public spending in these areas.

Water Management

Certain regions of the country like Bihar and Assam are constantly affected by floods every year, and we are witnessing that even now there is a need to find a long-term solution to control floods and to store and utilize surplus water for usage during the dry season and also the linking of regional river basins. In the Gangetic plain and in the Northeastern region, I would recommend the construction of layered wells at the entry points of the Kosi River flowing from Nepal and the Brahmaputra River flowing from Tibet. These layered wells will store floodwater at different levels and will control the intensity of damage in low-lying areas by reducing the velocity of the flow. In addition we may consider the possibility of underground water storage systems at river basin sites and also at other places. The water thus stored will be useful during the time of need. A Water Mission has been rightly identified as a priority area by my government.

Employment Generation

Our employment generation system has not kept pace with the inflow of educated youth. A three-pronged strategy is needed to make education more attractive and simultaneously create employment potential – how do we do that? Firstly, the education system should highlight the importance of entrepreneurship and prepare students right from college education to get oriented towards setting up of enterprises. Diversity of skills and perseverance in work makes an entrepreneur. In addition, college syllabi even for arts, science and commerce courses should include topics and practicals where such entrepreneurship is possible. Secondly, the banking system should provide venture capital right from the village level to prospective entrepreneurs for undertaking new enterprises. Banks have to be proactive in supporting innovative products for enabling wealth generation by young entrepreneurs by setting aside the "conventional tangible asset syndrome". Thirdly, there has to be an economic pull for generation of marketable products and enhancement of purchasing power among the people. This can come through the implementation of mega programmes such as rural connectivity, regional linking of rivers, infrastructural missions, power missions and tourism.

We need the education system to focus on high value and productive employment opportunities. A recent study indicates that the unemployment level in the country is 9 percent of 400 million employable people. That is around 36 million. We can definitely find productive employment for all 36 million people by launching certain missions like bio-diesel generation through plants such as Jatropha, dry land and herbal farming in the available 33 million hectares of waste land earmarked for cultivation.

Mission of Education

Education is the most important element for growth and prosperity of a nation. India is in the process of transforming itself into a developed nation by 2020. Yet we have 350 million people who need literacy and many more who have to acquire employable skills to suit the emerging modern India and the globe. Children who belong to weaker sections of our society are undernourished and only a small percentage of them manage to complete 8 years of satisfactory education. We need to think specifically about them. Education is indeed a fundamental right of every Indian child. Can we allow the situation to continue in which millions of these children are forced into life long poverty? The requirement is that the parents should be able to go to any school nearby and admit their children and happily come back home with the confidence that their children will get a good and value based quality education in that school. The conditions of differently-abled children require equally important attention. In view of such critical issues and their importance and also to break out of our historical mindset, an effective and self renewing education system is therefore fundamental to the survival and growth of civilizations. Therefore, I now propose to address the issues pertaining to education in some detail and suggest some solutions which can be considered for implementation.

Inequality of Access To Educational Resources: Let me share with you one important concern: unequal access to educational resources still exist due to a variety of reasons. For example, I have seen in our villages three types of families. The fortunate ones who realise the importance of educating the young ones at any cost, guide them at all critical stages due to their economic well-being. There are those families, who might realise the importance of education, but are not aware of the opportunities in time, nor the procedures and ways to realise these opportunities for their children. There is a third category of families who are economically weak and do not realise the value of education and hence for generations together, their children are neglected and continue to live in poverty. It is essential that we enlighten and create widespread awareness of education among all sections of society particularly in rural areas and among the urban poor. We should use technology for this important social purpose. It is possible for NGOs, other social and philanthropic institutions and the media to focus on this area of creating awareness. We should also mobilise necessary resources for providing education to the underprivileged people. Let us elaborate the way ahead.

Mobilising Resources For The Mission Of Education: Over the last 50 years, successive Governments have been committed to achieving the national goal of universal education and have steadily increased the budgetary allocation for education. However, 35 percent of our adult population is yet to achieve literacy. The expenditure on education as a percentage of our Gross Domestic Product has a direct impact on our literacy. Today our expenditure on education in India is little more than 4 percent of our GDP. If we have to achieve nearly 100 percent literacy, it is necessary to increase expenditure on education to about 6 to 7 percent of GDP. This 2 to 3 percent increase has to be sustained only for a few years. Thereafter, a lower percentage of GDP allocation to education will be adequate to sustain the high degree of literacy in this country for all time to come.

Clearly public expenditure alone from governments at the Centre and in the States might not able to meet the challenge of mobilising an additional 2 to 3 percent of GDP for the mission of education. It is here that we have to generate additional resources for this noble mission. Expenditure on education, whether in the Centre or in the States can no longer be provided only by respective ministries or departments for human resource development. Indeed, every department of the Government must play a significant role as a partner in human resource development organisation and contribute resources in terms of budget and infrastructure for implementing the mission of providing quality education to the whole nation.

To augment Government resources, I appeal to the entire corporate sector to emulate the example set by some corporate leaders who have focused on education to make a national difference. Different regions of the country may be adopted by the corporate sector within an overall national mission for education. The mechanism should enable persons to have freedom to innovate and deliver directly.

Standardisation Of Teaching: The preferred school concept is arising because of differential quality and standards of teaching. There is a need to make the quality of teaching high in all schools. There also is a need for preparatory education even in rural areas to make the child competitive when he or she joins the regular school. NGOs and the corporate sector can play a vital role in running such schools in rural areas. Rich parents who can afford can also adopt a certain number of rural children for educating them in preparatory schools.

Planning For Good Education For Children In Villages: I would like to recall a question asked by Master Kuldeep Yadav of Class Ten from Etawah during my visit to Saifai, he asked me:

"Mr. President, villages are also full of talent but facilities are available in the towns and cities only. Have you planned something for these children so that they can get good education in villages"?

I was glad to see a child's concern for his rural counterparts. We need to address this problem, which has multiple dimensions. It tells us about the non-availability of infrastructural facilities in schools, the problem of syllabi followed in the school and the non-availability of quality teachers.

Job opportunities being national, the syllabus should be structured in such a manner that it should meet changing societal needs, fulfill the needs of the occupation and inculcate high moral values among students in addition to learning skills. The delivery of quality education is possible only through quality teachers. The teacher has to be a committed teacher who loves teaching and children. The teacher also has to be equipped with all the knowledge required for effective teaching. The self-esteem of the teacher must be high and the teacher must have the quality to become a role model for children. Some element of competitive reward is to be done based on performance. This competency has to be built up throughout the country through a massive teachers education programme delivered through a tele-education system and continuously updated. This can be funded and implemented by a consortium of Government and educational institutions with the corporate sector providing value added services.

There is an urgent need that every school should have basic amenities such as a good building equipped with ventilation and lighting. The rooms should be airy and have spacious classrooms. The school should also have a library, laboratories including the latest Information Technology tools and infrastructure, safe drinking water, clean toilets and a playground. This is possible by earmarking the additional 2 to 3 percent of GDP.

The Role Of Parents: Parents have an important role in the education of their children and making them enlightened citizens. They must be aware of the need for good education of the child, male or female. Like teachers, parents also should set an example for the child in their overall behaviour and conduct. This will enable the child to develop love and respect for their parents and see them as role models.

Reducing Dropouts: It is reported that 39 percent of children, drop out from school after studying 5th Class and 55 percent drop out after studying up to 8th Class. This situation needs remedial action, especially since assent has been accorded to the 86th Constitution Amendment Act – The Right to Education Bill for children between the age group of 5 and 14 years. But an Act alone cannot achieve the goal, unless education is delivered in a manner, which will take into account the socio-ecnomic reality and perception of the people to whom it is addressed. Apart from attracting children to schools, the education system should be able to provide nourishment and inject creativity among them. The aim of the education system should also be to build character, human values, enhance learning capacity through technology and build confidence among children to face the future.

I have seen an education model implemented in Karnataka, which provides accelerated learning using computer aids so that children can have creative learning with the tools of creative animation through computers. Dropouts are identified and brought to the school. This holistic phenomenon of learning once ingrained in the primary stage, where there is a happy learning process and non-threatening evaluation, has led to voluntary learning by the participants.

System Of Entrance Examination: I recently received many e-mails from children and parents regarding too many entrance examinations which children have to appear in from nursery up to plus two level for entry into schools, colleges, universities and professional courses. I consider this as a heavy burden on children. It also has led to the proliferation of tuition and coaching institutes for preparing students for entrance examinations. We have to devise a common All India examination to be conducted by a nominated institution of the Government for entry into universities and professional colleges. Examinations must also be so designed that attending a coaching course would not provide undue advantage to privileged students. Entrance tests should be more in the nature of aptitude assessment rather than creating a seniority list.

Examination Reforms: I find there is a demand for a more transparent and reliable system of examination, evaluation and reporting. It is also noticed that examinations primarily test the memory of students. I remember during my studies at the Madras Institute of Technology in Chennai in the mid 1950s, that they used to conduct open book examinations. This used to be one of the toughest examinations for students. I would recommend that examining bodies may consider the introduction of the open book system of examinations. This will promote creativity among teachers in setting questions and the evaluation of the creative ability of the students. A secure examination system is the need of the hour.

Renewal Of Evaluation System: The examining bodies should have a reliable evaluation system and timely declaration of results. After the initial evaluation of the answer paper, a centralised core group can draw random samples from each batch and carry out independent evaluations. If there is no discrepancy between the initial evaluation and the core group evaluation and it is consistent with the performance of the students, it will be presumed that the batch marking is satisfactory. In case of a discrepancy further samples should be drawn for verification. Special training must be carried out by examining bodies for certifying the examiners in the evaluation process. In short the examining bodies must evolve very good procedures and then get ISO Certification for their evaluation system.

Need For Adoption Of Safety Measures: The recent tragedy involving school children at Kumbakonam must have rung some bells in all educational institutions in the country. It is the responsibility of sponsoring organisations to see that their schools maintain basic minimum norms both in the academic field as well as in the physical facilities which they provide on their campuses. Certain safety features must be built-in our school buildings without which it should not be possible to get affiliation by these schools. There should not be any discretion available with anyone to waive off these conditions. Honesty in implementation is vital at all levels.

Technology Enhanced Education

Constraints of time and space together with the rapid obsolescence of knowledge in some areas of science and technology, have created a huge demand for different courses from different institutions in the distance mode. There is a need for a working digital library system that alone can, in the long run, provide the kind of access required for a Knowledge

Society. Technology Enhanced Learning is a solution. It attempts to exploit the rapid developments in Information and Communication Technology. As the communications band-width continues to increase and the cost of computer power continues to drop, Technology Enhanced Learning will become an economically viable solution. Virtual classrooms of the future will have students from many locations taught by a team of geographically distributed instructors through the tele-education delivery system.

Conclusion

Ultimately, education in its real sense is the pursuit of truth. It is an endless journey through knowledge and enlightenment. Such a journey opens up new vistas of development of humanism where there is no scope, nor room for pettiness, disharmony, jealousy, hatred or enmity. It transforms a human being into a wholesome whole, a noble soul and an asset to the universe. Universal brotherhood in its true sense becomes the sheet anchor for such an education. Real education enhances the dignity of a human being and increases his or her self-respect. If only the real sense of education could be realised by each individual and carried forward in every field of human activity the world will be so much a better place to live in.

The mission of education by the government at the Centre or States or their combination is the foundation to ensure the creation of enlightened citizens who will make a prosperous, happy and strong nation. May God bless you.

❮29❯

Statement made by Prime Minister Shri Atal Bihari Vajpayee at the 12th SAARC Summit (04.01.2004)

> The Prime Minister suggested the setting up of a task force to implement the recommendations of the Commission on Poverty Alleviation and conveyed India's willingness to make an initial contribution of US $ 100 million to a proposed Poverty Alleviation Fund. He also praised "the courageous action" taken by the King of Bhutan against Indian insurgent groups.

"I join my other colleagues in congratulating the Prime Minister of Pakistan on his taking over as Chairman of SAARC. I would like to convey our sincere appreciation to the Government of Pakistan for the excellent arrangements made for this Summit, and for the warm hospitality extended to our delegation.

I also join other delegations in commending the immediate past Chairman – Nepal – for the energy and dedication with which it guided SAARC activities during these last two years. This was in spite of the many important domestic preoccupations of His Majesty's Government of Nepal. The spadework for many of today's successful outcomes was done in the various meetings of Ministers and officials in Kathmandu.

At the last Summit in Kathmandu, I had said that, at sixteen years of age, SAARC needed a dose of economic and social realism to move from adolescence to adulthood. Our organization is now 18 years old. I think we can look back with considerable satisfaction over what we have achieved since the last Summit. We have finalized a Social Charter. We have moved forward on Preferential Trading arrangements and have concluded a framework agreement for SAFTA.

We have agreed on an additional protocol, which significantly updates our 1987 Convention against Terrorism. Our Independent Commission on Poverty Alleviation has done sterling work in putting together a set of substantive recommendations for a regional approach to poverty alleviation.

Much more remains to be done. In its 18 years of existence, SAARC has created high expectations amongst the people of the region. We should be candid in accepting that these expectations have not been fulfilled in the measure of the potential. The benefits of SAARC have not yet touched the lives of ordinary people.

A Group of Eminent Persons, which we set up after the Male Summit, had reviewed the strengths and weaknesses of SAARC and made certain recommendations for its improvement. We are still debating how to make progress on many of these recommendations. We need to move from the realm of ideas to plans of action. Our statements of good intentions have to be translated into programmes for implementation.

The work of our Independent Commission on Poverty Alleviation illustrates this point. The Commission has noted that in spite of the endemic and widespread poverty in all our countries, South Asia has a rich tapestry of best practices, cutting across sectors and regions. Many of these practices have attracted global renown.

Yet we have done almost nothing to document them systematically, to disseminate the lessons from them and to expand their application to regional poverty alleviation programmes.

I would urge all our fellow South Asian countries that we should now act with purpose and focus to implement the Commission's recommendations.

Let us set up a dedicated Task Force – with representatives from each of our countries – to carry forward this implementation work. This Task Force can be set up either under the umbrella of the SAARC Secretariat, or independently. In the latter event, India is willing to host the task force. In either case, we are willing to fund the establishment and logistical costs of establishing and running such a task force.

I would propose, in addition, a Poverty Alleviation Fund, which can be professionally managed and can fund specific poverty alleviation programmes and projects in our countries. Once we have agreed on the modalities of creation of such a fund, and on its charter, India would be willing to make an initial contribution of US $ 100 million to this Fund, on the understanding that this money would be used entirely on projects within SAARC, but outside India.

The Poverty Alleviation Commission has proposed that before 2010 South Asia could reduce poverty by half, and also reduce by half the number of people without safe drinking water and sanitation.

The UN Millennium Development Goals aim to achieve these targets by 2015. With our rich natural resources, our technical manpower base, and our recent economic resurgence, South Asia can – and should – achieve these targets faster.

Let us now resolve that we will try to achieve all the Millennium Development Goals by 2010.

Again, India is willing to support the establishment of a SAARC Group, which could draw up strategies to ensure this, and would specially support those countries which are falling behind this schedule.

Any joint endeavour needs mutual trust and confidence. For many decades, South Asian countries – which have a complex and troubled colonial legacy

– have been unable to forge an integrated economic understanding, circumventing political differences.

Mutual suspicions and petty rivalries have continued to haunt us. As a result, the peace dividend has bypassed our region.

History can remind us, guide us, teach us or warn us; it should not shackle us. We have to look forward now, with a collective approach in mind.

Not very long ago, I had visited the Andaman Islands, where during our colonial days, political prisoners were kept in confinement. On the inscriptions in the Cellular Jail there, I found many names of brave martyrs and freedom fighters from what are today three South Asian countries.

Our forefathers fought side by side, transcending religious, regional and linguistic differences against a common colonial oppressor in our first war of Independence in 1857. It reminds us that many of us have a shared history, which pre-dates our more recent divisions.

In two years' time, we will enter the 150th Anniversary of that stirring uprising. Perhaps India, Pakistan and Bangladesh can together celebrate that anniversary, in remembrance of our joint struggle against a common adversary.

We have to learn appropriate lessons from the experience of other countries. After centuries of fratricidal conflicts and wars, Europe is now uniting to emerge as the world's most powerful economic grouping. Closer home, the ASEAN countries have found it possible not to allow their political problems to come in the way of economic cooperation.

Examples of ever deepening regional cooperation can be seen in Africa, Latin America and the Caribbean region where also countries have a long history of bitter hostility towards each other. All these examples remind us that rational economics should triumph over political prejudice in South Asia.

We should undoubtedly encourage free movement of people across the SAARC region. At the same time, we need sufficiently strong controls so that illegal migration is prevented.

We have to create more opportunities for free commercial interaction between us. This also requires jointly tackling smuggling, drug trafficking, money laundering and gun running, all of which today flourish across our borders because of our mutual rivalries and inadequate coordination.

The development of greater economic stakes in each other would naturally result in greater sensitivity to the concerns of each other. This would pave the way for the more ambitious – but entirely achievable – goals such as a Free Trade Area, an Economic Union, open borders and a common currency for our region.

In this context, I would like to draw attention to the courageous action taken by His Majesty the King of Bhutan and his government against insurgent groups, which were trying to use Bhutanese territory to launch terrorist activities in India. It is an outstanding example of sensitivity to the security concerns of a neighbour, which is at the same time in the direct long-term security interest of Bhutan itself.

World-class connectivity is key to faster development. The establishment of a modern Multi-modal Transport Infrastructure of road, rail, air, waterways and sea-links should be one of our priority objectives.

Again, a SAARC Task Force can be formed, with representatives from all our countries, which could commission or prepare techno-economic feasibility studies of major transportation links. India would be willing to fully support this venture; we would also be ready to make a substantial contribution to actually creating the viable infrastructure links recommended by the Task Force.

Development is increasingly dependent on free information flows. An information society is emerging all over the world. A digital divide between and within SAARC countries could retard development and raise social tensions.

SAARC countries have to transform their societies into "knowledge economies". India is prepared to share its recent experiences with other SAARC countries in this regard. We are willing to contribute to the widest possible cooperation in the use of IT, bio-technology and other S&T inputs for achieving our priority goals in socio-economic development.

Regional water and energy cooperation projects merit high priority. Our common rivers are a valuable resource for energy, irrigation and transportation. We have vast untapped hydro-carbon resources. A rational exploitation of these shared resources, with equal benefit to all stakeholders, can take us a long way towards real integration of South Asian economies.

When I landed in Islamabad yesterday, a hoarding near the airport caught my attention. It said, "Together we stand a better chance in the world". This is not a mere slogan. It aptly expresses a profound truth, which south Asia is still to grasp fully.

We have to change South Asia's image and standing in the world. We must make the bold transition from mistrust to trust, from discord to concord, and from tension to peace.

The bonds of religion, language, ethnicity and culture which hold us together as a South Asian family are far more enduring than the relatively recent barriers of political prejudice that we have erected. We should renew these bonds to jointly overcome poverty, disease and hunger.

Our region is blessed with rich and varied human resources, a young population, vast markets for intra-regional trade, large energy resources and a rich biodiversity.

In other words, we have the potential, talent and resources to make south Asia an economic powerhouse of the world. We only need the necessary political will to make this happen. This is the agenda which we leaders of SAARC should strive to advance in the coming years."

❮30❯

Statement made by the Prime Minister Shri Atal Bihari Vajpayee on "Next Steps in Strategic Partnership with USA" (13.01.2004)

> The Prime Minister announced the "next steps in strategic partnership" between India and the US for expanded cooperation in civilian nuclear activities, civilian space programme and high technology trade. He stated that relevant laws, regulations and procedures will be strengthened in accordance with respective national laws and international obligations.

"In November 2001, President Bush and I committed our countries to a strategic partnership. Since then, our two countries have strengthened bilateral cooperation significantly in several areas. Today we announce the next steps in implementing our shared vision.

India and the United States of America agree to expand cooperation in three specific areas: civilian nuclear activities, civilian space programmes, and high technology trade. In addition, we agree to expand our dialogue on missile defence. Cooperation in these areas will deepen the ties of commerce and friendship between our two nations, and will increase stability in Asia and beyond.

The proposed cooperation will progress through a series of reciprocal steps that will build on each other. It will include expanded engagement on nuclear regulatory and safety issues and missile defence, ways to enhance cooperation in peaceful uses of space technology, and steps to create the appropriate environment for successful high technology commerce. In order to combat the proliferation of weapons of mass destruction, relevant laws, regulations and procedures will be strengthened, and measures to increase bilateral and international cooperation in this area will be employed. These cooperative efforts will be undertaken in accordance with our respective national laws and international obligations.

The expanded cooperation launched today is an important milestone in transforming the relationship between India and the United States of America. That relationship is based increasingly on common values and common interests. We are working together to promote global peace and prosperity. We are partners in the war of terrorism and we are partners in controlling the proliferation of weapons of mass destruction and the means to deliver them.

The vision of the India-US strategic partnership that President Bush and I share is now becoming a reality".

❮31❯

Address to the Nation by Prime Minister Dr. Manmohan Singh (24.06.2004)

The Prime Minister reiterated the government's commitment to giving a "new deal" to rural India and emphasized the need to adopt a comprehensive approach to national security through greater synergy between intelligence agencies and internal security structures, civil-military interface and use of technology for national security management.

"My Fellow Citizens,

I speak to you with a deep sense of humility, fully conscious of the sacred responsibility entrusted to me. You have assigned the task of governance of our country to the United Progressive Alliance and its supporting parties. You have delivered your verdict and the verdict is clear. You have sought a change in the manner in which this country is run, a change in national priorities, and a change in the processes and focus of governance. You have, through your mandate, made it clear that economic growth has to be accompanied by equity and social justice. You have expressed concern for the poor and disadvantaged sections of our society and for minorities and backward regions to be at the heart of all policies of the government.

As I share with you the priorities of our government, I am reminded of the Father of our Nation, Mahatma Gandhi. Gandhiji had said that his mission in life was 'to wipe every tear from every eye.' Think of the poorest person you have ever seen, Gandhiji would say, 'and ask if your next act will be of any use to him.' That message of Bapu resonates in our ears as we settle down to the business of government.

The National Common Minimum Programme has been prepared by us keeping in mind the priorities brought into focus by your mandate. The Address of the President of India to Parliament outlines a comprehensive agenda for the nation to which our government is committed. The country would have benefited if Parliament had been allowed to discuss the President's Address. I was eagerly looking forward to contributions from all parties in this discussion. Unfortunately, this was not allowed to happen. It should be a matter of deep concern for all of us when established mechanisms for a constructive dialogue and critique, which are vital for a parliamentary democracy, are disrupted and not allowed to operate.

Parliament is a forum, which is sacred, and it must be our collective endeavour to ensure that we maximize its effectiveness. I request parties across the entire political spectrum to respect Parliament as an essential forum for public debate so that we can move forward on the task of nation-building which is a common goal for one and all. We can justly take pride in the fact that since Independence we have been able, with our efforts, to build the foundations of a modern economy and record an acceleration in the rate of economic growth. There have been impressive gains in terms of the educational and health status of the nation. However, the benefits of this performance have not touched all our citizens in equal measure. Growth is not an end in itself. It is a means to generate employment, banish poverty, hunger and homelessness and improve the standard of living of the mass of our people. It must also be environmentally sustainable.

Equity and efficiency are complimentary, not contradictory, and we must move forward on both these while maintaining a high degree of fiscal and financial discipline, and a robust external economic profile.

To be able to devote our attention and energy to economic development that improves the lives of our people, we must ensure social and political stability, communal harmony and respect for the rule of law. We must put in place policies and programmes, which empower all our citizens to lead a life of dignity and self-respect. Our government is committed to the security and welfare of all minorities, the protection of the interests of the scheduled castes and scheduled tribes, of backward classes and all weaker sections. Equally we are committed to the empowerment of women. We will ensure equal participation of all in the processes of governance.

The essence of the National Common Minimum Programme is the recognition that policies that are aimed at promoting economic growth must also advance the cause of distributive justice and create new employment opportunities. Economic reform is not only about freeing private enterprise from the shackles of bureaucratic control. It is also about making the government more effective, efficient and people friendly so that it can handle better the many tasks that only Governments can perform. And, it is also about ensuring fair and transparent regulation of the market where this is necessary. While many in our country are benefiting from their integration into the market and the global economy, millions of our citizens are still plagued by illiteracy, disease, want, hunger and malnutrition. Gender disparities are high and educational, nutritional and health levels of women are much lower than of men. Chronic poverty afflicts millions who lack income and food security. This is particularly acute among the scheduled castes, other backward castes and scheduled tribes. At a regional level, too, the disparities are high and while some regions of the country seem to be on an accelerating growth path, there is a concern that other regions are not only lagging but are also falling behind. Regrettably, minorities suffer from not only economic insecurity but also a sense of marginalization from political and governance processes.

As a nation, we cannot accept such disparities. We have been given a mandate, which enjoins us to be sensitive to the concerns of these deprived sections and regions. We have an obligation to ensure that they too benefit from growth in full measure. Our commitment to investments in the social sectors is rooted in this reality. It is the responsibility of government, at all levels, at the Centre, in the States and at the level of the community, to address each of these economic and social challenges. However, I am convinced that the government, at every level, is today not adequately equipped and attuned to deal with this challenge and meet the aspirations of the people. To be able to do so, we require the reform of government and of public institutions. Much of the focus of economic reforms in the past decade has been on reducing the role of the government in controlling the Private Sector; controls that hampered entrepreneurial dynamism and often bred corruption. This was necessary. Yet, there are many areas, critical areas, that directly affect the quality of life of every citizen, where the government has a role, and is expected by every citizen to have a role. These include the provision of social and physical infrastructure for development, the provision of elementary education and public health, providing drinking water and sanitation. They also include economic infrastructure, which in our country in large part must be provided by the Government such as irrigation, power, roads and railways. Our people expect the government to be pro-active and sensitive to their needs. In each of these areas, at every level of governance, the reform of government is today an urgent task before us.

We will pursue economic reform and widen the space for individual initiative and enterprise, but even as we do so, we cannot forsake the obligation of running a government that works, and works for the people. The reform of administration and of public institutions to improve efficiency and the quality of delivery services will be our immediate priority.

There has been a neglect of the interests of the farmers in recent years and this is reflected in a significant slowing down in agricultural growth in the past five years. Farmers in many parts of the country have faced distress and there has been no helping hand. The National Common Minimum Programme of the United Progressive Alliance is committed to giving a "New Deal" to rural India. Agriculture must receive the priority attention it deserves. Public and private investment in agriculture has to be greatly increased. A key concern in recent years has been the lack of access to credit. Our government is already addressing this issue directly by pursuing policies that improve the farmer's access to affordable credit. Agricultural research, training and extension also require much greater attention. I would like to see the emergence of new centers of excellence in agriculture, as we have in technology and management. There has to be a sharper focus on expanding opportunities for gainful employment in agriculture and in off-farm rural activities. Food for work programme, efficiently implemented, can greatly assist in achieving this objective.

The Indian farmer has also suffered from too many controls and restrictions. There are still far too many internal barriers to trade that must go. We must also re-examine those aspects of our policies that prevent a creative interaction between farmers and agro-industries. I would like to see the creation of a "Single Market" across the country for both manufactured and agricultural produce with encouragement of agro-industry linkages. With the introduction of value-added taxation this integration of the Indian market will be further enabled.

A striking feature of development in our country has been the rapid increase in urbanization. There are now more than 30 cities with a population of more than one million. The rapid and unplanned growth of these cities has contributed to increased urban pollution, crime, the absence of the required infrastructure like access to drinking water, sanitation, roads, footpaths for pedestrians and public spaces, parks and greenery is making life in urban India a living hell for many. Most of the responsibility for this rests with States and Municipal Governments. It will be our effort to give special attention to policies that can encourage urban development and urban renewal. We will actively seek public-private partnership in building urban infrastructure in a planned manner.

Higher rates of economic growth, urbanization and the modernization of agriculture will continue to increase the demand for energy. This demand can only be met with new investment, increased efficiency and rational pricing. Even as we plan to make more efficient use of conventional sources of energy, we must invest in the development of non-conventional sources. We will evolve an Energy Policy package that will cover all sources of energy and will address all aspects like energy security, access and availability, affordability and pricing, efficiency and environment.

Water has emerged as a critical and contentious issue across the country. Even access to safe drinking water remains a problem in many parts of our country. Water management policies have to be so formulated as to address the needs of farmers and weaker sections, especially women, as well as those of city-dwellers. We will have to find innovative, cost-effective and community-based solutions. Groundwater replenishment and management and rainwater harvesting require close cooperation between government, panchayati raj institutions and non-governmental organizations. The government will reverse the neglect of public investment in irrigation, addressing the specific problems of each river basin, in an environment and people friendly manner.

We need new thinking in health policy. While the government will continue to help in the growth of private and community based health and medical care, there is a crying need for the reform of public health and public hospitals. We will make public hospitals more efficient and accessible, through public-private partnership aimed at offering affordable and humane healthcare. We need community based and public health-oriented solutions to tackling communicable diseases, epidemics, especially HIV/AIDS, and disability management and population stabilization.

People are a nation's greatest resource. Our greatest asset will be an educated and capable work force. Our government will work along with State governments to step up public spending on education, to universalize access to elementary education and to improve the quality of our education. We shall make effective use of mid-day meals programme for school children to achieve this objective. I am particularly concerned about the access to schooling and higher education of children belonging to scheduled castes and scheduled tribes, weaker sections and minorities.

The education of the girl child and female literacy will be priority areas for us. We will do our utmost to provide scholarships to help them acquire the training and skills that can make them self-reliant and proud citizens. Our children need modern and relevant education aimed at making them concerned, capable and caring citizens of the Republic.

Our economy has been rapidly integrating with the global economy over the past decade, with a growing sense of self-confidence. However, domestic enterprise needs world class and cost-effective infrastructure. Better roads, better connectivity, modern airports and railways, efficient ports and affordable and reliable power are all the basic requirements for a competitive economy. For centuries India has been a trading nation, actively engaged in the movement of goods and people across continents and high seas. We will pursue policies that enable our economy to be better integrated with the world economy without hurting the interests of our people. We will create an environment conducive to the utilization of the talent pool of the vast and diverse Indian diaspora. We greatly value their participation in the development of our nation.

No objective in this development agenda can be met if we do not reform the instrument in our hand with which we have to work, namely the government and public institutions. Clearly, this will be my main concern and challenge in the days to come.

We will maintain our tradition of an independent foreign policy, built on a national consensus and based on our supreme national interests. We will expand our network of international relationships – preserving solidarity with traditional allies and strengthening new partnerships. We will work with like-minded nations for an equitable, multi-polar world order, which takes into account the legitimate aspirations of developing countries.

We desire to live in a neighbourhood of peace and prosperity. We will actively pursue the composite dialogue with Pakistan. We are sincere about discussing and resolving all issues, including Jammu & Kashmir. We recognize that resolution of major issues requires national consensus and accommodation of public sentiment in both countries. It is self-evident that terrorism and violence would cast a dark shadow over this process. With our other South Asian neighbours, it will be our sincere effort to jointly realize the vast potential for cooperation, and to ensure mutual security, stability and development.

In our relations with China, we are encouraged by positive developments, which we are committed to strengthening. Bilateral economic cooperation has shown remarkable growth and diversification. We shall carry forward the process of discussion to resolve the boundary question from the political perspective of our bilateral relations.

As two of the world's great democracies, our strengthened relationship with the USA is a fact of considerable importance. The transformation of our relations with USA has been supported by the expansion of economic links and people to people ties. We will welcome the expansion of cooperation between the two Governments to include new and mutually beneficial areas, particularly high technology.

The strength and vibrancy of our partnership with Russia has withstood the flux of the post-Cold War world. We will accelerate the diversification of our relationship, particularly in defence, high technology, space and nuclear energy, while intensifying economic cooperation.

We have traditionally strong relations with the countries of Southeast and West Asia, based on cultural affinities, economic interaction and a vibrant Indian expatriate community. We aim to build upon these. While speaking of West Asia, I must share our deep concern about developments in Iraq and the suffering of the people of that country. It is our earnest hope that democracy would be restored and full sovereignty transferred to a truly representative Government of Iraq. India is committed to participate in all endeavours aimed at bringing stability and to ensure the well being of the Iraqi people.

We will also strengthen our bilateral relations with developing countries of Latin America and Africa. Similarly, strong ties with the nations of Central Asia are of importance for our international trade, as well as for our strategic and energy security.

We will actively pursue a cooperative relationship with the European Union to expand the political and economic frontiers of collaboration. We welcome the inclusion of many new member states, with whom we have a long tradition of cooperation.

I wish to place on record the nation's deep sense of gratitude and pride in the valour, professionalism and the spirit of self-sacrifice of our armed forces. I assure the nation that we will not be found wanting in providing for our armed forces, or in caring for our ex-servicemen. We will streamline defence acquisition procedures, so that our forces obtain the modern weapon systems and technologies. Our government will ensure that the necessary funds are made available for these purposes.

We will maintain a credible minimum nuclear deterrent, along with a policy of 'no first use' is our nuclear doctrine. India is a responsible nuclear power, and we will continue to work to prevent proliferation of weapons of mass destruction. At the same time, we remain committed to the goal of universal nuclear disarmament.

Internal security remains an important challenge. Terrorism poses a grave threat to the unity and progress of our nation. We shall combat it with all the resources at our command. There shall be no doubt whatsoever about our resolve to deal with this insidious threat to our nation.

The government will continue the process of dialogue with the Hurriyat and all other groups in Jammu and Kashmir. The Government is willing to talk with all disaffected groups provided they shun the path of violence.

We will adopt a comprehensive approach to the problem of national security, to create greater synergy between our intelligence agencies, closer coordination between internal security structures, more efficient civil-military interface and more effective harnessing of technology to national security management.

My fellow citizens, I share the feeling of well-meaning citizens when they express pained concern about the decline of morals and ethics in public life. There is, however, no better way to deal with this incipient threat to our democracy than to meet it head on by joining public life ourselves.

When I chose to enter public life, I did so because I was convinced that our democracy needs more professionals to become more engaged and active in politics.

I therefore appeal to each one of you to also participate in our public life so that governments at all levels – central, state and local - are all constantly put on notice and not just tested once in five years.

When I travel across the country, I am always heartened by the increasing number of young and idealistic people I meet, who work with voluntary organizations, empowering the dispossessed and the dis-franchised. We shall make effective use of the resources of the civil society to improve the quality of governance and delivery of important public services.

Fellow citizens, I urge you to come forward and take an active role in the nation's public affairs. Each one of you can make a difference. I seek your support to restore to our public life a greater sense of purpose and a renewed commitment to decency, morality and the hard work needed to take our country and every one of our citizens forward. We must re-capture the spirit of idealism and self-sacrifice, which characterized the high noon of our freedom struggle. Working together, we shall ensure that this ancient, sacred land of ours regains its rightful place in the comity of nations.

Jai Hind."

❮32❯

Inaugural address by Prime Minister Dr. Manmohan Singh at BIMST-EC Summit, Bangkok (31.07.2004)

The Prime Minister stated that India's participation in BIMST-EC was "a key element in our Look East Policy" and stressed that interconnectivity-physical economic and technological- is of prime importance. He identified the trilateral India-Myanmar-Thailand Highway and optical fibre telecommunication link as important projects in the BIMST-EC context.

Mr. Chairman,

Excellencies,

Ladies and Gentlemen,

I begin by congratulating the Prime Minister of Thailand for assuming the Chairmanship of the first BIMST-EC Summit and for his inspiring Opening Address. I also wish to thank the Government of Thailand for its warm and gracious hospitality. This is my first overseas visit as the Prime Minister of India and I am gratified to be here in this beautiful land of Thailand. Mr. Chairman, yours is a country with which we have enduring and historical bonds and this occasion represents a new phase in a partnership, which has been mutually enriching. I take this opportunity to extend a very hearty welcome to Nepal and Bhutan as new members of BIMST-EC.

Excellencies, we in India view our quest for closer and mutually beneficial ties with all our neighbours as a logical response to the challenges with which contend. These challenges that we must address and overcome are varied and disparate. The world continues to be riven by poverty, inequity, disease and highly skewed access to resources at a time when science and technology have placed solutions within our reach. The global political environment fosters insecurity, making our task even more complex, and our endeavours more urgent. The intolerance bred by religious extremism can divide societies and people and we neglect it at our own peril. The scourge of terrorism is unfortunately one with which we all must grapple as a global phenomenon and as an everyday reality. The areas of conflict are coming closer to us.

But, Mr. Chairman we cannot stay our efforts. We have to work—we have to work for peace and for security, and to create a new climate in which we can concentrate on our primary responsibility—a better life for all our peoples. The solutions to some of these problems lie with Governments. Equally, we have to reach out beyond, to find imaginative answers to intractable issues. This is the way we have chosen in India. It is this perspective—that the many dimensions of the challenges we face can only be solved by working together that brings us here today in this beautiful city of Bangkok. A global order, which is better representative and more responsive to the needs of our times, must include the reform of the United Nations and a restructuring of the Security Council.

Excellencies, in that spirit, I deem it a privilege to be present on this occasion along with our close neighbours and friends representing the BIMST-EC countries. We belong to a region with many natural complementarities. Our bonds run deep in time, strengthened by strong economic, cultural and civilizational links. The colonial intervention over the last two centuries may have weakened these links somewhat, but has not in any way diminished the yearning of our people to revive them. We see BIMST-EC as a collective and effective forum for giving full expression to widely rediscover the coherence of our region based on the commonality of many linkages around the Bay of Bengal.

Regional integration is not antithetical to globalisation, but can be a useful building block. Our collective endeavours can be more than the sum of our individual efforts. BIMST-EC offers us the hope and the opportunity to fulfil this imperative of our times.

We consider our participation in BIMST-EC as a key element in our 'Look East Policy' and long standing approach of good neighbourliness towards all our neighbours — by land and sea.

The challenge before us is to transform the richness of our human and natural resources into cooperative regional activities promoting development, enhancing prosperity and the well-being of our people, and ensuring our collective security in all its multifarious dimensions.

We need to translate our inherent strengths of geographical contiguity into a community of prosperity and goodwill. Interconnectivity — physical, economic or technological — is of prime importance in building bridges of understanding. We can achieve this long-term vision of shared prosperity and growth through cooperative action based on dialogue and fostering mutual confidence, focussing on aspects that unite us.

Considerable progress has already been achieved in terms of a Framework Agreement on Free Trade and valuable expert-level studies under the six listed areas of cooperation. For instance, we consider the trilateral India-Myanmar-Thailand Highway proposal and the proposed Optical Fibre Telecommunication Link alongside the Highway as projects, which would have considerable importance in the BIMST-EC context.

For a region that is so richly endowed with energy resources, it is imperative that we address the need for their optimal utilization to meet our growing energy demands. In this context, India would be happy to host a Ministerial Conference on Energy Cooperation in the year 2005 to provide an impetus to our joint efforts in this area.

The vagaries of climate and weather in our region concern us all. We have had floods in some places and drought in others. To enable all BIMST-EC countries to pool their scientific resources and to benefit from weather forecasting India is prepared to set up a BIMST-EC Centre on Weather and Climate in New Delhi. India would also be willing to share its expertise in remote sensing for agriculture, environment and disaster management.

To further explore the vast potential that exists for increasing tourism within our region, India proposes to host a Round Table and Workshop of Tourism Ministers of BIMST-EC countries, with the participation of tour operators, hotel representatives and others associated and with the tourism industry with the objective of at least doubling tourism within BIMST-EC region in the next five years.

We are also happy to announce 150 scholarships for next year under the ITEC Programme for BIMST-EC countries, in addition to the 150 scholarships offered by India at the Ministerial Meeting in Phuket in February this year. All our countries are richly endowed in traditional systems of meuicine. Mr. Chairman, you referred to the vast potential of our herbal resources to find new remedies to HIV/AIDs. India offers 30 scholarships in this field to enable a productive partnership amongst BIMST-EC countries.

The statement to be issued on the conclusion of this Summit should reflect, as I am sure it will, the collective will of our Governments to carry forward the BIMST-EC vision of mutually beneficial regional cooperation through specific projects. Our mutual confidence would of course be greatly enhanced if we were able to forge a common front against terrorism, gun running, narcotics trafficking, which in varying degrees affect us all.

Mr. Chairman, Thailand has played a pioneering role in bringing the BIMST-EC idea to fruition and we thank you for staying the course and for your leadership role. It is now our collective responsibility to carry it forward towards purposeful cooperation. In achieving the objectives of BIMST-EC, I would like to reaffirm India's firm political commitment to regional cooperation for mutual benefit and wholehearted support and cooperation with our BIMST-EC partners so that we succeed in our efforts to translate ideals into meaningful cooperation on the ground.

❮33❯

Address to the Nation by Prime Minister Dr. Manmohan Singh (15.08.2004)

The Prime Minister urged the political leaders to take "a national and a holistic view" of managing water resources and pay special attention to governance in the North East and J&K. He identified agriculture, water, education, health care, employment, urban renewal and infrastructure as the seven priority sectors for focused attention.

Following is the free rendering of the Prime Minister's address to the nation, in Hindi, from the ramparts of the Red Fort on the 58th Independence Day, today:

"My dear countrymen, brothers, sisters, and dear children—Greetings to all of you on this day, the anniversary of our Independence.

This is a day we salute our Tiranga and feel pride and joy in watching it fly high in the blue sky. This is a day we remember and honour the leaders of our Freedom Movement for the struggle they waged under the inspiring leadership of Mahatma Gandhiji and for the victory they won against foreign rule. This is a day we thank our soldiers and security forces for their bravery and commitment. We salute them for their dedication and discipline—farmers, workers, teachers, professionals, scientists and our elected representatives.

In every walk of life, each one of us contributes in our own way to the building of our dear Bharat. What is that Bharat that we all wish to build?

A Bharat that is just and humane.

A Bharat that treats all its citizens as equals.

A Bharat that is prosperous.

A Bharat that lives in peace.

A Bharat in which every person is literate and healthy.

A Bharat in which everyone who seeks work is able to find it, and works for a brighter future for all of us. My greetings to all of you.

As I stand here before you, I am reminded of the words of our first Prime Minister Pandit Jawaharlal Nehru, when he spoke to the Nation on the first anniversary of our Independence in 1948. At that time I was a young student, and looked upon the dawn of Independence as the opening up of new vistas of opportunities to build an India of our dreams. Panditji had then said, "All of us talk of India and all of us demand many things from India. What do we give her in return?" Panditji asked, and he said, "India will ultimately give us what we give her of love and service and productive and creative work. India will be what we are: our thoughts and actions will shape her."

Friends, I ask each one of you to remember these wise words of Panditji as you go about doing your work, be it on farms, in factories, in schools, in colleges, in government offices, in shops, in research laboratories. Our Nation is what we are. It will become what we make of ourselves.

Brothers and sisters, it is one brick after another that helps make a building. Millions of bricks go to make a great building. In the same manner, the efforts of millions of people go into the formation of a nation. The process of nation building is a great enterprise of adventure and creativity. It requires all of us to work together, bonded by our love for our Motherland. This love flows from our identity as Indians. Whatever be our religion, region, language, caste or culture, we are all Indians and India is ours.

Our strength derives from our unity in diversity. The principles of secularism, social justice and the equality of all before law are the defining feature of our nation. Today is a day we re-dedicate ourselves to the service of our Nation, and of each and every citizen, especially those less fortunate than us.

This day comes for us in the middle of the monsoons. Each year when we meet here and see the Tiranga being unfurled on the Red Fort, we also look at the clouds above and wonder whether it would rain. This year too we have looked at the skies with anxiety.

In Andhra Pradesh I went to understand the problems of farmers, suffering from the impact of drought, and to hold the hands of the families that had lost their breadwinner due to the unbearable burden of debt. For miles together I could see no water. In Assam and Bihar I went to share the concern of people whose lives have been dislocated by floods. For miles without end I could see only water. Drought and floods are two fundamental problems that continue to bring suffering to our rural population. We need concerted action to deal with these perennial problems.

Our government has already taken some steps to deal with them. We intend to take more steps in future. We need to insulate our people from the impact of drought by creating local level water security. We have to mobilize our people to come forward to take up the challenge of water conservation and management. We are committed to increasing public investment in irrigation and addressing the specific problems of each river basin, in an environment and people friendly manner.

Water is a national resource, and we have to take an integrated view of our country's water resources, our needs and our policies and water utilization practices. We need to ensure the equitable use of scarce water resources.

The waters of our sacred rivers have for centuries nurtured our civilization. They are the threads that run through the fabric of our nation. We cannot allow these waters to divide us. I urge you and all our political leaders to take a national and a holistic view of the challenge of managing our water resources.

Dealing with the problem of water is an important commitment we have made as part of our "New Deal for Rural India". We have also taken steps to address the problem of availability and access to credit in rural areas. The "New Deal" that rural India needs must encompass investment in irrigation, credit delivery, healthcare, availability of electricity, primary education, rural roads and the modernization of the infrastructure for agriculture.

We must increasingly use modern science and technology to address the needs of dry land farming, the diversification of our cropping pattern, micro-irrigation and the quality of our livestock. Improving rural connectivity and access to information can enrich the farm community. Here Governmental initiative can be multiplied by the effort of private enterprise and community action.

Friends, more than three decades ago, Smt. Indira Gandhiji had given the call "Garibi Hatao". We have reduced the incidence of poverty to some extent, but there is much more remaining to be done. While liberalizing and modernizing our economy and enabling individual enterprise to blossom, we must pay special attention to the elimination of poverty and the empowerment of Scheduled Castes, Scheduled Tribes, Other Backward Castes and minorities. Our development strategies for tribal areas must be adequately sensitive to their felt needs and aspirations.

The empowerment of women is an important priority and the education of the girl child is vital to it. Our children are our future. In framing our policies we must keep the interests of future generations in mind. The Government will pursue social and economic policies that are conducive to the proper growth and development of our children, investing in their education, health and nutrition. A healthy child makes a healthy nation.

Employment generation has not kept pace with demand for jobs. Government will address this deficiency in the growth process by encouraging the growth of small and medium enterprises, agro industries and sectors like tourism, where there is a high job potential. There is also an urgent need to provide employment in rural areas especially in areas suffering from prolonged drought. The "Food For Work Programme" will be an important part of our strategy to deal with this challenge. New investment in the infrastructure sector will also help generate new jobs.

Our approach has to be one of seeking faster growth while ensuring that the benefits of growth are more evenly distributed. Our policies for higher economic growth and modernization will be combined with an emphasis on social justice, communal harmony, rural development, regional balance and concern for the environment.

Dear Countrymen, from the National Common Minimum Programme, I have identified seven priority sectors for focused attention. These are agriculture, water, education, healthcare, employment, urban renewal and infrastructure. These Seven Sectors (*saat sutra*) are the pillars of the development bridge we must cross to ensure higher economic growth and more equitable social and economic development.

The concerns of most of our citizens revolve around what we do for agriculture, water, education, health and employment. We recognize that for the development of the country what we are able to do in the key infrastructure sectors like power, roads, railways, ports and airports is also critical.

The plans and priorities of our government have been outlined in detail in the National Common Minimum Programme, in my first address to the nation and in the Finance Minister's recent Budget speech. Today, I have no promises to make, but I have promises to keep.

The real challenge for me and for the Government at all levels is the challenge of implementation of our stated policies and programmes. Central, State and local bodies have to work together for Government to be an effective instrument of development for the benefit of our people. There are areas, in which the Government has to be actively engaged, like education, healthcare, roads, railways, high technology and defence.

However, for Government to be able to deliver results, we must reform the functioning of government. We have to make officials accountable—make Government more transparent. We have to make public enterprises more efficient. Citizens increasingly demand governments that are accountable to them. They have a concern both for probity and efficiency in public affairs.

Fellow Citizens, the question of ethics in public life has repeatedly agitated our people and we have tried to find Constitutional, legislative and administrative devices to deal with the challenge. The time has come for us to consensually evolve a code of conduct for all political parties, a code of ethics for all individuals in public life, and a code of best practices for the Government at all levels. On this solemn occasion let us resolve to work together to develop such a code of conduct in a consensual way so as to uphold the values enshrined in our Constitution.

We must also look within our parties, and ourselves and ask ourselves what is the root cause of the decline in values in public life? How do we reform our public institutions, our political parties, and our government at various levels? When we launched economic reforms over a decade ago, we tried to liberate individual enterprise from the stranglehold of bureaucracy. We will continue to widen the space available for private enterprise and individual initiative.

But governments cannot be wished away, especially in a developing country like ours where the government has an important role to play. The challenge for economic reform today is to breathe new life into government so that it can play a positive role where it must.

But what is government? Government comprises people's representatives and civil servants. The reform of government is, therefore, a reform of the way we, the elected representatives and officials, work in government. It is you, fellow citizens, as members of the civil society, who must mobilize your enormous resources in support of such reform. To make democratic institutions more accountable we are committed to take several steps to strengthen the lowest tier of panchayats and urban local bodies. We need to build the capacity of decentralized bodies and their elected representatives and this is best done through effective transfer of funds and functions to them.

Today if we effectively utilize our decentralised system of governance through panchayat raj, we can take concerted action for more effective delivery of basic services such as primary education, public health and healthcare, providing safe drinking water and sanitation.

When we talk of reforming government and of Panchayat Raj we are reminded of Rajiv Gandhi who took pioneering initiatives in both these areas. Also, nearly twenty years ago, Rajiv Gandhi first drew the nation's attention to the newly emerging electronics and computer revolution then underway. The enthusiastic manner in which the young people of our country have participated in the information technology revolution, turning India into an "IT super power", is a tribute to the farsightedness of Rajivji.

It is a matter of satisfaction today that IT is enabling us to improve the standard of living of ordinary people even in remote areas. We will continue to explore ways in which modern technology can improve the lives of ordinary people. We will improve broadband access and enable the required investment in IT infrastructure.

We live in an age where science and technology have become an important determinant of power and wealth. For our country to attain its due place in the 21st century, it is necessary to integrate science and technology into all our development processes. The promotion of scientific temper must truly become a massive national movement.

We cannot make higher education a prisoner of either bureaucracy or ideology. It must develop on the foundations of professional excellence and intellectual integrity. The pursuit of excellence and concern for social equity must inform all our educational processes. The revered Dr. Ambedkar recognized very early the importance of education in the empowerment of the under-privileged. "We may forego material benefits", observed Dr Ambedkar, "but we cannot forego our right and opportunities to reap the benefit of the highest education to the fullest extent."

Dear Countrymen, ours is a vast country in which many States are as big as some countries of the world. For the benefits of development to reach all corners of the country the Centre and States have to work in a spirit of cooperative federalism. It is the responsibility of the central government to help States to realize our common and shared objectives of development. But, there is much that State and local governments can do to promote growth, social justice and welfare. They must raise the required resources to the extent feasible. Equally important, attention must also be paid to the quality and effectiveness of Government.

I am concerned about the slow rate of growth of the backward regions, just as I am concerned about the economic distress of the less privileged sections of our society.

We will encourage new investment in less developed regions. We will help in strengthening developmental institutions there. Special attention must continue to be paid to governance and development in the North-Eastern States and in Jammu and Kashmir. The pattern of development must be such as to create new opportunities for job creation so that the youth of these regions can look to the future with renewed hope and confidence. These regions of our country can benefit by improving rail and road connectivity and encouraging new investment.

Both the North-East and Jammu and Kashmir are the most beautiful regions of our country. If we can work together to create an environment conducive to development and tourism, these regions will prosper more. Peace, social and political stability and communal harmony are essential for economic development. People want such peace and stability so that they can lead safe, secure and normal lives and go about their work, relax and enjoy life.

We must fight all anti-national and anti-social forces that try to disrupt normal life. Be they terrorists or communal and other such divisive forces. Terrorism is a threat to our normal lives and we must all unite in fighting it. Violence has never helped in the progress and prosperity of any society. We will fight this menace to civilized existence with determination. There should be no doubts on this score. However, we are willing to talk to any group provided they abjure the path of violence.

Friends, today I want each of you to show the same degree of self-confidence that our freedom fighters showed, when they led our country to freedom, in your encounters with new markets and new opportunities. We have been an open society. But, in being open to the world, we have not lost our identity as a people. Again I remind you of what Gandhiji taught us. That our nation must be like a house built on firm foundations, whose windows are wide open to let the winds blow freely in every direction.

"I want the winds from every corner to blow through my house" Gandhiji said, “but I refuse to be swept off my feet by any of them”. That has been our attitude to the world, culturally and economically, for centuries. We must continue to adopt that attitude even as we seek to build a more self reliant and modern economy.

It is such focused attention to development that will address the real concerns of our people today. It is by strengthening our economy and making our democracy more inclusive that we can walk tall in the comity of nations. It is because of our commitment to democracy and development that we also wish to live in peace in our neighbourhood and with the world as a whole.

As a people we have always lived in peace with our neighbours in Asia and the Indian Ocean region. For centuries we welcomed with open arms both travellers and traders from different parts of the world. We ourselves set sail in search of markets and to spread the philosophies of our wise men. Even today we want to live in a neighbourhood of peace and prosperity.

I assure our armed forces and security forces our unstinted support to their welfare and to the modernization of our defences. They have played an admirable role in the defence of our unity and integrity. Not only have they defended our frontiers but also at home they have readily helped whenever their services have been sought in rescue and relief operations and in the protection of the life and property of fellow Indians.

Even as we devote our attention to defence, we must pay heed to the needs of development. All our neighbours are, like us, developing countries whose priority will also have to be the improvement of the quality of life of their citizens. We are not only bound together by our common borders but also by our common destiny. The assurance of peace and prosperity in our neighbourhood is an important priority for us. Our Government will give the highest priority to building closer political, economic and cultural ties with all our neighbours.

We have always been in favour of a purposive bilateral dialogue with Pakistan to resolve all outstanding issues. It is our intention to carry forward with firm resolve and sincerity the composite dialogue process with Pakistan. The edifice of peace that we wish to build must stand on the twin pillars of mutual trust and confidence. Of course, trends of cross-border terrorism and violence make our task more difficult and complex.

As far as our relations with China are concerned, the positive trends which commenced with Shri Rajiv Gandhi's visit to China in 1988, have provided a sound basis for later trends in our bilateral ties. We are committed to strengthening and expanding these relations. We shall carry forward the process of discussion to resolve the boundary question with political vision and a practical approach.

We value the friendship of all nations, big and small and we will seek closer economic relations with all countries. As a democratic country of more than a 100 crore people we are destined to play an important and positive role in world affairs, in structuring a just international order.

As a people, Indians have contributed a great deal to the advancement of knowledge. We value the positive role that the people of Indian origin have played in other countries. People of Indian origin are our cultural ambassadors wherever they live. We value their contribution to the societies they now live in just as much as we value the contribution they make to India, the land of their ancestors. Indians abroad are our "Brain Bank". They have shown how enterprising we Indians can be if the environment is conducive. If the required infrastructure is provided and individual initiative is rewarded we can be as good as the best in the world.

At home, this is the challenge for our Government. To create the environment in which merit is recognized, hard work and creativity are rewarded.

My dear countrymen, brothers and sisters, there are many things we must do in government to be able to meet your needs and fulfill your aspirations. This is a responsibility we have taken upon ourselves and as your representatives in government we are ultimately answerable to you. This is the essence of a democracy and I have accepted this responsibility with all humility.

The power of the people, however, is infinitely greater than the power of governments. But, it is by combining the two that we can make our nation truly great. However, as I have said already, there are limits to how much the government can do. Part of the solution lies in each one of us, in our families, in our communities. If we can all cooperate with one another and work together as a community there is much we can do without looking for intervention by the government. We have to revive the spirit of community service and the spirit of nationalism, especially among our youth.

Our national movement is unique in world history because we secured our freedom through non-violent means and by igniting hope in the minds of ordinary people. Generations of young people have been inspired by the Mahatma, a frail and soft-spoken man who shook the foundations of the mighty British Empire.

I want our youth to understand Mahatma Gandhiji's message that each one of us has the power to do good for our nation if we are only so determined. Let us all work together to revive that spirit of idealism, self-sacrifice, discipline and unity of purpose that characterized our freedom struggle. I am confident that the people of this great nation have the will, determination and the resources to meet this challenge. India's destiny beckons us to pool all our wisdom, experience and knowledge to make this future happen.

I am confident that this is possible and within our reach. Our government will do all that lies within its power to convert this dream into a living reality so that this ancient land of Bharat once again becomes a major powerhouse of both knowledge and creativity. I commit our government to the fulfillment of this sacred national task.

Dear Children, join me now and say: Jai Hind! Jai Hind! Jai Hind!"

❮34❯

Opening Remarks by Prime Minister Dr. Manmohan Singh during working lunch for Nepalese Prime Minister (09.09.2004)

> The PM highlighted the imperative of enhanced cooperation in water resources and emphasized the importance of a comprehensive Master Plan to manage and control floods. He also hoped that the operationalisation of the Inland Container Depot in Birgunj would facilitate transit as well as bilateral traffic.

Excellency, Members of the Nepalese delegation

I take this opportunity to welcome you once again. We have a long history of close and friendly times characterized by open borders and deep rooted people-to-people contacts of kinship and culture.

Our Government has accorded the highest priority to the development of relations with our neighbours. Nepal was the first destination for the visit of our External Affairs Minister after we took office.

We are committed to further development of our relations in the spirit of equality and mutual respect.

As I mentioned to you in our discussions earlier today, India is committed to providing all possible assistance to your Government in addressing the difficult challenges that it presently faces.

I am happy that we have been able to conclude two important agreements during your visit, relating to Cooperation in Culture and Sports as well as in the field of Weather Forecasting.

The recent floods highlighted the imperative of enhanced cooperation in water resources. I would like to emphasise the importance of comprehensive Master Plan to manage and control floods.

India is also deeply involved in developmental projects in Nepal and I would like to give my assurance that this will continue.

We hope that the operationalization of the Inland Container Depot in Birgunj will facilitate transit as well as bilateral traffic.

We are happy that the Consulate General of India in Birgunj has been functioning since February 2004.

Our trade treaty provides non-reciprocal duty free access to Nepalese exports to India. We hope that Nepal will soon overcome its present problems and be able to join the trend of enhanced growth rates in the region. I am glad that a large business delegation is accompanying you and will have meetings with their Indian counterparts during this visit. This is essential to foster a climate of business and investor confidence between our two countries.

Let me welcome you one again Excellency. My colleagues present here will be very happy to respond to points made by your colleagues on the Nepalese delegation.

❮35❯

Address to the UN General Assembly by Prime Minister Dr. Manmohan Singh (23.09.2004)

The PM stressed the need for evolving "a more cooperative and consensual international security order" which must differentiate between states whose actions strengthen non-proliferation and those that weaken them. He also stated that "representative institutions" rather than "exclusive clubs of privileged countries" can address threats posed by proliferation of WMDs.

Mr. President,

Allow me to congratulate you on your election as President of the 59th Session of this August Assembly. May I assure you of India's full support in ensuring its success.

Sir, as we gather here on the 60th year of the United Nations, we might perhaps pause to reflect on the fate of the ideas and ideals of the international community that animated its creation.

The post-war generation had already become aware that the world which had emerged from the ashes of the global war could no longer be a peaceful world unless the underlying forces of conflict were addressed effectively by the entire community of nations as a collectivity.

Nations, therefore, were united together to make the world a safer and more peaceful place, a world in which a free people could together pursue a destiny of shared prosperity.

Mr President, the impulse behind the creation of global institutions nearly sixty years ago has become even more pressing reality today. If we look around us, the single most defining characteristic of our contemporary world is the global, transnational character of the many challenges we confront, whether these are in the realm of international security or development.

Virtually every major issue that we face as nation states, has both a domestic as well as a transnational dimension. It is becoming increasingly apparent as never before that unless we fashion a global response, based on a meaningful consensus, to these challenges, we would not succeed in creating a world that truly manifests the ideals of the United Nations.

Sir, terrorism is one such challenge for which many of us have paid an unacceptable price. We shall not forget that three years ago, it was this great city that witnessed the single most horrendous terrorist act in human history.

About three weeks ago, the world saw another brutal act of terror, in Russia, which took the lives of hundreds of innocent civilians, including a large number of young children.

Terrorism exploits the technologies spawned by globalisation, recruits its foot soldiers on ideologies of bigotry and hatred, and directly targets democracies.

And yet it is a sad reality that international networks of terror appear to cooperate more effectively among themselves than the democratic nations that they target.

We speak about cooperation, but seem often hesitant to commit ourselves to a truly global offensive to root out terrorism, with the pooling of resources, exchange of information, sharing of intelligence, and the unambiguous unity of purpose that is required. This must change, Mr. President.

We do have a global coalition against terrorism. We must now give it substance and credibility, avoiding selective approaches and political expediency.

Mr. President, let me turn to other major challenges we face today, such as the proliferation of weapons of mass destruction. There is an increasing reliance on restrictive regimes and the use of punitive action to confront this threat to international peace and security. While India is firmly opposed to proliferation and has an impeccable record in this respect, we believe, Mr. President, that it is only a global consensus of willing nations that would ultimately prove to be truly effective in this regard.

The Chemical Weapons Convention is a good model to follow in respect of other weapons of mass destruction including nuclear weapons.

It is through representative institutions rather than through exclusive clubs of privileged countries that we can address global threats posed by the proliferation of weapons of mass destruction and their means of delivery.

Sir, as far back as in 1988, Prime Minister Rajiv Gandhi had outlined a series of specific steps in an Action Plan, whose central proposition remains valid even today that progressive steps towards the elimination of weapons of mass destruction must be based on a balance of obligations between those who possess such weapons and those who do not.

It is quite evident today that a global discourse is required for evolving a more cooperative and consensual international security order.

India believes that this consensus must differentiate between states whose actions strengthen non-proliferation and those that weaken realization of its objectives.

Mr. President, let me now turn to the central theme for the vast majority of UN members; the challenge of development and the eradication of mass poverty.

Globalization has undoubtedly brought enhanced effectiveness and efficiency in the functioning of our economies. It has integrated market places, higher standards of living and a revolution in global connectivity.

But, Sir, there is also the phenomenon of widening economic disparities, both within and among countries. Connectivity also means that the people are painfully aware in real time of how far and how fast they are falling behind in their relative conditions of living.

Development today is no longer a function of domestic resources and national policies alone. It is a process that is vitally linked to the international economic environment that the developing countries face.

Sir, the international community must find ways to contract the circles of exclusion. We need to find innovative sources of financing and access to new technologies that are necessary to assist those who are on the margins of globalization.

Just as prosperity cannot be sustained by being walled in, poverty cannot be banished to some invisible periphery. Development, therefore, must return to the centre of the global discourse.

We must evolve equitable and rule-based regimes to manage global trade, investment flows and movement of services.

Sir, four years ago, at our Millennium Summit, we adopted ambitious global development goals, but it is a matter of concern that we have already fallen behind in their implementation.

While globalization has generated new challenges, it has also given us new technologies to deal with these massive challenges.

The world faces looming pandemics such as HIV/AIDS, but it today also possesses remedies and skills that can rid the world of this scourge. We face problems of environmental degradation in many parts of our planet, but we also have available safe and environment-friendly technologies.

Many countries are beset by problems of hunger and malnutrition, but we possess modern techniques of food production and processing to make a hunger-free world a credible and realistic dream.

Although our excessive dependence on hydrocarbons raises concerns about the long-term availability of energy and about security of supplies, technology has made available many environmentally sound alternative technologies.

What we lack, however, is a truly global concert and a mobilization of the international community to overcome these massive challenges.

Mr President, Sir, the experience of the decades since the inception of the United Nations demonstrates the great significance of democracy as an instrument for achieving both peace and prosperity.

While it is gratifying that the frontiers of democracy have expanded dramatically in the last decade and a half, they still exclude significant numbers.

Only a few months ago, in India's 14th General Elections, our country went through the largest exercise of popular will in the world. I can, therefore, assert with confidence the importance of national articulations in global forums truly reflecting the democratically expressed will of their people.

We choose to overlook the absence of democracy in too many cases for reasons of political expediency.

Sir, democracy's representative nature validates the commitment we take on as countries; it should also determine the manner in which the architecture of international institutions evolves.

For what is required for the international community to successfully deal with global challenges, whether they be security challenges, economic challenges or challenges in the sphere of the environment are the existence of international institutions and a culture of genuine multilateralism.

The United Nations and its specialized agencies are the only instruments available for responding effectively to the challenges we face.

But what is missing is our sustained commitment to democratize the functioning of the United Nations.

Sir, it is common knowledge that the UN is often unable to exert an effective influence on global economic and political issues of critical importance.

This is due to its what may be called as "democracy deficit", which prevents effective multilateralism, a multilateralism that is based on a democratically-evolved global consensus.

Therefore, reform and restructuring of the United Nations system can alone provide a crucial link in an expanding chain of efforts to refashion international structures, imbuing them with a greater degree of participatory decision-making, so as to make them more representative of contemporary realities.

Mr. President, Our Millennium Declaration had recognized the urgency of the reform of the United Nations Security Council. An overwhelming majority of the world's population cannot be excluded from an institution that today legislates on an increasing number of issues, with an ever-widening impact.

The expansion of the Security Council, in the category of both permanent and non-permanent members, and the inclusion of countries like India as permanent members, would be a first step in the process of making the United Nations a truly representative body.

Mr President, I would like to make brief references to two countries with which India has had historically friendly ties and whose early return to political normalcy is the focus of the world's attention.

The situation in Iraq causes us great concern. The United Nations has a central role to play in erasing the discord of the recent past and in ensuring that the Iraqi people can soon exercise effective sovereignty, preserving the country's unity and territorial integrity.

An end to the suffering of the Iraqi people and recognition of their aspirations should be the guiding objectives.

Consistent with our long standing ties of friendship with the Iraqi people, India will contribute to Iraq's humanitarian and economic reconstruction.

Sir, in the past three years, the international community has assisted Afghanistan in pulling back from the brink of chaos and chronic instability.

We sincerely hope that the forthcoming Presidential elections and the subsequent Parliamentary elections will allow the Afghan people to express their will, free from interference and intimidation. India's assistance to Afghanistan's reconstruction and development will continue.

Relations between India and Pakistan have been a matter of attention for the international community. It is known that since January this year India and Pakistan have initiated a composite dialogue to resolve all issues, including Jammu and Kashmir. Sir, I reaffirm our determination to carry forward this dialogue to a purposeful and mutually acceptable conclusion.

In closing, Mr. President, I would like to reaffirm India's commitment to the principles that have brought us together in this Organisation.

These principles retain their relevance and validity even while the global economy and the international political order pose new and very different challenges.

All of us have to grow out of the comfort of the predictable, discard constraining habits of thought and move forward with confidence to meet the demands of the present and the future.

Each of us has to be prepared to take on new obligations and larger responsibilities relevant to the needs of our times.

Sir, I deem it a privilege to say unhesitatingly that India is conscious of the responsibilities that lie ahead. I speak of an India on the move, on the cutting edge of economic, technological and developmental transformations.

This is an India endowed with outstanding human resources, and we are putting in place policies which will respond to emerging and critical tasks. We have the capability and the capacity to take these on, and to participate in the re-structuring of a just and dynamic world order.

We are confident that in an inextricably interdependent world that we live in, our commitment to the common good, which this organization embodies, will be resolute and firm.

In this, we are inspired by the vision of internationalism bequeathed to us by India's first Prime Minister the great Jawaharlal Nehru his vision of a world order whose pillars are peace, harmony, cooperation and development.

This vision needs to reanimate the collective wisdom of the world community for a new partnership to meet the unprecedented challenges we face.

Thank you

❮36❯

Address by Prime Minister Dr. Manmohan Singh to Indian American CEOs in New York (23.09.2004)

The Prime Minister expressed the view that migration of talent does not necessarily constitute a "brain drain" but can in fact help create a "brain bank" from which India can draw provided it puts in place the required policies and infrastructure. He reiterated the government's commitment to policies that enable the "two way flow of ideas and opportunities".

"It gives me great pleasure to speak to a gathering of Indians and the Indian American community here on my first visit to the United States as Prime Minister.

I have long recognized that the Indian community in the United States is a very unique bridge between our two countries. I was delighted that President Bush shared this view when we met a couple of days ago. In American history, no group of immigrants have achieved as much success and respect within the span of one generation, that too the very first, as have Indian Americans. You play a role in US society and economy far beyond what may have been expected given the size of the community and its relatively recent arrival here. Your skills help to make America competitive, your minds are at the cutting edge of research, your services in a wide variety of professions enhance the quality of life in this country. Increasingly, your entrepreneurship has assumed a sharper profile in the American corporate world.

I am delighted to learn that Indian Americans are now also active in creative fields ranging from media to cinema. You have all earned for yourself an enviable reputation for diligence, for creativity, for enterprise, for commitment to the core values of democracy and pluralism that bind our Nations together. This has enabled you to shape favourably the larger American perception of India, among your colleagues at work, your neighbours in your communities and your elected representatives.

Emigrants have come to the shores of America for over half a millennia. Some have come in search of adventure, some in search of treasure, some escaped persecution and some others escaped hardship and deprivation. The Indian American community is again unique in this regard for most of you have come here in search of knowledge, skills, training and professional opportunity. You arrived here not just with hope, but with purpose and this has shaped the nature of your contribution to this great land of enterprise and opportunity.

The psyche of the migrant is a complex one. I understand and appreciate this, having myself migrated from the place of my birth under difficult circumstances and in times of strife. As migrants in search of a home and a living, my family and families like mine had to work that much harder. We had to have faith in the future, for the past was bleak and our present was trying. This was true of many migrant communities in the United States also. However, you, Ladies and Gentlemen, have succeeded here thanks to the foundation in education and skills your home country gave you, and the opportunities for further development your host country has given you. It is, for this reason, that I have always been impressed by the optimism that characterizes the psyche of the Indian American. You have echoed the "Can Do" spirit of the American people. It is also for this reason that you continue to look back at your home country, at India, with love, affection and longing; albeit with an understandable degree of impatience!

I feel particularly happy that the economic policies we initiated at home in the past decade have enabled us to reconnect with you more positively and re-engage you in meaningful ways in the reconstruction of our Motherland. The benign impact of these new economic policies has been supplemented by the new technologies that have contributed to the intimacy and immediacy of inter-continental contact.

When the first wave of migrants came to the shores of the United States they hardly ever went back to their home countries. When the first generation of Indians came to the US over a half-century ago travel was still largely by sea and contact with friends and relatives at home was still limited and cumbersome. According to one study the single largest item of monthly expenditure for Indians who had come to live here in the US in the 1970s and even into the 1980s was the phone bill for calls made home. So it is not surprising that an innovation like Hotmail, the free e-mail facility, was first thought up by an Indian American, Sabeer Bhatia! Millions of families in India and across the world must be grateful to him for having contributed to the creation of a global cyber-community, bringing People of Indian Origin closer to India.

It is this spirit of enterprise and adventure that I want you to inject back into India and I am here to ensure you that our Government is fully committed to the pursuit of such policies that enable this two-way flow of ideas and opportunities. I have always shared the view long expressed by my friend Jagdish Bhagwati, of Columbia University, that the migration of talent like yours does not necessarily constitute a "Brain Drain" but can in fact help create a "Brain Bank" from which we can draw provided we put in place at home the required policies and infrastructure. It will be our sincere endeavour to pursue such policies and programmes at home that will in fact enable a more productive and creative engagement between you and us, between the United States and India.

I am aware of the fact that even from this distance you still do remain concerned about the welfare and prosperity of our people. I would like to assure you that our Government is committed to taking forward the programme of reform and liberalization we initiated over a decade ago. What we must appreciate, however, is that the reforms we need to re-invigorate our economy and unleash the "animal spirits" of our entrepreneurs and the creative potential of our professionals, also involve a transformation of our society and a change of mindset. Our accomplishments, although not meager, pale before what lies ahead. India needs to educate its young, ensure their health, provide every job-seeker reasonable hope, and improve the quality of life of its people. We must emerge as a competitive manufacturing power as well as a knowledge-driven economy. These aspirations are increasingly those of the common man. The message from the recent General Elections, we believe, was an affirmation of faith in the policies we initiated a decade ago but combined with an urgent plea for a more equitable and socially just development process. I am committed to that process and our Government will pursue policies that restore to India its rightful place in the comity of Nations. The accomplishments of Indians abroad convince me that the fault lies not in our individual capabilities but in our collective endeavours and in our institutional structures. I am committed to a reform of the government, and to increased investment – domestic and foreign, private and public – in infrastructure, especially power, communications, airports and urban amenities.

Cities like Hyderabad and organizations like Infosys are already showing the rest of the country the way forward and setting the pace and direction of change. To be able to move at a faster pace we must ensure social and political stability, communal harmony and the fostering of a more inclusive economy and society. India and the United States have had a rich tradition of actively building a plural and liberal democracy. Open societies and free markets are but two sides of the same coin. They are kept in balance by their being inclusive, socially and economically.

With the exception of information technology and more recently the financial sector and management studies, the two way traffic in ideas between India and the Untied States has been limited and far below potential. There is no doubt that some of our policies and attitudes are in part to blame. However, there has also been inadequate initiative taken here in the US. I believe you can play an important role in bringing the knowledge economy in its wider scope in both countries closer. The recent agreements between the two countries relating to the first phase of the Next Steps In

Strategic Partnership should help bridge this gap partly. We would also like to see closer interaction in the fields of research, higher education and the development of our infrastructure and financial sectors. People to people contacts are the real cement that bind our Nations together.

I urge you to join us and strengthen our hands in our attempt to build a stronger and more open economy that is also committed to the principles of democracy and pluralism. India and the United States are, in that sense, on the same side of history. We are both equally committed to rid the world of the threat of terrorism, that is both a threat to peace and security and a challenge to the way both our countries want our world to be. That is, a world of freedom and plurality, of inclusiveness and equity. You can play a unique and important role by being the developmental and intellectual bridge between our two great democracies. I invite you to participate in this creative adventure. I assure you that we are committed to taking the necessary policy steps that will enable you to be part of this process more actively."

❮37❯

Address by Prime Minister Dr. Manmohan Singh to the Council on Foreign Relations (24.09.2004)

The PM emphasized that real partnership between India and the US "requires more than just a shared commitment to democracy". He believed that the time was ripe for US to seriously consider further enhancing the partnership on major international issues like nuclear non-proliferation and arms control by recognizing India's due place in global councils.

Dr. Haass, Dr. Bollinger, Professor Frankel, Dr. Desai, Ladies and Gentlemen.

It is a privilege to have this opportunity to share with this distinguished gathering my thoughts on the prospects for a stronger and mutually enriching partnership between India and the United States in the years ahead.

Commonality of values and factors driving a shared world view

It is usual for speakers on India US relations to stress the fact that we are both democracies and that this provides an essential commonality of values between our two countries which should lead naturally to a strong partnership. I do believe that this approach is fundamentally right. A commitment to a genuinely democratic society, which is also an open, liberal and tolerant society, represents a basis of shared values between us which is very important. But we must also realistically recognize that this by itself does not ensure or guarantee a close relationship as is evident from the fact that India US relations have had their ups and downs in the past.

Real partnership requires more than just a shared commitment to democracy. A real partnership requires the commonality of values to be supplemented by an awareness of converging interests, and a shared worldview. I believe that the changes that have occurred in the world in the past fifteen years or so have brought us much closer to such an awareness than ever in the past. In my view, there are at least three major elements that have driven this process of redefining world views.

Firstly, the cold war ended. Old threats receded and new threats emerged. Strategic equations began to be reevaluated, in Delhi, in Washington, and in other capitals too. The second factor is the accelerating pace of globalization. This had profound implications for economic policy in developing countries, and of course for India in particular. Thirdly, the nearly two million strong Indian American community carne of age in the US. They began to develop a prominent presence in this country, with greater involvement in mainstream America. They have become a potent voice for promoting stronger bilateral ties. These three factors, I believe, point to a future of accelerated engagement based on partnership.

Our democratic polity and commitment to pluralism liberalism. For India, our response to these factors is powerfully affected by our democratic structures and the underlying commitment to the deeper values of pluralism and liberalism. Let me elaborate.

As in other developing countries, our primary challenge is one of economic development. We are determined to improve the conditions of life for our people and this can only be done by transforming our economy into a modern, middle income economy as swiftly as possible. However, we have chosen to work towards this goal within the framework of parliamentary democracy. We adopted parliamentary democracy, based on universal suffrage, at per capita income levels which were: a fraction of those in industrialized countries and with levels of literacy as low as 18%, at the time India became independent.

The task of economic development, never an easy one, is especially challenging when it is to be realized through a functioning democracy in a low income environment. Economic transformation requires difficult choices in which short term goals often have to be sacrificed for longer term objectives. The pressures of politics do not always afford the luxury of the long view. Many observers had doubts on whether democratic India could deliver results and there have been periods when our performance has been less impressive than we would have wished. Yet, on the whole, we can be proud of what we have achieved.

We today are an economy which has grown at close to 6% per annum. over twenty years. We have the fourth largest GDP in the world in terms of purchasing power. We have a confident, competitive private sector, which displays remarkable entrepreneurial energy. India is well endowed with human resources of a very high order and an infrastructure of law and commercial accounting conducive to modern business. Our economy has shown dynamism in many areas of advanced technology.

This is the result of sustained efforts over the past fifty years to build institutions that provide the underpinning of economic development over the longer term efforts that began early on as a part of the vision of Jawaharlal Nehru. It is also the result of economic reforms which have greatly increased our competitiveness in recent years. Economic analysts today agree that India has the potential to achieve 8% growth for a sustained period. The fact that this achievement has drawn on, and reinforced our democracy is an achievement of which all Indians are justly proud.

Elections are the very essence of a democracy. We take pride in the unaffected regularity of our electorate voting their representatives into and out of office quite matter of factly. The United States is keen to support the promotion of democratic values around the world. India is a living example of how democratic institutions can flourish in developing countries and in a manner which achieves developmental objectives.

Our commitment to democracy is conjoined with a commitment to the deeper values of pluralism and liberalism. India's embrace of diversity as an essential ingredient of our democracy what today is characterised as multiculturalism is deeply rooted in our culture. The effort to preserve it in the process of building a modern state is a socio-political experiment on a massive scale. Its success is a validation of our underlying philosophy. This is a model of democratic practice that has great relevance to this fractured world, in which we often hear seductive arguments equating ethnicity or language or religion with nationhood. Such flawed hypotheses do not create states or civilizations. Democracy cannot be based on exclusion; it has to be inclusive because it celebrates plurality. Threatening this plurality is extremism and terrorism, now on a global scale, from which no one can be safe or insulated. Acts of violence and terror in the name of religion and ideology are sometimes projected as a clash of cultures, instead of what they actually are attempts to impose bigotry on tolerance. Multi-cultural nations like ours, will remain the targets of the protagonists of bigotry because our societies invalidate their thesis. We in India have suffered from such violence. The wounds inflicted on this city too, are still seared in our memory.

Earlier this week, I conveyed to President Bush that India's determination to confront and vanquish global terrorism is second to none. For a decade and a half, India has paid a price in human lives that cannot be equalled anywhere. We have not let it weaken our resolve, or undermine the fundamental values on which our society and yours is based. This is a shared struggle and one in which we should find it possible to do a great deal more together.

Globalisation: The other challenge

Globalisation is the other international development that influences our world view. As trade barriers have dropped sharply, global economic integration has encouraged an expansion in trade, foreign direct investment and flows of technology and people. The explosion of information technology has created new business opportunities undreamt of ten years ago. India, like other developing countries, stands to benefit enormously from this explosion of economic opportunities and indeed has done so in several respects.

As I have already mentioned, the economic reforms we introduced in 1991 and which have been continued by successive governments, laid the foundations of an economy poised to reap the potential benefits of globalization. Our trade has expanded and we have done exceptionally well in certain areas such as IT-enabled services. India is now seen as having the potential to emerge as a major player in the knowledge economy. Business Process Outsourcing a phrase which has spawned a number of emotive myths is only one indicator of the potential. Each day, Indian companies are proving themselves to be credible partners for American enterprises. Time and distance, the handicaps of the past, have become the advantages of our times. Our skills have helped to sharpen the competitive edge of American companies.

While globalisation presents many potential benefits, it also poses special challenges. In a democracy, it is necessary that the process of reform be perceived as equitable and caring. In a world in which information flows are unfettered, growth processes in which some are seen to benefit while others are excluded are not viable. This is particularly sensitive in a democratic polity in which public dissatisfaction can be quickly converted into electoral defeat. This is indeed the message of the recent elections in India. They were not, as some have said, a vote against reforms. They were a vote against a process of reform that was seen to be unbalanced, a process which neglected the needs of our rural areas and the agricultural economy.

My government is committed to addressing these problems. We will strengthen and deepen reforms so that India can benefit from the tremendous opportunities which the global economy offers today, but we will also ensure that there is a better distribution of benefits. Our vision of 'inclusive politics' is rooted in a vision of liberal economics.

The integration of the Indian economy with the world, opens new vistas of potential cooperation with the United States. The United States is potentially a major investor, but the volume of US investment in India is as yet modest. Our growth ambitions need massive investments, particularly in infrastructure, and much of this will have to come from public private partnerships. We believe the United States can play a major role in this area. The United States can also help in sustaining India's efforts to globalise by remaining true to your own traditional commitment to freer trade. I must confess that at times we see disturbing signs of protectionism in the US which run counter to everything this country has stood for. Let me just say that at this point in time when India and other developing countries are beginning to be won over by the persuasiveness of the case for globalisation, I hope the argument will not be lost here. We count on the United States standing firm in its commitment to free trade and open access.

Role of the Indian community in the USA

The Indian American community in this country is the third significant factor in a much stronger India US partnership in the future. I would like to use this opportunity to pay tribute to this community and to recognize their contribution to strengthening our bilateral relations. Indian Americans have shown the exceptional characteristic of being able to integrate fully into American life while also maintaining a close cultural and economic connection with India. They serve as a bridge between our national interests. They are an inspiration to our younger people. Often their regional roots in India makes them a special bridge to individual states. They also, we hope, speak for India, helping to explain some of our concerns, constraints and perceptions to their fellow Americans.

Recent trends in India US cooperation

Happily, the last decade and a half has seen a progressive transformation in our bilateral engagement. This process began during the visit of Prime Minister Indira Gandhi in 1983 and Prime Minister Rajiv Gandhi in 1986. The reevaluation on both sides of the India America equation has yielded encouraging results in recent years, and the canvas is still unfolding.

We have recently embarked on a forward looking programme which envisages cooperation in civilian space applications, nuclear energy, high technology commerce and a dialogue on missile defence. As we move forward on the basis of trust and confidence there are ever widening prospects for cooperation in these areas.

Our scientific and technological interaction is more and more wider ranging, with increasing global applications. It has also been energized by new prospects in industry. Information technology, advanced materials research, medicine and vaccine development are a few of the frontier areas of our collaboration.

Our defence, cooperation is growing rapidly. We also have close cooperation on counter terrorism, whose benefits are extensive and measurable.

In Nepal and Sri Lanka, the US has supported India's approach in strengthening peace and stability by supporting democratic forces, constitutional processes and political dialogue. In Afghanistan, India strongly supported US led efforts to replace the repressive Taliban regime and to eliminate the AI Qaeda menace. We remain deeply involved in assisting the democratic Government of Afghanistan in its national reconstruction efforts.

New partnerships have to escape the straitjacket of old paradigms. Looking beyond our bilateral relationship, I believe we can also be partners in developing a global perspective on creating a new and durable structure for international cooperation. It is remarkable that the world order of 1945 dominates global decision making even today. The architecture of all our major international organizations has remained virtually immune to the momentous political, economic, social and demographic changes of the second half of the twentieth century. It is not only the agencies and councils of the United Nations, which are outdated. So too are many nuclear proliferation and arms control regimes and a number of other alliance systems. They were all designed to address threats that either no longer exist or have been so fundamentally altered that their neutralization calls for innovative approaches. I believe the time is ripe for the United States to seriously consider the advantages of further enhancing' our partnership on major international issues by recognizing India's due place in global councils.

India's geographical location and security environment have confirmed our concern at the unrestrained proliferation of nuclear and missile technology. Our responsible record underscores the logic of India's partnership with the United States to make the world a safer place. Together, our governments can address threats from proliferation of weapons of mass destruction and their delivery systems. The Next Steps in Strategic Partnership, to which President Bush and I have committed our countries, would raise our cooperation in these areas to higher levels.

Friends,

I come to you with the conviction that an extraordinary responsibility rests upon our two nations to ensure that the future of mankind is not afflicted by the two paramount ills that made the previous century such a cruel one the scourge of violence that made the last century one of the most brutal known to mankind; and chronic and large scale deprivation that denied millions of human beings the dignified lives they deserve. History will judge us by our efforts to rid the world of the twin menaces of violence and exclusion.

I believe that the India US relationship has reached a stage where it can serve this larger global cause. Our polities are founded on similar principles and shared values. Our relations have reached a stage of maturity, in which we can manage our differences in a rational and practical manner. There is a mutuality of interests and a complementarity of major objectives. This is a sound basis for a durable partnership in the enterprise we are engaged in the building of a stable, secure, prosperous and equitable world order. In essence, therefore, my message is simple we are on the same side. And as I have said before the best is yet to be.

Thank You.

❮38❯

Address by Prime Minister Dr. Manmohan Singh at the Golden Jubilee Commemoration function of the DAE at the Indira Gandhi Centre for Atomic Research (IGCAR) in Kalpakkam (23.10.2004)

> The PM stated that the launching of the commercial phase of India's Fast Breeder Programme marked "a new and more advanced stage of nuclear energy production". He further stated that the limitations of the present non-proliferation regime should not be further accentuated by artificial restrictions on genuine peaceful nuclear applications.

Chairman of the Atomic Energy Commission, Dr. Kakodkar, Director General of IGCAR (and other dignitaries….) Friends,

It is a pleasure to be present on this historic occasion which marks the Golden Jubilee of the Department of Atomic Energy and coinciding with the commencement of Fast Breeder Technology (FB Tech).

Our nuclear programme takes a major step forward today with launching of the commercial phase of the fast breeder programme. This is an occasion to celebrate and also to reflect on our past achievements and also to look to the future with hope, courage and confidence. The progress during past 50 years as made us proud.

Under Jawaharlal Nehru's wise leadership, India was among the first group of countries to recognize the vast potential of unlocking the powers of the atom. The Department of Atomic Energy was established in August 1954. Even prior to that, as early as 1948, steps were already afoot to develop our country's capabilities in harnessing the tremendous potential of atomic energy for peaceful purposes.

In the last 50 years, we have crossed several milestones in this arduous journey. This has been a tireless quest for scientific and technological excellence some of which I would like to recall. APSARA, set up in Trombay was the first research reactor in Asia. Trombay was also the site where the first lot of fuel elements for CIRUS was fabricated. It was as early as in 1965 that the plutonium plant started functioning. In 1974, the country conducted a peaceful nuclear explosion. In the mid-1980s, steps were taken to diversify our nuclear programme further. Some of these programmes have come to fruition today.

Our nation owes a debt of gratitude to the founders of our nuclear programme. Dr. Homi Bhabha, the father of India's atomic energy programme, was a great visionary. He laid the foundations of this national treasure of self-reliant development, nurturing a whole generation of outstanding scientists and engineers. As a former Member of the Atomic Energy Commission, I remember working with Dr. Homi Sethna and Dr. Raja Ramanna who played an outstanding role in the growth and development of our atomic energy programme. I also recall with gratitude and pride the excellent contributions made by Dr. Iyengar, Dr. Srinivasa, Dr. Chidambaram and now, Dr. Kakodkar. It is therefore sad that Dr. Ramanna is not with us at this juncture when we are celebrating the Golden Jubilee of the Department of Atomic Energy. I would also like to recognize the contributions of all the scientists and employees of the Department who have contributed so magnificently to the nation's achievements in this field of national endeavour.

The activities of the Department of Atomic Energy range from fundamental scientific research to developmental applications of use to the common man in the fields of health, industry, food preservation and water desalination projects. It is a matter of deep satisfaction that our scientists have mastered practically all the aspects related to the release of nuclear energy. This has contributed to our nation's security and well being in a fundamental sense.

Energy Security is an issue of vital importance, particularly in the context of the accelerating pace of our economic growth. If we succeed in instituting an optimal mix of energy resources in which nuclear energy is an important component, we will be able to ensure our energy security. India's low per capital energy consumption currently cannot for long go hand in hand with our quest for an accelerated pace of economic growth.

Energy Security is therefore a national imperative. We must break the constraining limits of power shortages, which retard our development. Nuclear energy is not only cost effective, it is also a cleaner alternative to fossil fuels. We are determined as a nation to utilize its full potential for the national good. It can also be a much needed cushion against fluctuations of prices of petroleum products.

Nuclear power today accounts for only two per cent of our overall installed capacity. We have now embarked on a major programme to generate 20,000 megawatts of nuclear power by the year 2020. By 2008, we hope to add 4000 megawatts including the two 1000-megawatt nuclear reactors coming up at Kudankulam in collaboration with the Russian Federation.

It is a matter of national pride that India has developed comprehensive capabilities in the entire gamut of fuel cycle operations. India is also among the select group of countries which have the ability to recover plutonium from irradiated nuclear fuel and use it to produce power in thermal as well as in fast reactors. This path will ensure for us a large quantum of nuclear power on a sustainable basis.

Ladies and gentlemen, India is uniquely placed to utilize technologies required for launching the third stage of our nuclear power programme based on the utilization of thorium. The technology roadmap prepared by the Department of Atomic Energy for this purpose will receive our Government's fullest support. Fast breeder reactor technology is of crucial importance in enhancing our nuclear power capacity. By launching its commercial applications, we are indeed entering a new and more advanced stage of nuclear energy production, a technology mastered only by a very small group of countries.

The Department of Atomic Energy has been able to consolidate and strengthen our indigenous capabilities in the face of externally imposed limitations and constraints. These have, however, spurred us to greater levels of achievement. The founding principles of 'Atoms for Peace" were subverted by restrictions derived from an ineffective non-proliferation regime. Despite these limitations, our scientists to their great credit have excelled time and again in demonstrating our indigenous capabilities measuring to the highest standards in the global nuclear industry.

India is a responsible nuclear power. We are fully conscious of the immense responsibilities that come with the possession of advanced technologies, both civilian and strategic. While we are determined to utilize our indigenous resources and capabilities to fulfill our national interests, we are doing so in a manner that is not contrary to the larger goals of nuclear nonproliferation.

India will not be the source of proliferation of sensitive technologies. We will also ensure the safeguarding of those technologies that we already possess. We will remain faithful to this approach, as we have been for the last several decades. We have dóne so despite the well-known glaring examples of proliferation which have directly affected our security interests.

The limitations of the present non-proliferation regime should not be further accentuated by artificial restrictions on genuine peaceful nuclear applications. Technology denial and closing avenues for international cooperation in such an important field is tantamount to the denial of developmental benefits to millions of people, whose lives can be transformed by the utilization of nuclear energy and relevant technologies.

We call upon other advanced nuclear powers, and all those who have a stake in the future of nuclear energy, to come together for a constructive dialogue to evolve more effective measures that would stem the tide of proliferation without unduly constraining the peaceful uses of nuclear energy. Constraining those who are responsible amounts, in effect, to rewarding those who are irresponsible. The international community must face up to the implications of this choice. We in India are willing to shoulder our share of international obligations provided our legitimate interests are met. India has actively embraced globalisation. There is no reason why nuclear energy production should be an exception.

These functions of the Department of Atomic Energy are closely intertwined with our nation's needs and aspirations. It is important to ensure that the nation's best scientific talent enters our research institutions, and that we develop an environment in which excellence is recognized, nurtured and rewarded. The nation expects that the Department of Atomic Energy, as one such center of excellence, will continue to be at the cutting edge of scientific pursuit, national dedication and social commitment. The nation is proud of your achievements and is grateful for your contribution. However, we have a long and arduous journey ahead of us and many milestones to cross. It is my sincere hope that the Department will live up to our expectations. In this task, the Department can count on the sustained support of our government and the people of our country.

Jai Hind.

39

Speech by Prime Minister Dr. Manmohan Singh at the Hindustan Times Leadership Initiative (05.11.2004)

> The PM emphasized that the defining feature of the 21st century is not marked by a "clash of civilizations", but by a "confluence of civilizations". India's commitment to the values of "inclusive pluralism" and "multi-culturalism" within the framework of an open society and an open economy would form the basis for India's engagement with the world.

Shobhana Bhartiaji,

(President Kumaratunge, Mr. Major, Dr. Kissinger),

Ladies and Gentlemen,

I am delighted to be here this morning to inaugurate the Hindustan Times Leadership Initiative Conference on the theme "India and the World: A Blueprint for Partnership and Growth". I am grateful to Shobhana Bhartiaji for giving me this opportunity to share my thoughts on the subject with such a distinguished audience of eminent scholars, political leaders and policy analysts. I commend her and the Hindustan Times for taking this initiative. Your conference has become an important annual feature in the intellectual calendar of our national capital. I am also delighted to see so many friends both among the participants and in the audience. I do wish I had the time to be here right through your deliberations so as to learn from the wealth of intellectual opinion gathered here.

The theme of "India and the World" has often been debated in this country over the past half century. From the time of our Independence, when we tried to re-fashion our interaction with the outside world, this has been a subject of considerable discussion. The intellectual foundation for this debate was laid by Mahatma Gandhi when he said, "I want the winds from every corner to blow through my house, but I refuse to be swept off my feet by any of them."

Pandit Jawaharlal Nehru echoed this idea, while emphasizing the importance of national sovereignty in shaping the interaction with the outside world, when he wrote in the *Discovery of India*, "Today India swings between a blind adherence to her old customs and a slavish imitation of foreign ways. In neither of these can she find relief or life or growth. India will find herself again when freedom opens out new horizons, and the future will then fascinate her far more than the immediate past of frustration and humiliation." Panditji hoped that with freedom gained India "will go forward with confidence, rooted in herself and yet eager to learn from others and co-operate with them. It is obvious that she has to come out of her shell and take full part in the life and activities of the modern age."

To 'take full part in the life and activities of the modern age' and to establish 'partnerships for growth' are, indeed, the challenges that we have been grappling with in our interaction with the world. Perhaps no other post-colonial nation has debated so intensely and in so open a manner the terms of engagement with the world as we have in India. In the early years of de-colonisation, later through the heat of the Cold War and, more recently through the rough and tumble of the post-Cold War era we have debated at length the nature of our relationship with the world, the possibilities of partnerships and the potential for growth. Broadly speaking the debate has been within two perspectives: the political and strategic and the economic and commercial. Even your conference has been conceptualized within this framework. When you title your conference theme as "India and the World: A Blueprint for Partnership and Growth", I believe you are looking at political and economic partnerships and would like to see how these will accelerate the process of economic growth.

Undoubtedly, these issues lie at the core of our concerns. Our foreign policy and our economic policy have evolved over the years to enable us to derive the benefits of our interaction with the world while addressing the challenges that have come our way. While there are bound to be party political differences in priorities and perceptions in a democracy, it must be recognized that there has been an element of continuity, mirroring an evolving consensus, on many aspects of our foreign and external economic policy. I draw your attention to the fact that the initial response of our Government in the early 1990s to the new post-Cold War world has since evolved, under successive governments, in a direction set by us at the time. Be it our foreign policy, both with respect to major powers and other nations, or our external economic policy, there has been continuity with change. I am sure your conference will devote time to a deeper consideration of these issues. Suffice it for me to say that in the heat and dust of our domestic debates on foreign and external economic policy we should not lose sight of the fact of this emerging consensus on our political and economic interaction with the world.

I sincerely believe that India's standing in the world will, in the final analysis, be defined by our domestic capabilities, by the well-being and creativity of our people, by the resilience of our political and social institutions. Our Government would like to give the highest priority to an acceleration of the rate of economic growth through a process of economic and social development that is equitable and just. As an open society and an open economy we will have to engage the world at all levels and in all spheres. It is with this understanding that we seek a larger role for ourselves in global institutions and would like to help strengthen and broad base multilateral institutions. India has to be an active trading nation and is therefore committed to strengthening a rule-based, transparent and consensual multilateral trading regime.

India's economic engagement of the world must match up to our size and scope. I would like to see closer and wider economic engagement between India and our Asian neighbourhood. I would like our business leaders to explore the full potential of the creation of an Asian Economic Community. We seek mutually beneficial relations with all our Asian neighbours and will work closely with Asia to realize our combined aspiration to make the 21st century an Asian century. We would like to see a widening and deepening of our economic relations with China, Japan, the member countries of ASEAN, the Central Asian Republics and our traditional friends in West Asia and Africa. We want a neighbourhood of peace and shared prosperity in which people, goods and services can travel with ease across borders. South Asia must regain its pre-eminence in the global economy as a sub-continent of creativity and enterprise. We would like to inject new energy into regional associations like the South Asian Association for Regional Cooperation and the Bay of Bengal Initiative for Multi-sectoral Technical and Economic Cooperation (BIMSTEC). It is in our shared interest to wage a joint struggle against poverty and ignorance.

We will continue to strengthen our wide-ranging and many-sided relationship with the United States, European Union and Russia. As a responsible nuclear power we are firmly committed to nuclear non-proliferation and will cooperate with the world community to prevent the proliferation of weapons of mass destruction and deal with the threat of terrorism. India is committed to work with the international community to make the world a safer place to live in. We will pursue energy security within a cooperative framework working with other countries to ensure the security of oil supplies, of pipelines and sea-lanes of communication. We are equally committed to working with the international community in tackling other global threats. The threats to the environment, the threat of communicable diseases and the pandemic of HIV/AIDS are all global challenges. The world is a "global village" and so we must address these challenges as members of a cooperative global community.

An important aspect of our interaction with the world is the role of the so-called Indian "diaspora". There is a strong emotional link between the global community of people of Indian origin and the Motherland. I am convinced that if we create at home the right environment and the required infrastructure we can draw on the creativity and enterprise of overseas Indians in building a more vibrant and dynamic economy at home.

Ladies and Gentlemen,

I would like to take this opportunity to focus your attention on an altogether different aspect of our interaction with the world. This pertains to the dialogue between nations and civilizations. An ancient, civilisational nation like ours, home to more than one great religion of the world and many philosophical traditions; a land of linguistic and cultural diversity; and, located at Asia's cultural crossroads, has quite naturally and understandably a unique position in the world. The world expects us to bring to the table of global discourse something more than strategic partnerships and market opportunities, important as both these are and open as we are to engaging the world on both these fronts.

I submit to you that India has something more to offer, that is specially relevant to the on-going global discourse pertaining to the two great challenges of our time, namely, globalisation and the notion of a "clash of civilizations". Both these debates have often been conducted as if the debate is a battle between contending world-views. The media has often succumbed to the temptation of turning every dialogue into a debate by defining the terms of the discussion in binary opposites. Are you "For" or "Against"? Are you with "Us" or "Them". Reality can never be captured in black and white. It is always represented in an array of colours.

India's unique contribution to the world has been the notion of the many-sidedness and the constant and continuing discovery of Truth. The idea of unity in diversity, drawing on the wisdom of our forefathers who spoke of "Vasudhaiva Kutumbakam" – that translates as "The Whole World Is One Family" – is a powerful yet practical political basis for dealing with these twin challenges of our times.

It is that philosophical tradition that inspired our freedom struggle and that enabled a peaceful transfer of power. It is that notion of cooperative pluralism that was the basis of our democracy. Our democracy, like our civilization, has been built on the notions of "unity in diversity" and inclusive pluralism.

The idea of a "clash of civilizations" goes against the grain of our civilizaton. Like many tributaries joining and flowing together as a mighty river, diverse religions and cultures have combined to form the mighty river called India. What is a river but a confluence of its tributaries. The Ganga and the Indus, the two rivers that play a central role in the very definition of our civilization and identity are made wide and deep by the coming together of so many tributaries. When we revere the Ganga at its widest expanse in the plains we recognize the many rivers and tributaries that over time and space join it. India too is defined in this manner. A land of diversity, through time and space, where modern democracy has come to be built on the notion of pluralism and inclusiveness.

Admittedly, there are those even among us who do not share this syncretic view of India. They not only believe in the "clash of civilizations" but wish to encourage it. They do not, indeed cannot, represent the true spirit of our ancient land. As Sunil Khilnani and Pratap Bhanu Mehta have so eloquently argued in their thoughtful books, India's most important contribution to the world is the idea of syncretic pluralism that has shaped the institutions of an inclusive democracy. I am aware of the skepticism expressed by Fareed Zakaria about the "illiberal" aspects of democracy. But with all our faults and limitations, with all the challenges and shortcomings we have succeeded in stabilizing representative democracy and ensuring the smooth transfer of power after every election at all levels of democratic representation in a country of continental dimensions with an electorate of over half a billion people.

That is the basis on which we can build a meaningful partnership with the world. We have, through history, approached the world as seekers of knowledge and opportunity. Indians have always reached out to the world as teachers and traders, as writers and workers, and never as conquerors.

The world has increasingly come to accept that open societies and open markets are the most natural and stable form of social and economic organization. What is now increasingly clear is that an inclusive democracy, based on the principles of pluralism and multi-culturalism, is the most enduring means of dealing with the challenges posed by open markets and open societies.

The world community has been actively engaged in recent years in dealing with the perceived threat of globalisation and of political extremism in its various manifestations, ranging from ethnic cleansing to Jehadism. There are no military solutions to such challenges. There are no unilateral solutions either. Any meaningful solution must be based on the principles of democratic pluralism and inclusivism, the respect of the rule of law and of diversity of opinion and faith. The voice of moderation has to be empowered in all societies to make the world a better place to live in. The principle of an "eye for an eye", as Gandhiji often reminded us, would leave us all blind.

Friends,

Economists quantify our engagement with the world in terms of our share of world trade and capital flows, while strategic analysts look at military and political alliances. I submit to you for your consideration the idea that the most enduring engagement of a people with the world is in the realm of ideas and the idea we must engage the world through is the "Idea of India", the idea of "Vasudhaiva Kutumbakam". The idea that even if nations may clash with one another, cultures and civilizations can co-exist.

The defining feature of the 21st century is not that it will be marked by a "clash of civilizations", but that it will be shaped by a "confluence of civilizations".

I believe the world community can deal more meaningfully with the challenge of globalisation and the threat of terrorism by enabling a dialogue between nations and a "confluence of civilizations". India must actively engage the world towards this end. By rejecting the politics of exclusion and voting in favour of the values of secularism and pluralism that we cherish, the people of India have once again given us a reason to hold our head high in the comity of nations.

Those of us who celebrated the end of the Cold War and hoped to reap a development dividend from it are today dismayed by the new ideological divides that threaten global peace and prosperity. The ideology of a "clash of civilizations" and of terrorism is a threat to world peace. We must empower the voices of moderation and of civilized discourse to enable a "confluence of civilizations" to make the world a better and safer place to live in.

Just as many developed industrial economies assisted the so-called "Economies in transition" to make the transition from centrally planned economies to open market economies, the experience of a democracy like ours can be of some help in enabling "Societies in Transition", to evolve into open, inclusive, plural, democratic societies.

When the United Nations and the Governments of other democracies reach out to our Election Commission seeking its assistance in conducting elections we feel a sense of pride in our democratic processes and institutions. Our Election Commission has no peers anywhere in the world. It has established an enviable record of efficiency and transparency in the conduct of elections from Kanyakumari to Kashmir.

Let me assure you that in putting forward my views on how we can contribute to the strengthening of democracy in the world, I am not advocating diplomatic activism, nor would we in India ever advocate any form of political interventionism. Far from it, we recognize the sovereign right of every country to order its affairs in the manner most desired by its people. But I do believe that our experience can be of some help to the world community in its quest to strengthen the institutions of democracy and the idea of inclusive pluralism.

The partnerships we seek and the basis of growth we wish to create should rest on this foundation of our commitment to the values of inclusive pluralism and multi-culturalism within the framework of an open society and an open economy. This is the promise our Government has made at home. This is the experience we should happily share with the world. Our nationhood and our Republic are intrinsically linked to our commitment to democracy and our democracy has endured because we have enabled at home a dialogue between civilizations.

This is our message to the world and we should not shy away from opportunities to strengthen the institutions of democratic pluralism whenever we are called upon to do so. We know from our own experience that the world would be a safer place and growth and prosperity would be ensured if we can enable the "confluence of civilizations" within the framework of democratic pluralism. The partnerships for growth that we can build on that basis will be truly enduring. I think the time has come, as Panditji long ago believed, for India to "come out of her shell and take full part in the life and activities of the modern age."

Friends,

I will be grateful to the many learned people assembled here if you will consider some of these ideas and educate me whether I am correct to view our engagement with the world in these terms. I wish the Conference all success and look forward to learning of its deliberations.

Thank you

‹40›

Convocation Address by Prime Minister Dr. Manmohan Singh at the Kashmir Institute of Medical Sciences (17.11.2004)

> Stressing the economic imperative to improve the process of governance in Kashmir, the PM unveiled his "Plan" to reconstruct the economy, revitalize institutions and reform the government. He emphasized the need to empower the youth, create first-rate educational institutions, and persuade top private companies, especially in the IT sector to make Kashmir a priority destination.

"Today is an important day for me. I have waited long to come to Jammu and Kashmir and I am so happy to be here just days after we have celebrated Id and Deepavali. If Deepavali is the festival of light and the celebration of prosperity, Ramzan is the month of peace, prayer and brotherhood. Jammu and Kashmir need all these in full measure – light, prosperity, peace, prayer and brotherhood. I am particularly pleased to be among students, the youth of Jammu and Kashmir, in whose lifetime I am sure this proud State will see great prosperity and lasting peace.

It is always for me a great pleasure to visit a University as I am basically myself a teacher, and especially an institution as beautiful as this. I still feel completely at home amongst academics, although I may seem, at the moment, to be far removed from the world of academia.

It is a joy to meet young scholars and students. You have embarked on a journey that will lead to the exploration of new ideas and many of you will chart fresh intellectual frontiers. The road to real scholarship is often arduous, but it is a deeply fulfilling one. You are indeed fortunate to have such a scenic campus. With the majestic Dal Lake and the magnificent chinars, there are few universities in the world that can claim to be located in such magical surroundings, or be as conducive to the development of the highest intellectual ideals.

As Prime Minister, this is my first Convocation Address and I am delighted that I am speaking to a community of doctors and health specialists. Health-care is one of the cornerstones of the programme of policy action outlined in the National Common Minimum Programme. It is now widely recognized that the two areas where we have lagged behind and where urgent and massive intervention is required are education and health. The people of

India deserve a world class educational system and the best yet affordable healthcare.

Our performance in the area of human development lags behind many newly industrializing economies. It is my sincere hope and commitment that our Government will make a difference in these two areas. We have strengthened the mid-day meals programme and are launching a rural healthcare mission to deal with the challenge of low levels of literacy and healthcare at the village level. However, the educational and healthcare system need urgent and wide-ranging reform at all levels. I have made this an area of urgent priority for my Government and have urged the Ministry of Health and Family Welfare to come up with practical ideas for improving the health status of our people.

Ours has always been a knowledge society where ideas have had a powerful appeal. However, for us to build a knowledge economy we must invest in the education and health of our people. An illiterate and poor people are a social and economic liability, while an educated and healthy people are a nation's asset. I want medical universities and institutions to throw up new ideas on how we can build a relevant and affordable healthcare system in the country. You doctors and educationists must examine how best we can use the funds available to both widen the scope and quality of medical education and the range and reach of an affordable healthcare delivery system.

Today, I want to speak in particular to the young men and women of Kashmir and address a subject that concerns us all: the future of Kashmir. I have come here not to lecture, but to seek your partnership in the building of a Naya Kashmir.

You are all the real stakeholders in the future of Kashmir, and it is only through your enthusiastic participation that a 'new' Kashmir can truly be built. Several decades ago, a bold vision of Naya Kashmir had been spelt out. The time has come to put forward a new blueprint, a fresh vision for Kashmir and for the Kashmiri people, free from the fear of war, want and exploitation.

The Kashmiri people have gone through a traumatic experience over much of the last decade and a half. Nearly every family has witnessed a tragedy, hundreds have been killed or injured and thousands have been displaced. Women and children have been the worst sufferers. My heart goes out to those innocent mothers and sisters, sons and daughters. I share your grief and understand how difficult it often can be to believe that a better future lies ahead. But I have a dream and a firm belief that working together we can build a new Kashmir, which can become – once again – a symbol of peace, prosperity and cultural pluralism.

I understand that all of you have suffered and are continuing to be scarred by the violence. We are working on our neighbour to put a permanent end to this mindless violence. If the violence ends, the security presence will be unnecessary. I have already issued instructions to reduce the number of troops deployed in the State. If conditions improve and if the incidence of infiltration and of violence remains under control it will make it easier for me to seek a further reduction of troops.

Our security forces have been deployed to protect the life and property of law abiding citizens. They have been performing this task under very difficult conditions. The honour and dignity of our security forces oblige us to deal firmly with all violations of human rights of citizens. Our Government remains committed to this ideal. I am firmly committed to peace, to a return to normalcy and to the assurance of a life of dignity and self respect for the people of Kashmir.

When I met President Musharraf of Pakistan last month, I impressed on him the need for our two countries to work together to create the conditions for sustainable peace in South Asia. Our Government is committed to a purposeful dialogue with Pakistan to resolve all outstanding issues. Our only condition is that, as agreed to by Pakistan, territory under control of Pakistan should not be used to promote cross-border terrorism directed against us. Our Government will work earnestly with the State Government and other political parties to improve the quality of governance to make it transparent, people friendly and corruption free.

Our Government is also committed to an unconditional dialogue with anyone and everyone in the State who abjures violence. This dialogue should be and will be carried forward. But the task of reconstructing Kashmir cannot wait until these dialogues arrive at a satisfactory conclusion. We cannot afford this luxury. The challenge is to begin peace building in Kashmir now, even while there may be forces that do not share our vision and actively seek to undermine it. I want the journey of development to begin here and now in Kashmir.

Even as we discuss the improvement of the processes of governance, the present economic imperative is clear. Kashmir needs more jobs, Kashmir needs better connectivity, Kashmir needs tourists, Kashmir needs credit and agro industries, Kashmir needs power and roads. Kashmir's women and children need a vastly improved system of education and healthcare and the empowerment that comes with these. For us to ensure all this faster, better, Kashmir needs peace. Come join me and support me so that we can together work to restore peace, prosperity and brotherhood to Kashmir.

Thinking about the future of Kashmir, I am inspired by Rabindranath Tagore's well known lines:

"Where the mind is without fear and the head is held high;

Where knowledge is free; where words come out from the depth of truth;

Where tireless striving stretches its arms towards perfection;

Where the clear stream of reason has not lost its way into the dreary desert sand of dead habit;

Where the mind is led forward by thee into ever widening thought and action.

Into that heaven of freedom, my Father, let my country awake".

To create a society that matches up to this 'heaven of freedom' is not easy. It requires, as its base, upright men and women who are willing to commit themselves selflessly to this goal. Those who are willing to give up negative emotions, and shed the hopelessness and pessimism of the past. I know that in Kashmir we have many such people. They need to be empowered.

Empowering the abundantly talented young men and women of this State must, therefore, surely be our first priority. I am particularly concerned about the educational and social status of women, across the entire sub-continent and not just in Kashmir. But Kashmir can show the way by focusing immediate attention on the education and empowerment of women. We must improve the human development profile of Jammu and Kashmir's people as a whole.

Our respected President has, on many occasions, emphasised the need to create a real 'knowledge economy.' We need to lay the foundations of precisely such an economy in the State through the dynamism of you all. And as a partner, I commit myself and my Government to creating institutions of excellence in the State, which can channelise the creativity and energy of the youth of Kashmir. We will together build and strengthen the cadre of extraordinarily skilled men and women who are dedicated to a vision of peaceful and prosperous Kashmir. That alone is a guarantee for sustainable peace in Kashmir.

I am fully aware of the great achievements of the men and women of Kashmir in all spheres: from the arts to the science. I count among my friends many from these parts who have made a name for themselves at home in India and abroad. Despite many odds, they have carved out a niche for themselves in the rest of India and many parts of the world. But the educational and skill-development institutions in the State have greatly been affected by the events over the last fifteen years. Schools have been burnt, teachers have been threatened and many have just left.

During the last two years, I understand, considerable progress has been made. The Kashmir University has been accredited by the National Assessment and Accreditation Council and given a five star rating. The neighbouring Regional Engineering College is now the National Institute of

Technology. Kashmir University is developing additional compuses in North and South Kashmir. The University of Jammu is seeking ISO certification. All this is satisfying, but much, much more needs to be done.

We need to create first-rate educational institutions all over the State. We need, as I said, to invest in the human resources of Kashmir. We will assist the State Government in improving the quality of primary and secondary education, help it to create post-school vocational institutions that can offer world-class training and skill development, and ensure that institutions of higher learning can provide the facilities for the best teaching and research in science and technology, in the arts and humanities, and in the social sciences.

Many Kashmiri young men have felt alienated because of lack of employment opportunities in the State. The Government cannot be the only source of employment; in fact the necessity is to reduce the size of the Government, not to enlarge it. A partnership for rebuilding Kashmir can only work once we include these unemployed men in our task of peace building. Many of them are highly trained and educated. We need to create new opportunities for them. To give just one example, Kashmir is ideal for outsourcing of services, particularly in the IT sector.

I assure you that I will seek to persuade the top private companies, especially in the IT sector, to make Kashmir a priority destination. We will strengthen the Software Technology Park in Srinagar and also create re-training centres for those whose skills need upgradation.

The tourism sector has traditionally been a source of employment. Tourism has flourished as much because of the breathtaking beauty of this land as because of the warmth and hospitality of the Kashmiri people. Fortunately, the tourist season this year has gone off well. Once there is a permanent end to the violence, the State will surely become one of the most attractive international destinations for tourists. Even now there is the possibility of promoting 'adventure' and 'pilgrimage' tourism more aggressively and improving the infrastructure. We remain committed to doing this.

But let me also urge you to make use of the wealth of economic opportunities that exist in the rest of India. Some of you are already doing this. India is changing and changing rapidly. There is a new energy, a new wave of entrepreneurship, which has been unleashed.

Become part of this process. By doing so you will carry forward the vision of 'peace building' in Kashmir into the rest of India. As I have said once before, I have come today to Kashmir not with a 'package' but with a 'plan'. A Plan to reconstruct the economy, reform the Government, regenerate entrepreneurship, revitalise the institutions of civil society and redefine the political paradigm and context in the sub-continent.

To help the State Government and guide the central Government in implementing an integrated plan of long term development of Jammu and Kashmir, I will be constituting a High-Powered Advisory Council on Economic Development of Jammu and Kashmir. This Council will help to evolve an integrated and holistic view of Jammu and Kashmir's long-term economic and social development. It will also help the State Government identify sources of finance locally, nationally and globally to fund this process of planned development of the State.

The culture and value system of Kashmir has always been a source of its strength. I know that this land of Sheikh Nurudin Nurani and Lal Ded can never succumb to extremism and fanaticism. Through all these years the Kashmiris, despite many onslaughts, have kept alive their culture of tolerance and pluralism. We need to now, in partnership, further strengthen Kashmir's civil society, its fabulous traditional arts and crafts and the variety of music and dance that have enriched this beautiful valley. I am asking the State Government to put forward a proposal for setting up a Centre for Art and Culture. This institution will not just celebrate the State's rich diversity, but open to the world the richness of Kashmir's heritage.

My young friends, India is today on the cusp of a new wave of development. The world recognises that the 21st Century will be an Asian Century and that India and China will be the two Great Asian Nations and World Powers of the 21st century. Our destiny beckons us.

There is new ray of hope for an ancient civilisational nation that ours is. It is our good fortune that our forefathers helped build here in this sub-continent a truly multi-cultural, multi-religious, multi-lingual and multi-ethnic nation on the principles of parliamentary democracy, secularism and the rule of law. The Indian sub-continent consisting of India, Pakistan, Bangladesh, Nepal and Sri Lanka is on the threshold of a new awakening to realise its vast latent development potential. All of us have an obligation to make the future happen.

I am convinced that Kashmir will find peace and prosperity within this framework of pluralism and of unity in diversity. I come with the assurance that Kashmir is safe in our hearts and in our minds and should, therefore, feel safe in our secular, plural and democratic framework. You, the young men and women of Kashmir, have an enormous stake in the collective future of our diverse sub-continent. India is many things to many people, but it is home for us all—the land of our birth, of our dreams and our destiny. Come join me in this new adventure of building a new India and a new Kashmir.

❮41❯

Opening Remarks by External Affairs Minister, Shri Yashwant Sinha at the 9th Meeting of India-Mauritius Joint Commission (08.01.2004)

India expressed satisfaction with the developments in the strategic partnership in high technology and expressed the need to intensify cooperation in the areas of oceanography including hydrographic studies, exploration of hydrocarbon resources and generation of ocean thermal power.

Your Excellency, Mr. Jaya Krishna Cuttaree, distinguished members of the Mauritian delegation and friends,

1. I extend a warm welcome to you and your delegation and I hope your stay would be pleasant and our deliberations fruitful.
2. The Ninth session of the Indo-Mauritian Joint Commission is meeting after a hiatus of seven years. During my visit to Mauritius in July last year, we had taken the important decision of upgrading the JCM so that it could be co-chaired at the level of Foreign Ministers of two countries. This is an important development in our bilateral relations. Over the years, we have been able to foster a privileged and close relationship based on historical and cultural ties. We share a common commitment to the ideals of peace, non-violence and democracy. Both our countries pride themselves in being multi-ethnic, multi-religious, multi-cultural societies based on the principles of democracy, socialism and the rule of law. Mauritius has always been supportive of our concerns both in the global and regional context. Our relations are underpinned by close coordination and understanding on all global and bilateral issues. In this background, the upgradation of the Joint Commission and its regular meetings will provide added momentum to our unique partnership.
3. We have been able to cement the close ties through frequent high-level political exchanges. The recent successful visit of your Prime Minister, Mr. Paul Raymond Berenger has served to further consolidate our cooperation, which encompasses diverse areas such as cultural, educational, scientific, technical, defense and commercial. The setting up of a number of Joint Working Groups in these areas would enable

us to move forward on the decisions that were taken during the high level exchanges. I am glad to know that the Joint Working Groups in some areas such as science and technology have already commenced deliberations and that many other JWGs are in the advanced stages of finalisation.

4. Our bilateral relations are extensive and our cooperation is intensive. We are working to implement a number of bilateral projects discussed at different levels in the past. We are happy that the Cyber City, which is a manifestation of the new face of our bilateral cooperation, is nearing completion. It is an important project in establishing our strategic partnership in high technology. We are also happy to assist you in the establishment of an International Convention Centre in Mauritius and I hope that the Mauritian government will expeditiously complete all the work connected with the conclusion of the contract so that we could move ahead at our end. The recently concluded agreement on the establishment of the World Hindi Secretariat in Mauritius will further strengthen our cultural ties.

5. In the domain of Science & Technology, we have commenced work on Bioinformatics institute in Mauritius which would enable both sides to take advantage of the rich biodiversity resources in both countries, and to assist in research related to diabetes and bio-technology including food technology. In the area of Oceanography, we need to intensify our cooperation, which could include hydrographic studies, exploration of hydrocarbon resources and generation of ocean thermal power. Our National Institute of Oceanography has already commenced discussions with its counterpart in Mauritius. Recently, we have proposed that our Navy should also be involved since it has a great deal of expertise in conducting hydrographic surveys.

6. Our excellent bilateral relations are not matched by an equal expansion of economic and commercial relationship. Our bilateral trade in the past three years has been almost static hovering around US $ 185 million. We firmly believe that there is tremendous potential to increase bilateral trade in all sectors. During the visit of Hon. PM Berenger to India, he extended an invitation to Indian businessmen to use Mauritius as a gateway to jointly enter Southern African markets. In this context, the Joint Study Group which we have decided to set up to explore the proposal for concluding a Comprehensive Economic Cooperation Agreement should complete its task expeditiously. I am happy that the first meeting of this Joint Study Group was held on the sidelines of the Joint Commission. We should also examine appropriate joint ventures in Mauritius with potential for exports to India. Our Joint Council needs to identify new ways of expanding trade.

Many Indian companies are desirous of participating in various projects in Mauritius through competitive bidding. The participation of Indian companies should not be limited to only those that are financed by grants and credits from India. As long as they submit competitive bids, the Indian companies should be facilitated to obtain these contracts in the true spirit of our friendly relations. We also need to create conducive atmosphere to facilitate trade and flow of investment between our countries by adopting liberal visa regime and creating favourable conditions for Indian companies to set up operations in Mauritius.

7. We have recently received your proposal for Indian assistance for the construction of a new Supreme Court building in Mauritius. We would favourably consider extending fresh credit lines on concessional terms. Similarly, we will be happy to work on other infrastructural projects such as Sewerage project at *Baie Du Tombeau* and to associate ourselves with the grand project of light rail transit system.

8. We also need to increase our cooperation in the area of Security. We are partners in the international coalition against terror and are now working towards bilateral mechanism to combat terrorism. We need to speed up the setting up of the Joint Working Group on Terrorism. We are also cooperating against drug trafficking. In this context, I would like to emphasise the importance of early conclusion of the Mutual Legal Assistance Treaty, which I believe is in the final stage of completion.

9. I hope the meeting of the JCM will invest our relations with greater focus and will lead to regular interaction between us at different levels to take our relations forward in all spheres.

Thank You.

❮42❯

Statement made by External Affairs Minister, Shri K. Natwar Singh on Departure from Islamabad (after the SAARC Council of Ministers Meeting) (23.07.2004)

> India's proposals for setting up a South Asian Parliamentary Forum, High Economic Council, Infrastructure Fund and Poverty Alleviation Fund were endorsed by SAARC countries. India and Pakistan also reiterated the importance of continuing the dialogue process and tackling the scourge of terrorism with renewed vigor.

I have had a productive and useful visit to Pakistan for the SAARC Council of Ministers meeting. The Council meeting has resulted in significant steps in key areas of regional cooperation. Our basic approach was to give SAARC greater relevance and meaning and to enable it to meet the aspirations of our peoples. As SAARC moves into its third decade, we hope to move from studies and meetings to implementation of projects.

2. At the Council of Ministers meeting, India made the following proposals:

   i) Setting up a South Asian Parliamentary Forum to deliberate on issues pertaining to regional cooperation endeavours. India also offered to host the next meeting of the South Asia Association of Speakers and Parliamentarians to consider the establishment of the Forum.

   ii) Establishment of a SAARC High Economic Council with Finance and Commerce Ministers of the SAARC Member Countries to promote ideas and initiatives related to regional integration in economic, trade, financial and monetary areas.

   iii) Setting up a SAARC Infrastructure Fund, which could have a corpus of about US $ 10 billion, to fund major infrastructure projects in the region.

   iv) Setting up National Committees in member countries to monitor and devise programmes to implement the goals of the SAARC Social Charter, and to promote collaborative poverty alleviation projects, including those under the SAARC Poverty Alleviation Fund.

   v) As part of the SAARC Awareness Year for TB and HIV/AIDS, the Council decided to give a SAARC Youth Award for "Dedicated Community Services in the field of TB and / or HIV/AIDS. India offered to host a meeting this year of experts and community workers, to train paramedics from SAARC countries, and offered to send medical vans and mobile awareness units to each SAARC country. We would also host a variety of youth activities, and promote youth and academic exchanges in the next twelve months.

The other SAARC countries endorsed these proposals.

3. On the margins of the Ministerial meeting, I had very useful bilateral discussions with my colleagues from Bangladesh, Bhutan, Maldives, Nepal and Sri Lanka. We discussed bilateral and SAARC related issues in detail. My colleagues and I called jointly on the President and Prime Minister of Pakistan.
4. I also utilized my presence in Pakistan for separate meetings on the sidelines with the leadership of Pakistan. I called on President Pervez Musharraf, Prime Minister Chaudhury Shujaat Hussain, senior Minister Shaukat Aziz and Foreign Minister Khurshid Kasuri. This was my third meeting with Foreign Minister Kasuri in the last month. These meetings were an opportunity to review our bilateral relations. I found the attitude of the Pakistani leadership constructive and positive. We discussed progress so far in the process of composite dialogue that began in February. As you are aware, the next three weeks will see intensive interaction between our countries, with six meetings on different subjects in the composite dialogue process. Thereafter, FM Kasuri and I will meet again on September 5 and 6 in New Delhi.
5. In my meetings, we shared perceptions on several issues. We expressed satisfaction at the wide range of contacts taking place at governmental and non governmental levels between India and Pakistan. India and Pakistan are committed to discuss and settle all bilateral issues, including that of Jammu & Kashmir, to the satisfaction of both sides.
6. During my call on President Musharraf earlier today, I mentioned our intention to carry on a sustained and steady dialogue with Pakistan. We reviewed all significant aspects of our relations. Both sides reiterated the importance of continuing the dialogue process in an atmosphere free of violence, and to tackling the scourge of terrorism with renewed vigour. I deeply appreciated the time and consideration shown to me and my delegation by H.E. the President of Pakistan. No aspect of our relationship including Jammu & Kashmir was left out of our warm, frank and realistic discussions. The meeting lasted one hour and thirty minutes.
7. I leave Pakistan with renewed determination to work with Pakistan, bilaterally, to normalize our relations and to resolve differences while building on many commonalities. I am grateful to the government of Pakistan for the excellent arrangements and many courtesies shown to me and my delegation during the visit. The warmth of our welcome by the Government and people of Pakistan touched us deeply.

❮43❯

Address by External Affairs Minister, Shri K. Natwar Singh at the Hindustan Times Leadership Initiative, (06.11.2004)

The EAM highlighted a number of reasons why India is destined to play a leading role in the transformation that the world is undergoing. Its abundance of skills suited for a knowledge society, its history of interaction and peaceful coexistence with Islam and its role as an indispensable partner in every key region of the world place it in a unique position to assist in this process.

Mr. Surakiart Sathirathai, the distinguished Foreign Minister of Thailand,
Mr. Vir Sanghvi,
Friends, Ladies and Gentlemen,

This session is devoted to discussing regional cooperation, but I would like to place my remarks in the larger context of a rapidly transforming global order and what India sees as its role in shaping the architecture of that emerging order.

The twenty first century is already beginning to look like a confused tangle of competing forces, confronting States with issues of governance for which there are few reference points, even in recent history. Our impulses remain rooted in our conception of nation states and yet there is virtually no challenge we are called upon to address, which does not have, at the same time, a regional or global dimension.

The line between what is the realm of domestic policy and what constitutes external affairs is constantly being eroded, demanding a degree of coordination and consultation within arms of government that are most comfortable working in compartmentalized hierarchies with clearly marked out territories. The challenge for India lies in its capacity to fashion a foreign policy that addresses concerns, which have multiple dimensions and evolve an efficient instrument to deliver that policy. To borrow an analogy from the military field, but with entirely peaceful intentions, not only do we need a potent warhead in the form of good policy; we also need an efficient delivery system in the shape of our external affairs establishment.

What is India's world vision, what is the place we wish to occupy in the emerging international landscape? It should come as no surprise that, as a flourishing democracy, India believes that democratic values are as relevant internationally as they are within our own country. We need a more equitable international order, where global challenges are addressed through collective decision-making, through the forging of broad consensus and not through a process dominated by the few. Just as the rule of law is essential to democratic functioning within countries, so is it necessary to restrain the strong and safeguard the weak in the community of nations.

We see a major role for the United Nations in the emerging international architecture, but we believe it can play this role only after significant reform, reform that makes its structure and its functioning much more democratic than it is currently. Most UN members today recognise the need for an enlarged and restructured Security Council, with representation by more developing countries. India's claims to permanent membership arise not just because of our civilizational legacy and our representation of one sixth of humanity. They arise because we are the world's largest, most vibrant democracy and the fourth largest economy in terms of purchasing power parity. They arise because of India's unswerving commitment to the ideals and activities of the UN. They arise because of India's impressive record of participation in UN Peacekeeping Operations.

We also believe that a more democratic international order is also integrally linked to a more equitable sharing of the world's resources, a recognition of our interdependence for sustainable development and the mobilization of our considerable scientific and technological resources for the banishment of poverty from our midst. Development must return to the center of our international discourse and we must endeavour to create, collectively, an economic environment, where each nation and peoples have a credible opportunity to seek a decent livelihood with a sense of dignity and self-respect. Just as we need an international political order that is based on law and accepted norms, so too, is there need for a rule-based multilateral trading system. We have to collectively acknowledge what has been increasingly evident for some time islands of prosperity in a sea of poverty, are simply unsustainable.

India wishes to play a leading role in shaping the global order that is in the making. We believe we can and must play this role not merely because we are a nation of a billion people, or because we are an emerging economic powerhouse or because we have always been active in the international scene. We bring to a troubled and divided world our unique civilizational attributes. India is a multi-ethnic, multi-cultural and multi-religious society where plural democracy has been, despite a few setbacks, an outstanding success. Through the centuries, India has been at the cross-roads of multiple influences and its creative genius has drawn strength from all the different cultures and religions that have found place in its welcoming fold. For India, diversity is strength, not a weakness. It is a source of creativity, not a threat to unity. At a time when the world is watching with anxiety the sharpening edge of assertive ethnic and religious identities, we are a living refutation of the pernicious theory of a clash of civilisations. We believe that in resolving the contradictions that a globalising world is confronting, India is uniquely placed to deliver a message of harmony and creative co-existence.

There is another reason why India is destined to play a leading role in the transformation that the world is undergoing. Classical economics made development the function of putting together land, labour and capital as the primary resources available to a country. Today, the critical resource for development is knowledge and the society of the future is the Knowledge Society. Countries which will be in the forefront of economic advancement and will lead change, instead of being overwhelmed by change, are those which have an abundance of human skills and command over knowledge. In this perspective, India with its vast pool of skilled manpower, covering the entire spectrum of human endeavour, and not merely information technology, is uniquely placed to make a significant contribution, by becoming a knowledge powerhouse for the entire world.

It is within this over-arching world vision and rooted in a unique civilizational ethos that we must conduct India's foreign policy. We have to recognize the ground realities, which we face, but we must also seek to transform them in line with our vision.

In international affairs, what are the challenges that confront us today? To my mind, the world must adjust to the emergence of both China and India as major actors on the global scene. There is a clear sense that the two Asian giants have much to gain by cooperating together in nudging the world towards multipolarity and multilateralism. And they are beginning to discover that each can contribute to the economic dynamism of the other as large developing economies. It is no accident that trade between us will probably exceed $ 12 billion this year and continue to grow at a breathtaking pace.

The world must also contend with the disappearance of the Soviet Union and its point of view. You may or may not have agreed with that point of view but at least it represented an alternative point of view. Its disappearance has led to unprecedented power and global influence being exercised by just one country today, the United States. For India, relations with the U.S. have a special flavour because we are both vibrant democracies. Our perspectives on specific issues may be different and that may lead to differences in policies. However, we share a great and enduring affinity as peoples wedded to democratic values and today there is such a broad range of interaction between the two countries across the board, that U.S. election results do not fill us with any great uncertainty or doubt. India-US relations are beginning to acquire a degree of stability and predictability and a willingness to work together on shared concerns.

For India, Russia is a key interlocutor and a reliable partner. The challenge for both countries has been to manage the transition from the Soviet Union to Russia, even while the strategic convergences that underlay Indo-Soviet friendship, continue to be valid. Today there is need for India to engage with Russia at many different levels, interacting with many newly emergent constituencies in a much more diffused polity. This will be one of the major policy objectives of our Government.

Another area of pre-eminent challenge for us is to create a congenial neighbourhood with peaceful and tranquil borders, and the pursuit of a common destiny of shared prosperity for the 1.5 billion people who inhabit the sub-continent. This has to be pursued in a complex environment, where the sub-continent is dominated in terms of area, population and economic resources, by India and where India has land or maritime boundaries with all its South Asian neighbours. It is only natural, but not necessarily inevitable, that our smaller neighbours look upon India with some degree of apprehension and fear of domination by it. A key objective of our policy is to reassure our neighbours, and anchor this assurance in a virtuous web of cross-border, economic and commercial linkages. Once India is looked upon as an opportunity, then India's size and its economic strength would become an asset rather than a liability in dealing with our neighbours. The road to a South Asia, which is at peace with itself, lies in economic integration. It is in this spirit that we will be approaching the forthcoming 13th SAARC Summit in Dhaka in January 2005.

Yet another challenge that the world confronts is dealing with the menace of international terrorism. Terrorism threatens not only growth and prosperity, but the very foundation of civilised, democratic societies. This scourge respects no boundaries. The same bomb that kills and maims in Mumbai today can cause death and destruction in another part of the world tomorrow. For this reason, there can never be a category of good terrorists and bad terrorists.

The events following September 11 have created yet another challenge—how to deal with the problem of extremism and fundamentalism without wounding the self respect of the Islamic world. Today, there are 54 Muslim countries which are members of the United Nations. There is no doubt that the unfortunate juxtaposition of terrorism and Islam has hurt Muslim psyche across the world from Mauritania to Medan. It is the responsibility of all of us to provide the healing touch. India with its history of interaction and peaceful coexistence with Islam for more than a thousand years is again uniquely placed to assist in this process.

In pursuing all these objectives, the Ministry of External Affairs will coordinate policy with a number of other actors. At the central level, this involves working together with the Ministries of Home and Defence, the

Economic Ministries and security agencies. Equally important is regular consultation and coordination with the Governments of bordering States. Currently, our effort is precisely to promote such consultation and coordination, make it a regular habit, rather than a sporadic event. In a very real sense, we are witnessing a domestication of diplomacy, which is changing the way we conduct our foreign policy.

Ours is a coalition Government and it has been in office for less than six months. When it came to office, there were doubts expressed on whether it would have the capacity and even coherence to deal with emerging challenges. The first diplomatic crisis we faced was the hostage crisis in Iraq, and we came out successfully having saved the lives of our citizens without compromising our principles. With Pakistan, not only have we carried forward the dialogue process, but have also replaced a reactive mindset with a pro-active, forward looking strategy which is beginning to yield results. We did not let the change in Government disturb the tempo of our engagement with the U.S., and it is our Government, which was able to move decisively to conclude the Next Steps in Strategic Partnership (NSSP). It is this UPA Government which has brought India to the threshold of UNSC permanent membership using skilful diplomacy to get the four major aspirants, India, Brazil, Germany and Japan, on the same platform. Our ability to mobilize a majority of UN members in India's support was again on display when India won the highest number of votes in the recent elections to ECOSOC - 174 as against 152 by even a UNSC permanent member China. We have used all the tools of our diplomacy to support India's quest for reliable energy supplies, seeking and obtaining opportunities in Angola and Sudan in Africa, Kazakhstan in Central Asia and Myanmar in South East Asia. We have made India an indispensable partner in every key region of the world. In two days from now, India and the EU will announce a Strategic Partnership, which will transform our relationship with an expanded union of 25 European countries. By any yardstick, this is a significant achievement for a Government, which has been in office for only five months, and I can promise that there will be many more successes in the days to come.

❮44❯

Address by External Affairs Minister, Shri K. Natwar Singh at the seminar on "Europe and Asia: Perspectives on the Emerging International Order" (19.11.2004)

> The EAM stated that the most persuasive argument for engagement between Europe and Asia is the economic one. Asia with its large population offers attractive markets for European products, and its large young populations with adequate skills make them attractive locations for manufacturing.

Shri R.K. Mishra, Chairman of the Observer Research Foundation General V.P. Malik, President ORF. Distinguished guests, ladies and gentlemen. It gives me great pleasure to be here today. The 'Observer Research Foundation' has emerged as one of our premier think tanks. You undertake rigorous research oriented projects to provide inputs into policy making both at the domestic and international levels. I am also glad that ORF has chosen such an important topic—"Europe and Asia: Perspectives on the Emerging International Order".

Why Europe, and indeed, why Asia? After all, there are seven continents on the earth. The reason, I suppose, is obvious. Dr. Henry Kissinger predicted a few years ago that the future world will have six poles—America, Japan, China, Russia, the European Union, and India. If we take away America, which, in any case, is the pre-eminent power in the world, all the other countries belong to either Europe or Asia. Thus, the future history of the world will be largely determined by the interplay of relations between Europe and Asia. Pt. Jawaharlal Nehru was prescient enough to have seen this as early as in 1951. He said and I quote, "Asia has a very long history behind it and for long ages it has played an outstanding part in the world. Its emergence from colonial status is making a great difference to the balance of forces in the world. The old equilibrium has been upset and can never be restored…. Therefore ... it is of the utmost importance that Europe and Asia should understand each other."

Let's first talk of Asia which Jawaharlal Nehru described as "the mother of continents and the cradle of history's major civilizations". Today, Asia is the continent where two-thirds of the world's population resides. The debate on whether the 21st century belongs to Asia or not is an on-going one, but there is no denying the fact that Asia is poised to play a significant role in international relations. Asia is now the center of economic growth and commercial dynamism. It has the world's most youthful populations. Asia is the fastest growing continent, with China and India set to emerge as the world's second and third largest economies over the next few decades. Yet the region is also prone to instability from national strategic rivalries, economic and political transitions and rapid social transformations. Hence, the emergence of Asia is in reality the sum of the success of each of its parts. The economic dynamism of Asia will be sustained by growing connectivity and infrastructure development. It will also be reinforced by the evident emphasis on integrating markets through free trade arrangements and restructuring and reforms in individual economies.

Asia is also the principal source of world's energy supply. There are ever new and impressive discoveries of oil and gas not only in the Persian Gulf region but also in India, Bangladesh, Myanmar, Indonesia and Vietnam. China sits on foreign exchange reserves of nearly three 300 billion dollars. India on the other hand is emerging as the major hub of international technology products and services. Our foreign exchange reserves have crossed the 120 billion mark and exports have recorded a steady growth of 10% in recent years. Some of the smaller countries like Vietnam and Thailand are also growing very fast, at the rate of more than 6%.

Nehru's vision of resurgent Asia and India's critical engagement in reshaping its destiny was based on three basic assumptions. First, that India was geo-strategically central to Asia, for being "so situated as to be the meeting point of western and northern, and eastern and southeastern Asia." Secondly, its historical and cultural roots were deeply embedded into the larger evolution of Asia over the centuries. Nehru was acutely conscious of these roots when he said : "If you should know India, you have to go to Afghanistan and Western Asia, to Central Asia, to China and Japan and to the countries of South Asia."

The third assumption underlying Nehru's approach to Asia was that the decolonized and newly independent countries of Asia would like to keep off from great power rivalries and conflicts and also free themselves for ever, from political and economic bondage. In this freedom, Nehru saw a constructive and decisive possibility of Asia lending its legitimate weight in world politics in favour of peace and stability. But for this, Asian solidarity was a precondition and India was willing to work for it. In so doing, Nehru also underlined the role of regionalism and institutionalization of cooperation and mutual understanding.

Now let me now turn to Europe. Today, the European Union has become virtually synonymous with Europe. The recent developments in the EU are of great importance to the world community. The bold and dynamic steps taken by the EU such as the Enlargement, the EU Constitution and the Euro have enabled the EU to carve out for itself a distinct personality. With the accession of ten new Member States, in terms of population, the EU has become bigger than NAFTA, with a combined population of over 450 million. By the time the EU enlargement process reaches conclusion, the EU's borders will extend from Belarus to the Black Sea to Iraq, increasing the EU's population by 50%. But the process is not going to be easy. Europe is deeply divided, for instance, on the issue of Turkey's accession to the EU. If Turkey is admitted, it will mean the entry of the first Muslim country into the EU. If it is not, the EU will be perceived as an exclusively Christian Club. The enlargement of the European Union will, therefore, not only have a profound effect on the world, but on Europe itself.

There can thus be no doubt that both Asia and Europe have to work together. The question before us is how will the partnership between Asia and Europe unfold? As the elections in India and the more recent ones in the US have shown, crystal gazing is a rather hazardous occupation. Nevertheless, I feel that there are sufficient pointers for us to outline the dynamics which will shape the partnership between Asia and Europe in the first quarter of the 21st century.

On the political side, I think both Asia and Europe have a shared interest in strengthening multilateralism. The developments in Iraq have reiterated the need for effective multilateralism. The EU will continue to seek outside support for strengthening multilateralism and countries like India and China and the regional blocks such as ASEAN are increasingly seen as promoters of this idea. The ongoing debate on the relevance of the UN in the 21st century assumes significance in this context. Both Europe and Asia share the view of the need for UN reform and restructuring of the UNSC. Although the EU does not have a common position on UNSC reform, it has taken note of India's credentials to be a UNSC member. Most EU member states are supportive of an expanded and restructured UNSC consisting of India, Japan, Germany and Brazil. The EU's desire for greater engagement with Asia is also driven by their concerns over growing regional uncertainties. The situation in Afghan, developments in Iraq, the Middle East Peace Process and the continuing international debate on the Iranian and North Korean nuclear ambitions make it inevitable for EU to stay engaged with Asia and maintain a dialogue process with its strategic partners such as India, China and Japan and also with regional groups. We are already seeing concrete results of this engagement in the form of the agreement which the EU-3 (France, Britain and Germany) were able to broker with Iran last week on its nuclear programme. A variation on this engagement is the dialogue of three civilizations—India-Russia-China. They represent nearly three billion of today's humanity and the best of Europe and Asia. I participated in the

Fourth Meeting of the Trilateral Forum in Almaty last month. We had a meeting of minds on virtually all issues. We agreed to intensify the fight against terrorism and drug-trafficking and emphasised the need for multilateralism and greater UN role in world affairs.

The EU is also seriously concerned about the growing menace of terrorism. With the increasing realization of its repercussions to Europe, the EU is serious about involving Asian states in the fight against terrorism. The EU recognizes now that all terrorism is interlinked and open and democratic societies are particularly vulnerable since terrorists abuse the very freedom and liberty offered by these societies. The need for cooperation with regard to WMDs, narcotics, hawala transactions and cyber crime, besides terrorism, will all lead to a strengthened dialogue between Asia and Europe.

Asia, with its diverse religions, ethnicities and cultures has provided a model of syncretic evolution of civilization. India, with the second largest Muslim community in the world, is a paradigm of Asia's syncretic culture, and of how Islam can flourish in a plural, democratic and open society. The problems of religious extremism and fundamentalism also beset Europe with its expanding and increasingly diversifying population. This is an area where Europe and India could dialogue in order to benefit from their respective experiences.

The most persuasive argument for engagement between Europe and Asia is the economic one. Globalization is a fact of life. In the evolving interdependent linkages, the Asian nations are placed at a vantage point, which will make it inevitable for the EU to stay engaged. A large population of over 3 billion with significant consumer power will make them attractive market destinations for EU products. In the areas of manufacturing and investment, the demographics will significantly change the way EU does its business with the outside world. Here again regions with significant and large young populations with adequate skills will make them attractive locations for manufacturing, i.e., if we are to believe that the market forces will determine the future. A graying Europe will seek to shift its manufacture base to Asian countries, taking advantage of their large skilled, reasonably salaried manpower not only for local consumptions but also for exports to third countries, including to the European markets, themselves. This would entail greater cooperation between Asia and Europe in the WTO.

Science and Technology provides yet another meeting ground for Europe and Asia. Both in fundamental and applied research there will be greater synergies between EU and Asian enterprises. India has already leap-frogged to the front ranks of nations engaged in cutting edge technologies. Our skills in IT and Bio-technology are world renowned. China, Japan, South Korea and South East Asian countries will all become hubs for germinating new ideas and conceptualizing them. All these are also interlinked to management of migration flows. Movement of natural persons in a seamless environment would become a logical fallout and therefore the challenge ahead for both EU and Asia is how to manage migration flows.

Environment, sustainable development and energy are interlinked. While Asia will continue to depend on greater energy sources, including alternative sources such as renewable energy, it will also continue to depend a great deal on the technology of Europe for harnessing them. This dependence will inevitably forge a synergic relationship in energy. The EU's concern over environment is another factor which will bring it closer for a dialogue with Asia because, through sustainable development, it seeks to minimize the negative fallouts on climate change.

It therefore appears safe to say that as the 21st century enters its first decade, both Asia and Europe will come together as natural partners. The foundation for this partnership has already been laid through the varied dialogue processes: ARF, the EUs Summit level interactions with India, China and Japan, APEC, ASEM, and the EU's intensified interaction with regional groupings including with SAARC and OIC.

Now for a word on India's own ties with the European Union. These relations are broad-based and intensive. As Prime Minister Manmohan Singh said in the Hague on November 8: "India and EU are natural partners. Our relations are based on shared values of democracy, pluralism, rule of law, a free press and an independent judiciary. Our partnership has evolved over the years from economic and development cooperation to a broad based engagement on a wide range of issues." Closer political consultations and a dynamic business relationship, underpinned by a shared commitment to democracy, are the main pillars of our engagement with the EU. The Summit at The Hague endorsed the decision to launch a strategic partnership between India and the EU. This is significant, given that the EU has strategic partnerships with only five other countries in the world – USA, Russia, China, Japan and Canada. We now intend to take this partnership to even higher levels, especially in hi-technology such as the energy sector and in space where India is presently in an advanced stage of negotiations regarding its participation in the Galileo Satellite Navigation Project.

In the end I would like to convey my best wishes to the eminent scholars and participants gathered in the Conference. I am confident that the proceedings will not only enrich our knowledge of the dynamics of international relations between Asia and Europe, but also provide us guidelines to making that relationship stable and mutually beneficial so that it contributes to a more peaceful, cohesive and prosperous world.

❮45❯

Inaugural address by National Security Advisor, Shri Brajesh Mishra at the ORF conference on Iran: Twenty-five Years after the Revolution (07.03.2004)

The NSA highlighted that "there is a fresh yearning in Iran to view the significance of the events of the 1979 Islamic Revolution through the prism of contemporary realities and pragmatic possibilities". This evolutionary process in Iran must be allowed to go forward without external interference.

Shri Hamid Ansari, Shri R.K. Mishra,
Distinguished scholars from Iran, India and other countries,
Excellencies, ladies and gentlemen.

I congratulate the ORF for this initiative of inviting such a distinguished galaxy of scholars to discuss where Iran stands today – 25 eventful years after the revolution, which transformed its religious, political and social life. For obvious reasons, it is a subject of absorbing interest to religious historians, social scientists, political analysts and strategic thinkers.

No objective scholar of history can deny the fact that the Islamic Revolution of 1979 was one of the seminal events of the twentieth century. The overthrow of a strong monarchy, commanding a formidable military machine, by a popular revolution that united diverse strands of Iranian society under the iconic leadership of Ayatollah Khomeini, sent political ripples around the world.

The Iranian Revolution was an assertion of national independence and an expression of indigenous political traditions. It was, in a sense, a successor to the Mossadeq period of Iran's search for a nationalist framework to accommodate its unique historical and religious ethos. There was appreciation – including in India – for the new Iran's foreign policy choice of "na sharghi na gharbi" (neither West nor East), which mirrored our policy of non-alignment. In tandem with this foreign policy, Iran's new leaders adopted a model of development based on self-reliance and economic justice, which found a sympathetic echo in much of the developing world.

Of course, there was also a tinge of concern, based on the world's past experience of Revolutions driven by ideology. Also after many centuries, the twentieth century rediscovered the unique experience of a revolution driven by religion.

Where have the last twenty-five years taken Iran? I will only take a few snapshots of prominent events and trends over this quarter century.

- The Revolution was challenged virtually from the start. Eight years of a brutal and destructive war with Iraq retarded development and denied an entire generation the opportunity of national and social reconstruction.
- The rise of the extremist and obscurantist Taliban in neighbouring Afghanistan aroused both theological and security concerns in Iran.
- The military action in Iraq last year aggravated Iranian apprehensions about external influences in the region. But in the aftermath, Iran finds itself in a position to make a key contribution to the sovereignty and territorial integrity of Iraq by promoting a democratic, secular polity in that country, which would shun extremism, sectarianism and terrorism and would provide irrevocable constitutional guarantees to all its minority groups.
- Iran's position, posture and actions in the other West Asian processes are also of crucial importance for the success of the efforts to bring enduring peace to the Middle East.
- The course of recent discussions and arguments over Iran's nuclear programme have illustrated both an encouraging trend of "normalization" of Iran's relations with some of the western countries and some persisting contradictions with others. It is important to emphasise that these contradictions can be resolved only through cooperative effort of the concerned parties and sincere implementation of the commitments made in the recent past.
- Iran now faces the daunting challenge of fulfilling the aspirations of a largely post-Revolution generation, The political awareness of this generation has been shaped by the experiences of Iranian nationalism, but its economic and social expectations flow from the reality of globalization.
- The message of the Revolution has evolved over the last decade to a call for a 'Dialogue among Civilizations', which has been widely welcomed. The relevance of this message has been reinforced after 9/11.
- The memories of the past, the compulsions of the present and the aspirations for the future were all reflected in the fierce debates and emotional polemics, which marked the run up to the recent Parliamentary elections in Iran. There is a fresh yearning to view the significance of the events of 1979 through the prism of contemporary realities and pragmatic possibilities. This evolutionary process in Iran must be allowed to go forward on its own without external interference of any kind or in any manner.

So, I think there is a lot for scholars to discuss and analyze on modern-day Iran.

For us in India, Iran is an important neighbour. We shared a border till 1947. The Indian and Persian civilizations enriched each other and the world around them. You can see the pervasive Persian influence on our languages – particularly Urdu – and in our art, architecture and music.

Engagement with Iran is an important component of India's strengthening interaction with its extended neighbourhood. Despite the distractions of some regional developments – and because of the convergences created by others – the bilateral relations of the two countries have shown a consistently upward trajectory.

India and Iran were among a handful of countries to warn the world of the dangers from Taliban-ruled Afghanistan, well before 9/11. We cooperated in working for the ouster of the Taliban. Today, we share common perspectives on the future course of Afghanistan's development and reconstruction.

Iran is a vital energy partner for us. We are exploring long-term, cost-effective and secure modes for transfer of gas from Iran to India. We see a synergy between the energy resources in Iran and energy markets in India, which we should exploit through commercial arrangements.

The complementarities in our economies have taken our bilateral trade to nearly US $3 billion by last year. We have begun functional cooperation in areas such as IT, science & technology and health. We are also working together for new transit corridors from India to Afghanistan, Central Asia and Russia, through Iran.

The high-level visits between India and Iran testify to our strengthening bilateral relations. Our Prime Minister visited Iran in 2001. We had the honour to welcome President Khatami as the Chief Guest at our Republic Day Celebrations last year. Our two National Security Councils have a regular dialogue. My Iranian counterpart was here in Delhi less than two weeks ago. Later this week, we will receive another important Iranian dignitary – Ayatollah Shahroudi, the Head of the Judiciary.

Ladies and gentlemen,

Jawaharlal Nehru wrote in his "Discovery of India" that few people have been more closely associated in origin and throughout history than the people of India and Iran. Today, we are engaged in exploiting the contemporary relevance of our ancient links. For this, it is essential that the new India and the new Iran understand each other in the full range of our political, economic, social and cultural aspirations and perspectives. It is equally important that we put this understanding in the context of the changing contours of the international environment. Seminars such as this one, particularly with its eminent participation list, contribute to this process.

My best wishes to you for a successful conference. I would like to assure you that the Government of India will follow with interest your deliberations and conclusions.

Thank you.

❮46❯

Third Africa Day Lecture by Foreign Secretary Shri Shashank at India Council of World Affairs, New Delhi (02.06.2004)

The Foreign Secretary assured that India will be a reliable partner in the vision of the Africa Union of economic integration across the continent. He also highlighted India's pledge of US $ 200 million line of credit for NEPAD, US $ 500 million for TEAM-9 countries and a proposal for US $ 1.5 billion to combat HIV/AIDS in Africa.

H.E. Mrs. M.E. Nkoana Mashabane, High Commissioner of the Republic of South Africa; H.E. Major General Charles Dickson Ndaxu P. Namoloh, High Commissioner of the Republic of Namibia; Mr. Butshikan Singh, Deputy Director- General of ICWA; Excellencies, Ladies and Gentlemen,

I am proud and honoured to deliver the Third Africa Day Lecture here at the Indian Council of World Affairs.

India and Africa have been close, and our relations are built on strong political foundations. We have been co-travellers in the anti-apartheid and anti-colonial struggle for centuries. We recognise each other's voices, and hear in the heartbeats of our peoples their hope for a life filled with greater opportunity and security.

I have had the good fortune to visit several African countries, and I have interacted closely with many people at several levels. These visits have deepened my knowledge of developments in Africa, and hence I understand African people's vision for Africa in the 21st century. India wishes to be their reliable partner in helping achieve this vision.

We see two recent developments as being of fundamental importance for Africa's future. First, with the transformation of the OAU into the African Union (AU), the African countries have embarked on the course for a stronger integration of their great continent. For us in India, it will be a privilege to interact with the African Union at all levels including the Summit level.

On the other hand, there is the New Partnership for Africa's Development (NEPAD). It has been crafted by reform-oriented African leaders who have a vision for Africa. The prospects offered by this partnership and the vast potential for sustainable progress inherent in African initiative show that there is room for other countries, such as India, to share and be part of this new dynamism.

In a knowledge society, sustainable economic and social development rely significantly on individual and collective creativity, and thus on the freedom of the citizens. Freedom depends on the rule of law, on open democratic societies. Good governance, is therefore, one of the critical issues of today, because it holds the key to peace and economic success. It is striking how NEPAD emphasises this idea. Without forgetting the consequences of colonialism in terms of resource impoverishment and denial of intrinsic development rights, NEPAD concentrates on the problems of today and on the necessary approaches to solve them. India will lend its support in Africa's determination to take its political and social destiny in its own hands, in forging African ownership of Africa in material and intellectual terms.

Africa Day, which the African states celebrate as a joint event, is a prime symbol of African unity. Since last year's Africa Day, there have been significant developments such as the election and appointment of the African Union Commission, the adoption of a common defence and security policy, the forming of the Pan-African Parliament, and the entry into force of the protocol establishing the African Court of Human Rights. The solemn launching also took place of the Peace and Security Council of the African Union last month on Africa Day in Addis Ababa.

These important advances bear witness to enhanced activity and consensus among the member states, on which India congratulates the AU warmly. As well as these institutional successes, India is also keenly interested in the programmes that the AU will plan and adopt at its summit in Addis Ababa this July. India is, and wishes to be recognised as a genuine and true friend of Africa, one that has stood by it over the years.

The African Union, all African states, their governments and citizens know that India has stood by them as a friend and partner during the past decades. Together Africa and India look to a future that will be characterised by cooperation and friendship. Decades of partnership and of trust lie behind us, as they do before us, for a future to be jointly crafted.

India's relations with the countries of Africa have been constructed on the twin pillars of peace and development. The two are mutually interdependent. India's commitment to the peace agenda in Africa is manifest in our substantial contribution to UN peacekeeping and monitoring operations in the past. On the development front, India's approach is to strengthen South-South horizontal linkages and to promote self-reliance through transfer of intermediate technologies appropriate to the needs of recipient countries India views South-South Cooperation as the embodiment of a new spirit, of a proven alternate cooperative approach to development.

We have also been close partners in the nonaligned movement and stood together to safeguard our freedom of option in conducting our foreign policy. That freedom still underpins our interaction with the world, whether it pertains to political, security, or economic choices.

We would like to be considered as a serious development partner for the African countries. We have so far extended about US$ 1 billion worth of technical assistance including training, deputation of experts and projects to African countries. Currently, for example, about 450 personnel from sub-Saharan Africa are receiving training in civilian and defence fields every year under the ITEC and SCMP programme. Both Africa and India have shared common views in several multilaterals such as the UN, NAM, Commonwealth, WTO, etc. to defend the interests of the developing countries.

There is a drive towards regionalism in Africa that reflects the natural urge of the African countries towards better economic and, eventually, political integration. There is also the important need to address the problem of market fragmentation. The East African Community (EAC), Southern African Development Community (SADC), Common Market of Eastern and Southern Africa (COMESA) are indicators of this trend. While these may be nascent regional groupings, their agenda and ambition can assure their long future.

As elsewhere in the world, there are considerable unexploited opportunities in Africa to promote growth through regional cooperation. Creating larger and more integrated markets, facilitating cross-border investment, and allowing the free movement of people and exchange of ideas, carries economic, as well as political benefits. Boosting South-South trade carries a dual benefit – it strengthens our local basis for generating growth and jobs, and it also gives all of us a stronger voice when urging advanced economies to reform their trade practices. We see that, step by step, Africa is constructing an architecture of institutions to promote peace, security and development on the continent.

As this meeting takes place, the world economy is showing marked signs of recovery. There is now substantial stimulus in national economies and greater availability of resources for development initiatives. In Africa, as a whole, it is said that the average growth is likely to climb to over 5 per cent in 2004.

Indeed, NEPAD itself aims at raising growth to 7 per cent per year. This is an ambitious goal, but one which Africa has the potential to achieve. India would like to congratulate you on NEPAD, with which Africa assumes responsibility for its own transformation, renewal, and development. Partnership and peer review are integral parts of NEPAD, and, I believe, that they will foster a critical element of the development process – the ability to learn from each other. Most importantly, we understand that the leadership in Africa is getting the people of Africa, to understand, accept, and be involved in NEPAD's implementation.

We note the progress being made in its implementation, especially in priority areas of agriculture, infrastructure, environment and health and all key areas in reducing poverty, promoting social stability and improving the quality of life.

India has signed MoUs for cooperation with SADC and COMESA, and is in the process of establishing a dialogue with ECOWAS. Recently, the SADC Council of Ministers has agreed to set up an India-SADC Forum for regular political and economic dialogue between India and SADC. Similar arrangements will be worked out with other regional groupings such as COMESA and ECOWAS.

We are also hoping to have a forum for regular interaction at the Summit level with the leaders of the African Union to better integrate, structure and guide this partnership between Africa and India.

The year 2003-2004 was, indeed, a momentous year as far as evolution of relations between India and Africa was concerned. A strong impetus to the growth of this relationship was given during this period. At the political level, this year had the highest frequency of bilateral WIP exchanges. Within the last year, we were honoured to receive several Heads of States and Governments from Africa including those from Djibouti, Mauritius, Namibia, Zambia, Mozambique, Senegal, South Africa, Zanzibar, and Lesotho. More such visits are planned for future.

Our engagement with the North African region has consolidated during the past few years. Our President visited Sudan and our Prime Minister visited Syria during 2003. In addition, ministerial delegations were received from Egypt, Tunisia, Algeria and Sudan. Bilateral political consultations were held with several countries on bilateral, regional and international issues. Joint Working Group meetings on specific issues also took place.

Our Vice President has also recently attended the celebrations in South Africa on their 10th Freedom Day, as well as to mark the inauguration of their new Presidency. President Thabo M. Mbeki became President for the second term and this is a happy development for us, considering we always had excellent relations with the ANC. Next year, South Africa will be the partner country for CII's India Engineering Trade Fair 2005.

Interaction with African leaders through meetings on the sidelines of important international gatherings such as NAM, UN and CHOGM has been strengthened. Joint Commissions are being revived/set up with sub-Saharan African countries.

Africa-India relations are now poised to enter a new and exciting phase.

Various programmes of cooperation between our countries in a wide range of areas including agriculture, health, IT, small/medium industries, show considerable promise. Many countries of Africa are now increasingly aware that Indian technology and goods are better suited for them. There is recognition that what India can offer, both in products and services, is not only very competitive but also excellent in terms of quality. We are also very pleased that there is a genuine demand for and appreciation of our experts being sent under the ITEC.

Our bilateral trade with Africa has expanded rapidly. Our exports to countries in southern Africa in 2002-2003 showed a rise of 36.55 per cent over the corresponding figure for 2001-2002. Similarly, our exports to East Africa grew by 13.97 per cent over the same period.

Regarding West Africa, a region with which India's interaction was thus far rather limited, we have started a new venture called TEAM-9. The first ministerial meeting of TEAM-9 was held recently in New Delhi. We are hopeful that this new organisation would pave the way for greater cooperation with West Africa.

The Ministry of External Affairs, along with other ministries, is in the process of devising suitable financial mechanisms, which can underpin the expansion of our economic cooperation with Africa. We are working on suitable lines of credit through EXIM Bank. As you are aware, we have pledged US$ 200 million line of credit for NEPAD. These funds are the first demonstration of India's support to the African Union. Similarly, India has recently pledged US$ 500 million for TEAM-9 countries. Another proposal is being processed to extend a line of credit of US$1500 million to combat HIV/AIDS in Africa. It is gratifying to observe that both the public and the private sector in India are very happy with India's involvement with NEPAD and other regional initiatives.

Last year India offered new credit lines to a number of countries in East and South Africa. While some of these credit lines have not become fully operational, it is hoped that these credits on highly concessional terms by us will go a long way in giving a boost to our economic ties with this region.

A major new initiative undertaken by India last year was the offering of food aid to a number of African countries suffering from drought. Substantial donations of anti-HIV drugs were also made to some countries in Africa.

In spite of various constraints, India's trade with sub-Saharan African region increased from US$ 893 million in 1991-92 to US$ 4.2 billion in 2001-2002. This represents increase of over 350% in ten years. Africa is abundantly endowed with a variety of natural resources and is potentially a large market. Countries like Nigeria can emerge as important suppliers of minerals to India.

.There are more than 60 Indian joint ventures operating in Africa in many sectors like banking, textiles, steel, agro processing etc. This is despite the fact that FDI inflows into Africa have shown a declining trend.

Africa's share of FDI flows to developing countries has declined from about 30 per cent in 1970 to less than 4 per cent in 2002.

Some countries in sub-Saharan Africa face shortages today, owing to low rates of growth in agriculture. The Indian experience in green revolution would be very relevant for Africa.

The Sirte Declaration by the leaders of the African Union signed recently at the Extraordinary Summit in Libya focuses entirely on agriculture and irrigation. India has already signed MoUs for cooperation in agriculture with many African countries. We can go beyond these limited assurances of cooperation. India is ready to share its experiences in these areas with African countries, whether it be in mega ventures, small extension and demonstration projects, or in terms of agricultural research. Our terrains are very similar, from lush rain fed and irrigated lands to semi-arid and desert tracts. There is much we can do together to produce food, distribute food and to export food. The area of agricultural research requires agricultural processing techniques, where both Africa and India can share their knowledge and experience.

I may as well mention our experience with self-help groups, which has been a pioneering initiative to take village development programmes to the poor and un-empowered women, which can be a very workable strategy for the African countries as well. It assigns the task of development directly in the hands of those who need it. Herein lies the benefit of sharing of best practices that have proved their efficacy in the Indian rural set up, and which can be adapted in the African countries, given our common problems in the field of agriculture and rural development.

We all recognise that for a sustainable industrial policy, the development of micro-enterprises and small and medium enterprises play a "key role". Let us work together in this area as well. It is now a well-recognised fact, that information and communication technology (ICT) play a crucial role in the promotion of social and economic development. India can contribute immensely in this sector to the multifaceted development of African countries. This has potential to provide effective tools to job creation, economic growth and poverty eradication along with giving an overall boost to the whole process of socio-economic development.

In the ambit of our exchanges, we should also look at the crucial role that our private sectors can play in economic growth and poverty reduction. This, of course, is in the broader context of sustainable development. Strong private sector cooperation can make money for both partners and, at the same time, create wealth for the society, and provide jobs and skills to our people.

These are just some areas that I have outlined. We are drafting a fairly comprehensive document on the areas of our cooperation which we hope to submit soon for the consideration of the African Union.

In all this, I believe that this Africa Centre set up in Sapru House under the Indian Council of World Affairs in June 2002 will allow for a greater interaction between India and Africa on a sustained basis. The Government of India has launched a "Focus Africa" programme and its endeavour is to enhance and deepen engagement with Africa in the political and economic fields. Setting up of the Africa Centre in ICWA is, thus, a step forward to promote understanding and interaction with various countries in Africa. Some activities have already been initiated such as the Africa Day Lecture each year by an eminent personality.

I would like to mention that this Africa Centre has an exclusive section where a large number of books and journals on Africa are kept and a large number of scholars specialising in studies on Africa use this Centre.

In consonance with the Government's policy of having a special focus on Africa, the Indian Council of World Affairs envisions greater interaction with similar institutions in various countries in Africa. Efforts are afoot to invite dignitaries and scholars to visit India and deliver special addresses at Sapru House.

You have recently celebrated Africa Day. Today we are doing it here by talking of Africa-India cooperation. I would like to congratulate you on this anniversary on behalf of the Government and people of India and convey to you our sincere wishes for peace, security, and sustained development.

Your Excellencies, ladies and gentlemen, the vision of the African Union, of economic integration across the continent, must inspire all of us. And you may rest assured that on this path of yours, India will be a reliable partner. We will stand committed to support you with our goodwill, our expertise and whatever economic and financial resources that we can muster to help you realise your aspirations.

Thank you.

〈47〉

Speech on "Indirect Threats to Global Security: Climate Change and Avian Flu Pandemics" delivered by the Deputy to the National Security Advisor, Shri Satish Chandra at the 21st International Workshop on Global Security, Berlin (08.05.2004)

> Deputy to the NSA warned that the threat of a Flu Pandemic could become a reality if the highly pathogenic form of bird flu-H5N1- becomes human to human transmittable. He also warned that the continuous build up of green house gases and the resultant global warming were serious security threats that could be more appropriately termed as non-conventional threats.

Indirect Threats to Global Security: Climate Change and FLU Pandemics

I am glad that the organizers of this Workshop on Global Security have slotted at least one full session to "indirect threats" to global security. Such threats arise not from issues customarily associated with security such as wars, regional conflicts, civil strife, proliferation of nuclear weapons, terrorism etc. but from those which traditionally are not considered to impact significantly on security like climate change, disease, poverty, economic inequities, etc. Accordingly, such threats could perhaps more appropriately be termed as non-conventional threats. These threats are not really "indirect" as failure to address them can have as disastrous an impact on our existence and well being as the failure to address the more conventional threats.

2. In my talk, I will attempt to highlight the grave dangers posed to us by climate change and flu pandemics and outline briefly as to what we can and need to do. Both these can within the next few years inflict upon us a devastation of an order hitherto never visited upon mankind. In each case, I will now paint an entirely plausible hypothetical scenario designed to bring home the gravity of the threat posed to us.

3. It is 2015. Despite much debate and warning, the world has in the preceding years done little to address the build-up of green house gases and the consequent acceleration in the process of global warming which is accompanied by increasing unpredictability of world weather patterns. Extreme heat conditions, storms and droughts create havoc for farmers. Mega droughts affect major granaries. The world's

agricultural production and fresh water resources are seriously stretched thereby reducing the planet's carrying capacity. Deaths from famine and drought run into hundreds of thousands. Violent and frequent storms lash western Europe leading to the abandonment of low lying cities like the Hague. Rising sea level makes countries like Bangladesh nearly uninhabitable leading to mass migration.

4. The 2015 scenario projected above, scary as it is, pales in comparison with what could overtake us by 2007 if the highly pathogenic form of bird flu – H5N1 – becomes human to human transmittable. A simple gene shift of the bird flu virus is all that it would take to make it transmittable from human to human and this could happen any day. In a globalised world linked by rapid air travel, the disease would spread like a raging forest fire. Should this happen with an estimated 60% mortality rate, it would overwhelm our public health system, cripple our economies and wipe out a billion people within the space of a few months.

5. Both these scenarios might seem alarmist but they are within the realm of possibility. We are, however in a position to put in place structures and programmes to mitigate and possibly even prevent such disasters. A no regrets strategy demands that this be done before it is too late. In examining what we need to do, we must dwell in greater depth on the nature and extent of the threat of climate change and of flu pandemics.

Climate change

6. It is well established that global warming experienced by us today is the direct result of the increased concentration of greenhouse gases caused by human activity. The Inter-Governmental Panel on Climate Change (IPCC) has stated that since 1750 AD atmospheric concentrations of methane are up by 151 percent and those of carbon dioxide by 31 percent. Current levels of carbon dioxide and methane concentrations (viz. 375 ppm and 1760 ppb) have not been exceeded during the past 420000 years. The current rate of increase of atmospheric $C0_2$ concentrations viz. 1.5 ppm per year over the past two decades is unprecedented at least over the last 20000 years. 75% of the anthropogenic CO_2 emissions in the last 2 decades are due to fossil fuel burning and the rest mainly due to land use change, particularly deforestation.

7. The fact of global warming is self-evident. We can all feel it. Maximum summer temperatures in Europe in 2003 were unlike anything seen in the preceding 100 years—6°C higher than the 1961-91 average. On an average, Europe was 2°C hotter last summer than average summer temperature over the entire 20th century. In North India, March 2004 temperatures were 5° to 7°C above normal.

8. The IPCC has pointed out that global average surface temperature increased by about 0.6°C during the 20th xcentury and that the 1990s were warmest decade since instrumental records were kept beginning 1861. As a result of global warming, snow-cover since the late 1960s has declined by 10%. The thickness of Arctic Sea ice during late-summer/autumn declined 40% in recent decades. There has been a widespread retreat of mountain glaciers in non-polar regions. Global average sea level has increased between 0.1 and 0.2 meters during the 20th century. El-Nino events, which bring severe droughts in some parts and floods in others, have become more frequent and intense during last 30 years compared to the previous 100 years. Coral reef bleaching, which leads to major loss of biodiversity in coastal areas has become more frequent.
9. Some scientists believe that the extreme weather phenomenon witnessed in the 1990s are an indication of the fact that the 0.6 degree centigrade warming in the 20th century may have already led to the crossing of the threshold beyond which global warming has entered an upward and accelerating spiral. The declining snow cover, increased precipitation which in turn increases water vapor and the fact that the CO_2 emissions of yesterday continue to have an impact on the future, are all contributors to increasing warming. Indeed, even if we were able hypothetically to freeze carbon dioxide concentrations at the current levels of 375 parts per million (ppm), global temperatures will rise another 1°C on top of what we have already experienced. Should this happen, according to a special report on Climate Change in the February 2004 edition of the *Ecologist*, glaciers and sea-ice would in all probability vanish and the number of extreme events such as floods, landslides, heat-waves and violent storms would increase. These would inevitably have catastrophic effect on global food supplies. The report further postulates that if carbon dioxide emissions are curbed so that carbon dioxide concentrations only increase to 550 ppm or roughly double pre-industrial levels, global temperatures would rise two degrees Centigrade over the next 100 years. In this scenario, our current climate system would probably still be able to cope "without jumping unexpectedly to a very different and hard to predict state". It would nevertheless result in sea level increase of a foot or more and even stronger climate events, including storms, sea-surges, torrential rains and droughts. If, however, energy use continues to grow at current rates, there could be a four-fold increase in greenhouse gases compared to pre-industrial times. This could result in 8°C rise in global average temperatures which would produce sea levels 12 meters higher than those existing today and the complete elimination of permanent polar ice-zones. In this eventuality, we would lose our major capital cities, much of our best farm land and be subjected to violent weather

conditions which together would make survival virtually impossible. The IPCC after gaming a number of global warming scenarios has projected global average surface temperatures increase of the order of between 1.4° to 5.8°C over the period 1990 to 2100. The *Ecologist's* February 2004 special report on Climate Change contends that these projections are perhaps far too optimistic.

10. In this context, it would be germane to refer to a study on 'Abrupt Climate Change' developed in October 2003 by Peter Schwartz and Doug Randall which was commissioned by Andrew Marshall for the US Government. The study projects a sharp acceleration in atmospheric warming in the first decade of the 21st century. Average temperatures worldwide increase by 0.5° F and in the harder hit regions by as much as 2° F. Most of North America, Europe and parts of South America experience 30% more days with peak temperatures of over 90°F than a century ago. Weather patterns become much more erratic – more floods in mountainous regions and prolonged droughts in grain producing and coastal agricultural areas. Climate shift becomes an economic nuisance generally affecting local areas as storms, droughts and hot spells impact on agriculture and other climate-dependent activities. More severe storms and typhoons bring about higher storm surges and floods and in 2007, a few coastal cities such as the Hague become uninhabitable, melting along the glaciers accelerates, floating ice in the North Polar seas disappears, sea levels rise, oceanic waves increase in intensity damaging coastal cities. As a result of the freshening of the North Atlantic waters due to higher precipitation and melting of the polar sea ice, the thermohaline circulation system begins to collapse starting 2010. This collapse disrupts the temperate climate of Europe which has been made possible by the warm flows of the Gulf Stream.

11. With the collapse of the thermohaline circulation system under the impact of global warming, the report projects Europe as being hit hardest by climate change in the period 2010-2020. Average annual temperatures drop 6° F in a decade making north west Europe colder and in fact more like Siberia. Reduced precipitation causes soil loss contributing to food shortages. Europe struggles to stem emigration out of Scandinavian and Northern European nations. Colder, windier and drier weather makes growing seasons shorter and less productive throughout the northeastern United States and longer and drier in the southwest. Coastal areas remain at risk as rising ocean levels continue along shores. China is hit hard by a decreased reliability of the monsoon rains. Longer colder winters and hotter summers with reduced precipitation stress already tight energy and water supplies, widespread famine causes chaos and internal conflict. Bangladesh becomes nearly uninhabitable due to persistent typhoons and sea level rise. The report projects that as a result of these climatic

changes, there is a significant drop in the planet's ability to carry the existing population and future wars would be fought over the issue of survival rather than religion, ideology or national honour and that deaths from wars and famine will run into millions.

12. The extreme view projected in this study is as yet a minority view. It is, however, serious enough for the US Senate Commerce Committee to have approved $60 million for further research and for Hollywood to work on the climate catastrophe film "The Day-after-Tomorrow" which will be on the screens shortly. Whether or not the collapse of the thermohaline circulation system actually occurs in as short a time as projected in the study climate change as reportedly pointed out by Sir David King, the British government's chief scientist, is "the most severe problem we are facing today, more serious even than the threat of terrorism".

13. Even if this planet does not in the next decade or two undergo a thermohaline circulation system collapse, the consequences of global warming will be sufficiently serious in our own life time. Two top US Government experts – Dr. Thomas Karl of the National Atmospheric and Oceanic Administration and Dr. Kevin Trenberth of the National Centre for Atmospheric Research -published a paper in the December 5,2003 issue of *Science* warning that on our current course, the likely result is more frequent heat-waves, droughts, extreme precipitation events related impacts such as wild fires, heat stress, vegetation changes and sea level rise. A leading reinsurer Swiss Re has released a report predicting that the financial costs of global warming will double every decade rising to $ 150 billion year over the next 10 years. A major study published in *Nature* magazine projects that in the next 50 years climate change is expected to drive a quarter of land, animals and plants to extinction or more than a million species. Much of that loss – more than one in 10 of all plants and animals – is irreversible because of the extra green house gases already discharged into the atmosphere. A recent study undertaken by WHO finds climate change responsible for 2.4% of diarrhea cases worldwide and for 2% of all cases of malaria. In 2000, it estimates that 150,000 deaths were caused by climate change.

14. The economic impact of climate change will be enormous. Physical infrastructure – energy transmission systems, buildings, urban infrastructure etc., are directly affected by extreme events like floods and cyclones. Extreme weather episodes also lead to migrations. Urban flooding has already become a major issue on most continents. Agricultural, forestry, fisheries and tourism, on which the livelihood of billions of people depends are all highly sensitive to climate change. The insurance and finance services sector has been adversely affected by weather related events which are perceived to be linked to climate change.

15. As stated earlier, we today have the technological means to fix the problem. The extent of climate change is directly linked to the increase in CO_2 concentrations which in turn are determined by trends in carbon emissions from fossil fuel burning. Naturally, the lowering of global carbon emissions would require major changes in existing patterns of energy resource development. We need to utilize the full potential of a host of new technologies such as wind-turbines, highly efficient hybrid electric cars, fuel cell technologies, solar energy etc. together with those designed to eliminate industrial byproduct gases. Greater use of natural gas, nuclear energy and hydropower would further reduce the utilisation of fossil fuels. Moreover, there are innumerable low cost opportunities that need to be seized for promotion of efficient energy use in buildings, transportation and manufacturing. There are enormous possibilities to reduce the extent of forest biomass burning and the cutting down of methane and nitrous oxide emissions which also contribute to global warming. In addition we can also build carbon sinks through judicious re-afforestation programmes. The IPCC has assessed that it is entirely possible through such actions to reduce global emissions well below 2000 levels between 2010 and 2020 and much of this could be achieved in a cost effective manner.
16. While the entire planet is vulnerable to the shifts in climate, the capacity to adapt and meet the challenges of climate change varies vastly from region-to-region. Simply put, developing countries and poorer populations have limited adaptive capacity to adjust to climate change. According to TAR the adaptive capacity of human systems is high in Australia, New Zealand, Europe and North America while low in Asia, Latin American and the polar regions. Small island states are considered to be the most vulnerable to climate change.
17. It was with this in mind that the international community concluded the UN Framework Convention on Climate Change at the 1992 Earth Summit and subsequently, the Kyoto Protocol in 1997. These two understandings show the way for addressing the dangers of climate change based on the following principles:
    - *Based on the "precautionary principle"*, Immediate efforts must be made to halt, if not reverse, global warming.
    - All countries should take action to respond to climate change in accordance with their differentiated responsibilities and differing capabilities. It is on this basis that the Kyoto Protocol imposed binding commitments only on developed countries to reduce their greenhouse gas emissions. It may in this context be underlined that the responsibility for global warming rests in the main with the industrialized countries whose historic and current per capita emission

levels are at unsustainable level and far in excess of those of developing countries. Climate change is being caused not per se by greenhouse gas emissions but by excessive levels of anthropogenic greenhouse gas emissions and the responsibility for this lies on industrialized countries. For instance, while India's current per capita carbon emissions are 0.3 tons, far below the global average of 1.1 tons, those of the US are of the order of about 5 tons. Moreover, developing countries lack the financial and technological capability for addressing global warming. Any binding commitments on developing countries to reduce greenhouse gas emissions would thus not only be iniquitous but also be detrimental to the attainment of their primary goals, namely, economic and social development.

- The industrialized nations with the greatest historical contribution to climate change must take the lead in addressing the problem and therefore at Kyoto they undertook to reduce by 2012 their greenhouse gas emissions by 5.2% below their 1990 levels. In order to lessen their difficulty in meeting the agreed targets several measures were agreed upon such as 'flexibility mechanisms', that allow the trading of emission permits, the use of forests and other carbon 'sinks' and the earning of credits through a Clean Development Mechanism or joint implementation projects.
- Developing countries committed themselves to monitor and address their CO_2 emissions and even to enter into contractual and conditional commitments to implement specific mitigation measures provided the full incremental costs are met by developed countries.

18. Regrettably the Kyoto Protocol has been stymied as both the US and Russia have refused to ratify it. The protocol can only be an instrument of international law if ratified by 55 countries representing 55% of the emissions of the industrialised world. As USA and Russia together account for 53% of the industrialised world's emissions, Kyoto protocol cannot enter into force. It is also disturbing that global carbon emissions from fossil fuel consumption have gone up by 9.1% between 1990 to 2000 and those of the US from 22% to 24% of global carbon emissions. As against the Kyoto emission target of reducing total greenhouse gases by industrialised countries by 5.2% below 1990 level, actual carbon emissions are down by only 1.7%. The reductions achieved are largely due to a 30% reduction in the carbon emissions by Russia, and a 1.4% decline in the carbon emission levels in the EU. The Russian declines may be largely attributed to the slow down in its economy and closure of inefficient industries. Other major industrialised countries like Japan, Canada, Australia have seen massive increase in carbon emissions in the period 1990 to 2000. European countries in

general and UK and Germany in particular have performed fairly well in curbing carbon emissions through curtailing coal utilisation and promoting more efficient and eco-friendly technologies. Many developing countries notably Mexico, China, India and the Philippines have also taken some commendable steps to reduce carbon emissions growth. While individual countries can and must do whatever is possible to reduce greenhouse gas emissions, progress in the matter can most effectively be undertaken only within the framework of an international and legally binding agreement which clearly sets out the obligations and responsibilities of the parties concerned in the achievement of clearly defined benchmarks and objectives. In this context, there can be no substitute for the agreement enshrined in the Kyoto Protocol and it is in our common interest that the Protocol is ratified by all concerned. Failure to do so will condemn us to the perils of climate change.

19. In conclusion, one needs to recognise that global warming is like cancer: difficult to detect in the early stages and difficult to cure if detected late. Regrettably, we have detected global warming late and there are some who feel that the consequences of global warming are reaching the point of irreversibility. Even if we were to cut back emissions *to the levels* suggested in the Kyoto Protocol, we would be merely scratching the surface of the problem. The stabilization of greenhouse gas concentrations at 450 ppm would require annual carbon emissions to drop to less than 1 billion tons over the next century. This would entail a cut of around 80% in global carbon emissions from present levels – much larger than what is being contemplated in the Kyoto Protocol. However, in the absence of anything better, we need to go along the Kyoto Protocol as it constitutes the first step in seriously addressing climate change in a truly global manner which is the only way in which an issue of this nature can be addressed. Pending its ratification, the international community must in any case push ahead with the implementation of the Clean Development Mechanism which should be enshrined in an international agreement as it would facilitate investment and technology flows to developing countries in exchange for carbon credits.

20. In the effort to maximize the use of clean energy technologies, India believes that nuclear power can play a major role. Whenever mention is made of India's nuclear programme, immediate linkage is made to our nuclear weapons development. However, our nuclear programme has always been primarily anchored in the developmental applications of nuclear energy. Nuclear power today accounts for only about 3% of our total power production, but we have an ambitious growth programme. To put the scale of the problem in perspective, if India has to achieve a per capita energy consumption level commensurate

with even the lower end of the present standard of living in developed countries, it would need to increase its electricity generation capacity from today's level of around 100,000 Mwe to around 1.5 million Mwe i.e. to 15 times present capacity. If we did so using fossil fuels alone, this would mean additional CO_2 emissions equal to roughly the entire existing global level.

21. Every effort by us to increase the proportion of nuclear energy in our total energy output should, therefore, be supported wholeheartedly. Instead, the pretext of non-proliferation concerns is frequently used to deny cooperation with India in this area. The irony is that India, with its impeccable record on non-proliferation, is denied access to technology and investment important for its development in a manner which protects the global climate, while clandestine transfers of nuclear, missile and dual-use technologies have escaped unpunished even when exposed. This has served neither non-proliferation goals, nor the objectives of environment-friendly development. Nuclear power has to be recognized as clean energy and should be brought within the purview of CDM.

Flu Pandemic

22. If the possibility of the collapse of the thermohaline circulation system is alarming, the possibility of a human to human transmittable bird flue pandemic is positively a nightmare. What makes it even more frightening is the fact that it could happen any time and that we are ill prepared to face it. At current levels of mortality rate, it could result in "sudden death" for 15 to 20 percent of mankind.

23. The most severe health crisis in terms of death toll in recent times was the 1918-19 influenza epidemic which in the space of one year caused an estimated 40 million deaths worldwide. Starting in March 1918 in Kansas, it spread to Europe and then to India, Australia and New Zealand. The virulence and mortality rate of first wave of influenza in Spring of 1918 was only slightly above normal levels but the second wave beginning in the fall of 1918 was extraordinarily deadly with mortality rates of 5 to 20% above the normal levels. It is believed that the fall strain of the virus occurred through genetic mutation and the genetic structure of the virus was a form of swine and avian influenza strain.

24. Since 1918, the world has seen several influenza outbreaks, most notably the 1957 Asian flu and the 1968 Hong Kong flu each killing a million people. Accordingly, WHO has in position an Influenza Surveillance programme and an Influenza Pandemic Preparedness Plan. Nevertheless, we need to examine the possibility of the highly pathogenic H5N1 bird flu becoming human to human transmittable, the outcome of such an eventuality and as to what needs to be done to address this possibility.

25. Since the end of last year, outbreaks of the highly pathogenic avian influenza or bird flu caused by H5N1 strain have occurred in 8 Asian countries resulting in the loss of 100 million poultry birds. The implications for human health are worrisome on account of the extreme pathogeniticity of this virus as it has the capability to infect humans causing severe illness with mortality rates of 60 to 70%. It has done so thrice in the recent past in 1997 and 2003 in Hong Kong and since mid-January this year in Vietnam and Thailand. So far the transmission of this virus to humans has occurred only to those who came into contact with dead or diseased poultry. It has not so far mutated to achieve the capability of human to human transmission. Since the H5N1 strain has not been eliminated from its avian hosts, it is obviously endemic. The risk, therefore of the H5N1 virus taking on a new form which would give it the capability of human to human transmission is considerable. This is all the more so as the mass vaccination of chickens with a view to mitigating the disaster facing poultry farmers has allowed the virus to continue to circulate amongst the vaccinated birds. It can thus continue to linger indefinitely in poultry and the required gene mutation for making H5N1 human to human transmittable becomes an even greater possibility.

26. It could be said that there are three prerequisites for the start of a pandemic notably, (i) a new virus must emerge to which general population has little or no immunity; (ii) the new virus must be able to replicate in humans and cause disease; and (iii) the new virus must be efficiently transmitted from one human to another. Dr. Anarji Asamoa Baah, Assistant Director General, Communicable Diseases, WHO, asserts that in respect of H5N1, the first two prerequisites have already been met and it is known that the virus can improve its transmittability via two mechanisms, namely, "adaptive mutation" and "genetic re-assortment". He has further contended that re-assortment of H5N1 with a human influenza virus can take place in humans without prior adaptation in other species such as swine.

27. It is clear, therefore, that (a) the H5N1 virus will continue to circulate for a very long time in poultry birds; (b) the threat to public health will be there as long as the virus continues to circulate in poultry birds; (c) should the virus become human to human transmittable, the consequences for human health worldwide in the words of Mr. Baah "could be devastating"; and (d) the world needs to be prepared to respond to the next influenza outbreak. During an Influenza Pandemic Preparedness meeting in mid March in Geneva, the head of the World Health Organisation warned "We know another pandemic is inevitable. It is coming" and that when it happens "we also know that we are unlikely to have enough drugs, vaccines, healthcare workers and hospital capacity to cope in an ideal way".

28. WHO scientists on the basis of epidemiological model project that an influenza pandemic will result in 57 million to 132 million outpatient hospital visits plus 1 million to 2.3 million admissions and between 280,000 to 650,000 deaths in less than 2 years. The impact on poor nations would be much greater. It is submitted that these projections are gross underestimates given the fact that when the 1918-19 influenza epidemic with mortality rates of a maximum of 20% above normal level caused as many as 40 million deaths. H5N1 virus with mortality rates in excess of 60% is bound to prove to be much more deadly. This is all the more so as in today's world of air connectivity, the spread of H5N1 would be much more rapid than that of the 1918 influenza epidemic. Indeed, the death toll could run into hundreds of millions.
29. In order to prepare ourselves for the coming H5N1 flu pandemic, we need to consider the following measures:
    i) Upgraded surveillance systems to ensure real-time detection of avian flu when it infects both poultry and humans. The surveillance challenge as so well put by Aileen Plant of Australia's Curtin University of Technology is to "identify the first case, the first time humans are infected, the first time the disease goes from human to human, and then to identify when it starts to spread quickly". For surveillance to work, it must be transparent and based on regional and international cooperation.
    ii) Once avian flu is detected in poultry, rather than going in for poultry vaccination, it would be more prudent to engage in culling.
    iii) On detection of bird flu in humans, quarantines and travel advisories should be rigorously imposed with a view to containing the disease.
    iv) As the pandemic would quickly exhaust healthcare system resources, plans need to be activated to develop back up facilities and staff.
    v) Massive investment is required in influenza vaccine programmes so that vaccines could be developed in shorter timeframes and greater quantities.
    vi) Vaccine production capacity currently ranges from about 260 million to 280 million doses. In the event of a major pandemic, we would need at least a billion doses. We need, therefore, to augment our vaccine manufacturing capacities. Moreover, once a virus has been isolated, vaccine development today takes between 4 to 6 months. We will not have the luxury of so much time to effectively cope with a deadly pandemic. Accordingly, we need to devise ways and means of reducing the timeframe for developing a vaccine.
    vii) Stocks of anti-viral influenza drugs need to be built up.

‹48›

Keynote address by the Deputy to the National Security Advisor, Shri Satish Chandra at the Delhi Policy Group Seminar on Nuclear Weapons Security (30.08.2004)

> Deputy to the NSA stated that "as long as control regimes remain discriminatory, horizontal proliferation is an inevitability". He recommended the need for a nuclear weapons convention, similar to the chemical weapons convention, "which first de-legitimizes the use and threat of use of nuclear weapons and then goes on to eliminate them."

It is both a privilege and pleasure for me to be here today to interact with the Delhi Policy Group on the subject of "Nuclear Weapons and Security". The title of the seminar is well chosen because momentous developments have taken place in this field in the last few years which pose serious challenges. Apart from India and Pakistan having gone nuclear, there are several other countries knocking on the doors of the nuclear club. WMD terrorism has become an imminent threat and *ad hoc* regimes are being developed to cope with it. Doctrinal evolution in the US is blurring the distinction between conventional and nuclear weapons, and the concept of 'deterrence' is being dethroned by that of 'pre-emption'.

2. The title of this seminar is also apt because there is much divergence of view on whether or not nuclear weapons contribute to security. Some believe that security cannot be guaranteed without nuclear weapons while others feel that nuclear weapons make for insecurity. There would, I believe, be nothing better than living in a nuclear weapon free world. Since, however, a nuclear weapon free world is not on the cards and nuclear weapons are here to stay, it is inevitable that some States, given their security environment, would feel impelled to go nuclear.

3. In my talk, I will attempt to very briefly touch upon some of the issues just cited as well as the nuclear arms race, efforts at arms control, the doctrinal evolution from MAD to NUTS and the rationale for our having gone nuclear.

Nuclear Arms Race

4. As is well known, notwithstanding the horrors of Hiroshima and Nagasaki, the super powers proliferated both vertically and spatially carrying the nuclear threat around the globe. Thus, by the mid 1980s, they had between them at least 24,000 nuclear warheads with yields ranging from few kilotons to thousands of kilotons. This mega tonnage was sufficient to destroy the world 100 times over.
5. Proponents of nuclear weapons and deterrence would argue that their buildup made the world more secure. The fact that there hasn't been a world war since the advent of nuclear weapons would seem to bear this out. This line of argumentation will always be hypothetical for we will never know as to whether or not the superpowers would have gone to war in the absence of nuclear weapons. However, it cannot be said that nuclear weapons ensured peace or security. While nuclear deterrence prevailed at the central level the US and the USSR fought their wars by proxy in several parts of the world.
6. Since the US first began work on nuclear weapons in 1940 the arsenal has cost at least $ 4 trillion, approximately three times more (in 1995 dollars) than what was spent on procurement for the whole of the second world war. Analysts estimate that another $500 billion to $1 trillion could be added once the known costs for operating and maintaining the arsenal are documented and added up. This would amount to $5 trillion; approximately equal to the US national debt. The USSR could have been expected to have incurred similar expenses.

Nuclear Arms Control

7. Though the nuclear weapon States, particularly the super powers, have long discussed nuclear arms control and entered into several agreements, none of these has been aimed at eliminating nuclear weapons. On the contrary, they were directed at perpetuating the nuclear status quo and maintenance of the exclusivity of the nuclear club. Only horizontal proliferation was a concern to them and vertical proliferation was at best addressed only marginally.
8. The PTBT was entered into only after the nuclear weapon States did not have any more need to resort to atmospheric testing and the Outer Space Treaty merely banned the placing of nuclear weapons on celestial bodies and in outer space. The NPT which entered into force in March 1970 is, as we are all aware, a discriminatory treaty which helped legitimize the retention of nuclear weapons by a few 'haves' and deprived the 'have-nots' of the option of going nuclear. The SALT-I agreement of May 1972 merely limited the land based ballistic missiles of the super powers to existing levels and the caps placed on

their sea based missiles were above existing levels. Furthermore, the agreement permitted MIRVing leading to the proliferation of nuclear warheads. It was only in 1987 that the US and the USSR formalized their first real disarmament treaty for the elimination of intermediate nuclear missiles. While much has been made of the START-I and START-II agreements, placing caps on warheads and delivery vehicles (6000 warheads and 1600 delivery vehicles under START-I and 3000-3500 warheads and 1700-1750 SLBMs under START-II), the concept of 'the hedge' dilutes this effort at disarmament. Accordingly, the US to-date retains in its inventory about 10,700 warheads. It is estimated that even in 2007, taking into account 'the hedge' the USA would have as many as the 6200 warheads. Moreover, START does not place any restrictions on technological modernization. Development of nuclear weapon technologies to cater to new threat scenarios is still continuing apace. I have gone into some detail in this matter to underline that much of the disarmament that has been undertaken is in fact illusory and the super powers continue to retain an overkill capability and have done little to diminish the value of nuclear weapons as a currency of power.

Doctrinal evolution from MAD to NUTS

9. The doctrine of Mutual Assured Destruction (MAD) which was in place by the mid-60s was designed to hold population centers of either side hostage to destruction. As technology gave the superpowers access to newer types and more accurate nuclear weapons MAD was replaced by more aggressive doctrines entailing counter-force targeting. Growing technological sophistication gave the US options of Flexible response of the McNamara years (1970s) which advocated graduated nuclear attacks. The 1980s saw the US propagating the theory that a nuclear war could stay limited and that nuclear wars could actually be fought and won.

10. The disappearance of the political and strategic confrontation between the US and the USSR (Russia) should have eliminated the rationale for nuclear weapons and deterrence. It should have led to a realization that a nuclear weapon free world could indeed be achieved. The greatest beneficiary would have been the United States which by the early 1990s enjoyed a conventional margin of superiority which no other military power could hope to contest. This holds true to this day with perhaps even greater validity.

11. Instead of moving in this direction, US strategists since the mid 1990s have been advocating new rationales for the retention of nuclear weapons and developing new types of nuclear weapons. As early as 1996, the US doctrine for Joint Theatre Nuclear Operations postulated that non-

State actors in possession of weapons of mass destruction could be likely targets for use of nuclear weapons. The doctrine further argued that US nuclear weapons could be used to ensure the success of US conventional forces and to counter enemy weapons of mass destruction. In the section in targeting, the doctrine stated that enemy combat forces and facilities, including WMD and their delivery systems, ground combat units, air defence facilities, underground facilities and even non-State actors, etc. could be targets for US nuclear forces.

12. The US Nuclear Posture Review (NPR) 2002 further refines and formalizes this line of thinking. It advocates a shift in US strategy from a country based to a capabilities based approach focusing on variable threats, allowing for flexibility and adaptation to cater for and target these threats. It talks of use of nuclear weapons (a) against hardened targets which can withstand a conventional attack, (b) in retaliation against an attack by nuclear, chemical or biological weapons and (c) in the event of surprising military developments. It advocates the retention of the nuclear hedge adding that nuclear warheads disabled as a result of arms control treaties would be added to the already existing hedge of 2500 warheads. It talks of a new triad of weapons comprising a mix of nuclear and non-nuclear forces, defensive systems and the responsive infrastructure (the hedge). It also advocates maintaining nuclear test site readiness so as to be able to resume nuclear testing at short notice.

13. The nuclear posture review clearly views nuclear weapons as more usable than has been the case so far. The fact that the NPR talks of nuclear and non-nuclear weapons together as constituting the first leg of the new triad indicates that the US military planners view these weapons as one continuum where thresholds for use are not clearly defined. To fit this more pro-active approach, the United States is building new types of nuclear weapons, notably bunker buster nuclear bombs. Small low-yield nuclear weapons are being developed for use in scenarios envisaged under the Nuclear Posture Review. Precisely for this reason these weapons where yield and fallout is limited would be more usable than their thermonuclear predecessors of yester years. The annulment of the ABM treaty and the US moves to develop ballistic missile defences are clear indicators that the strategic thinking in the United States is undergoing a paradigm shift whereby it could consider resorting to the use of nuclear weapons in a pre-emptive mode. Thus, while the nuclear weapon build up of the 1970s and 1980s was justified mainly on grounds of deterrence, the Nuclear Use Theorists (NUTS) envisage the actual utilisation of these weapons in situations short of nuclear war whether limited or all out.

14. It may not be out of place to mention here that the UK seems to be following the US line. It has been reported that it is upgrading the Fylingdales radar station in North Yorkshire to accommodate the US nuclear missile defence programme. Furthermore, it has earmarked 2 billion pounds to equip the Atomic Weapons Establishment at Aldermaston to design and build a new generation of tactical nuclear weapons.

15. The US is not relying on diplomatic means alone to contain proliferation. The doctrine of pre-emption – viz. to take out an adversary's WMD capabilities before they mature is latent in the NPR. The Doctrine of Counter proliferation first advocated in the early 1990s, which advocates use of military means to "take out" the capabilities of potential proliferators is now a well established doctrine in US military strategy.

Rationale for India's going Nuclear

16. The fact that India went nuclear should have been no cause for surprise since its neighbourhood was awash with nuclear weapons, there was clear evidence of ongoing Sino-Pak collusion, Pakistan had time and again sought to exercise nuclear blackmail, and, above all, the nuclear weapon States had no intention of moving towards complete elimination of nuclear weapons. Conclusive proof on the latter, if any was required, was the indefinite extension of the NPT at the 1995 NPT Review Conference. Any surprise relating to India's going nuclear must be as to why in the face of so much provocation, it did not do so earlier.

17. India's Nuclear Doctrine as enunciated in early January 2003 following a CCS meeting, presents no surprises and is clearly built around pronouncements made by the Government over the preceding few years following Pokhran-II. The Doctrine embraces the concept of "No First Use" and of "No-Use" of nuclear weapons against non-nuclear weapon states (NNWS). It elaborates that India would use nuclear weapons only in retaliation against a nuclear attack on Indian territory or on Indian forces abroad and it would retain the option of using such weapons in the event of a major attack against India or Indian forces abroad by biological or chemical weapons. While underlining that use of nuclear weapons could only be authorized by the civilian political leadership, it unambiguously asserts that retaliation to a first strike would be massive and designed to inflict unacceptable damage. The fact that India is a mature and responsible nuclear weapon State is borne out not only by the incorporation in its Nuclear Doctrine of elements such as "No First Use" and "Non-use" of nuclear weapons against non-nuclear weapon States but also by a clear indication that India would build and maintain a credible minimum deterrent, would continue to observe a moratorium on nuclear tests, maintain strict

control on export of nuclear and missile related technologies etc. The doctrine furthermore reiterates India's continued commitment to the goal of a nuclear weapon free world through global, verifiable and non-discriminatory nuclear disarmament.

18. The doctrine is reflective of India's resolve not to engage in arms racing, not to emulate the nuclear war fighting doctrines expounded by some other nuclear weapon States and to envisage the role of nuclear weapons purely as a deterrent.

New Challenges

19. The interplay of the forces generated by the erosion of the non-proliferation regime coupled with the emergence of WMD terrorism on the one hand and the somewhat ad hoc responses thereto, together with the determination of the P5 to maintain the exclusivity of the nuclear club within the framework of the inherently flawed NPT regime on the other, is inevitably throwing up new challenges which the world will be faced with and would need to address with finesse. I cannot give any definitive responses at this stage to some of these challenges but must at least flag them for what I am sure would constitute the subjects for animated and useful discussion.

I. Horizontal Proliferation

20. As stated earlier, several countries are knocking on the doors of the nuclear club. This is inevitable given the inherently flawed nature of the NPT regime. It is clear that in the absence of any serious moves towards the complete elimination of nuclear weapons, horizontal proliferation will take place. What does this mean for the world? I would venture to suggest that while proliferation per se increases risks, these are greatly minimised if the concerned nuclear weapon States are governed by democratic civilian regimes which are sensitive to the importance of ensuring the safe custody of their nuclear arsenals and regard these as nothing more than instruments for deterrence. The risks would be even further reduced if nuclear weapon States adopt appropriate 'no-first-use' and 'non-use' policies. The dangers emanating from nuclear arsenals are greatly enhanced should these be under the control of military regimes which are prone to be adventurist and which see in them instruments of blackmail and as weapons for achieving politico-military objectives. These dangers are even further enhanced if nuclear arsenals are under the custody of military regimes which have long had close linkages with terrorist groups and which are not sufficiently sensitive to the need for ensuring foolproof safe custody of nuclear weapons. Much has been made of nuclear CBMs as stabilizing and risk reduction measures. While they certainly have a role in the ultimate analysis, nuclear stability rests on deterrence.

II. Measures to curb Horizontal Proliferation

21. The US today is taking a series of ad hoc initiatives based on the existing NPT regime designed to strengthen controls on technology transfers, universalize additional safeguards protocol of the IAEA move towards an FMCT sans verification, criminalisation of proliferation, etc.

22. Although we are against proliferation, have exercised maximum restraint in export of sensitive technologies and materials and will continue tightening up our export control regimes in accordance with our own laws and systems, we have been at the receiving end of existing export control regimes.

23. Accordingly, US moves need to be analysed closely with a view to ensuring that the new systems being contemplated do not hurt us. It may be mentioned that the technology controls which have hurt us, have not similarly hurt countries like Pakistan and other rogue States which have clandestinely been able to get around these restraints. The complicity of some of the P5 States in this exercise needs also to be borne in mind. The US, for instance, has tended to turn a blind eye to such illicit moves by countries like Pakistan in pursuance of other objectives. One wonders, therefore, whether the enhanced technology controls being proposed will achieve the desired ends? Our faith in such ideas would have been immeasurably greater had punitive action been taken against States clearly guilty of wilfully undertaken illicit transactions.

III. WMD Terrorism

24. The threat of WMD terrorism is an unfortunate reality of the 21st century. It is now commonly accepted that terrorist groups have had access to WMD materials. It is no longer a question of whether they will use these but only a question about when and where such weaponry will be used. Apart from taking measures to handle WMD terrorist threat, it is imperative that the international community joins hands to prevent such activities. The manner in which Pakistan's complicity in the AQ Khan transactions and its contribution to WMD terrorism have been brushed under the carpet do not give credence to the international community's resolve to deal seriously with this issue. The United States has of course announced several measures most notably the Proliferation Security Initiative as well as the Container Security Initiative to address this threat. Some of the measures contained in these proposals are per se commendable but some others could pose problems. For instance, there are obviously problems of legality in the interdictions envisaged under the Proliferation Security Initiative. There are also

problems as to what would trigger these interdictions. I wonder whether rather than ad hoc, piecemeal measures suggested, it would not be better if the international community would take concerted action through universally negotiated programmes and systems designed to contain WMD terrorism?

Conclusion

25. In conclusion, I would like to underline the following:
   i) The focus of the NWS has been on arms control rather than on disarmament. The motive: Maintenance of dominance.
   ii) As long as control regimes remain discriminatory, horizontal proliferation is an inevitability. This is likely to increasingly become clandestine particularly with the tightening up of such regimes.
   iii) In view of the foregoing, non-State actors getting possession of weapons of mass destruction will become an incremental possibility.
   iv) Discriminatory regimes impede the peaceful uses of nuclear energy and space technologies in many non-nuclear weapon States. This has an adverse fall out on their economic development.
   v) The ideal solution would be to have a nuclear weapon free world. This is not all that utopian. Chemical weapons have been outlawed under the Chemical Weapons Convention and a viable verification mechanism established to ensure they stay that way. A similar Nuclear Weapon's Convention which first de-legitimizes the use and threat of use of nuclear weapons and then goes on to eliminate them from the face of the earth is the only sure path to completely do away with the risk of nuclear annihilation.

❮49❯

Statement by Permanent Representative of India to the UN, Shri V.K. Nambiar on Non-Proliferation of WMDs (22.04.2004)

Taking note of the observations of the co-sponsors of UNSC Resolution 1540 that the resolution "does not prescribe adherence to treaties to which we are not a State party", India's Permanent Representative stated that "on our part, we shall not accept any interpretation of the resolution that imposes obligations arising from treaties that India has not signed or ratified...".

Mr. President,

We appreciate this opportunity to express our views on the vital issue of the nonproliferation of weapons of mass destruction in an open session of the Security Council today. The threat of terror and WMD proliferation coming together is a real one and should clearly be an issue of the highest priority for the international community.

As a victim of terrorism for almost two decades, India understands the dangers that the transfers of such weapons of mass destruction to non-state actors could entail.It is this realization that prompted India to pilot a resolution on "measures to prevent terrorists from acquiring weapons of mass destruction", adopted by consensus by the last two sessions of the General Assembly.

We perceive today's discussion as a logical continuation of the process initiated in the General Assembly. Hence the validity of the focus on 'non-state actors' in the draft resolution. However, this in no way diminishes state accountability on combating terrorism, in eliminating its support infrastructure or linkages with WMD. As in the case of terrorism, state accountability cannot be absolved on grounds that proliferation was the result of private enterprise.

The co-sponsors of this draft resolution have stated that the intention behind their initiative is to fill a gap in the non-proliferation regime, one that, if negotiated through the multilateral framework, could take years. In our view, the issue should ideally have been addressed through existing international instruments and by building on them. The BWC and CWC, the only two non-discriminatory, disarmament treaties, provide for international cooperative efforts for assistance and protection against these mass destruction weapons. We have also supported addressing the issue of radiological weapons at the Conference on Disarmament, in view of the growing concern about radiation dispersal devices.

Our recognition of the time imperative in seeking recourse through the Security Council does not, however, obscure our more basic concerns over the increasing tendency of the Council, in recent years, to assume new and wider powers of legislation on behalf of the international community, and binding on all states. In the present instance, the Council seeks to both define the non-proliferation regime and monitor its implementation. But who will monitor the monitors? We are concerned that the exercise of legislative functions by the Council, combined with recourse to Chapter VII mandates, could disrupt the balance of power between the General Assembly and the Security Council, as enshrined in the Charter.

The issue goes beyond a mere legal consideration of the Council's allocated powers under the Charter. The credibility and even respect that the Security Council can garner would depend on its actions being the product of internal cohesion and universal acceptability. Though resolutions such as 1373 were adopted unanimously, the limitations in their implementation underscore the need for caution on the Security Council being used as a route to short-circuit the process of creating an international consensus. Exhaustive and excessive reporting obligations resulting from UNSC 1267 and 1373 have led to repetitive reporting exercises and burdensome bureaucratic structures without commensurate results on the ground.

In returning to the theme of non-proliferation after 1992 after a over 12 years the Council's credentials are not helped by its track record. Exclusive focus on nonproliferation does disservice to the essential principle of the mutually reinforcing linkage between disarmament and non-proliferation, recognized since SSOD-I. Such approaches erode the collective effort essential for building confidence among states and enabling them to focus on common threats. International treaties or agreements in this field should be multilaterally negotiated not imposed. They should be based on a balance of obligations to ensure universal adherence- the true test of legitimacy and credibility.

To our mind, export controls are not an issue on which the Security Council should prescribe norms. There is tension between ad hoc arrangements on harmonizing export controls among a select few countries on the one hand, and measures being put forward by the Council, on the other hand, intended for universal application. The flip side of export controls is indiscriminate technology - denial, to states with legitimate socio-economic needs. Recent cases have thrown the spotlight once again on the inadequacies of the current regime. They have also shown that far from effectively addressing genuine proliferation concerns, export controls on sensitive technology and materials have served to deny these technologies to responsible nations who play the game by the rules.

India has taken note of the observations of the co-sponsors that the resolution does not prescribe adherence to treaties to which we are not a State party. On our part, we shall not accept any interpretation of the resolution that imposes obligations arising from treaties that India has not signed or ratified, consistent with the fundamental principles of international law and the law of treaties. India will not accept externally prescribed norms or standards, what ever their source, on matters pertaining to domestic jurisdiction of its Parliament, including national legislation, regulations or arrangements which are not consistent with its Constitutional provisions and procedures or contrary to its national interests, or infringe on its sovereignty.

A word of caution on the definitions and terms will be in order. By applying traditionally understood categories of arms control in novel areas in which definitions are not well established we may be creating grounds for differing interpretations. This problem can be compounded by differing national capacities among states to carry out their obligations. A 'one-size-fits-all' approach will not work. The draft makes a reference to "non-state actors" as those identified in the UN list, which may not be exhaustive.

While being under Chapter VII, the resolution ought to steer clear of any coercive or punitive approach or follow-up mechanism, which would defeat its very purpose. We have noted the sponsors' assurance that the use of force is not envisaged or authorized by this resolution. Transparency and inclusiveness in this regard is crucial. Given the far reaching scope of the resolution, it stands to reason that membership of the relevant Committee is not restricted to that of the Council, but also includes member states which have significant capabilities and expertise in related fields.

Having said this, it must also be stated that a resolution which enjoins States to adopt and enforce effective laws to negate transfer of WMD for terrorist purposes and to establish effective domestic controls to prevent WMD proliferation, cannot but be supported by the international community. Most Member States see the undoubted utility of urgent measures to foster cooperative actions at a multilateral level as envisaged in the resolution.

As a matter of national policy, conscious of its responsibilities arising from the possession of advanced technologies, India is committed to an effective and comprehensive system of export controls, to deny unlawful access-whether to states or non-state actors. Our national effort is based on a policy anchored on a conscious decision to prohibit or control export of WMD-usable materials, equipment or technologies or their delivery systems.

Mr. President,

The crisis underlying the non-proliferation order is a matter of deep concern to India since the infirmities of the present order have adversely impacted on our security. It would be a precarious paradox if individual state actions, despite this resolution, condone instances of proliferation or reward proliferant states by other means.

We believe that meeting new proliferation challenges requires fresh approaches, pooling together the efforts and resources of the international community. In the 1992 Security Council Summit on Non-proliferation, in which India participated, we had called for a new international consensus on non-proliferation. We renew that call today, with the hope that our endeavors will spur common efforts for mutual benefit and in the interests of a safe and secure world.

Thank you.

❮50❯

Letter by Permanent Representative of India to the UN, Shri V.K. Nambiar on WMDs to the President of the UN Security Council (27.04.2004)

Shri V.K. Nambiar stated that India perceives the draft resolution on non-proliferation of WMDs "as a further step in the process initiated by India in the General Assembly on measures to prevent terrorists from acquiring weapons of mass destruction, and as such we generally support it". At the same time, he highlighted India's concern "at the increasing tendency of the Security Council in recent years to assume legislative and treaty making powers..." not envisaged in the UN Charter and observed that "India will not accept externally prescribed norms or standards... on matters within the jurisdiction of its Parliament...".

Excellency,

The delegation of India has learnt that the Security Council is scheduled to take action shortly on the draft resolution on Non-Proliferation contained in document S/2004/326 of April 26, 2004.

2. India has conveyed its position on the draft resolution in the open debate of the Security Council on April 22. As mentioned in that statement, we perceive the draft resolution as a further step in the process initiated by India in the General Assembly on measures to prevent terrorists from acquiring weapons of mass destruction, and as such we generally support it. Our approach has been that of a responsible State possessing nuclear weapons. We take note of the recognition in the draft of the inherent and mutually reinforcing linkage between disarmament and non-proliferation.

3. My government would like to reiterate its unwavering commitment to contributing to global efforts for preventing the proliferation of Weapons of Mass Destruction and their means of delivery.

4. At the same time, I wish to state the following:

   India is concerned at the increasing tendency of the Security Council in recent years to assume legislative and treaty-making powers on behalf of the international community, binding on all States, a function not envisaged in the United Nations Charter.

India has taken note of the observation of co-sponsors that the resolution contained in document S/2004/326 does not prescribe adherence to treaties to which a State is not a State Party. India cannot accept any obligations arising from treaties that India has not signed or ratified. The position is consistent with the fundamental principles of international law and the law of treaties.

India will not accept externally prescribed norms or standards, whatever their source, on matters within the jurisdiction of its Parliament, including national legislation, regulations or arrangements which are not consistent with India's constitutional provisions and procedures, or are contrary to India's national interests, or infringe on its sovereignty.

5. In view of the importance of the subject, I would request that this letter be circulated as a document of the Security Council.

❮51❯

Statement by the Ambassador and Permanent Representative of India to the Conference of Disarmament, Shri Jayant Prasad, (06.12.2004)

Ambassador Prasad highlighted that India favours "the inclusion of provisions of a adequate and effective verification mechanism in the BTWC" and sought international cooperation in transfers and exchanges of biological materials and technologies for peaceful purposes. He also called for national and international efforts to strengthen existing mechanisms for the surveillance, detection, diagnosis and combating of infectious diseases.

Mr. Chairman,

Allow me, first of all, to express the pleasure of my delegation in seeing you in the Chair. We are happy indeed that you are maintaining the high standards of leadership set last year by Ambassador Tibor Toth. We assure you of our fullest cooperation in the discharge of your responsibilities.

India believes that norms against biological weapons enshrined in the Biological and Toxin Weapons Convention must be upheld, particularly at a time of heightened threat of biological weapons proliferation and bio-terrorism. Meaningful multilateral efforts should be pursued to strengthen these norms, since biological weapons could well become the weapon of choice for the terrorists due to ever increasing access to requisite technologies, materials and equipment. We have to guard against the increased risk, in this context, of hostile use of advances in biotechnology and the constant need to prevent misuse of biological agents.

The BTWC is the first disarmament instrument that bans the development, production, stockpiling and use of an entire class of weapons. India fully supports initiatives to strengthen the Convention, ensure its full implementation by all States Party and make it universal. In this context, my delegation fully subscribes to the statement made by the Ambassador of Malaysia on behalf of the non-aligned movement.

Mr. Chairman,

India has been playing a constructive role in international efforts aimed at enhancing the effectiveness of BTWC. It is committed to the ongoing process, established by the resumed session of the 5th review Conference in 2002, anchored in the multilateral framework, which is a prerequisite for addressing issues that affect the security of all nations. In our assessment, both Meetings held last year, that of Experts in August and of the States Party in December, were productive. They gave delegations the opportunity to exchange views and to promote, thereby, common understanding and effective action on national implementation of the prohibitions set forth in the Convention and national mechanisms to establish and maintain bio-security. This year as well there were useful exchanges among the States Party during the July Meeting of Experts, as also good presentations by the concerned international organisations, the World Health Organisation, Food and Agricultural Organisation and World Organisation for Animal Health.

Indian experts have actively participated in these exchanges and shared information on India's capabilities for responding to and investigating and mitigating the effects of cases of alleged use of biological and toxin weapons or suspicious outbreak of diseases and on our existing national efforts and mechanisms for the surveillance, detection, diagnosis and combating of infectious diseases affecting humans, animals and plants.

We have keenly followed the national overview statements and thematic presentations by other delegations. Their working papers and presentations contain many useful ideas and suggestions. We appreciate your initiative, Mr. Chairman, to compile and present them in your paper in a succinct and synthesised format. We hope that delegations will find your paper useful in considering measures to strengthen national disease surveillance mechanisms.

Mr. Chairman,

We are, first, considering the promotion of common understanding and effective action on enhancing international capabilities for responding to investigating and mitigating the effects of cases of alleged use of biological or toxin weapons or suspicious outbreaks of disease. Articles VI and VII of the Convention provide the mechanism for investigation into alleged use of biological and toxin weapons and to provide assistance in such cases. Thus, in cases of alleged use of biological weapons, there is a standing mandate from the Convention for the UN Security Council to initiate appropriate international procedures, including investigation of the allegations and provision of assistance in such cases. This has been supplemented by the specific tasking of the UN Secretary General by relevant General Assembly and Security Council resolutions.

It is, indeed, a matter of satisfaction that provisions of Article VI and VII have not been invoked. However, this also has resulted in the efficacy and adequacy of the prevailing mechanism remaining untested. We remain, therefore, in uncharted territory in considering how to enhance the international capabilities for responding to, investigating and mitigating the effects of cases of alleged use of biological or toxin weapons or suspicious outbreak of diseases.

It is the lack of a mechanism for verification of compliance, that diminishes the Convention's effectiveness. India is willing to consider all efforts to strengthen the Convention within a multilateral framework. We favour the inclusion of provisions of an adequate and effective verification mechanism in the BTWC. We also seek increased international cooperation in transfers and exchanges of biological materials and technologies for peaceful purposes.

Meanwhile, several new suggestions were made at the Meeting of Experts on strengthening the provisions of Articles VI and VII. These could be an important input for the next Review Conference, which is mandated to consider the work under the present process and decide possible follow-on action.

The second agenda item, strengthening and broadening national and international efforts and existing mechanisms for the surveillance, detection, diagnosis and combating of infectious diseases is closely linked to the first agenda item. The institutional mechanisms for surveillance and combating of outbreaks of infectious diseases remain the same, irrespective of whether the outbreak is a result of natural causes or an outcome of deliberate use of biological weapons. As we have stressed before, the primary responsibility for surveillance and combating of outbreak of infectious diseases rests with the States Parties, who require to develop national capabilities for the purpose.

Given the asymmetries among the States Party, it is unrealistic to expect all developing countries to have congruent or identical set of standards and institutional mechanisms to deal with surveillance, detection, diagnosis and combating of infectious diseases. The need to provide assistance to them in the development of these capabilities has been recognised by the States Party to the Convention as well as by international organisations such as the WHO, FAO and OIE. We would, therefore, encourage the States Party and the concerned international organizations to provide ready assistance to other States Parties in accordance with the provisions of the Convention.

Mr. Chairman,

We are all aware of the circumstances that led to evolution of the present process, which essentially aims at promoting implementation of the provisions of BTWC by the States Party. The 5th Review Conference clearly spelt out the mandate, process and authority of decision making.

The purpose of the present process is to promote common understanding and effective action and not to seek or agree upon or arrive at any new common understandings. Since both aspects are interconnected and we are treading a fine line here, we should tread with care. Promoting effective action does indeed imply making the implementation of BTWC more precise, effective and operational. One way of so doing would be to assist States Parties to undertake full and effective implementation of their obligations under the Convention, including in relation to the two agenda items before us, but it must be left to their own national decision-making processes.

In our view, in the present circumstances, common understanding and effective action can best be promoted through an exchange of views and learning from each others national experiences and best practices. Besides, the agenda items being considered under the present process cover only some and not all the aspects of implementation of BTWC. The 6th Review Conference will be the proper forum to review the implementation of the Convention in its entirety, achieve overall balance in its results, and draw up recommendations, take decisions and undertake fresh commitments to strengthen the Convention and promote its implementation.

Thank you, Mr. Chairman

❮52❯

Remarks of the Co-Chairman, Indo-US Cyber Security Forum, Shri Arvind Gupta at the 2nd plenary meeting (09.11.2004)

Shri Arvind Gupta highlighted the fact that India's approach to the Indo-US Cyber Security Forum would focus on capacity building including training, exchange of experts, sharing of technology, joint collaboration in specific R&D projects and establishing contacts between law enforcement agencies and technical institutions. He also suggested setting up of a Indo-US Cyber Security Fund and Training Institute.

Dear Mr. Bloomfield, Friends and Colleagues.

1. It is a matter of great pleasure for me and my delegation to participate in the 2nd plenary session of the Indo-US Cyber Security Forum. I wish to thank you for the excellent arrangements and the warm hospitality extended to us during our stay here.
2. Ms. Michelle Markoff and her colleagues visited New Delhi in October and did some very useful preparatory ground work for this meeting. I thank her for that.
3. Indo-US Cyber Security Forum, which enjoys high level political support in both countries, is emerging as an important bilateral mechanism for exchange of views on cyber security, development of cooperative mechanisms *and* as a source of new ideas. We, therefore, readily agreed to the US suggestions for holding the 2nd meeting of the Forum and also about the restructuring of the working groups. We have brought a large delegation of experts and industry representatives to discuss the future action plan of the Forum.
4. In our previous meeting in New Delhi, you had pointed out the growing interdependence of the US and Indian interests and infrastructures across various sectors. Under Secretary Mr. Juster, when he was in India, underlined the importance of our two countries developing appropriate standards for cyber security and strengthening of national laws and enforcement capabilities. Michelle Markoff, speaking at the India-US information security summit 2004 in New Delhi, stressed the borderless nature of cyber space between US and India and advocated the creation of a culture of cyber security.

5. We are in agreement. The rapid growth of ITES Sector in India in recent years, the increasing use of information technology in e-governance projects in India, the opening of R&D facilities and business operations by multinationals in India have made both the government and industry extremely conscious of the need for a strong cyber security culture in the country. The government has taken a series of legal technical and administrative steps to ensure that cyber security is factored into e-governance. Likewise, the Indian industry has also taken cyber security on board in a big way. Many of these issues were discussed at the Indo-US cyber security summit.
6. A lot has been mentioned about data protection. This is a matter of intense debate in India at present. While there is a general agreement that protection of data in law is necessary, precise approach as to data protection issues is to be evolved. Both the US and EU approaches to the issue are being studied. It has been pointed out that there is no separate law in the US on data protection. In India the thinking at this stage is that there may not be a need for a separate data protection law. The existing laws could be amended to incorporate the necessary elements required for giving adequate data protection. Data protection issues involve some aspects of intellectual property rights. Even the legal definition of data protection is not clear. Therefore, it seems to us that there needs to be more debate amongst experts on these issues. Industry will have an important say on this issue. I would, therefore, like to suggest that an Indo-US legal workshop of interested stakeholders may be held in India in the near future so that both sides can exchange views on the issues involved.
7. In India we have also been discussing the European Convention on Cybercrime and its relevance for India. We have done a detailed analysis of Indian law and how it compares with the European Convention. Our finding is that a large section of the convention is taken care of in the various Indian laws and that the proposed amendments in Indian law will provide an adequate legal framework for cyber security. There may be some elements of the cyber crime convention which may be difficult for us to incorporate in our laws. Mrs. Renuka Muttoo, Co-chair of the Legal Working Group and her team of officials from the Ministry of Home Affairs, Ministry of External Affairs and security agencies would discuss in detail the legal and law enforcement issues involved in cybersecurity.
8. We have taken note of US suggestions made from time to time to strengthen cyber security cooperation. For instance, we are agreeable to setting up of 24x7 contacts between US and Indian law enforcement agencies to deal with cyber security issues. The Central Bureau of Investigation (CBI) will be the nodal point from Indian side.

9. India has recently set up a Computer Emergency Response Team (CERT-In). They will be the nodal point for 24x7 interaction with the US CERT. Dr. K.K.Bajaj, the Director of CERT-In, is with us in the delegation. Dr. Bajaj is the Co-chair of the working group on Critical Infrastructure, Watch and Warning and Emergency Response. His team includes the representatives of some of the critical infrastructure sectors like the Railways, Telecom and Civil Aviation. They are looking forward to a meaningful interaction with his counterparts.
10. I would also like to take this opportunity to tell this distinguished gathering briefly about how cyber security is being handled in India.

Excellency,

11. Since we met the last time, a number of important developments have taken place in India in the field of cyber security. At the policy level, a National Information Board, chaired by the National Security Adviser, presently, Mr. J.N. Dixit, has been set up to coordinate all aspects of information related policies in the country. Information Security, including cybersecurity, is an extremely important area of the NIB's remit. The Indian approach to Indo-US Cybersecurity Forum has been discussed and approved at the National Information Board.
12. The Department of Information Technology has set up a number of high-level Working Groups of officials and experts to look into a range of issues pertaining to cyber security. These include working groups on Legal framework and Cyberforensic, the National Assurance Programme, Training and Awareness and Encryption policy. The Department has also set up an Information Security Technology Development Council consisting of government and private sector representatives to look at the cybersecurity R&D and development of cybersecurity technology in the country.
13. The National Security Council Secretariat, a part of the National Security Council, is coordinating a National Information Security Policy in the country. The NSCS has also set up a group of senior cybersecurity officials who oversee the implementation of Information Security Policy in different critical sectors of the economy.
14. Some progress has been made in evolving cybersecurity standards and best practices in the country. Dr. S.L. Sarnot, Director General of STQC, the organisation tasked with developing suitable technical capabilities in the country in the area of Assurance and setting up Common Criteria Lab and training facilities is also a member of the delegation. We also have a representative of the Institute of Development and Research in Banking Technology, which has done useful work in the development of technologies in the Banking sector.

15. In India we are paying a great deal of attention to cybersecurity R&D. We have with us Dr. N. Sitaram, Director, Centre of Artificial Intelligence and Robotics as well as Dr. Krishnan, Senior Director in the Department of Information Technology who are doing a lot of research in Cybersecurity. We also have with us Prof. Veni Madhavan, of the Indian Institute of Science, Bangalore who is a noted expert on cryptology. We would be interested in developing cooperation with US R&D & academic institute in areas like cryptoanalysis and cyberforensics. We would recommend academic exchanges and hands on experience. The R&D Working Group have come with specific proposals to develop cooperation in Cyber security R&D.
16. Cybersecurity has become an urgent issue with our defence forces in the context of RMA. India has made detailed proposals for training of service officers in cybersecurity. We have a substantial delegation of the representatives of Indian defence forces headed by Mr. S.K. Sharma, Joint Secretary in the MoD. He is accompanied by Rear Admiral R Chopra of the Integrated Defence Staff and other representatives of defence services. They will be looking forward to meaningful exchanges with their counterparts in Cyber security.
17. Finally, we also have included for the first time the representatives of the industry in our delegation to address the concerns of the US industry in Cyber security. Mr. Felix Mohan, a former Naval Officer, is representing the CII. He also heads an information security company and would be discussing information security with his counterparts. The Industry delegation includes Mr. Amitabh Singhal President, Internet Service Providers Association of India, and Mr. Sunil Gujral Vice President of Wipro Spectramind, a BPO company. They will also be exploring commercial opportunities during their brief visit here.
18. I would like to dwell briefly on our approach to the Indo-US Cybersecurity Forum.

Excellency,

19. As I had mentioned on the previous occasion during our first meeting, India's focus will be on capacity building. We believe this is in our mutual interest. We are concentrating on training, exchange of experts, sharing of technology, joint collaboration in specific R&D projects, sharing of best practices and establishing close contacts between the law enforcement agencies of both sides as well as technical institutions like the CERTs.
20. We feel that for the success of Indo-US Cyber security Forum both sides should have equal stakes in the action plans and implementation mechanisms. In this context, we believe the Forum should:

(i) Lay greater emphasis on training. The proposals already made need to be pursued and new areas for training to be explored.

(ii) Promote short and medium term exchange of technical experts in each others' institutions. This should include hands on experience for experts. We are prepared to begin these exchanges immediately.

(iii) Set up a joint Indo-US Cybersecurity Fund to which the two governments can contribute initially. Other stakeholders could also be invited to contribute. The fund will be used to finance the activities of the Indo-US Cybersecurity Forum. The size and other modalities of the fund can be decided in further negotiations.

(iv) Set up a joint Indo-US Cybersecurity Training Institute. One branch of the Institute can be in India, the other in the US. Modalities can be decided through further negotiations.

Excellency,

21. I thank you for giving me an opportunity to share with you our views on Cybersecurity. We look forward to fruitful discussions.

Part 2 A
Documents International

❮53❯

UNSC Resolution 1536 (extending the mandate of UN Assistance Mission in Afghanistan) (26.03.2004)

Stressing the importance of extending Central Government authority to all parts of Afghanistan and re-constitution of the new Afghan National Army, the resolution decides to extend the mandate of the United Nation Assistance Mission in Afghanistan (UNAMA) for an additional period of 12 months. It encourages the UNAMA and Afghan authorities to accelerate voter registration in preparation for elections.

Adopted by the Security Council at its 4937th meeting, on 26 March 2004

The Security Council,

Reaffirming its previous resolutions on Afghanistan, in particular its resolution 1471 (2003) extending the mandate of the United Nations Assistance Mission in Afghanistan (UNAMA) through 27 March 2004,

Reaffirming its strong commitment to the sovereignty, independence, territorial integrity and national unity of Afghanistan,

Welcoming the Constitution adopted by the Loya Jirga on 4 January 2004 which reflects the determination of the Afghan people to ensure the transition of their country towards a stable and democratic State,

Recognizing that the United Nations must continue to play its central and impartial role in the international efforts to assist the Afghan people in consolidating peace in Afghanistan and rebuilding their country,

Reaffirming the Transitional Administration as the sole legitimate government of Afghanistan pending the democratic presidential and parliamentary elections envisioned in the Bonn Agreement as in the Afghan constitution,

Reiterating its strong support for the full implementation of the Bonn Agreement (S/2001/1154) and *supporting also* the objectives of the international conference scheduled to take place in Berlin from 31 March to 1 April 2004 to allow the Afghan authorities and the international community to reaffirm their long-term commitment to take the transitional process in Afghanistan forward, including by demonstrating support for the Afghan political process and its national security, as well as by confirming and generating international financial and other donations,

Recalling the importance of the coming elections to establish democratic Afghan authorities as a further step towards implementation of the Bonn Agreement and *welcoming* in that regard the creation of a Joint Electoral Management Body and the initial progress made in voter registration,

Recalling and emphasizing the importance of the Kabul Declaration of 22 December 2002 on Good-Neighbourly relations (S/2002/1416), and encouraging all States concerned to continue to follow up on the Kabul Declaration and the Declaration on Trade, Transit and Inward Investment signed in Dubai in September 2003,

Stressing also the importance of extending central government authority to all parts of Afghanistan, of comprehensive nationwide disarmament, demobilization and reintegration of all armed factions, and of security sector reform including reconstitution of the new Afghan National Army and Afghan National Police,

Welcoming the visit of the Security Council Mission to Afghanistan in October-November 2003 and takes note of its report and recommendations,

1. *Decides* to extend UNAMA for an additional period of 12 months from the date of adoption of this resolution;
2. *Welcomes* the report of the Secretary-General of 23 March 2004 (S/2004/230) and the recommendations contained therein;
3. *Stresses* the importance of the provision of sufficient security and of significant donor support for the holding of credible national elections in accordance with the Afghan constitution and the Bonn Agreement and to this end *urges* member states and international organizations to coordinate closely with UNAMA and the Transitional Administration;
4. *Encourages* Afghan authorities to enable an electoral process that provides for voter participation that is representative of the national demographics including women and refugees and *calls upon* all eligible Afghans to fully participate in the registration and electoral processes;
5. *Encourages* UNAMA and the Afghan authorities, in this regard, to accelerate voter registration efforts in preparation for elections and urges close coordination between Afghan and UN authorities;
6. *Welcomes* the progress made since the commencement of the Disarmament, Demobilization and Reintegration (DDR) process in October 2003 and the contribution of the International Observer Group in this regard; *stresses* that efforts on the part of the Afghan Authorities and all Afghan parties, supported by the international community, to achieve further progress on DDR are critical, particularly for the creation of an environment more conducive to the conduct of free and fair elections; and in this regard, calls upon all Afghan parties to abide by commitments made in the Bonn Agreement including its Annex 1;
7. *Welcomes* the efforts to date of the Afghan authorities to implement their National Drug Control Strategy adopted in May 2003 and *urges* the

Afghan authorities to make further efforts in that regard and Member States to support its implementation with the necessary resources;

8. *Stresses* that tackling the drugs trade cannot be separated from creating a strong economy and a secure environment in Afghanistan and cannot be achieved without increased cooperation among neighbouring states and countries along trafficking routes to strengthen anti-narcotic controls to curb the drug flow, and *notes* with concern in this regard the assessment made by UNODC in its last Afghan opium survey;
9. *Welcomes* the appointment of Jean Arnault as new Special Representative of the Secretary-General (SRSG) for Afghanistan; *reaffirms* its continued strong support for the SRSG and the concept of a fully integrated mission and *endorses* his full authority, in accordance with all relevant resolutions, over all United Nations activities in Afghanistan;
10. *Requests* UNAMA, with the support of the Office of the United Nations High Commissioner for Human Rights, to continue to assist the Afghan Independent Human Rights Commission in the full implementation of the human rights provisions of the new Afghan constitution, in particular those regarding the full enjoyment by women of their human rights; *requests* also that UNAMA support the establishment of a fair and transparent judicial system, and work towards the strengthening of the rule of law;
11. *Calls upon* all Afghan parties to cooperate with UNAMA in the implementation of its mandate and to ensure the security and freedom of movement of its staff throughout the country;
12. *Welcomes* the progress made by the International Security Assistance Force (ISAF), in expanding its presence outside of Kabul and in implementing its mandate in accordance with resolutions 1444 (2002) and 1510 (2003), requests that ISAF continue working in close consultation with the Secretary-General and his Special Representative; *calls upon* troop contributors to provide the necessary resources to ensure the full implementation of the mandate of ISAF;
13. *Welcomes* the development of the new Afghan National Army and Afghan National Police as important steps towards the goal of Afghan security forces providing security and ensuring the rule of law throughout the country, and *also welcomes* the readiness of ISAF to provide security assistance for the organization of the forthcoming elections in support of the Afghan authorities and UNAMA in accordance with resolution 1510;
14. *Requests* the Secretary-General to report to the Council in a timely manner on developments in Afghanistan, including, after elections, on the future role of UNAMA;
15. *Decides* to remain actively seized of the matter.

❮54❯

UNSC Resolution 1540 (non-proliferation of WMD) (28.04.2004)

Acting under Chapter VII of the UN Charter the resolution calls on states to refrain from providing support to non-state actors in the development, acquisition or use of WMDs and their means of delivery. It also calls upon states to present a "national implementation report" within 6 months of the adoption of the resolution.

Adopted by the Security Council at its 4956th meeting, on 28 April 2004

The Security Council,

Affirming that proliferation of nuclear, chemical and biological weapons, as well as their means of delivery,* constitutes a threat to international peace and security,

Reaffirming, in this context, the Statement of its President adopted at the Council's meeting at the level of Heads of State and Government on 31 January 1992 (S/23500), including the need for all Member States to fulfil their obligations in relation to arms control and disarmament and to prevent proliferation in all its aspects of all weapons of mass destruction,

Recalling also that the Statement underlined the need for all Member States to resolve peacefully in accordance with the Charter any problems in that context threatening or disrupting the maintenance of regional and global stability,

Affirming its resolve to take appropriate and effective actions against any threat to international peace and security caused by the proliferation of nuclear, chemical and biological weapons and their means of delivery, in conformity with its primary responsibilities, as provided for in the United Nations Charter,

Affirming its support for the multilateral treaties whose aim is to eliminate or prevent the proliferation of nuclear, chemical or biological weapons and the importance for all States parties to these treaties to implement them fully in order to promote international stability,

Welcoming efforts in this context by multilateral arrangements which contribute to non-proliferation,

---

* Means of delivery: missiles, rockets and other unmanned systems capable of delivering nuclear, chemical, or biological weapons, that are specially designed for such use.

Affirming that prevention of proliferation of nuclear, chemical and biological weapons should not hamper international cooperation in materials, equipment and technology for peaceful purposes while goals of peaceful utilization should not be used as a cover for proliferation,

Gravely concerned by the threat of terrorism and the risk that non-State actors[†] such as those identified in the United Nations list established and maintained by the Committee established under Security Council resolution 1267 and those to whom resolution 1373 applies, may acquire, develop, traffic in or use nuclear, chemical and biological weapons and their means of delivery,

Gravely concerned by the threat of illicit trafficking in nuclear, chemical, or biological weapons and their means of delivery, and related materials,[‡] which adds a new dimension to the issue of proliferation of such weapons and also poses a threat to international peace and security,

Recognizing the need to enhance coordination of efforts on national, subregional, regional and international levels in order to strengthen a global response to this serious challenge and threat to international security,

Recognizing that most States have undertaken binding legal obligations under treaties to which they are parties, or have made other commitments aimed at preventing the proliferation of nuclear, chemical or biological weapons, and have taken effective measures to account for, secure and physically protect sensitive materials, such as those required by the Convention on the Physical Protection of Nuclear Materials and those recommended by the IAEA Code of Conduct on the Safety and Security of Radioactive Sources,

Recognizing further the urgent need for all States to take additional effective measures to prevent the proliferation of nuclear, chemical or biological weapons and their means of delivery,

Encouraging all Member States to implement fully the disarmament treaties and agreements to which they are party,

Reaffirming the need to combat by all means, in accordance with the Charter of the United Nations, threats to international peace and security caused by terrorist acts,

Determined to facilitate henceforth an effective response to global threats in the area of non-proliferation,

Acting under Chapter VII of the Charter of the United Nations,

1. *Decides that* all States shall refrain from providing any form of support to non-State actors that attempt to develop, acquire,

† Non-State actor: individual or entity, not acting under the lawful authority of any State in conducting avtivities which come within the scope of this resolution.

‡ Related materials: materials, equipment and technology covered by relevant multilateral treaties and arrangements, or included on national control lists, which could be used for the design, development, production or use of nuclear, chemical and biological weapons and their means of delivery.

manufacture, possess, transport, transfer or use nuclear, chemical or biological weapons and their means of delivery;

2. *Decides also* that all States, in accordance with their national procedures, shall adopt and enforce appropriate effective laws which prohibit any non-State actor to manufacture, acquire, possess, develop, transport, transfer or use nuclear, chemical or biological weapons and their means of delivery, in particular for terrorist purposes, as well as attempts to engage in any of the foregoing activities, participate in them as an accomplice, assist or finance them;
3. *Decides also* that all States shall take and enforce effective measures to establish domestic controls to prevent the proliferation of nuclear, chemical, or biological weapons and their means of delivery, including by establishing appropriate controls over related materials and to this end shall:
   (a) Develop and maintain appropriate effective measures to account for and secure such items in production, use, storage or transport;
   (b) Develop and maintain appropriate effective physical protection measures;
   (c) Develop and maintain appropriate effective border controls and law enforcement efforts to detect, deter, prevent and combat, including through international cooperation when necessary, the illicit trafficking and brokering in such items in accordance with their national legal authorities and legislation and consistent with international law;
   (d) Establish, develop, review and maintain appropriate effective national export and trans-shipment controls over such items, including appropriate laws and regulations to control export, transit, trans-shipment and re-export and controls on providing funds and services related to such export and trans-shipment such as financing, and transporting that would contribute to proliferation, as well as establishing end-user controls; and establishing and enforcing appropriate criminal or civil penalties for violations of such export control laws and regulations;
4. *Decides* to establish, in accordance with rule 28 of its provisional rules of procedure, for a period of no longer than two years, a Committee of the Security Council, consisting of all members of the Council, which will, calling as appropriate on other expertise, report to the Security Council for its examination, on the implementation of this resolution, and to this end calls upon States to present a first report no later than six months from the adoption of this resolution to the Committee on steps they have taken or intend to take to implement this resolution;
5. *Decides* that none of the obligations set forth in this resolution shall be interpreted so as to conflict with or alter the rights and obligations of State Parties to the Nuclear Non-Proliferation Treaty, the Chemical

Weapons Convention and the Biological and Toxin Weapons Convention or alter the responsibilities of the International Atomic Energy Agency or the Organization for the Prohibition of Chemical Weapons;

6. *Recognizes* the utility in implementing this resolution of effective national control lists and calls upon all Member States, when necessary, to pursue at the earliest opportunity the development of such lists;
7. *Recognizes* that some States may require assistance in implementing the provisions of this resolution within their territories and invites States in a position to do so to offer assistance as appropriate in response to specific requests to the States lacking the legal and regulatory infrastructure, implementation experience and/or resources for fulfilling the above provisions;
8. *Calls upon* all States:
   (a) To promote the universal adoption and full implementation, and, where necessary, strengthening of multilateral treaties to which they are parties, whose aim is to prevent the proliferation of nuclear, biological or chemical weapons;
   (b) To adopt national rules and regulations, where it has not yet been done, to ensure compliance with their commitments under the key multilateral nonproliferation treaties;
   (c) To renew and fulfil their commitment to multilateral cooperation, in particular within the framework of the International Atomic Energy Agency, the Organization for the Prohibition of Chemical Weapons and the Biological and Toxin Weapons Convention, as important means of pursuing and achieving their common objectives in the area of non-proliferation and of promoting international cooperation for peaceful purposes;
   (d) To develop appropriate ways to work with and inform industry and the public regarding their obligations under such laws;
9. *Calls upon* all States to promote dialogue and cooperation on nonproliferation so as to address the threat posed by proliferation of nuclear, chemical, or biological weapons, and their means of delivery;
10. Further to counter that threat, *calls upon* all States, in accordance with their national legal authorities and legislation and consistent with international law, to take cooperative action to prevent illicit trafficking in nuclear, chemical or biological weapons, their means of delivery, and related materials;
11. *Expresses* its intention to monitor closely the implementation of this resolution and, at the appropriate level, to take further decisions which may be required to this end;
12. *Decides* to remain seized of the matter.

❮55❯

UNSC Resolution 1546 (Iraq) (08.06.2004)

Acting under Chapter VII of the UN Charter the resolution endorses the formation of a sovereign interim government of Iraq "which will assume full responsibility and authority by 30th July 2004" thereby ending the occupation. The resolution also calls for holding direct democratic elections to a transitional national assembly by 31 January, 2005 that will draft a permanent constitution for Iraq leading to a constitutionally elected government by 31 December, 2005.

Adopted by the Security Council at its 4987th meeting, on 8 June 2004

The Security Council,

Welcoming the beginning of a new phase in Iraq's transition to a democratically elected government, and *looking forward* to the end of the occupation and the assumption of full responsibility and authority by a fully sovereign and independent Interim Government of Iraq by 30 June 2004,

Recalling all of its previous relevant resolutions on Iraq,

Reaffirming the independence, sovereignty, unity, and territorial integrity of Iraq,

Reaffirming also the right of the Iraqi people freely to determine their own political future and control their own natural resources,

Recognizing the importance of international support, particularly that of countries in the region, Iraq's neighbours, and regional organizations, for the people of Iraq in their efforts to achieve security and prosperity, and *noting* that the successful implementation of this resolution will contribute to regional stability,

Welcoming the efforts of the Special Adviser to the Secretary-General to assist the people of Iraq in achieving the formation of the Interim Government of Iraq, as set out in the letter of the Secretary-General of 7 June 2004 (S/2004/461),

Taking note of the dissolution of the Governing Council of Iraq, and *welcoming* the progress made in implementing the arrangements for Iraq's political transition referred to in resolution 1511 (2003) of 16 October 2003,

Welcoming the commitment of the Interim Government of Iraq to work towards a federal, democratic, pluralist, and unified Iraq, in which there is full respect for political and human rights,

Stressing the need for all parties to respect and protect Iraq's archaeological, historical, cultural, and religious heritage,

Affirming the importance of the rule of law, national reconciliation, respect for human rights including the rights of women, fundamental freedoms, and democracy including free and fair elections,

Recalling the establishment of the United Nations Assistance Mission for Iraq (UNAMI) on 14 August 2003, and *affirming* that the United Nations should play a leading role in assisting the Iraqi people and government in the formation of institutions for representative government,

Recognizing that international support for restoration of stability and security is essential to the well-being of the people of Iraq as well as to the ability of all concerned to carry out their work on behalf of the people of Iraq, and *welcoming* Member State contributions in this regard under resolution 1483 (2003) of 22 May 2003 and resolution 1511 (2003),

Recalling the report provided by the United States to the Security Council on 16 April 2004 on the efforts and progress made by the multinational force,

Recognizing the request conveyed in the letter of 5 June 2004 from the Prime Minister of the Interim Government of Iraq to the President of the Council, which is annexed to this resolution, to retain the presence of the multinational force,

Recognizing also the importance of the consent of the sovereign Government of Iraq for the presence of the multinational force and of close coordination between the multinational force and that government,

Welcoming the willingness of the multinational force to continue efforts to contribute to the maintenance of security and stability in Iraq in support of the political transition, especially for upcoming elections, and to provide security for the United Nations presence in Iraq, as described in the letter of 5 June 2004 from the United States Secretary of State to the President of the Council, which is annexed to this resolution,

Noting the commitment of all forces promoting the maintenance of security and stability in Iraq to act in accordance with international law, including obligations under international humanitarian law, and to cooperate with relevant international organizations,

Affirming the importance of international assistance in reconstruction and development of the Iraqi economy,

Recognizing the benefits to Iraq of the immunities and privileges enjoyed by Iraqi oil revenues and by the Development Fund for Iraq, and *noting* the importance of providing for continued disbursements of this fund by the Interim Government of Iraq and its successors upon dissolution of the Coalition Provisional Authority,

Determining that the situation in Iraq continues to constitute a threat to international peace and security,

Acting under Chapter VII of the Charter of the United Nations,

1. *Endorses* the formation of a sovereign Interim Government of Iraq, as presented on 1 June 2004, which will assume full responsibility and authority by 30 June 2004 for governing Iraq while refraining from taking any actions affecting Iraq's destiny beyond the limited interim period until an elected Transitional Government of Iraq assumes office as envisaged in paragraph four below;
2. *Welcomes* that, also by 30 June 2004, the occupation will end and the Coalition Provisional Authority will cease to exist, and that Iraq will reassert its full sovereignty;
3. *Reaffirms* the right of the Iraqi people freely to determine their own political future and to exercise full authority and control over their financial and natural resources;
4. *Endorses* the proposed timetable for Iraq's political transition to democratic government including:
   (a) formation of the sovereign Interim Government of Iraq that will assume governing responsibility and authority by 30 June 2004;
   (b) convening of a national conference reflecting the diversity of Iraqi society; and
   (c) holding of direct democratic elections by 31 December 2004 if possible, and in no case later than 31 January 2005, to a Transitional National Assembly, which will, inter alia, have responsibility for forming a Transitional Government of Iraq and drafting a permanent constitution for Iraq leading to a constitutionally elected government by 31 December 2005;
5. *Invites* the Government of Iraq to consider how the convening of an international meeting could support the above process, and *notes* that it would welcome such a meeting to support the Iraqi political transition and Iraqi recovery, to the benefit of the Iraqi people and in the interest of stability in the region;
6. *Calls on* all Iraqis to implement these arrangements peaceably and in full, and on all States and relevant organizations to support such implementation;
7. *Decides* that in implementing, as circumstances permit, their mandate to assist the Iraqi people and government, the Special Representative

of the Secretary- General and the United Nations Assistance Mission for Iraq (UNAMI), as requested by the Government of Iraq, shall:

(a) play a leading role to:

(i) assist in the convening, during the month of July 2004, of a national conference to select a Consultative Council;

(ii) advise and support the Independent Electoral Commission of Iraq, as well as the Interim Government of Iraq and the Transitional National Assembly, on the process for holding elections;

(iii) promote national dialogue and consensus-building on the drafting of a national constitution by the people of Iraq;

(b) and also:

(i) advise the Government of Iraq in the development of effective civil and social services;

(ii) contribute to the coordination and delivery of reconstruction, development, and humanitarian assistance;

(iii) promote the protection of human rights, national reconciliation, and judicial and legal reform in order to strengthen the rule of law in Iraq; and

(iv) advise and assist the Government of Iraq on initial planning for the eventual conduct of a comprehensive census;

8. *Welcomes* ongoing efforts by the incoming Interim Government of Iraq to develop Iraqi security forces including the Iraqi armed forces (hereinafter referred to as "Iraqi security forces"), operating under the authority of the Interim Government of Iraq and its successors, which will progressively play a greater role and ultimately assume full responsibility for the maintenance of security and stability in Iraq;

9. *Notes* that the presence of the multinational force in Iraq is at the request of the incoming Interim Government of Iraq and therefore *reaffirms* the authorization for the multinational force under unified command established under resolution 1511 (2003), having regard to the letters annexed to this resolution;

10. *Decides* that the multinational force shall have the authority to take all necessary measures to contribute to the maintenance of security and stability in Iraq in accordance with the letters annexed to this resolution expressing, inter alia, the Iraqi request for the continued presence of the multinational force and setting out its tasks, including by preventing and deterring terrorism, so that, inter alia, the United Nations can fulfil its role in assisting the Iraqi people as outlined in paragraph seven above and the Iraqi people

can implement freely and without intimidation the timetable and programme for the political process and benefit from reconstruction and rehabilitation activities;

11. *Welcomes,* in this regard, the letters annexed to this resolution stating, inter alia, that arrangements are being put in place to establish a security partnership between the sovereign Government of Iraq and the multinational force and to ensure coordination between the two, and *notes also* in this regard that Iraqi security forces are responsible to appropriate Iraqi ministers, that the Government of Iraq has authority to commit Iraqi security forces to the multinational force to engage in operations with it, and that the security structures described in the letters will serve as the fora for the Government of Iraq and the multinational force to reach agreement on the full range of fundamental security and policy issues, including policy on sensitive offensive operations, and will ensure full partnership between Iraqi security forces and the multinational force, through close coordination and consultation;
12. *Decides further* that the mandate for the multinational force shall be reviewed at the request of the Government of Iraq or twelve months from the date of this resolution, and that this mandate shall expire upon the completion of the political process set out in paragraph four above, and *declares* that it will terminate this mandate earlier if requested by the Government of Iraq;
13. *Notes* the intention, set out in the annexed letter from the United States Secretary of State, to create a distinct entity under unified command of the multinaticnal force with a dedicated mission to provide security for the United Nations presence in Iraq, *recognizes* that the implementation of measures to provide security for staff members of the United Nations system working in Iraq would require significant resources, and *calls upon* Member States and relevant organizations to provide such resources, including contributions to that entity;
14. *Recognizes* that the multinational force will also assist in building the capability of the Iraqi security forces and institutions, through a programme of recruitment, training, equipping, mentoring, and monitoring;
15. *Requests* Member States and international and regional organizations to contribute assistance to the multinational force, including military forces, as agreed with the Government of Iraq, to help meet the needs of the Iraqi people for security and stability, humanitarian and reconstruction assistance, and to support the efforts of UNAMI;

16. *Emphasizes* the importance of developing effective Iraqi police, border enforcement, and the Facilities Protection Service, under the control of the Interior Ministry of Iraq, and, in the case of the Facilities Protection Service, other Iraqi ministries, for the maintenance of law, order, and security, including combating terrorism, and *requests* Member States and international organizations to assist the Government of Iraq in building the capability of these Iraqi institutions;
17. *Condemns* all acts of terrorism in Iraq, *reaffirms* the obligations of Member States under resolutions 1373 (2001) of 28 September 2001, 1267 (1999) of 15 October 1999, 1333 (2000) of 19 December 2000, 1390 (2002) of 16 January 2002, 1455 (2003) of 17 January 2003, and 1526 (2004) of 30 January 2004, and other relevant international obligations with respect, inter alia, to terrorist activities in and from Iraq or against its citizens, and specifically *reiterates* its call upon Member States to prevent the transit of terrorists to and from Iraq, arms for terrorists, and financing that would support terrorists, and *re-emphasizes* the importance of strengthening the cooperation of the countries of the region, particularly neighbours of Iraq, in this regard;
18. *Recognizes* that the Interim Government of Iraq will assume the primary role in coordinating international assistance to Iraq;
19. *Welcomes* efforts by Member States and international organizations to respond in support of requests by the Interim Government of Iraq to provide technical and expert assistance while Iraq is rebuilding administrative capacity;
20. *Reiterates* its request that Member States, international financial institutions and other organizations strengthen their efforts to assist the people of Iraq in the reconstruction and development of the Iraqi economy, including by providing international experts and necessary resources through a coordinated programme of donor assistance;
21. *Decides* that the prohibitions related to the sale or supply to Iraq of arms and related material under previous resolutions shall not apply to arms or related material required by the Government of Iraq or the multinational force to serve the purposes of this resolution, *stresses* the importance for all States to abide strictly by them, and *notes* the significance of Iraq's neighbours in this regard, and *calls upon* the Government of Iraq and the multinational force each to ensure that appropriate implementation procedures are in place;

22. *Notes* that nothing in the preceding paragraph affects the prohibitions on or obligations of States related to items specified in paragraphs 8 and 12 of resolution 687 (1991) of 3 April 1991 or activities described in paragraph 3 (f) of resolution 707 (1991) of 15 August 1991, and *reaffirms* its intention to revisit the mandates of the United Nations Monitoring, Verification, and Inspection Commission and the International Atomic Energy Agency;
23. *Calls on* Member States and international organizations to respond to Iraqi requests to assist Iraqi efforts to integrate Iraqi veterans and former militia members into Iraqi society;
24. *Notes* that, upon dissolution of the Coalition Provisional Authority, the funds in the Development Fund for Iraq shall be disbursed solely at the direction of the Government of Iraq, and *decides* that the Development Fund for Iraq shall be utilized in a transparent and equitable manner and through the Iraqi budget including to satisfy outstanding obligations against the Development Fund for Iraq, that the arrangements for the depositing of proceeds from export sales of petroleum, petroleum products, and natural gas established in paragraph 20 of resolution 1483 (2003) shall continue to apply, that the International Advisory and Monitoring Board shall continue its activities in monitoring the Development Fund for Iraq and shall include as an additional full voting member a duly qualified individual designated by the Government of Iraq and that appropriate arrangements shall be made for the continuation of deposits of the proceeds referred to in paragraph 21 of resolution 1483 (2003);
25. *Decides further* that the provisions in the above paragraph for the deposit of proceeds into the Development Fund for Iraq and for the role of the IAMB shall be reviewed at the request of the Transitional Government of Iraq or twelve months from the date of this resolution, and shall expire upon the completion of the political process set out in paragraph four above;
26. *Decides* that, in connection with the dissolution of the Coalition Provisional Authority, the Interim Government of Iraq and its successors shall assume the rights, responsibilities and obligations relating to the Oil-for-Food Programme that were transferred to the Authority, including all operational responsibility for the Programme and any obligations undertaken by the Authority in connection with such responsibility, and responsibility for ensuring independently authenticated confirmation that goods have been delivered, and *further decides* that, following a 120-day transition period from the date of adoption of this resolution, the Interim Government of Iraq and its

successors shall assume responsibility for certifying delivery of goods under previously prioritized contracts, and that such certification shall be deemed to constitute the independent authentication required for the release of funds associated with such contracts, consulting as appropriate to ensure the smooth implementation of these arrangements;

27. *Further decides* that the provisions of paragraph 22 of resolution 1483 (2003) shall continue to apply, except that the privileges and immunities provided in that paragraph shall not apply with respect to any final judgement arising out of a contractual obligation entered into by Iraq after 30 June 2004;

28. *Welcomes* the commitments of many creditors, including those of the Paris Club, to identify ways to reduce substantially Iraq's sovereign debt, *calls on* Member States, as well as international and regional organizations, to support the Iraq reconstruction effort, *urges* the international financial institutions and bilateral donors to take the immediate steps necessary to provide their full range of loans and other financial assistance and arrangements to Iraq, *recognizes* that the Interim Government of Iraq will have the authority to conclude and implement such agreements and other arrangements as may be necessary in this regard, and *requests* creditors, institutions and donors to work as a priority on these matters with the Interim Government of Iraq and its successors;

29. *Recalls* the continuing obligations of Member States to freeze and transfer certain funds, assets, and economic resources to the Development Fund for Iraq in accordance with paragraphs 19 and 23 of resolution 1483 (2003) and with resolution 1518 (2003) of 24 November 2003;

30. *Requests* the Secretary-General to report to the Council within three months from the date of this resolution on UNAMI operations in Iraq, and on a quarterly basis thereafter on the progress made towards national elections and fulfilment of all UNAMI's responsibilities;

31. *Requests* that the United States, on behalf of the multinational force, report to the Council within three months from the date of this resolution on the efforts and progress of this force, and on a quarterly basis thereafter;

32. *Decides* to remain actively seized of the matter.

Annex

Text of letters from the Prime Minister of the Interim Government of Iraq Dr. Ayad Allawi and United States Secretary of State Colin L. Powell to the President of the Council

5 June 2004

Republic of Iraq
Prime Minister Office
Excellency:

On my appointment as Prime Minister of the Interim Government of Iraq, I am writing to express the commitment of the people of Iraq to complete the political transition process to establish a free, and democratic Iraq and to be a partner in preventing and combating terrorism. As we enter a critical new stage, regain full sovereignty and move towards elections, we will need the assistance of the international community.

The Interim Government of Iraq will make every effort to ensure that these elections are fully democratic, free and fair. Security and stability continue to be essential to our political transition. There continue, however, to be forces in Iraq, including foreign elements, that are opposed to our transition to peace, democracy, and security. The Government is determined to overcome these forces, and to develop security forces capable of providing adequate security for the Iraqi people.

Until we are able to provide security for ourselves, including the defence of Iraq's land, sea and air space, we ask for the support of the Security Council and the international community in this endeavour. We seek a new resolution on the Multinational Force (MNF) mandate to contribute to maintaining security in Iraq, including through the tasks and arrangements set out in the letter from Secretary of State Colin Powell to the President of the United Nations Security Council. The Government requests that the Security Council review the mandate of the MNF at the request of the Transitional Government of Iraq, or twelve months from the date on which such a resolution is adopted.

In order to discharge the Iraqi Government's responsibility for security, I intend to establish appropriate security structures that will allow my Government and Iraqi security forces to progressively take on that responsibility. One such structure is the Ministerial Committee for National Security, consisting of myself as the Chair, the Deputy Prime Minister, and the Minister of Defense, Interior, Foreign Affairs, Justice, and Finance. The National Security Advisor, and Director of the Iraqi National Intelligence Service will serve as permanent advisory members of the committee. This forum will set the broad framework for Iraqi security policy. I intend to invite, as appropriate, the MNF commander, his Deputy, or the MNF

His Excellency Mr. Lauro L. Baja, Jr.
President of the Security Council
United Nations
New York, New York

Commander's designative representative, and other appropriate individuals, to attend and participate as well, and will stand ready to discuss mechanisms of coordination and cooperation with the MNF. Iraqi armed forces will be responsible to the Chief of Staff and Minister of Defense. Other security forces (the Iraqi police, border guards and Facilities Protection Service) will be responsible to the Minister of the Interior or other government ministers.

In addition, the relevant ministers and I will develop further mechanisms for coordination with the MNF. Intend to create with the MNF coordination bodies at national, regional, and local levels, that will include Iraqi security forces commanders and civilian leadership, to ensure that Iraqi security forces will coordinate with the MNF on all security policy and operations issues in order to achieve unity of command of military operations in which Iraqi forces are engaged with MNF. In addition, the MNF and Iraqi government leaders will keep each other informed of their activities, consult regularly to ensure effective allocation and use of personnel, resources and facilities, will share intelligence, and will refer issues up the respective chains of command where necessary, Iraqi security forces will take on progressively greater responsibility as Iraqi capabilities improve.

The structures I have described in this letter will serve as the fora for the MNF and the Iraqi government to reach agreement on the full range of fundamental security and policy issues, including policy on sensitive offensive operations, and will ensure full partnership between Iraqi forces and the MNF, through close coordination and consultation. Since these are sensitive issues for a number of sovereign governments, including Iraq and the United States, they need to be resolved in the framework of a mutual understanding on our strategic partnership. We will be working closely with the MNF leadership in the coming weeks to ensure that we have such an agreed strategic framework.

We are ready to take sovereign responsibility for governing Iraq by June 30. We are well aware of the difficulties facing us, and of our responsibilities to the Iraqi people. The stakes are great, and we need the support of the international community to succeed. We ask the Security Council to help us by acting now to adopt a Security Council resolution giving us necessary support.

I understand that the Co-sponsors intend to annex this letter to the resolution on Iraq under consideration. In the meantime, I request that you provide copies of this letter to members of the Council as quickly as possible.

(*Signed*) Dr. Ayad Allawi

The Secretary of State
Washington

5 June 2004

Excellency:

Recognizing the request of the government of Iraq for the continued presence of the Multi-National Force (MNF) in Iraq, and following consultations with Prime Minister Ayad Allawi of the Iraqi Interim Government, I am writing to confirm that the MNF under unified command is prepared to continue to contribute to the maintenance of security in Iraq, including by preventing and deterring terrorism and protecting the territory of Iraq. The goal of the MNF will be to help the Iraqi people to complete the political transition and will permit the United Nations and the international community to work to facilitate Iraq's reconstruction.

The ability of the Iraqi people to achieve their goals will be heavily influenced by the security situation in Iraq. As recent events have demonstrated, continuing attacks by insurgents, including former regime elements, foreign fighters, and illegal militias challenge all those who are working for a better Iraq.

Development of an effective and cooperative security partnership between the MNF and the sovereign Government of Iraq is critical to the stability of Iraq. The commander of the MNF will work in partnership with the sovereign Government of Iraq in helping to provide security while recognizing and respecting its sovereignty. To that end, the MNF stands ready to participate in discussions of the Ministerial Committee for National Security on the broad framework of security policy, as referred to in the letter from Prime Minister of the Interim Government of Iraq Allawi dated June 5, 2004. On the implementation of this policy, recognizing that Iraqi security forces are responsible to the appropriate Iraqi ministers, the MNF will coordinate with Iraqi security forces at all levels — national, regional, and local — in order to achieve unity of command of military operations in which Iraqi forces are engaged with the MNF. In addition, the MNF and the Iraqi government leaders will keep each other informed of their activities, consult regularly to ensure effective allocation and use of personnel, resources, and facilities, will share intelligence, and will refer issues up the respective chains of command where necessary. We will work in the fora described by Prime Minister Allawi in his June 5 letter to reach agreement on the full range of fundamental security and policy issues, including policy on sensitive offensive operations, and will ensure full partnership between MNF and Iraqi forces, through close coordination and consultation.

His Excellency
Mr. Lauro L. Baja, Jr.
President of the Security Council
United Nations
New York, New York

Under the agreed arrangement, the MNF stands ready to continue to undertake a broad range of tasks to contribute to the maintenance of security and to ensure force protection. These include activities necessary to counter ongoing security threats posed by forces seeking to influence Iraq's political future through violence. This will include combat operations against members of these groups, internment where this is necessary for imperative reasons of security, and the continued search for and securing of weapons that threaten Iraq's security. A further objective will be to train and equip Iraqi security forces that will increasingly take responsibility for maintaining Iraq's security. The MNF also stands ready as needed to participate in the provision of humanitarian assistance, civil affairs support, and relief and reconstruction assistance requested by the Iraqi Interim Government and in line with previous Security Council Resolutions.

In addition, the MNF is prepared to establish or support a force within the MNF to provide for the security of personnel and facilities of the United Nations. We have consulted closely with UN officials regarding the United Nations' security requirements and believe that a brigade-size force will be needed to support the United Nations' security effort. This force will be under the command and control of the MNF commander, and its missions will include static and perimeter security at UN facilities, and convoy escort duties for the UN mission's travel requirements.

In order to continue to contribute to security, the MNF must continue to function under a framework that affords the force and its personnel the status that they need to accomplish their mission, and in which the contributing states have responsibility for exercising jurisdiction over their personnel and which will ensure arrangements for, and use of assets by, the MNF. The existing framework governing these matters is sufficient for these purposes. In addition, the forces that make up the MNF are and will remain committed at all times to act consistently with their obligations under the law of armed conflict, including the Geneva Conventions.

The MNF is prepared to continue to pursue its current efforts to assist in providing a secure environment in which the broader international community is able to fulfil its important role in facilitating Iraq's reconstruction. In meeting these responsibilities in the period ahead, we will act in full recognition of and respect for Iraqi sovereignty. We look to other member states and international and regional organizations to assist the people of Iraq and the sovereign Iraqi government in overcoming the challenges that lie ahead to build a democratic, secure and prosperous country. The co-sponsors intend to annex this letter to the resolution on Iraq under consideration. In the meantime, I request that you provide copies of this letter to members of the Council as quickly as possible.

Sincerely,

(*Signed*) Colin L. Powell

❮56❯

G-8 Action Plan on Nonproliferation (09.06.2004)

The G-8 members announced new actions to reduce the risk of proliferation while allowing the world to enjoy the benefits of peaceful nuclear technology. These included amending NSG guidelines, developing new measures to ensure reliable access to nuclear materials including nuclear fuel and universal adherence to IAEA comprehensive safeguards and the Additional Protocol.

At Evian, we recognized the proliferation of weapons of mass destruction and their delivery systems, together with international terrorism, as the pre-eminent threat to international peace and security. This challenge requires a long-term strategy and multi-faceted approaches.

Determined to prevent, contain, and roll back proliferation, today, at Sea Island, we announce an action plan to reinforce the global nonproliferation regime. We will work together with other concerned states to realize this plan.

All states must fulfill their arms control, disarmament, and nonproliferation commitments, which we reaffirm, and we strongly support universal adherence to and compliance with these commitments under the relevant multilateral treaties. We will help and encourage states in effectively implementing their obligations under the multilateral treaty regimes, in particular implementing domestically their obligations under such treaties, building law enforcement capacity, and establishing effective export controls. We call on all states that have not already done so to subscribe to the Hague Code of Conduct against Ballistic Missile Proliferation.

We strongly support UN Security Council Resolution 1540, calling on all states to establish effective national export controls, to adopt and enforce effective laws to criminalize proliferation, to take cooperative action to prevent nonstate actors from acquiring weapons of mass destruction, and to end illicit trafficking in such weapons, their means of delivery, and related materials. We call on all states to implement this resolution promptly and fully, and we are prepared to assist them in so doing, thereby helping to fight the nexus between terrorism and proliferation, and black markets in these weapons and related materials.

1. Nuclear Nonproliferation

The trafficking and indiscriminate spread of sensitive nuclear materials, equipment, and technology that may be used for weapons purposes are a threat to us all. Some states seek uranium enrichment and plutonium reprocessing capabilities for weapons programs contrary to their commitments under the Treaty on the Non- Proliferation of Nuclear Weapons (NPT). We reaffirm our commitment to the NPT and to the declarations made at Kananaskis and Evian, and we will work to prevent the illicit diversion of nuclear materials and technology. We announce the following new actions to reduce the risk of nuclear weapons proliferation and the acquisition of nuclear materials and technology by terrorists, while allowing the world to enjoy safely the benefits of peaceful nuclear technology.

- To allow the world to safely enjoy the benefits of peaceful nuclear energy without adding to the danger of weapons proliferation, we have agreed to work to establish new measures so that sensitive nuclear items with proliferation potential will not be exported to states that may seek to use them for weapons purposes, or allow them to fall into terrorist hands. The export of such items should only occur pursuant to criteria consistent with global nonproliferation norms and to states rigorously committed to those norms. We shall work to amend appropriately the Nuclear Suppliers Group (NSG) guidelines, and to gain the widest possible support for such measures in the future. We aim to have appropriate measures in place by the next G-8 Summit. In aid of this process, for the intervening year, we agree that it would be prudent not to inaugurate new initiatives involving transfer of enrichment and reprocessing equipment and technologies to additional states. We call on all states to adopt this strategy of prudence. We will also develop new Sea Island Summit measures to ensure reliable access to nuclear materials, equipment, and technology, including nuclear fuel and related services, at market conditions, for all states, consistent with maintaining nonproliferation commitments and standards.
- We seek universal adherence to IAEA comprehensive safeguards and the Additional Protocol and urge all states to ratify and implement these agreements promptly. We are actively engaged in outreach efforts toward this goal, and ready to offer necessary support.
- The Additional Protocol must become an essential new standard in the field of nuclear supply arrangements. We will work to strengthen NSG guidelines accordingly. We aim to achieve this by the end of 2005.
- We support the suspension of nuclear fuel cycle cooperation with states that violate their nuclear nonproliferation and safeguards

obligations, recognizing that the responsibility and authority for such decisions rests with national governments or the Security Council.

- To enhance the IAEA's integrity and effectiveness, and strengthen its ability to ensure that nations comply with their NPT obligations and safeguards agreements, we will work together to establish a new Special Committee of the IAEA Board of Governors. This committee would be responsible for preparing a comprehensive plan for strengthened safeguards and verification. We believe this committee should be made up of member states in compliance with their NPT and IAEA commitments.
- Likewise, we believe that countries under investigation for non-technical violations of their nuclear nonproliferation and safeguards obligations should elect not to participate in decisions by the IAEA Board of Governors or the Special Committee regarding their own cases.

2. Proliferation Security Initiative

We reiterate our strong commitment to and support for the Proliferation Security Initiative (PSI) and the Statement of Interdiction Principles, which is a global response to a global problem. We will continue our efforts to build effective PSI partnerships to interdict trafficking in weapons of mass destruction, their delivery systems, and related materials. We also will prevent those that facilitate proliferation from engaging in such trafficking and work to broaden and strengthen domestic and international laws supporting PSI. We welcome the increasing level of support worldwide for PSI, which now includes all G-8 members. The Krakow meeting commemorating PSI's first anniversary, attended by 62 countries, evidences growing global support.

We will further cooperate to defeat proliferation networks and coordinate, where appropriate, enforcement efforts, including by stopping illicit financial flows and shutting down illicit plants, laboratories, and brokers, in accordance with national legal authorities and legislation and consistent with international law. Several of us are already developing mechanisms to deny access to our ports and airports for companies and impose visa bans on individuals involved in illicit trade.

We encourage all states to strengthen and expand national and international measures to respond to clandestine procurement activities. Directly, and through the relevant international mechanisms, we will work actively with states requiring assistance in improving their national capabilities to meet international norms.

3. The Global Partnership Against Weapons and Materials of Mass Destruction

Since its launch by G-8 Leaders two years ago at Kananaskis, the Global Partnership has become a significant force worldwide to enhance international safety and security. Global Partnership member states, including the six new donors that joined at Evian, have in the past year launched new cooperative projects in Russia and accelerated progress on those already underway. While much has been accomplished, significant challenges remain. We recommit ourselves to our Kananaskis Statement, Principles, and Guidelines as the basis for Global Partnership cooperation.

- We recommit ourselves to raising up to $20 billion for the Global Partnership through 2012.
- Expanding the Partnership to include additional donor countries is essential to raise the necessary resources and to ensure the effort is truly global. Today we welcome the decisions of Australia , Belgium, the Czech Republic, Denmark, Ireland, the Republic of Korea, and New Zealand to join.
- We will continue to work with other former Soviet states to discuss their participation in the Partnership. We reaffirm that Partnership states will participate in projects according to their national interests and resources.
- We reaffirm that we will address proliferation challenges worldwide. We will, for example, pursue the retraining of Iraqi and Libyan scientists involved in past WMD programs. We also support projects to eliminate over time the use of highly-enriched uranium fuel in research reactors worldwide, secure and remove fresh and spent HEU fuel, control and secure radiation sources, strengthen export control and border security, and reinforce biosecurity. We will use the Global Partnership to coordinate our efforts in these areas.

4. Nonproliferation Challenges

- The DPRK's announced withdrawal from the NPT, which is unprecedented; its continued pursuit of nuclear weapons, including through both its plutonium reprocessing and its uranium enrichment programs, in violation of its international obligations; and its established history of missile proliferation are serious concerns to us all. We strongly support the Six-Party Process, and strongly urge the DPRK to dismantle all of its nuclear weapons-related programs in a complete, verifiable, and irreversible manner, a fundamental step to facilitate a comprehensive and peaceful solution.
- We remain united in our determination to see the proliferation implications of Iran's advanced nuclear program resolved. Iran must be in full compliance with its NPT obligations and safeguards agreement. To this end, we reaffirm our support for the IAEA Board of Governors' three Iran resolutions. We note that since Evian, Iran has signed the Additional Protocol and has committed itself to cooperate with the Agency, and to suspend its enrichment and reprocessing

related activities. While we acknowledge the areas of progress reported by the Director General, we are, however, deeply concerned that Iran's suspension of enrichment-related activity is not yet comprehensive. We deplore Iran's delays, deficiencies in cooperation, and inadequate disclosures, as detailed in IAEA Director General reports. We therefore urge Iran promptly and fully to comply with its commitments and all IAEA Board requirements, including ratification and full implementation of the Additional Protocol, leading to resolution of all outstanding issues related to its nuclear program.

- We welcome Libya's strategic decision to rid itself of its weapons of mass destruction and longer-range missiles, to fully comply with the NPT, the Additional Protocol, the Biological and Toxin Weapons Convention (BWC), and the Chemical Weapons Convention (CWC), and to commit not to possess missiles subject to the Missile Technology Control Regime. We note Libya has cooperated in the removal of nuclear equipment and materials and taken steps to eliminate chemical weapons. We call on Libya to continue to cooperate fully with the IAEA and the Organization for the Prohibition of Chemical Weapons.

5. Defending Against Bioterrorism

Bioterrorism poses unique, grave threats to the security of all nations, and could endanger public health and disrupt economies. We commit to concrete national and international steps to: expand or, where necessary, initiate new biosurveillance capabilities to detect bioterror attacks against humans, animals, and crops; improve our prevention and response capabilities; increase protection of the global food supply; and respond to, investigate, and mitigate the effects of alleged uses of biological weapons or suspicious outbreaks of disease. In this context, we seek concrete realization of our commitments at the fifth Review Conference of the BWC. The BWC is a critical foundation against biological weapons' proliferation, including to terrorists. Its prohibitions should be fully implemented, including enactment of penal legislation. We strongly urge all non-parties to join the BWC promptly.

6. Chemical Weapons Proliferation

We support full implementation of the CWC, including its nonproliferation aspects. We strongly urge all non-parties to join the CWC promptly, and will work with them to this end. We also urge CWC States Parties to undertake national legislative and administrative measures for its full implementation. We support the use of all fact-finding, verification, and compliance measures, including, if necessary, challenge inspections, as provided in the CWC.

7. Implementation of the Evian Initiative on Radioactive Source Security

At Evian we agreed to improve controls on radioactive sources to prevent their use by terrorists, and we have made substantial progress toward that goal. We are pleased that the IAEA approved a revised Code of Conduct on the Safety and Security of Radioactive Sources in September 2003. We urge all states to implement the Code and recognize it as a global standard.

We have agreed to export and import control guidance for high-risk radioactive sources, which should only be supplied to authorized end-users in states that can control them. States should ensure that no sources are diverted for illicit use. We seek prompt IAEA approval of this guidance to ensure that effective controls are operational by the end of 2005 and applied in a harmonized and consistent manner. We support the IAEA's program for assistance to ensure that all countries can meet the new standards.

8. Nuclear Safety and Security

Since the horrific 1986 accident at Chornobyl, we have worked with Ukraine to improve the safety and security of the site. We have already made a large financial contribution to build a safe confinement over the remnants of the Chornobyl reactor. We are grateful for the participation and contributions made by 21 other states in this effort. Today, we endorse international efforts to raise the remaining funds necessary to complete the project. We urge Ukraine to support and work closely with us to complete the confinement's construction by 2008 in a way that contributes to radiological safety, in particular in Ukraine and neighboring regions. An effective, efficient nuclear regulatory system is essential for our safety and security. We affirm the importance for national regulators to have sufficient authority, independence, and competence.

❮57❯

Implementation of the NPT Safeguards agreement in Iran, Resolution adopted by the IAEA Board (18.06.2004)

The IAEA Resolution called on Iran to take necessary steps to help resolve all outstanding questions, especially that of LEU and HEU contamination and also the question of the nature and scope of Iran's P-2 centrifuge programme.

The Board of Governors,

(a) Recalling the resolutions adopted by the Board on 13 March 2004 (GOV/2004/21), 26 November 2003 (GOV/2003/81), and on 12 September 2003 (GOV/2003/69) and the statement by the Board of 19 June 2003 (GOV/OR.1072),

(b) Noting with appreciation the Director General's report of 1 June 2004 (GOV/2004/34), on the implementation of safeguards in Iran,

(c) Reiterating its appreciation that Iran has continued to act as if its Additional Protocol were in force, and noting with satisfaction that Iran has submitted to the Agency the initial declarations pursuant to that Protocol,

(d) Noting, however, that Iran has yet to ratify the Protocol as called for in previous Board resolutions,

(e) Recalling Iran's voluntary decisions to suspend all enrichment-related and reprocessing activities and to permit the Agency to verify that suspension; noting with concern that, as detailed in the Director General's report, this verification was delayed in some cases, and that the suspension is not yet comprehensive because of the continued production of centrifuge equipment; also noting with concern that Iran's decision to proceed with the generation of UF_6 is at variance with the Agency's previous understanding as to the scope of Iran's decision regarding suspension; and further noting that Iran has withheld 10 assembled centrifuge rotors for research activities,

(f) Encouraged by the Director General's assessment that there has been good progress on the actions agreed during the Director General's visit to Tehran in early April 2004 and that the Agency continues to make progress in gaining a comprehensive understanding of Iran's nuclear programme, but noting with concern that after almost two years from when Iran's undeclared programme came to the Agency's knowledge a number of questions remain outstanding, and in particular two questions that are key to understanding the extent and nature of Iran's enrichment programme: the sources of all HEU contamination in Iran and the extent and nature of work undertaken on the basis of the P-2 advanced centrifuge design,

(g) Noting in this context with serious concern that important information about the P-2 centrifuge programme has often been forthcoming only after repeated requests, and in some cases has been incomplete and continues to lack the necessary clarity and also that the information provided to date relating to contamination issues has not been adequate to resolve this complex matter,

(h) Noting with appreciation that the Agency has received some information from other states that may be helpful in resolving some contamination questions,

(i) Noting with concern that the Agency's investigations have revealed further omissions in the statements made by Iran, including in the October declaration, in particular concerning the importation of P-2 components from abroad and concerning laser enrichment tests, which have produced samples enriched up to 15%, and also that Agency experts have raised questions and doubts regarding the explanations provided by Iran concerning those programmes, which require further clarification,

(j) Recognising the inalienable right of states to the development and practical application of atomic energy for peaceful purposes, including the production of electric power, consistent with their treaty obligations, with due consideration for the needs of the developing countries,

(k) Stressing the need for effective safeguards in order to prevent the use of nuclear material for prohibited purposes in contravention of safeguards agreements and underlining the vital importance of effective safeguards for facilitating cooperation in the field of nuclear energy, and

(I) Acknowledging the statement by the Director General on 14 June that it is essential for the integrity and credibility of the inspection process to bring these issues to a close within the next few months,

1. Acknowledges that Iranian cooperation has resulted in Agency access to all requested locations, including four workshops belonging to the Defence Industries Organisation;
2. Deplores, at the same time, the fact that, overall, as indicated by the Director General's written and oral reports, Iran's cooperation has

not been as full, timely and proactive as it should have been, and, in particular, that Iran postponed until mid-April visits originally scheduled for mid-March including visits of Agency centrifuge experts to a number of locations involved in Iran's P-2 centrifuge enrichment programme—resulting in some cases in a delay in the taking of environmental samples and their analysis;

3. Underlines that, with the passage of time, it is becoming ever more important that Iran work proactively to enable the Agency to gain a full understanding of Iran's enrichment programme by providing all relevant information, as well as by providing prompt access to all relevant places, data and persons; and calls on Iran to continue and intensify its cooperation so that the Agency may provide the international community with required assurances about Iran's nuclear activities;

4. Calls on Iran to take all necessary steps on an urgent basis to help resolve all outstanding questions, especially that of LEU and HEU contamination found at various locations in Iran, including by providing additional relevant information about the origin of the components in question and explanations about the presence of a cluster of 36% HEU particles; and also the question of the nature and scope of Iran's P-2 centrifuge programme, including by providing full documentation and explanations at the request of the Agency;

5. Welcomes Iran's submission of the declarations under Articles 2 and 3 of its Additional Protocol; and stresses the importance of Iran complying with the deadlines for further declarations required by Articles 2 and 3 of the Protocol, and that all such declarations should be correct and complete;

6. Emphasises the importance of Iran continuing to act in accordance with the provisions of the Additional Protocol to provide reassurance to the international community about the nature of Iran's nuclear programme; and urges Iran to ratify without delay its Protocol;

7. Recalls that in previous resolutions the Board called on Iran to suspend all enrichment-related and reprocessing activities; welcomes Iran's voluntary decisions in that respect; regrets that those commitments have not been comprehensively implemented and calls on Iran immediately to correct all remaining shortcomings, and to remove the existing variance in relation to the Agency's understanding of the scope of Iran's decisions regarding suspension, including by refraining from the production of UF6 and from all production of centrifuge components, as well as to enable the Agency to verify fully the suspension;

8. In the context of Iran's voluntary decisions to suspend all enrichment-related and reprocessing activities, calls on Iran, as a further confidence-building measure, voluntarily to reconsider its decision to begin production testing at the Uranium Conversion Facility and also, as an additional confidence building measure, to reconsider its decision to start construction of a research reactor moderated by heavy water, as the reversal of those decisions would make it easier for Iran to restore international confidence undermined by past reports of undeclared nuclear activities in Iran;
9. Recalls that the full and prompt cooperation with the Agency of all third countries is essential in the clarification of certain outstanding questions, notably contamination;
10. Commends the Director General and the Secretariat for their professional and impartial efforts to implement Iran's safeguards agreement, and, pending its entry into force, Iran's Additional Protocol, as well as to verify Iran's suspension of enrichment-related and reprocessing activities, and to investigate supply routes and sources;
11. Requests the Director General to report well in advance of the September Board—or earlier if appropriate—on these issues as well as on the implementation of this and prior resolutions on Iran; and
12. Decides to remain seized of the matter.

‹58›

Chairman's Statement at the end of 6-Party Nuclear Talks on North Korea in Beijing (26.06.2004)

> The parties stressed the need for a step by step process of "words for words" and "action for action" and noted some common elements, which would provide a useful basis for future work. The parties authorized the working group to define "corresponding measures" for first steps for de-nuclearisation.

The four-day third round of six-party talks on the Korean Peninsula nuclear issue concluded in Beijing Saturday morning and the parties made public a Chairman's Statement.

Following is the full text of the statement:

1. The third round of the six-party talks was held in Beijing among the People's Republic of China (PRC), the Democratic People's Republic of Korea (DPRK), Japan, the Republic of Korea (ROK), the Russian Federation (Russia) and the United States of America (USA) from June 23 to 26, 2004.
2. The heads of delegations were Mr. Wang Yi, vice-foreign minister of China; Mr. Kim Kye-gwan, vice-foreign minister of DPRK; Ambassador Mitoji Yabunaka, director-general for Asian and Oceanian Affairs of Ministry of Foreign Affairs of Japan; Ambassador Lee Soo-Hyuck, deputy minister of Foreign Affairs and Trade of ROK; Ambassador Alexander Alekseyev, special envoy of the Ministry of Foreign Affairs of Russia; Mr. James A. Kelly, assistant secretary of State for East Asian and Pacific Affairs, United States Department of State.
3. In preparation of the third round of the six-party talks, two sessions of the Working Group were held in Beijing from May 12 to 15 and from June 21 to 22, 2004. The parties approved the Concept Paper on the Working Group in the plenary.
4. During the third round of the talks, the parties had constructive, pragmatic and substantive discussions. Based on the consensus reached at the second round of the talks, as reflected in its Chairman's Statement, they reaffirmed their commitments to the goal of

denuclearization of the Korean Peninsula and stressed the need to take first steps toward that goal as soon as possible.

5. The parties stressed the need for a step-by-step process of "words for words" and "action for action" in search for a peaceful solution to the nuclear issue.
6. In this context, proposals, suggestions and recommendations were put forward by all parties. The parties welcomed the submission of those proposals, suggestions and recommendations, and noted some common elements, which would provide a useful basis for future work, while differences among the parties remained. The parties believed that further discussions were needed to expand their common ground and reduce existing differences.
7. The parties agreed in principle to hold the fourth round of the six-party talks in Beijing by the end of Sept. 2004, at a date to be decided through diplomatic channels with due consideration to the proceedings of the working group. The parties authorized the working group to convene at the earliest possible date to define the scope, duration and verification as well as corresponding measures for first steps for denuclearization, and as appropriate, make recommendations to the fourth round of the talks.
8. The delegations of the DPRK, Japan, the ROK, Russia and the USA expressed their appreciation to the Chinese side for its efforts for the success of the third round of the six-party talks.

‹59›

NATO: Istanbul Summit Communique (28.06.2004)

The 26 nations of the North Atlantic Alliance decided to expand NATO-led ISAF in Afghanistan, including through Provincial Reconstruction Teams; agreed to conclude the successful SFOR operation in Bosnia and Herzegovina and welcomed the readiness of EU to deploy a new UN mandated Chapter VII mission in the country; and decided to offer assistance to Iraq with the training of its security forces.

Istanbul Summit Communiqué

Issued by the Heads of State and Government participating in the meeting of the North Atlantic Council

1. We, the Heads of State and Government of the member countries of the North Atlantic Alliance, reaffirmed today the enduring value of the transatlantic link and of NATO as the basis for our collective defence and the essential forum for security consultation between Europe and North America. Our 26 nations are united in democracy, individual liberty and the rule of law, and faithful to the purposes and principles of the United Nations Charter. Inspired by the common vision embodied in the Washington Treaty, we remain fully committed to the collective defence of our populations, territory and forces. Transatlantic cooperation is essential in defending our values and meeting common threats and challenges, from wherever they may come.
2. At our last Summit, in Prague in 2002, we agreed to transform our Alliance with new members, new capabilities, and new relationships with our partners. Just a few months ago, seven new member countries – Bulgaria, Estonia, Latvia, Lithuania, Romania, Slovakia and Slovenia — joined our Alliance in the most robust round of enlargement in NATO's history. Today at our Istanbul Summit, we have given further shape and direction to this transformation in order to adapt NATO's structures, procedures and capabilities to 21st century challenges. We underscore that these efforts should not be perceived as a threat by any country or organisation. Our Alliance is taking on a full range of missions, promoting stability where it is needed to defend our security and our values.

3. Today, we have:

- decided to expand the NATO-led International Security Assistance Force (ISAF) in Afghanistan, including through several more Provincial Reconstruction Teams (PRTs) and by enhancing our support for the upcoming elections;
- agreed to conclude the Alliance's successful SFOR operation in Bosnia and Herzegovina, and welcomed the readiness of the European Union to deploy a new and distinct UN-mandated Chapter VII mission in the country, based on the Berlin+ arrangements agreed between our two organisations;
- confirmed that a robust KFOR presence remains essential to further enhance security and promote the political process in Kosovo;
- decided to enhance the contribution of Operation Active Endeavour, our maritime operation in the Mediterranean, to the fight against terrorism;
- decided to offer assistance to the Government of Iraq with the training of its security forces, in conformity with the separate statement that we have issued on Iraq;
- agreed on an enhanced set of measures to strengthen our individual and collective contribution to the international community's fight against terrorism;
- decided to further the transformation of our military capabilities to make them more modern, more usable and more deployable to carry out the full range of Alliance missions;
- reaffirmed that NATO's door remains open to new members, and encouraged Albania, Croatia and the former Yugoslav Republic of Macedonia to continue the reforms necessary to progress towards NATO membership;
- taken a number of steps to further strengthen the Euro-Atlantic Partnership, in particular through a special focus on engaging with our Partners in the strategically important regions of the Caucasus and Central Asia; and
- decided to enhance our Mediterranean Dialogue and to offer cooperation to the broader Middle East region through the "Istanbul Cooperation Initiative".

4. Contributing to peace and stability in Afghanistan is NATO's key priority. NATO's leadership of the UN-mandated International Security Assistance Force demonstrates the readiness of the North Atlantic Council to decide to launch operations to ensure our common security. NATO's aim is to assist in the emergence of a secure and stable Afghanistan, with a broad-based, gender sensitive, multi-ethnic and fully representative government, integrated into the international

community and cooperating with its neighbours. Establishing and sustaining peace in Afghanistan is essential to the well-being of the Afghan people and to our shared struggle against terrorism. We remain committed to that cause and pledge to contribute to ISAF the forces necessary for successful completion of our mission in Afghanistan.

5. In consultation with the Afghan authorities, we will continue to expand ISAF in stages throughout Afghanistan, through the establishment by lead nations of additional Provincial Reconstruction Teams. We will continue to coordinate and cooperate with Operation Enduring Freedom, as appropriate. The successful conduct of nation-wide elections will be a crucial milestone in the democratic development and peaceful evolution of Afghanistan. In response to President Karzai's request, ISAF is currently supporting the voter registration process and will provide enhanced support to the Afghan authorities in providing security during the election period, within means and capabilities. After the election, it will be for the government of Afghanistan to develop a forward-looking plan that fulfils the vision of the Bonn Agreement to promote national reconciliation, lasting peace, stability, and respect for human rights. ISAF has been assisting in disarming the militias and securing weapons. The Bonn process is on track and legitimate political institutions are developing. Reconstruction projects, security sector reform and other initiatives are improving the daily lives of many citizens. We strongly condemn the increasing attacks on civilian aid workers, who are making a valuable contribution to Afghanistan's future.
6. We call on the Afghan authorities to energetically pursue the disarmament, demobilisation and reintegration process, and particularly the withdrawal of military units from Kabul and other urban centres. We will provide appropriate support, within ISAF's mandate, to the Afghan authorities in taking resolute action against the production and trafficking of narcotics. We are prepared to help the Afghan government to build a better future for Afghanistan, together with Operation Enduring Freedom, the UN Assistance Mission to Afghanistan, the European Union, and other international organisations on the ground. We also call on Afghanistan's neighbours to contribute to this effort consistent with the wishes of the Afghan authorities. We commend the role of Canada in ISAF and look forward to the future role of the Eurocorps.
7. The security environment in the strategically important region of the Balkans is stable but remains fragile. The Alliance remains committed to peace and stability in the Balkans, and the territorial integrity and sovereignty of all the countries in the region. We will remain

committed until peace and security are firmly established and the progressive integration of all Balkan countries into Euro-Atlantic structures is achieved. All the countries of the region must assume ownership of, and implement, pressing reforms. Closer cooperation in their own region will help to promote stability and prosperity. While welcoming improvement in cooperation with the International Criminal Tribunal for the Former Yugoslavia (ICTY), where it has occurred, we stress that all countries concerned must cooperate fully with the ICTY, in particular bringing to justice all those who are indicted by the Tribunal, notably Radovan Karadzic and Ratko Mladic, as well as Ante Gotovina, in accordance with United Nations Security Council Resolutions 1503 and 1534.

8. As the security situation in Bosnia and Herzegovina has evolved positively, we have decided to conclude the Alliance's successful SFOR operation by the end of this year. We welcome the readiness of the European Union to deploy a new and distinct UN-mandated robust Chapter VII mission in the country, based on the Berlin+ arrangements agreed between our two organisations, and look forward to continued close cooperation. NATO's long-term political commitment to Bosnia and Herzegovina remains unchanged and the establishment of a NATO headquarters will constitute NATO's residual military presence in the country. NATO HQ Sarajevo, which has the principal task of providing advice on defence reform, will also undertake certain operational supporting tasks, such as counter-terrorism whilst ensuring force protection; supporting the ICTY, within means and capabilities, with regard to the detention of persons indicted for war crimes; and intelligence sharing with the EU. The Dayton/Paris Accords remain in force as the basis for peace and stability in Bosnia and Herzegovina.

9. In Kosovo, a robust KFOR presence remains essential to further enhance security and promote the political process. We reaffirm our commitment to a secure, stable and multi-ethnic Kosovo, on the basis of full implementation of United Nations Security Council Resolution 1244, the agreed Standards before Status Policy and the Standards Review Mechanism. We strongly condemn the outbreak of violence resulting in the loss of lives and the destruction of religious and cultural heritage sites in March 2004, and will not tolerate any such actions intended to undermine the political process. We call on all parties to speed up the reconstruction and to create conditions for the safe return of displaced persons. We urge all communities to work constructively towards meeting the internationally endorsed standards, to engage in dialogue at all levels, and to participate in local civic institutions. We also call on them to

conduct, and participate in, the upcoming October elections in a fair and peaceful manner. We welcome the appointment by the UN Secretary General of Mr. Søren Jessen-Petersen as his Special Representative in Kosovo. To further progress, NATO will continue to work with the UN, the EU, the OSCE and other international organisations, as well as the Contact Group, including, as appropriate, attendance at its meetings.

10. NATO's maritime surveillance and escort operation, Operation Active Endeavour, demonstrates the Alliance's resolve and ability to respond to terrorism. In March of this year, the operation was extended to the whole of the Mediterranean. Work is underway to further enhance its contribution to the fight against terrorism, including through the contributory support of partner countries, including the Mediterranean Dialogue countries. We welcome the offers of contributory support by Russia and Ukraine and have invited both countries to discuss the modalities of their participation. All such offers of support, including by other interested countries, will be considered on a case-by-case basis. In reviewing Operation Active Endeavour's mission, NATO may consider addressing, in accordance with international law, the risk of terrorist-related trafficking in, or use of, nuclear, chemical and biological weapons, their means of delivery and related materials.

11. We pay tribute to the men and women of all nations serving in NATO-led operations for their professionalism and dedication to the cause of peace and security. We appreciate how much the success of our operations depends on the bonds they build with the governments and peoples in the various theatres of operation. We are profoundly grateful for the sacrifice of those who have lost their lives or been injured in the course of their mission, and extend our deepest sympathies to their families and loved ones.

12. Terrorism and the proliferation of Weapons of Mass Destruction (WMD) and their means of delivery currently pose key threats and challenges to Alliance and international security.

13. We strongly condemn terrorism, whatever its motivations or manifestations, and will fight it together as long as necessary. The Alliance provides an essential transatlantic dimension to the response against terrorism, which requires the closest possible cooperation of North America and Europe. We are committed to continue our struggle against terrorism in all its forms, in accordance with international law provisions and UN principles. Our approach to terrorism, and its causes, will include the full implementation of United Nations Security Council Resolution 1373 on the fight against terrorism, and will continue to be multi-faceted and comprehensive, including political,

diplomatic, economic and, where necessary, military means. Continuing terrorist acts, including in Istanbul last year and in Madrid in March of this year, have shown the acute threat which terrorism continues to pose around the world. Defence against terrorism may include activities by NATO's military forces, based on decisions by the North Atlantic Council, to deter, disrupt, defend and protect against terrorist attacks, or threat of attacks, directed from abroad, against populations, territory, infrastructure and forces of any member state, including by acting against these terrorists and those who harbour them. We have accordingly agreed today an enhanced set of measures to strengthen our individual and collective contribution to the international community's fight against terrorism, including the need to prevent WMD from being acquired by terrorists. These measures include:

- improved intelligence sharing between our nations, including through our Terrorist Threat Intelligence Unit and a review of current intelligence structures at NATO Headquarters;
- a greater ability to respond rapidly to national requests for assistance in protecting against and dealing with the consequences of terrorist attacks, including attacks involving chemical, biological, radiological and nuclear (CBRN) weapons and, in this regard, continued robust support for the NATO Multinational CBRN Defence Battalion;
- assistance to protect selected major events, including with NATO Airborne Early Warning and Control Aircraft;
- an enhanced contribution to the fight against terrorism by Operation Active Endeavour;
- a continued robust effort through our operations in the Balkans and Afghanistan to help create conditions in which terrorism cannot flourish;
- enhanced capabilities to defend against terrorist attacks, including through our programme of work to develop new, advanced technologies; and
- increased cooperation with our partners, including through the implementation of our Civil Emergency Action Plan and the Partnership Action Plan on Terrorism, and with other international and regional organisations, including the active pursuit of consultations and exchange of information with the European Union.

14. The Alliance's policy of support for arms control, disarmament and non-proliferation will continue to play a major role in the achievement of the Alliance's security objectives, including preventing the proliferation of Weapons of Mass Destruction and their means of delivery. We stress the importance of all states abiding by, and fully implementing, their arms control, disarmament, and non-proliferation

commitments, and of strengthening existing international arms control and disarmament accords and multilateral non-proliferation and export control regimes. In this regard, early admission of all NATO members into all appropriate existing non-proliferation regimes would play a positive role. Today, we:

- underline our commitment to reinforcing the Nuclear Non-Proliferation Treaty, the cornerstone of non-proliferation and disarmament, and ensuring the full compliance with it by all states Party to the Treaty;
- underline the importance of related other international accords, including the Biological and Toxin Weapons Convention, the Chemical Weapons Convention and the Hague Code of Conduct against the Proliferation of Ballistic Missiles;
- strongly support United Nations Security Council Resolution 1540, calling on all states to establish effective national export controls, to adopt and enforce laws to criminalise proliferation, to take cooperative action to prevent non-state actors from acquiring WMD, and to end illicit trafficking in WMD and related materials;
- resolve to strengthen our common efforts to reduce and safeguard nuclear and radiological material;
- resolve to prevent and contain proliferation of WMD and their means of delivery, and to work together to achieve these objectives;
- welcome the adoption by the G-8 of its Action Plan on Non-Proliferation adopted on 10 June; and
- welcome the discovery and ongoing investigation of the A.Q. Khan proliferation network.

15. The Alliance underscores its strong support for the aims of the Proliferation Security Initiative (PSI) and its Statement of Interdiction Principles to establish a more co-ordinated and effective basis through which to impede and stop shipments of WMD, delivery systems, and related materials flowing to and from states and non-state actors of proliferation concern. The Alliance welcomes PSI efforts which are consistent with national legal authorities and relevant international law and frameworks, including United Nations Security Council Resolutions. We call on our partners and other countries to join us in supporting and implementing the objectives of the PSI.

16. The Alliance welcomes the steps taken by Libya to implement its decision, announced on 19 December 2003, to dismantle its WMD programmes under international supervision, and to limit its missiles to a range less than 300 kilometres. We look forward to continued progress. At the same time, we urge Libya to respect fundamental human rights.

17. We reiterate our commitment to the CFE Treaty as a cornerstone of European security, and reaffirm our attachment to the early entry into force of the Adapted Treaty. We recall that fulfilment of the remaining Istanbul commitments on the Republic of Georgia and the Republic of Moldova will create the conditions for Allies and other States Parties to move forward on ratification of the Adapted CFE Treaty. We note the progress that was made in 2003 on withdrawal of Russian military forces from the Republic of Moldova. We regret that this progress has not continued in 2004 and that the extended 31 December 2003 completion date, agreed in the framework of the OSCE, was not met. It is essential that efforts be intensified to complete the withdrawal as soon as possible. We will continue, via the OSCE, to monitor and assist in this process. We urge a swift resolution of the outstanding issues between Georgia and Russia as set out in their Istanbul Joint Statement of 17 November 1999, and to this end, call upon the parties to resume negotiations at an appropriately senior level. We welcome the approach of non-CFE Allies who have stated their intention to request accession to the Adapted CFE Treaty upon its entry into force. Their accession would provide an important additional contribution to European security and stability.

18. We welcome the progress made in the transformation of the Alliance's military capabilities. This is a long-term endeavour which must continue if NATO is to be able to perform the full range of its missions in a challenging security environment and respond to its operational commitments and the threats we face today, including terrorism and the proliferation of weapons of mass destruction. NATO must be able to field forces that can move quickly to sustain operations over distance and time.

19. In realising the goals we set at the Prague Summit in November 2002:
   - the NATO Multinational CBRN Defence Battalion has just become fully operational;
   - as planned, the operationally flexible NATO Response Force (NRF) will reach initial operational capability later this year;
   - the implementation of NATO's streamlined command arrangements is on track, including the establishment of Allied Command Transformation;
   - the implementation of national Prague Capabilities Commitments (PCC) is progressing, and multinational activities – in strategic sealift and airlift, air-to-air refuelling, and the Alliance Ground Surveillance system – continue to make progress and will enhance our military capabilities in many areas; and

- we are examining options for addressing the increasing missile threat to Alliance territory, forces and population centres through an appropriate mix of political and defence efforts, along with deterrence. We note the initiation of the feasibility study on missile defence decided at Prague to examine options, and we continue to assess the missile threats.

20. In order to meet today's challenges, we need the right capabilities. In some cases nations could free up resources from no longer needed national force structures and/or capabilities and reinvest them in deployable capabilities. We need greater willingness and preparedness of nations to provide these forces and capabilities. NATO needs to be able to act quickly and is configured to do so. At the same time, we are determined to further enhance our political decision-making process through in-depth consultations facilitating a common sense of purpose and resolve, the definition of clear strategies and objectives before launching an operation, as well as enhanced planning to support nations' contributions to operations – recognising the sovereign right of each of our nations to decide upon the use of its forces.

21. In order to enhance our ability to conduct operations successfully and strengthen the link between political agreement to commence operations and the provision of the necessary forces, we have today:

- welcomed the commitments made by the seven new Allies in the framework of the Prague Capabilities Commitment, and reaffirmed our support for it; we welcomed the cooperation between PCC and European Capabilities Action Plan groups; we will give special emphasis in our national plans to overcoming remaining critical shortages, implementing our national commitments, further advancing the multinational cooperation projects in which our countries participate, and making our capabilities interoperable and adapting them to the evolving security environment;
- welcomed the report from our Defence Ministers on further steps to increase the usability of our forces through the adoption in Istanbul of high-level political targets and to supplement such targets through individual national usability targets, and agreed to intensify our efforts, taking account of national priorities and obligations, to structure, prepare and equip land forces for deployed operations under NATO or other auspices;
- welcomed changes to the Alliance's planning processes, making them more responsive to current and future operational requirements. We have directed the Council in Permanent Session to produce for our consideration comprehensive political guidance in support of the Strategic Concept for all Alliance capabilities issues, planning disciplines

and intelligence, responsive to the Alliance's requirements, including for forces which are interoperable and deployable, able to carry out major operations as well as smaller ones, to conduct them concurrently if necessary, as well as to operate jointly in a complex security environment. The interfaces between the respective Alliance planning disciplines, including operational planning, should be further analysed;

- welcomed progress in the work to improve the force generation process for NATO-agreed operations and the NATO Response Force, including by moving towards a longer-term and more comprehensive and pro-active approach, and facilitating decisions that are matched at each stage with the requisite military capabilities; and
- directed that work on theatre ballistic missile defence be taken forward expeditiously. In this context we noted the approval of the principle of the establishment of a NATO Active Layered Theatre Ballistic Missile Defence programme; welcomed the willingness of nations to make the tri-national Extended Air Defence Task Force available to the Alliance; and noted ongoing work by the NATO Military Authorities in relation to the defence of deployed NATO forces, including the NRF, against theatre ballistic missiles.

22. With the decisions taken here in Istanbul and the further improvements we have put in train and which we have directed the Council in Permanent Session to pursue, we are ensuring that Allied capabilities will be modern, efficient and flexible, fully appropriate to the challenges we face now and may face in the future.

23. We have invited the Secretary General and the Council in Permanent Session to take the steps necessary to ensure that the transformation process, including on questions of management and funding, is fully implemented. We look forward to the outcome of the NATO Agencies Review which should provide a sound basis for the next decade of support activity. We encourage the Secretary General to carry forward the new NATO Headquarters project in a timely and effective way.

24. NATO's armament activities must meet the Alliance's evolving military needs. We therefore reaffirm the importance we attach to mutually advantageous transatlantic defence industrial cooperation.

25. We celebrate the success of NATO's Open Door policy, and reaffirm today that our seven new members will not be the last. The door to membership remains open. We welcome the progress made by Albania, Croatia and the former Yugoslav Republic of Macedonia in implementing their Annual National Programmes under the Membership Action Plan, and encourage them to continue pursuing the reforms necessary to progress towards NATO membership. We also commend their contribution to regional stability and cooperation. We want all

three countries to succeed and will continue to assist them in their reform efforts. NATO will continue to assess each country's candidacy individually, based on the progress made towards reform goals pursued through the Membership Action Plan, which will remain the vehicle to keep the readiness of each aspirant for membership under review. We direct that NATO Foreign Ministers keep the enlargement process, including the implementation of the Membership Action Plan, under continual review and report to us. We will review at the next Summit progress by aspirants towards membership based on that report.

26. The recent enlargements of NATO and the European Union are a major step towards a Europe whole and free, and a strong confirmation that our organisations share common values and strategic interests. We are pleased with the progress made in developing the NATO-EU strategic partnership on the basis of and since the conclusion of the Berlin+ arrangements. NATO and the EU continue to cooperate effectively in the Western Balkans, and are committed to assist the countries of the region in their further integration into Euro-Atlantic structures. NATO-EU relations now cover a wide range of issues of common interest relating to security, defence and crisis management, including the fight against terrorism, the development of coherent and mutually reinforcing military capabilities, and civil emergency planning. We are determined to work together to further develop the NATO-EU strategic partnership as agreed by our two organisations, in a spirit of transparency, and respecting the autonomy of our two organisations.

27. Building on the progress made since our Prague Summit, we have today taken a number of steps to further strengthen the Euro-Atlantic Partnership. While taking these steps, we expect all Partners to fulfil their commitments to the protection and promotion of human rights and the other fundamental freedoms and values they have adhered to under the Euro-Atlantic Partnership Council and the Partnership for Peace. We support the independence, sovereignty and territorial integrity of all states in the Euro-Atlantic area.

28. We have launched today a Partnership Action Plan on Defence Institution Building. We encourage and support Partners to make full use of this new instrument to build democratically responsible defence institutions.

29. Military interoperability and transformation are central to the effectiveness of our Partnerships in helping us to meet evolving security challenges and to enable Allied and Partner forces to operate effectively in NATO-led operations. The value of this cooperation to the Alliance, in particular by the Western European Partners, is

continuously being demonstrated in the Balkans as well as in Afghanistan. We intend, therefore, to provide our Partners with increased opportunities to enhance their contributions to NATO-led operations, and to help transform their defences in keeping with NATO's own evolving operational roles and capabilities, including through enhancement of the Operational Capabilities Concept. We will seek the earliest possible involvement by troop-contributing nations in the decision-shaping process, including the possibility of political consultation. NATO's new command structure offers opportunities to increase the participation by Partners, including by offering them appropriate representation in the Allied Command Transformation.

30. NATO has adopted a comprehensive policy to contribute to international efforts to combat the trafficking in human beings, which constitutes a flagrant abuse of human rights and fuels corruption and organised crime. We are also determined to work together with our Partners to support international efforts, where NATO can add value, to combat this and other forms of illegal trafficking.

31. In enhancing the Euro-Atlantic Partnership, we will put special focus on engaging with our Partners in the strategically important regions of the Caucasus and Central Asia. Towards that end, NATO has agreed on improved liaison arrangements, including the assignment of two liaison officers, as well as a special representative for the two regions from within the International Staff. We welcome the decision by Georgia, Azerbaijan and Uzbekistan to develop Individual Partnership Action Plans with NATO. This constitutes a significant step in these countries' efforts to develop closer Partnership relations with the Alliance. We welcome the commitment of the new government of Georgia to reform.

32. We remain committed to partnership with the Republic of Moldova and encourage it to make use of Partnership instruments to take forward its aspirations of promoting stability in the region as a Partner of this Alliance.

33. We look forward to welcoming Bosnia and Herzegovina and Serbia and Montenegro into the Partnership for Peace once they have met the established NATO conditions. We want them to succeed in joining the Euro-Atlantic partnership and will assist them in this endeavour. We are prepared to assist the countries by including them in selected PfP activities. Each country will be judged on its own merits on the road to PfP.

34. We welcome Bosnia and Herzegovina's significant progress in defence reform, a key condition for PfP membership. We urge continued progress towards achieving a single military force. We have agreed

to designate a Contact Point Embassy in Sarajevo to increase understanding of NATO. We are concerned that Bosnia and Herzegovina, particularly obstructionist elements in the Republika Srpska entity, has failed to live up to its obligation to cooperate fully with ICTY, including the arrest and transfer to the jurisdiction of the Tribunal of war crimes indictees, a fundamental requirement for the country to join PfP. We also look for systemic changes necessary to develop effective security and law enforcement structures.

35. Serbia and Montenegro has also shown progress in defence reform, and the government has played a constructive regional role, improving relations with its neighbours. We look forward to further progress in these areas, in particular in relation to the government's engagement on Kosovo-related issues. At the same time, the International Court of Justice cases against several of the Allies still stand. We call on the government to fulfil its international obligations, in particular to cooperate with ICTY and render all necessary assistance to secure the arrest and transfer to the jurisdiction of the Tribunal of war crimes indictees.

36. From its inception in 1994, NATO's Mediterranean Dialogue has greatly contributed to building confidence and cooperation between the Alliance and its Mediterranean partners. In the current security environment there are greater opportunities for effective cooperation with Mediterranean Dialogue partners. Following our decision at Prague to upgrade the Mediterranean Dialogue, we are today inviting our Mediterranean partners to establish a more ambitious and expanded partnership, guided by the principle of joint ownership and taking into consideration their particular interests and needs. The overall aim of this partnership will be to contribute towards regional security and stability through stronger practical cooperation, including by enhancing the existing political dialogue, achieving interoperability, developing defence reform and contributing to the fight against terrorism. Our efforts will complement and mutually reinforce other Mediterranean initiatives, including those of the EU and the OSCE.

37. We have today also decided to offer cooperation to the broader Middle East region by launching our "Istanbul Cooperation Initiative". This initiative is offered by NATO to interested countries in the region, starting with the countries of the Gulf Cooperation Council, to foster mutually beneficial bilateral relationships and thus enhance security and stability. The initiative focuses on practical cooperation where NATO can add value, notably in the defence and security fields. This initiative is distinct from, yet takes into account and complements, other initiatives involving other international actors.

38. While respecting the specificity of the Mediterranean Dialogue, the enhanced Mediterranean Dialogue and the "Istanbul Cooperation Initiative" are complementary, progressive and individualised processes. They will be developed in a spirit of joint ownership with the countries involved. Continued consultation and active engagement will be essential to their success.

39. Since its creation two years ago, the NATO-Russia Council has raised the quality of the relationship between the Alliance and Russia to a new level, to the benefit of the entire Euro-Atlantic area. We reaffirm our determination to broaden our political dialogue and are committed to deepening our consultations on key security issues, including Afghanistan and the Balkans, and the fight against terrorism and against the proliferation of Weapons of Mass Destruction and their means of delivery. Our practical cooperation has progressed further, including in military-to-military projects. Through our efforts to improve interoperability, we have also laid the groundwork for future operational support to NATO forces, including for potential joint peacekeeping operations. We welcome the progress made in advancing practical cooperation on theatre missile defence, civil emergency planning, the Cooperative Airspace Initiative, and search and rescue at sea. We look forward to making further progress in implementing the Rome Declaration of May 2002, working together as equal partners in areas of common interest.

40. We welcome Ukraine's determination to pursue full Euro-Atlantic integration. In this context, we reaffirm the necessity to achieve consistent and measurable progress in democratic reform. We encourage Ukraine to accelerate the implementation of the objectives outlined in the NATO-Ukraine Action Plan, particularly regarding the conduct of free and fair elections, the guaranteeing of media freedoms, and implementation of the results of the Defence Review. We are determined to support Ukraine in these efforts, while noting that a further strengthening of our relationship will require stronger evidence of Ukraine's commitment to comprehensive reform, in particular with a view to the conduct of presidential elections this autumn. We welcome Ukraine's continued participation in KFOR within the Polish-Ukrainian Battalion. We note the progress made by Ukraine in defence reform and in strengthening defence and military cooperation with NATO, including in the area of host nation support and strategic airlift. With this understanding, we instruct the Council in Permanent Session to assess NATO-Ukraine relations, with a view to presenting recommendations to Foreign Ministers after the presidential elections.

41. We note the importance of the Black Sea region for Euro-Atlantic security. Littoral countries, Allies and Partners are working together

to contribute to further strengthening security and stability in the area. Our Alliance is prepared to explore means to complement these efforts, building upon existing forms of regional cooperation.

42. We welcome the interest shown by several countries who are developing individual, mutually beneficial dialogues on security matters with NATO as contact countries. In this context, we welcome the interest shown by Australia in closer cooperation with our Alliance.

43. NATO and the OSCE have largely complementary responsibilities and common interests, both functionally and geographically. NATO will continue to further develop the cooperation with the OSCE in areas such as conflict prevention, crisis management and post-conflict rehabilitation.

44. We welcome the role of the NATO Parliamentary Assembly in complementing NATO's efforts to promote stability throughout Europe. We also appreciate the contribution made by the Atlantic Treaty Association in promoting better understanding of the Alliance and its objectives among our publics.

45. Today's complex strategic environment demands a broad approach to security, comprising political, economic and military elements. We are united in our commitment to such an approach. The Alliance is conducting challenging operations in regions of strategic importance; transforming its capabilities to meet the new threats; and working ever more closely together with partner countries and other international organisations in a truly multilateral effort to address common security concerns. While NATO's transformation continues, its fundamental purpose – based on the common values of democracy, human rights and the rule of law – endures: to serve as an essential transatlantic forum for consultation and an effective instrument for Europe and North America to defend peace and stability, now and into the future.

46. We express our deep appreciation for the gracious hospitality extended to us by the Government of Turkey and the city of Istanbul. Here in Istanbul, a city that bridges two continents, we have reaffirmed the vital transatlantic link, and extended new offers of cooperation to countries and to regions of strategic importance.

❮60❯

Bangkok Leadership Statement at the end of AIDS Conference, Thailand (16.07.2004)

> Recognising that 38 million people are living with HIV/AIDS and that enough had not been done to protect them, the leaders committed themselves to coordinate efforts among themselves and with international organizations through mechanisms such as the World AIDS Campaign and strengthen the principles and implementation of the "three ones" as articulated by UNAIDS and its partners.

The leadership programme of the XV International AIDS Conference in Bangkok brought together leaders of people living with HIV, males who have sex with males, people who inject drugs, sex workers, women, young people, leaders from AIDS programmes, governments, NGOs/CBOs, the private sector, religion, science, uniformed services, and the world of work. This is our statement of commitment. Today we leaders remember the millions of people who have died as a result of AIDS and the millions of people who are living with HIV. These were and are the first AIDS leaders, struggling with neglect, social exclusion, discrimination, abuse and denial. We pay our respects to people living with HIV, who are the primary leaders in the fight against the epidemic. Most of them are unrecognized and their struggle is silent and invisible.

We are ashamed that in 2004 some 38 million people are living with HIV/AIDS and fighting the same battles after two decades. Despite all that we have learned about what works in prevention and treatment, the epidemic is on the rise in every region.

We recognise that we have not done enough to protect people from new infections. We have not done enough to provide access to affordable treatment and care to all those who need it. We have not done enough to combat stigma, unnecessary criminalization, and discrimination, or to reduce the risk and vulnerability of tens of millions of young people and adults.

We are also concerned that we have not succeeded in meaningfully involving infected and affected people in our response.

We acknowledge that **we have failed** to provide enough information, education, prevention tools and technologies, treatment, care and support. Our inability to ensure human rights, equity, opportunities, and a supportive and enabling environment for all has helped to fuel the epidemic.

Chapter 60 Bangkok Leadership Statement at the end of AIDS Conference

Today we as leaders from all levels and all sectors, have come together to commit to improving the quality of life of those people who are living with HIV/AIDS or, affected by it, and to prevent further infections. We hold ourselves accountable – collectively and individually—to strategies and actions including:

- Supportive policies and legislation
- Scaled up programmes in prevention, care, treatment and impact alleviation
- Increased financial and human resources
- Mobilizing other leaders in the response
- Accountability to fulfilling all commitments and promises made so far

We commit to transforming our world into a loving and caring one, and to working towards changing the attitude of everyone in the community, in order to eradicate stigma, unnecessary criminalization, and discrimination. The leaders among us from government, the private sector, the community and the world of work commit ourselves to coordinate efforts, not only among ourselves but also with international organizations and donors and through mechanisms such as the World AIDS Campaign. We also reaffirm and strengthen the principles and implementation of the "three ones" as articulated by UNAIDS and its partners. We commit to strengthen a broad-based multiministerial and multi-sectoral response.

We are deeply concerned that our response to the epidemic is often motivated by value judgments. We commit to base our actions on human rights, informed science and to implement evidence-based interventions.

We must acknowledge the threat to, and suffering, of all vulnerable people including children, young people, women, sex workers, people who inject drugs, males who have sex with males and migrant and displaced persons – and commit to reducing their vulnerability to HIV infection.

The world has agreed on the UNGASS Declaration of Commitments and other declarations that focus on achieving an exceptional response to HIV/AIDS. Our Leadership Statement supports these earlier commitments of the world's leaders and holds governments, the private sector, communities and international organizations accountable for its implementation.

We the leaders from various communities and groups gathered here have developed our own respective declaration of leadership commitments. These statements of commitment are an integral part of this Bangkok Leadership Statement and we want the world to pay special attention to them. The statements of each group will motivate the leaders from that group and will be their guide to action. Each group commits to develop mechanisms of accountability towards the fulfillment of their commitments.

Realising the urgency for action, we promise to start acting on our commitments immediately and to report on our progress at the XVI International AIDS Conference in Toronto.

(As presented at the XV International AIDS Conference by Ms. Graca Machel, Patron of the Leadership Programme on July *16, 2004 in Bangkok.*)

❮61❯

BIMST-EC Summit Declaration (31.07.2004)

> The leaders agreed that the grouping shall henceforth be known as Bay of Bengal Initiative for Multi-Sectoral Technical and Economic Cooperation. They agreed inter alia, to promote sustainable and optimal energy utilization through development of new hydrocarbon and hydropower projects, inter-connection of electricity and natural gas grids and renewable energy technologies.

Following is the text of the declaration issued at the conclusion of the first BIMSTEC Summit in Bangkok on July 31, 2004:

"We, the Prime Minister of the People's Republic of Bangladesh, the Prime Minister of the Kingdom of Bhutan, the Prime Minister of the Republic of India, the Prime Minister of the Union of Myanmar, the Prime Minister of the Kingdom of Nepal, the President of the Democratic Socialist Republic of Sri Lanka and the Prime Minister of The Kingdom of Thailand gathered in Bangkok, Thailand, on 31 July 2004 for the first BIMSTEC summit meeting;

Convinced that the geographical location of our countries and our rich natural and human resources provide a sound basis for mutually beneficial cooperation,

Recognizing that the pluralistic nature of our societies, our shared cultural heritage and the rich diversity of languages, arts, crafts and traditions provide ample opportunity for multi-dimensional cooperation within our region;

Convinced that regional and sub-regional economic cooperation such as ours contribute to efforts towards global free and fair trade being pursued under the multilateral trading regime,

Affirming that the above realities provide a firm foundation on which to build our partnership and overall cooperation;

Resolving to foster a sense of community that will lead to the economic and social development of the entire region;

Do hereby:

Agree that grouping shall henceforth be known as BIMSTEC or the Bay of Bengal Initiative for Multi-Sectoral Technical and Economic Cooperation.

Commit ourselves to the founding objectives and principles of BIMSTEC; to assess the challenges and opportunities for economic cooperation in our region; and to strengthen BIMSTEC's ability to find ways and means to realize those challenges and opportunities effectively and efficiently.

Note with satisfaction BIMSTEC's achievements so far, including the signing of the Framework Agreement for a BIMSTEC Free Trade Area, the launch of Visit BIMSTEC Year 2004-2005 and the year-long Plan of Action on tourism, the establishment of the BIMSTEC Chamber of Commerce, the first BIMSTEC Youth Football Tournament held in Phuket, the establishment of the BIMSTEC Center in Bangkok, and a biomass gasifier plant in Myanmar, and pledge to move forward with renewed vigor.

Agree to focus on specific areas of cooperation, including but not limited to trade & investment, transport & communications, tourism, energy, human resources development, agriculture, fisheries, science & technology and people-to-people contact.

Agree to explore the expansion of BIMSTEC cooperation into the areas of culture, education, public health, protection of biodiversity and traditional knowledge, rural community development, small and medium-scale enterprise, construction, environment, information and communications technology, biotechnology, weather & climate research, natural disaster mitigation & management.

Agree to take all possible steps including timely completion of the Free Trade Area negotiations for realization of the full potential of BIMSTEC trade and investment, taking into account the special needs of individual member countries.

Recognize that future cooperation under BIMSTEC requires the development of key infrastructure, in particular transportation & communication linkages, to facilitate tourism, trade and investment and accordingly agree to strengthen and accelerate cooperation for developing concrete regional project proposals such as the ongoing negotiations on road linkages between the member countries.

Agree to promote sustainable and optimal energy utilization through development of new hydrocarbon and hydropower projects, interconnection of electricity and natural gas grids, energy conservation, and renewable energy technologies.

Agree to coordinate our diverse strengths in the tourism sector to drive maximum benefit from our natural, cultural and historical attractions, and recognize the need to enhance inter-regional tourism through such strategies as joint marketing of intra-BIMSTEC tourism packages, exchange of visits and information as well as sub-regional tourism co-operation.

Agree to facilitate travel within the region for business travel, exchange programmes and tourism, including through the introduction of a BIMSTEC Business Travel Card/Visa.

Encourage the private sector to explore ways to tap the economic partnership potential of the member economies and make full use of BIMSTEC opportunities.

Agree to intensify cooperation to promote the sustainable use of the marine resources in the Bay of Bengal through effective management and conservation in close coordination with the already existing frameworks, including the Bay of Bengal Programme-Inter-Governmental Organisation (BOBP-IGO).

Agree to enhance technical cooperation aimed at capacity building, and recognize the potential for public and private organizations to expand existing cooperation in this area.

Express grave concern at the continuing threat of international terrorism and transnational crime that has adversely affected the economic and social progress of the peoples of the BIMSTEC region; recognize that the solidarity and friendship existing among member states could be utilized as a basis to counter this threat; agree, as an urgent priority, to co-ordinate our efforts to combat this menace, including through the exchange of information among concerned agencies, and other concrete programmes of co-operation, and resolve to continue active co-operation in ongoing efforts of the international community in combating terrorism in all its forms and manifestations, by whosoever it is perpetrated irrespective of its cause of stated rationale.

Agree to coordinate our efforts to address, as a matter of priority, transnational issues that threaten the economic and social progress of the peoples of the BIMSTEC region, including HIV/AIDS and other threats to public health such as malaria, tuberculosis, and polio; and encourage active cooperation among concerned agencies, including through the exchange of information, sharing of experiences and other concrete programmes.

Decide to proactively promote increased interaction among our peoples through programmes, such as exchanges of parliamentarians, media persons, students and faculty, sports persons, as well as exchanges in the fields of performing arts and entertainment, such as motion pictures, television programmes and music.

Decide to accord priority to projects that could be clearly conceptualized, adequately funded and effectively implemented, with well-defined goals and tangible results relevant to the needs of our peoples, based, as far as possible, on internal financing from within the BIMSTEC countries.

Agree to streamline procedures and protocols to make BIMSTEC more efficient and output-based.

Agree that once a clear and focused programme of cooperation is in place, appropriate formal institutional mechanisms would be established, jointly and within each member country, for effective coordination and implementation.

Agree to task their Foreign Ministers with the responsibility of coordinating overall BIMSTEC cooperation.

We express our gratitude to the Government of Thailand for the warm hospitality and excellent arrangements made for the Summit.

❮62❯

WTO Draft Framework Deal on Agriculture, Industrial Tariffs and Customs procedure, Geneva (01.08.2004)

Taking note of the report by the Chairman of the Trade Negotiations Committee (TNC) the General Council adopted a framework for establishing modalities in agriculture, cotton, and market access for non-agricultural products. The Council also suggested modalities for negotiations on trade facilitation and made recommendations for trade in services.

Doha Work Programme

Decision Adopted by the General Council on 1 August 2004

1. The General Council reaffirms the Ministerial Declarations and Decisions adopted at Doha and the full commitment of all Members to give effect to them. The Council emphasizes Members' resolve to complete the Doha Work Programme fully and to conclude successfully the negotiations launched at Doha. Taking into account the Ministerial Statement adopted at Cancún on 14 September 2003, and the statements by the Council Chairman and the Director-General at the Council meeting of 15-16 December 2003, the Council takes note of the report by the Chairman of the Trade Negotiations Committee (TNC) and agrees to take action as follows:
   - **a. Agriculture**: the General Council adopts the framework set out in Annex A to this document.
   - **b. Cotton**: the General Council reaffirms the importance of the Sectoral Initiative on Cotton and takes note of the parameters set out in Annex A within which the trade-related aspects of this issue will be pursued in the agriculture negotiations. The General Council also attaches importance to the development aspects of the Cotton Initiative and wishes to stress the complementarity between the trade and development aspects. The Council takes note of the recent Workshop on Cotton in Cotonou on 23-24 March 2004 organized by the WTO Secretariat, and other bilateral and multilateral efforts to make progress on the development assistance aspects and instructs the Secretariat to continue to

work with the development community and to provide the Council with periodic reports on relevant developments.

Members should work on related issues of development multilaterally with the international financial institutions, continue their bilateral programmes, and all developed countries are urged to participate. In this regard, the General Council instructs the Director General to consult with the relevant international organizations, including the Bretton Woods Institutions, the Food and Agriculture Organization and the International Trade Centre to direct effectively existing programmes and any additional resources towards development of the economies where cotton has vital importance.

c. **Non-agricultural Market Access**: the General Council adopts the framework set out in Annex B to this document.

d. **Development**:

Principles: development concerns form an integral part of the Doha Ministerial Declaration. The General Council rededicates and recommits Members to fulfilling the development dimension of the Doha Development Agenda, which places the needs and interests of developing and least-developed countries at the heart of the Doha Work Programme.The Council reiterates the important role that enhanced market access, balanced rules, and well targeted, sustainably financed technical assistance and capacity building programmes can play in the economic development of these countries.

Special and Differential Treatment: the General Council reaffirms that provisions for special and differential (S&D) treatment are an integral part of the WTO Agreements. The Council recalls Ministers' decision in Doha to review all S&D treatment provisions with a view to strengthening them and making them more precise, effective and operational. The Council recognizes the progress that has been made so far. The Council instructs the Committee on Trade and Development in Special Session to expeditiously complete the review of all the outstanding Agreement-specific proposals and report to the General Council, with clear recommendations for a decision, by July 2005. The Council further instructs the Committee, within the parameters of the Doha mandate, to address all other outstanding work, including on the cross-cutting issues, the monitoring mechanism and the incorporation of S&D treatment into the architecture of WTO rules, as referred to in TN/CTD/7 and report, as appropriate, to the General Council. The Council also instructs all WTO bodies to which proposals in Category II have been referred to expeditiously complete the consideration of these proposals and report to the General Council, with clear recommendations for a decision, as soon as possible and no later than July 2005. In doing so these bodies will ensure that, as far as possible, their meetings do not overlap so as to enable full and effective participation of developing countries in these discussions.

Technical Assistance: the General Council recognizes the progress that has been made since the Doha Ministerial Conference in expanding Trade-Related Technical Assistance (TRTA) to developing countries and low-income countries in transition. In furthering this effort the Council affirms that such countries, and in particular least-developed countries, should be provided with enhanced TRTA and capacity building, to increase their effective participation in the negotiations, to facilitate their implementation of WTO rules, and to enable them to adjust and diversify their economies. In this context the Council welcomes and further encourages the improved coordination with other agencies, including under the Integrated Framework for TRTA for the LDCs (IF) and the Joint Integrated Technical Assistance Programme (JITAP).

Implementation: concerning implementation-related issues, the General Council reaffirms the mandates Ministers gave in paragraph 12 of the Doha Ministerial Declaration and the Doha Decision on Implementation-Related Issues and Concerns, and renews Members' determination to find appropriate solutions to outstanding issues. The Council instructs the Trade Negotiations Committee, negotiating bodies and other WTO bodies concerned to redouble their efforts to find appropriate solutions as a priority. Without prejudice to the positions of Members, the Council requests the Director-General to continue with his consultative process on all outstanding implementation issues under paragraph 12(b) of the Doha Ministerial Declaration, including on issues related to the extension of the protection of geographical indications provided for in Article 23 of the TRIPS Agreement to products other than wines and spirits, if need be by appointing Chairpersons of concerned WTO bodies as his Friends and/or by holding dedicated consultations. The Director-General shall report to the TNC and the General Council no later than May 2005. The Council shall review progress and take any appropriate action no later than July 2005.

Other Development Issues: in the ongoing market access negotiations, recognising the fundamental principles of the WTO and relevant provisions of GATT 1994, special attention shall be given to the specific trade and development related needs and concerns of developing countries, including capacity constraints. These particular concerns of developing countries, including relating to food security, rural development, livelihood, preferences, commodities and net food imports, as well as prior unilateral liberalisation, should be taken into consideration, as appropriate, in the course of the Agriculture and NAMA negotiations. The trade-related issues identified for the fuller integration of small, vulnerable economies into the multilateral trading system, should also be addressed, without creating a sub-category of Members, as part of a work programme, as mandated in paragraph 35 of the Doha Ministerial Declaration.

Least-Developed Countries: the General Council reaffirms the commitments made at Doha concerning least-developed countries and renews its determination to fulfil these commitments. Members will continue to take due account of the concerns of least-developed countries in the negotiations. The Council confirms that nothing in this Decision shall detract in any way from the special provisions agreed by Members in respect of these countries.

e. **Services**: the General Council takes note of the report to the TNC by the Special Session of the Council for Trade in Services[1] and reaffirms Members' commitment to progress in this area of the negotiations in line with the Doha mandate. The Council adopts the recommendations agreed by the Special Session, set out in Annex C to this document, on the basis of which further progress in the services negotiations will be pursued. Revised offers should be tabled by May 2005.

f. **Other negotiating bodies**:

Rules, Trade & Environment and TRIPS: the General Council takes note of the reports to the TNC by the Negotiating Group on Rules and by the Special Sessions of the Committee on Trade and Environment and the TRIPS Council.[2] The Council reaffirms Members' commitment to progress in all of these areas of the negotiations in line with the Doha mandates.

Dispute Settlement: the General Council takes note of the report to the TNC by the Special Session of the Dispute Settlement Body[3] and reaffirms Members' commitment to progress in this area of the negotiations in line with the Doha mandate. The

1. This report is contained in document TN/S/16.
2. The reports to the TNC referenced in this paragraph are contained in the following documents: Negotiating Group on Rules - TN/RL/9; Special Session of the Committee on Trade and Environment - TN/TE/9; Special Session of the Council for TRIPS - TN/IP/10.
3. Thi//.,s report is contained in document TN/DS/10.

Council adopts the TNC's recommendation that work in the Special Session should continue on the basis set out by the Chairman of that body in his report to the TNC.

g. **Trade Facilitation**: taking note of the work done on trade facilitation by the Council for Trade in Goods under the mandate in paragraph 27 of the Doha Ministerial Declaration and the work carried out under the auspices of the General Council both prior to the Fifth Ministerial Conference and after its conclusion, the General Council decides by explicit consensus to commence negotiations on the basis of the modalities set out in Annex D to this document.

Relationship between Trade and Investment, Interaction between Trade and Competition Policy and Transparency in Government Procurement: the Council agrees that these issues, mentioned in the Doha Ministerial Declaration in paragraphs 20-22, 23-25 and 26 respectively, will not form part of the Work Programme set out in that Declaration and therefore no work towards negotiations on any of these issues will take place within the WTO during the Doha Round.

h. **Other elements of the Work Programme**: the General Council reaffirms the high priority Ministers at Doha gave to those elements of the Work Programme which do not involve negotiations. Noting that a number of these issues are of particular interest to developing-country Members, the Council emphasizes its commitment to fulfil the mandates given by Ministers in all these areas. To this end, the General Council and other relevant bodies shall report in line with their Doha mandates to the Sixth Session of the Ministerial Conference. The moratoria covered by paragraph 11.1 of the Doha Ministerial Decision on Implementation-related Issues and Concerns and paragraph 34 of the Doha Ministerial Declaration are extended up to the Sixth Ministerial Conference.

2. The General Council agrees that this Decision and its Annexes shall not be used in any dispute settlement proceeding under the DSU and shall not be used for interpreting the existing WTO Agreements.

3. The General Council calls on all Members to redouble their efforts towards the conclusion of a balanced overall outcome of the Doha Development Agenda in fulfilment of the commitments Ministers took at Doha. The Council agrees to continue the negotiations launched at Doha beyond the timeframe set out in paragraph 45 of the Doha Declaration, leading to the Sixth Session of the Ministerial Conference. Recalling its decision of 21 October 2003 to accept the generous offer of the Government of Hong Kong, China to host the Sixth Session, the Council further agrees that this Session will be held in December 2005.

Annex A

Framework for Establishing Modalities in Agriculture

1. The starting point for the current phase of the agriculture negotiations has been the mandate set out in Paragraph 13 of the Doha Ministerial Declaration. This in turn built on the long-term objective of the Agreement on Agriculture to establish a fair and market-oriented trading system through a programme of fundamental reform. The elements below offer the additional precision required at this stage of the negotiations and thus the basis for the negotiations of full modalities in the next phase. The level of ambition set by the Doha mandate will continue to be the basis for the negotiations on agriculture.
2. The final balance will be found only at the conclusion of these subsequent negotiations and within the Single Undertaking. To achieve this balance, the modalities to be developed will need to incorporate operationally effective and meaningful provisions for special and differential treatment for developing country Members. Agriculture is of critical importance to the economic development of developing country Members and they must be able to pursue agricultural policies that are supportive of their development goals, poverty reduction strategies, food security and livelihood concerns. Non-trade concerns, as referred to in Paragraph 13 of the Doha Declaration, will be taken into account.
3. The reforms in all three pillars form an interconnected whole and must be approached in a balanced and equitable manner.
4. The General Council recognizes the importance of cotton for a certain number of countries and its vital importance for developing countries, especially LDCs. It will be addressed ambitiously, expeditiously, and specifically, within the agriculture negotiations. The provisions of this framework provide a basis for this approach, as does the sectoral initiative on cotton. The Special Session of the Committee on Agriculture shall ensure appropriate prioritization of the cotton issue independently from other sectoral initiatives. A subcommittee on cotton will meet periodically and report to the Special Session of the Committee on Agriculture to review progress. Work shall encompass all trade-distorting policies affecting the sector in all three pillars of market access, domestic support, and export competition, as specified in the Doha text and this Framework text.
5. Coherence between trade and development aspects of the cotton issue will be pursued as set out in paragraph 1.b of the text to which this Framework is annexed.

Domestic Support

6. The Doha Ministerial Declaration calls for "substantial reductions in trade-distorting domestic support". With a view to achieving these substantial reductions, the negotiations in this pillar will ensure the following:

- Special and differential treatment remains an integral component of domestic support. Modalities to be developed will include longer implementation periods and lower reduction coefficients for all types of trade-distorting domestic support and continued access to the provisions under Article 6.2.
- There will be a strong element of harmonisation in the reductions made by developed Members. Specifically, higher levels of permitted trade-distorting domestic support will be subject to deeper cuts.
- Each such Member will make a substantial reduction in the overall level of its trade-distorting support from bound levels.
- As well as this overall commitment, Final Bound Total AMS and permitted *de minimis* levels will be subject to substantial reductions and, in the case of the Blue Box, will be capped as specified in paragraph 15 in order to ensure results that are coherent with the long-term reform objective. Any clarification or development of rules and conditions to govern trade distorting support will take this into account.

Overall Reduction: A Tiered Formula

7. The overall base level of all trade-distorting domestic support, as measured by the Final Bound Total AMS plus permitted *de minimis* level and the level agreed in paragraph 8 below for Blue Box payments, will be reduced according to a tiered formula. Under this formula, Members having higher levels of trade-distorting domestic support will make greater overall reductions in order to achieve a harmonizing result. As the first instalment of the overall cut, in the first year and throughout the implementation period, the sum of all trade-distorting support will not exceed 80 per cent of the sum of Final Bound Total AMS plus permitted *de minimis* plus the Blue Box at the level determined in paragraph 15.

8. The following parameters will guide the further negotiation of this tiered formula:

- This commitment will apply as a minimum overall commitment. It will not be applied as a ceiling on reductions of overall trade-distorting domestic support, should the separate and complementary formulae to be developed for Total AMS, *de minimis* and Blue Box payments imply, when taken together, a deeper cut in overall trade-distorting domestic support for an individual Member.
- The base for measuring the Blue Box component will be the higher of existing Blue Box payments during a recent representative period to be agreed and the cap established in paragraph 15 below.

Final Bound Total AMS: A Tiered Formula

9. To achieve reductions with a harmonizing effect:
   - Final Bound Total AMS will be reduced substantially, using a tiered approach.
   - Members having higher Total AMS will make greater reductions.
   - To prevent circumvention of the objective of the Agreement through transfers of unchanged domestic support between different support categories, product-specific AMSs will be capped at their respective average levels according to a methodology to be agreed.
   - Substantial reductions in Final Bound Total AMS will result in reductions of some product-specific support.
10. Members may make greater than formula reductions in order to achieve the required level of cut in overall trade-distorting domestic support.

De Minimis

11. Reductions in *de minimis* will be negotiated taking into account the principle of special and differential treatment. Developing countries that allocate almost all *de minimis* support for subsistence and resource-poor farmers will be exempt.
12. Members may make greater than formula reductions in order to achieve the required level of cut in overall trade-distorting domestic support.

Blue Box

13. Members recognize the role of the Blue Box in promoting agricultural reforms. In this light, Article 6.5 will be reviewed so that Members may have recourse to the following measures:
   - Direct payments under production-limiting programmes if:
     - such payments are based on fixed and unchanging areas and yields; or
     - such payments are made on 85% or less of a fixed and unchanging base level of production; or
     - livestock payments are made on a fixed and unchanging number of head.
   - Direct payments that do not require production if:
     - such payments are based on fixed and unchanging bases and yields; or
     - livestock payments made on a fixed and unchanging number of head; and
     - such payments are made on 85% or less of a fixed and unchanging base level of production.
14. The above criteria, along with additional criteria will be negotiated. Any such criteria will ensure that Blue Box payments are less trade-distorting than AMS measures, it being understood that:
   - Any new criteria would need to take account of the balance of WTO rights and obligations.
   - Any new criteria to be agreed will not have the perverse effect of undoing ongoing reforms.

15. Blue Box support will not exceed 5% of a Member's average total value of agricultural production during an historical period. The historical period will be established in the negotiations. This ceiling will apply to any actual or potential Blue Box user from the beginning of the implementation period. In cases where a Member has placed an exceptionally large percentage of its trade-distorting support in the Blue Box, some flexibility will be provided on a basis to be agreed to ensure that such a Member is not called upon to make a wholly disproportionate cut.

Green Box

16. Green Box criteria will be reviewed and clarified with a view to ensuring that Green Box measures have no, or at most minimal, trade-distorting effects or effects on production. Such a review and clarification will need to ensure that the basic concepts, principles and effectiveness of the Green Box remain and take due account of non-trade concerns. The improved obligations for monitoring and surveillance of all new disciplines foreshadowed in paragraph 48 below will be particularly important with respect to the Green Box.

Export Competition

17. The Doha Ministerial Declaration calls for "reduction of, with a view to phasing out, all forms of export subsidies". As an outcome of the negotiations, Members agree to establish detailed modalities ensuring the parallel elimination of all forms of export subsidies and disciplines on all export measures with equivalent effect by a credible end date.

End Point

18. The following will be eliminated by the end date to be agreed:
Export subsidies as scheduled.

- Export credits, export credit guarantees or insurance programmes with repayment periods beyond 180 days.
- Terms and conditions relating to export credits, export credit guarantees or insurance programmes with repayment periods of 180 days and below which are not in accordance with disciplines to be agreed. These disciplines will cover, *inter alia*, payment of interest, minimum interest rates, minimum premium requirements, and other elements which can constitute subsidies or otherwise distort trade.
- Trade distorting practices with respect to exporting STEs including eliminating export subsidies provided to or by them, government financing, and the underwriting of losses. The issue of the future use of monopoly powers will be subject to further negotiation.
- Provision of food aid that is not in conformity with operationally effective disciplines to be agreed. The objective of such disciplines will

be to prevent commercial displacement. The role of international organizations as regards the provision of food aid by Members, including related humanitarian and developmental issues, will be addressed in the negotiations. The question of providing food aid exclusively in fully grant form will also be addressed in the negotiations.

19. Effective transparency provisions for paragraph 18 will be established. Such provisions, in accordance with standard WTO practice, will be consistent with commercial confidentiality considerations.

Implementation

20. Commitments and disciplines in paragraph 18 will be implemented according to a schedule and modalities to be agreed. Commitments will be implemented by annual instalments. Their phasing will take into account the need for some coherence with internal reform steps of Members.

21. The negotiation of the elements in paragraph 18 and their implementation will ensure equivalent and parallel commitments by Members.

Special and Differential Treatment

22. Developing country Members will benefit from longer implementation periods for the phasing out of all forms of export subsidies.

23. Developing countries will continue to benefit from special and differential treatment under the provisions of Article 9.4 of the Agreement on Agriculture for a reasonable period, to be negotiated, after the phasing out of all forms of export subsidies and implementation of all disciplines identified above are completed.

24. Members will ensure that the disciplines on export credits, export credit guarantees or insurance programs to be agreed will make appropriate provision for differential treatment in favour of least-developed and net food-importing developing countries as provided for in paragraph 4 of the Decision on Measures Concerning the Possible Negative Effects of the Reform Programme on Least-Developed and Net Food-Importing Developing Countries. Improved obligations for monitoring and surveillance of all new disciplines as foreshadowed in paragraph 48 will be critically important in this regard. Provisions to be agreed in this respect must not undermine the commitments undertaken by Members under the obligations in paragraph 18 above.

25. STEs in developing country Members which enjoy special privileges to preserve domestic consumer price stability and to ensure food security will receive special consideration for maintaining monopoly status.

Special Circumstances

26. In exceptional circumstances, which cannot be adequately covered by food aid, commercial export credits or preferential international

financing facilities, ad hoc temporary financing arrangements relating to exports to developing countries may be agreed by Members. Such agreements must not have the effect of undermining commitments undertaken by Members in paragraph 18 above, and will be based on criteria and consultation procedures to be established.

Market Access

27. The Doha Ministerial Declaration calls for "substantial improvements in market access". Members also agreed that special and differential treatment for developing Members would be an integral part of all elements in the negotiations.

The Single Approach: a Tiered Formula

28. To ensure that a single approach for developed and developing country Members meets all the objectives of the Doha mandate, tariff reductions will be made through a tiered formula that takes into account their different tariff structures.

29. To ensure that such a formula will lead to substantial trade expansion, the following principles will guide its further negotiation:

- Tariff reductions will be made from bound rates. Substantial overall tariff reductions will be achieved as a final result from negotiations.
- Each Member (other than LDCs) will make a contribution. Operationally effective special and differential provisions for developing country Members will be an integral part of all elements.
- Progressivity in tariff reductions will be achieved through deeper cuts in higher tariffs with flexibilities for sensitive products. Substantial improvements in market access will be achieved for all products.

30. The number of bands, the thresholds for defining the bands and the type of tariff reduction in each band remain under negotiation. The role of a tariff cap in a tiered formula with distinct treatment for sensitive products will be further evaluated.

Sensitive Products

Selection

31. Without undermining the overall objective of the tiered approach, Members may designate an appropriate number, to be negotiated, of tariff lines to be treated as sensitive, taking account of existing commitments for these products.

Treatment

32. The principle of 'substantial improvement' will apply to each product.

33. 'Substantial improvement' will be achieved through combinations of tariff quota commitments and tariff reductions applying to each product.

However, balance in this negotiation will be found only if the final negotiated result also reflects the sensitivity of the product concerned.

34. Some MFN-based tariff quota expansion will be required for all such products. A base for such an expansion will be established, taking account of coherent and equitable criteria to be developed in the negotiations. In order not to undermine the objective of the tiered approach, for all such products, MFN based tariff quota expansion will be provided under specific rules to be negotiated taking into account deviations from the tariff formula.

Other Elements

35. Other elements that will give the flexibility required to reach a final balanced result include reduction or elimination of in-quota tariff rates, and operationally effective improvements in tariff quota administration for existing tariff quotas so as to enable Members, and particularly developing country Members, to fully benefit from the market access opportunities under tariff rate quotas.

36. Tariff escalation will be addressed through a formula to be agreed.

37. The issue of tariff simplification remains under negotiation.

38. The question of the special agricultural safeguard (SSG) remains under negotiation.

Special and differential treatment

39. Having regard to their rural development, food security and/or livelihood security needs, special and differential treatment for developing countries will be an integral part of all elements of the negotiation, including the tariff reduction formula, the number and treatment of sensitive products, expansion of tariff rate quotas, and implementation period.

40. Proportionality will be achieved by requiring lesser tariff reduction commitments or tariff quota expansion commitments from developing country Members.

41. Developing country Members will have the flexibility to designate an appropriate number of products as Special Products, based on criteria of food security, livelihood security and rural development needs. These products will be eligible for more flexible treatment. The criteria and treatment of these products will be further specified during the negotiation phase and will recognize the fundamental importance of Special Products to developing countries.

42. A Special Safeguard Mechanism (SSM) will be established for use by developing country Members.

43. Full implementation of the long-standing commitment to achieve the fullest liberalisation of trade in tropical agricultural products and for

products of particular importance to the diversification of production from the growing of illicit narcotic crops is overdue and will be addressed effectively in the market access negotiations.

44. The importance of long-standing preferences is fully recognised. The issue of preference erosion will be addressed. For the further consideration in this regard, paragraph 16 and other relevant provisions of TN/AG/W/1/Rev.1 will be used as a reference.

Least - Developed Countries

45. Least-Developed Countries, which will have full access to all special and differential treatment provisions above, are not required to undertake reduction commitments. Developed Members, and developing country Members in a position to do so, should provide duty-free and quota-free market access for products originating from least-developed countries.

46. Work on cotton under all the pillars will reflect the vital importance of this sector to certain LDC Members and we will work to achieve ambitious results expeditiously.

Recently Acceded Members

47. The particular concerns of recently acceded Members will be effectively addressed through specific flexibility provisions.

Monitoring and Surveillance

48. Article 18 of the Agreement on Agriculture will be amended with a view to enhancing monitoring so as to effectively ensure full transparency, including through timely and complete notifications with respect to the commitments in market access, domestic support and export competition. The particular concerns of developing countries in this regard will be addressed.

Other Issues

49. Issues of interest but not agreed: sectoral initiatives, differential export taxes, GIs.

50. Disciplines on export prohibitions and restrictions in Article 12.1 of the Agreement on Agriculture will be strengthened.

Annex B

Framework for Establishing Modalities in Market Access for Non-Agricultural Products

1. This Framework contains the initial elements for future work on modalities by the Negotiating Group on Market Access. Additional negotiations are required to reach agreement on the specifics of

some of these elements. These relate to the formula, the issues concerning the treatment of unbound tariffs in indent two of paragraph 5, the flexibilities for developing-country participants, the issue of participation in the sectorial tariff component and the preferences. In order to finalize the modalities, the Negotiating Group is instructed to address these issues expeditiously in a manner consistent with the mandate of paragraph 16 of the Doha Ministerial Declaration and the overall balance therein.

2. We reaffirm that negotiations on market access for non-agricultural products shall aim to reduce or as appropriate eliminate tariffs, including the reduction or elimination of tariff peaks, high tariffs, and tariff escalation, as well as non-tariff barriers, in particular on products of export interest to developing countries. We also reaffirm the importance of special and differential treatment and less than full reciprocity in reduction commitments as integral parts of the modalities.

3. We acknowledge the substantial work undertaken by the Negotiating Group on Market Access and the progress towards achieving an agreement on negotiating modalities. We take note of the constructive dialogue on the Chair's Draft Elements of Modalities (TN/MA/W/35/Rev.1) and confirm our intention to use this document as a reference for the future work of the Negotiating Group. We instruct the Negotiating Group to continue its work, as mandated by paragraph 16 of the Doha Ministerial Declaration with its corresponding references to the relevant provisions of Article XXVIII *bis* of GATT 1994 and to the provisions cited in paragraph 50 of the Doha Ministerial Declaration, on the basis set out below.

4. We recognize that a formula approach is key to reducing tariffs, and reducing or eliminating tariff peaks, high tariffs, and tariff escalation. We agree that the Negotiating Group should continue its work on a non-linear formula applied on a line-by-line basis which shall take fully into account the special needs and interests of developing and least-developed country participants, including through less than full reciprocity in reduction commitments.

5. We further agree on the following elements regarding the formula:

- product coverage shall be comprehensive without *a priori* exclusions;
- tariff reductions or elimination shall commence from the bound rates after full implementation of current concessions; however, for unbound tariff lines, the basis for commencing the tariff reductions shall be [two] times the MFN applied rate in the base year;
- the base year for MFN applied tariff rates shall be 2001 (applicable rates on 14 November);

- credit shall be given for autonomous liberalization by developing countries provided that the tariff lines were bound on an MFN basis in the WTO since the conclusion of the Uruguay Round;
- all non-*ad valorem* duties shall be converted to *ad valorem* equivalents on the basis of a methodology to be determined and bound in *ad valorem* terms;
- negotiations shall commence on the basis of the HS96 or HS2002 nomenclature, with the results of the negotiations to be finalized in HS2002 nomenclature;
- the reference period for import data shall be 1999-2001.

6. We furthermore agree that, as an exception, participants with a binding coverage of non-agricultural tariff lines of less than [35] percent would be exempt from making tariff reductions through the formula. Instead, we expect them to bind [100] percent of non-agricultural tariff lines at an average level that does not exceed the overall average of bound tariffs for all developing countries after full implementation of current concessions.
7. We recognize that a sectorial tariff component, aiming at elimination or harmonization is another key element to achieving the objectives of paragraph 16 of the Doha Ministerial Declaration with regard to the reduction or elimination of tariffs, in particular on products of export interest to developing countries. We recognize that participation by all participants will be important to that effect. We therefore instruct the Negotiating Group to pursue its discussions on such a component, with a view to defining product coverage, participation, and adequate provisions of flexibility for developing-country participants.
8. We agree that developing-country participants shall have longer implementation periods for tariff reductions. In addition, they shall be given the following flexibility:
   a) applying less than formula cuts to up to [10] percent of the tariff lines provided that the cuts are no less than half the formula cuts and that these tariff lines do not exceed [10] percent of the total value of a Member's imports; or
   b) keeping, as an exception, tariff lines unbound, or not applying formula cuts for up to [5] percent of tariff lines provided they do not exceed [5] percent of the total value of a Member's imports.

   We furthermore agree that this flexibility could not be used to exclude entire HS Chapters.
9. We agree that least-developed country participants shall not be required to apply the formula nor participate in the sectorial approach, however, as part of their contribution to this round of negotiations, they are expected to substantially increase their level of binding commitments.

10. Furthermore, in recognition of the need to enhance the integration of least-developed countries into the multilateral trading system and support the diversification of their production and export base, we call upon developed-country participants and other participants who so decide, to grant on an autonomous basis duty-free and quota-free market access for non-agricultural products originating from least-developed countries by the year [...].
11. We recognize that newly acceded Members shall have recourse to special provisions for tariff reductions in order to take into account their extensive market access commitments undertaken as part of their accession and that staged tariff reductions are still being implemented in many cases. We instruct the Negotiating Group to further elaborate on such provisions.
12. We agree that pending agreement on core modalities for tariffs, the possibilities of supplementary modalities such as zero-for-zero sector elimination, sectorial harmonization, and request & offer, should be kept open.
13. In addition, we ask developed-country participants and other participants who so decide to consider the elimination of low duties.
14. We recognize that NTBs are an integral and equally important part of these negotiations and instruct participants to intensify their work on NTBs. In particular, we encourage all participants to make notifications on NTBs by 31 October 2004 and to proceed with identification, examination, categorization, and ultimately negotiations on NTBs. We take note that the modalities for addressing NTBs in these negotiations could include request/offer, horizontal, or vertical approaches; and should fully take into account the principle of special and differential treatment for developing and least-developed country participants.
15. We recognize that appropriate studies and capacity building measures shall be an integral part of the modalities to be agreed. We also recognize the work that has already been undertaken in these areas and ask participants to continue to identify such issues to improve participation in the negotiations.
16. We recognize the challenges that may be faced by non-reciprocal preference beneficiary Members and those Members that are at present highly dependent on tariff revenue as a result of these negotiations on non-agricultural products. We instruct the Negotiating Group to take into consideration, in the course of its work, the particular needs that may arise for the Members concerned.
17. We furthermore encourage the Negotiating Group to work closely with the Committee on Trade and Environment in Special Session with a view to addressing the issue of non-agricultural environmental goods covered in paragraph 31 (iii) of the Doha Ministerial Declaration.

Annex C

Recommendations of the Special Session of the Council for Trade in Services

(a) Members who have not yet submitted their initial offers must do so as soon as possible.

(b) A date for the submission of a round of revised offers should be established as soon as feasible.

(c) With a view to providing effective market access to all Members and in order to ensure a substantive outcome, Members shall strive to ensure a high quality of offers, particularly in sectors and modes of supply of export interest to developing countries, with special attention to be given to least-developed countries.

(d) Members shall aim to achieve progressively higher levels of liberalization with no a priori exclusion of any service sector or mode of supply and shall give special attention to sectors and modes of supply of export interest to developing countries. Members note the interest of developing countries, as well as other Members, in Mode 4.

(e) Members must intensify their efforts to conclude the negotiations on rule-making under GATS Articles VI:4, X, XIII and XV in accordance with their respective mandates and deadlines.

(f) Targeted technical assistance should be provided with a view to enabling developing countries to participate effectively in the negotiations.

(g) For the purpose of the Sixth Ministerial meeting, the Special Session of the Council for Trade in Services shall review progress in these negotiations and provide a full report to the Trade Negotiations Committee, including possible recommendations.

Annex D

Modalities for Negotiations on Trade Facilitation

1. Negotiations shall aim to clarify and improve relevant aspects of Articles V, VIII and X of the GATT 1994 with a view to further expediting the movement, release and clearance of goods, including goods in transit.[4] Negotiations shall also aim at enhancing technical assistance and support for capacity building in this area. The negotiations shall further aim at provisions for effective cooperation between customs or any other appropriate authorities on trade facilitation and customs compliance issues.

4. It is understood that this is without prejudice to the possible format of the final result of the negotiations and would allow consideration of various forms of outcomes.

2. The results of the negotiations shall take fully into account the principle of special and differential treatment for developing and least-developed countries. Members recognize that this principle should extend beyond the granting of traditional transition periods for implementing commitments. In particular, the extent and the timing of entering into commitments shall be related to the implementation capacities of developing and least-developed Members. It is further agreed that those Members would not be obliged to undertake investments in infrastructure projects beyond their means.
3. Least-developed country Members will only be required to undertake commitments to the extent consistent with their individual development, financial and trade needs or their administrative and institutional capabilities.
4. As an integral part of the negotiations, Members shall seek to identify their trade facilitation needs and priorities, particularly those of developing and least-developed countries, and shall also address the concerns of developing and least-developed countries related to cost implications of proposed measures.
5. It is recognized that the provision of technical assistance and support for capacity building is vital for developing and least-developed countries to enable them to fully participate in and benefit from the negotiations. Members, in particular developed countries, therefore commit themselves to adequately ensure such support and assistance during the negotiations.[5]
6. Support and assistance should also be provided to help developing and least-developed countries implement the commitments resulting from the negotiations, in accordance with their nature and scope. In this context, it is recognized that negotiations could lead to certain commitments whose implementation would require support for infrastructure development on the part of some Members. In these limited cases, developed-country Members will make every effort to ensure support and assistance directly related to the nature and scope of the commitments in order to allow implementation. It is understood, however, that in cases where required support and assistance for such infrastructure is not forthcoming, and where a developing or least-developed Member continues to lack the necessary capacity, implementation will not be required. While every effort will be made to ensure the necessary support and assistance, it is understood that the commitments by developed countries to provide such support are not open-ended.

---

5. In connection with this paragraph, Members note that paragraph 38 of the Doha Ministerial Declaration addresses relevant technical assistance and capacity building concerns of Members.

7. Members agree to review the effectiveness of the support and assistance provided and its ability to support the implementation of the results of the negotiations.
8. In order to make technical assistance and capacity building more effective and operational and to ensure better coherence, Members shall invite relevant international organizations, including the IMF, OECD, UNCTAD, WCO and the World Bank to undertake a collaborative effort in this regard.
9. Due account shall be taken of the relevant work of the WCO and other relevant international organizations in this area.
10. Paragraphs 45-51 of the Doha Ministerial Declaration shall apply to these negotiations. At its first meeting after the July session of the General Council, the Trade Negotiations Committee shall establish a Negotiating Group on Trade Facilitation and appoint its Chair. The first meeting of the Negotiating Group shall agree on a work plan and schedule of meetings.

‹63›

UNSC Resolution 1563 (extending the authorization of ISAF in Afghanistan) (17.09.2004)

Acting under Chapter VII of the UN charter the Council decided to extend the authorization of the ISAF for a period of 12 months beyond 13 October 2004. It also called on member states to contribute to the ISAF and to the Trust Fund established pursuant to Resolution 1386 (2001).

The Security Council,

Reaffirming its previous resolutions on Afghanistan, in particular its resolutions 1386 (2001) of 20 December 2001, 1413 (2002) of 23 May 2002, 1444 (2002) of 27 November 2002 and 1510 (2003) of 13 October 2003,

Reaffirming its strong commitment *to* the sovereignty, independence, territorial integrity and national unity of Afghanistan,

Reaffirming also its resolutions 1368 (2001) of 12 September 2001 and 1373 (2001) of 28 September 2001 and *reiterating* its support for international efforts to root out terrorism in accordance with the Charter of the United Nations,

Recognizing that the responsibility for providing security and law and order throughout the country resides with the Afghans themselves and *welcoming* the continuing cooperation of the Afghan Transitional Administration with the International Security Assistance Force,

Reaffirming the importance of the Bonn Agreement and the Berlin Declaration, and recalling in particular annex 1 of the Bonn Agreement which, inter alia, provides for the progressive expansion of the International Security Assistance Force to other urban centres and other areas beyond Kabul,

Stressing also the importance of extending central government authority to all parts of Afghanistan, of conducting free and fair elections, of comprehensive disarmament, demobilization and reintegration of all armed factions, of justice sector reform, of security sector reform including reconstitution of the Afghan National Army and Police, and of combating narcotics trade and production, and recognizing certain progress that has been made in these and other areas with the help of the international community,

Recognizing the constraints upon the full implementation of the Bonn Agreement resulting from concerns about the security situation in parts of Afghanistan, in particular in the light of the upcoming elections,

Welcoming in this context the commitment by NATO lead nations to establish further Provincial Reconstruction Teams (PRTs), as well as the readiness of the International Security Assistance Force and the Operation Enduring Freedom Coalition to assist in securing the conduct of national elections,

Expressing its appreciation to Eurocorps for taking over the lead from Canada in commanding the International Security Assistance Force, to Canada for its leadership of the International Security Assistance Force during the past year, and recognizing with gratitude the contributions of many nations to the International Security Assistance Force,

Determining that the situation in Afghanistan still constitutes a threat to international peace and security,

Determined to ensure the full implementation of the mandate of the International Security Assistance Force, in consultation with the Afghan Transitional Administration and its successors,

Acting for these reasons under Chapter VII of the Charter of the United Nations,

1. *Decides* to extend the authorization of the International Security Assistance Force, as defined in resolution 1386 (2001) and 1510 (2003), for a period of twelve months beyond 13 October 2004;
2. *Authorizes* the Member States participating in the International Security Assistance Force to take all necessary measures to fulfil its mandate;
3. *Recognizes* the need to strengthen the International Security Assistance Force, and in this regard *calls upon* Member States to contribute personnel, equipment and other resources to the International Security Assistance Force, and to make contributions to the Trust Fund established pursuant to resolution 1386 (2001);
4. *Calls upon* the International Security Assistance Force to continue to work in close consultation with the Afghan Transitional Administration and its successors and the Special Representative of the Secretary-General as well as with the Operation Enduring Freedom Coalition in the implementation of the force mandate;
5. *Requests* the leadership of the International Security Assistance Force to provide quarterly reports on implementation of its mandate to the Security Council through the Secretary-General;
6. *Decides* to remain actively seized of the matter.

❮64❯

Implementation of the NPT Safeguards agreement in Iran, Resolution adopted by the IAEA Board (18.09.2004)

Noting that further work was required on a number of issues like contamination, the scope of the P2 centrifuge programme and the timeframe of Iran's plutonium separation experiments, the resolution urged Iran once again to ratify the Additional Protocol, suspend all enrichment related activities and "voluntarily" reconsider its decision to start construction of a research reactor moderated by heavy water.

The Board of Governors

(a) Recalling the resolutions adopted by the Board on 18 June 2004 (GOV/2004/49), 13 March 2004 (GOV/2004/21), 26 November 2003 (GOV/2003/81), and on 12 September 2003 (GOV/2003/69) and the statement by the Board of 19 June 2003 (GOV/OR.1072),

(b) Noting with appreciation the Director General's report of 1 September 2004 (GOV/2004/60), on the implementation of safeguards in Iran,

(c) Noting the Director General's assessment that the Agency is making steady progress towards understanding Iran's nuclear programmes, but that further work is still required on a number of questions and issues, notably contamination and the scope of the P2 centrifuge programme, and that there are other issues that will also require further follow-up, for example the timeframe of Iran's plutonium separation experiments,

(d) Noting with serious concern that, as detailed in the Director General's report, Iran has not heeded repeated calls from the Board to suspend, as a confidence building measure, all enrichment-related and reprocessing activities,

(e) Also concerned that, at its Uranium Conversion Facility, Iran is planning to introduce 37 tonnes of yellowcake, as this would run counter to the request made of Iran by the Board in resolution GOV/ 2004/49,

(f) Recognising the right of states to the development and practical application of atomic energy for peaceful purposes, including the production of electric power, consistent with their Treaty obligations, with due consideration for the needs of the developing countries, and

(g) Stressing the need for effective safeguards to prevent nuclear material being used for prohibited purposes, in contravention of agreements, and underlining the vital importance of effective safeguards for facilitating cooperation in the field of nuclear energy, International Atomic Energy Agency

1. Strongly urges that Iran respond positively to the Director General's findings on the provision of access and information by taking such steps as are required by the Agency and/or requested by the Board in relation to the implementation of Iran's Safeguards Agreement, including the provision of prompt access to locations and personnel, and by providing further information and explanations when required by the Agency and proactively, to assist the Agency to understand the full extent and nature of Iran's enrichment programme and to take all steps within its power to clarify the outstanding issues before the Board's 25 November meeting, specifically including the sources and reasons for enriched uranium contamination, and the import, manufacture, and use of centrifuges;
2. Emphasises the continuing importance of Iran acting in accordance with all provisions of the Additional Protocol including by providing all access required in a timely manner; and urges Iran once again to ratify its Protocol without delay;
3. Deeply regrets that the implementation of Iranian voluntary decisions to suspend enrichment related and reprocessing activities, notified to the Agency on 29 December 2003 and 24 February 2004, fell significantly short of the Agency's understanding of the scope of those commitments and also that Iran has since reversed some of those decisions; stresses that such suspension would provide the Board with additional confidence in Iran's future activities; and considers it necessary, to promote confidence, that Iran immediately suspend all enrichment-related activities, including the manufacture or import of centrifuge components, the assembly and testing of centrifuges, and the production of feed material, including through tests or production at the UCF, under Agency verification so that this could be confirmed in the reports requested in paragraphs 7 and 8 below;
4. Calls again on Iran, as a further confidence-building measure, voluntarily to reconsider its decision to start construction of a research reactor moderated by heavy water;
5. Underlines the need for the full and prompt cooperation with the Agency of third countries in relation to the clarification of outstanding

issues, and expresses appreciation for the cooperation received by the Agency to date;

6. Appreciates the professional and impartial efforts of the Director General and the Secretariat to implement Iran's NPT Safeguards Agreement, and, pending its entry into force, Iran's Additional Protocol, as well as to verify Iran's suspension of enrichment-related and reprocessing activities, and to investigate supply routes and sources;
7. Requests the Director General to submit in advance of the November Board:
   - a report on the implementation of this resolution;
   - a recapitulation of the Agency's findings on the Iranian nuclear programme since September 2002, as well as a full account of past and present Iranian cooperation with the Agency, including the timing of declarations, and a record of the development of all aspects of the programme, as well as a detailed analysis of the implications of those findings in relation to Iran's implementation of its Safeguards Agreement;
8. Also requests the Director General to submit in advance of the November Board a report on Iran's response to the requests made of it by the Board in previous resolutions, especially requests relating to full suspension of all enrichment-related and reprocessing activities;
9. Decides that at its November session it will decide whether or not further steps are appropriate in relation to:
   - Iran's obligations under its NPT Safeguards Agreement;
   - the requests made of Iran, as confidence building measures, by the Board in this and previous resolutions; and to remain seized of the matter.

<65>

UNSC Resolution 1566 (condemning terrorism) (08.10.2004)

Condemning all acts of terrorism "irrespective of their motivation", the UNSC requested the Counter-Terrorism Committee (CTC) to develop a "set of best practices" to assist states in implementing Resolution 1373 (2001). It also established a working group to suggest "practical measures" that will help in extradition, freezing of financial assets and preventing supply of arms and related material to terrorists.

The Security Council,

Reaffirming its resolutions 1267 (1999) of 15 October 1999 and 1373 (2001) of 28 September 2001 as well as its other resolutions concerning threats to international peace and security caused by terrorism,

Recalling in this regard its resolution 1540 (2004) of 28 April 2004,

Reaffirming also the imperative to combat terrorism in all its forms and manifestations by all means, in accordance with the Charter of the United Nations and international law,

Deeply concerned by the increasing number of victims, including children, caused by acts of terrorism motivated by intolerance or extremism in various regions of the world, *Calling upon* States to cooperate fully with the Counter-Terrorism Committee (CTC) established pursuant to resolution 1373 (2001), including the recently established Counter-Terrorism Committee Executive Directorate (CTED), the "Al-Qaida/Taliban Sanctions Committee" established pursuant to resolution 1267 (1999) and its Analytical Support and Sanctions Monitoring Team, and the Committee established pursuant to resolution 1540 (2004), and *further calling* upon such bodies to enhance cooperation with each other,

Reminding States that they must ensure that any measures taken to combat terrorism comply with all their obligations under international law, and should adopt such measures in accordance with international law, in particular international human rights, refugee, and humanitarian law,

Reaffirming that terrorism in all its forms and manifestations constitutes one of the most serious threats to peace and security,

Considering that acts of terrorism seriously impair the enjoyment of human rights and threaten the social and economic development of all States and undermine global stability and prosperity,

Emphasizing that enhancing dialogue and broadening the understanding among civilizations, in an effort to prevent the indiscriminate targeting of different religions and cultures, and addressing unresolved regional conflicts and the full range of global issues, including development issues, will contribute to international cooperation, which by itself is necessary to sustain the broadest possible fight against terrorism,

Reaffirming its profound solidarity with victims of terrorism and their families,

Acting under Chapter VII of the Charter of the United Nations,

1. *Condemns* in the strongest terms all acts of terrorism irrespective of their motivation, whenever and by whomsoever committed, as one of the most serious threats to peace and security;
2. *Calls upon* States to cooperate fully in the fight against terrorism, especially with those States where or against whose citizens terrorist acts are committed, in accordance with their obligations under international law, in order to find, deny safe haven and bring to justice, on the basis of the principle to extradite or prosecute, any person who supports, facilitates, participates or attempts to participate in the financing, planning, preparation or commission of terrorist acts or provides safe havens;
3. *Recalls* that criminal acts, including against civilians, committed with the intent to cause death or serious bodily injury, or taking of hostages, with the purpose to provoke a state of terror in the general public or in a group of persons or particular persons, intimidate a population or compel a government or an international organization to do or to abstain from doing any act, which constitute offences within the scope of and as defined in the international conventions and protocols relating to terrorism, are under no circumstances justifiable by considerations of a political, philosophical, ideological, racial, ethnic, religious or other similar nature, and *calls upon* all States to prevent such acts and, if not prevented, to ensure that such acts are punished by penalties consistent with their grave nature;
4. *Calls upon* all States to become party, as a matter of urgency, to the relevant international conventions and protocols whether or not they are a party to regional conventions on the matter;
5. *Calls upon* Member States to cooperate fully on an expedited basis in resolving all outstanding issues with a view to adopting by consensus the draft comprehensive convention on international terrorism and the draft international convention for the suppression of acts of nuclear terrorism;

6. *Calls upon* relevant international, regional and subregional organizations to strengthen international cooperation in the fight against terrorism and to intensify their interaction with the United Nations and, in particular, the CTC with a view to facilitating full and timely implementation of resolution 1373 (2001);
7. *Requests* the CTC in consultation with relevant international, regional and subregional organizations and the United Nations bodies to develop a set of best practices to assist States in implementing the provisions of resolution 1373 (2001) related to the financing of terrorism;
8. *Directs* the CTC, as a matter of priority and, when appropriate, in close cooperation with relevant international, regional and subregional organizations to start visits to States, with the consent of the States concerned, in order to enhance the monitoring of the implementation of resolution 1373 (2001) and facilitate the provision of technical and other assistance for such implementation;
9. *Decides* to establish a working group consisting of all members of the Security Council to consider and submit recommendations to the Council on practical measures to be imposed upon individuals, groups or entities involved in or associated with terrorist activities, other than those designated by the Al-Qaida/Taliban Sanctions Committee, including more effective procedures considered to be appropriate for bringing them to justice through prosecution or extradition, freezing of their financial assets, preventing their movement through the territories of Member States, preventing supply to them of all types of arms and related material, and on the procedures for implementing these measures;
10. *Requests* further the working group, established under paragraph 9 to consider the possibility of establishing an international fund to compensate victims of terrorist acts and their families, which might be financed through voluntary contributions, which could consist in part of assets seized from terrorist organizations, their members and sponsors, and submit its recommendations to the Council;
11. *Requests* the Secretary-General to take, as a matter of urgency, appropriate steps to make the CTED fully operational and to inform the Council by 15 November 2004;
12. *Decides* to remain actively seized of the matter.

<66>

China-Russia Joint Statement on Boundary (14.10.2004)

> Both sides agreed that the Complementary Agreement between China and Russia on the "Eastern Section" signed this time and the two boundary agreements signed prior to that mark the "complete identification of the trend of the over 4,300 km. long China-Russia border line".

At the invitation of President Hu Jintao of the People's Republic of China, President Vladimir Vladimirovich Putin of the Russian Federation paid a state visit to China from October 14 to 16, 2004.

The two heads of state hold that the celebration of the 55th anniversary of the establishment of China-Russia diplomatic ties is of special significance. The two sides hold comprehensive and in-depth discussions on the status quo and prospects of China-Russia relations, indicating that whatever changes take place in the international situation, to deepen China-Russia strategic cooperative partnership is the priority of the foreign policies of both countries. This serves the fundamental interests of the two countries and peoples and is conducive to safeguarding and promoting regional and world peace, stability and economic development. Based on the sincerer aspiration of continuing pushing for and strengthening bilateral cooperation and exchanges in various fields and in order to open up a new prospect for China-Russia relations, the two heads of state make a statement as follows.

I

After more than a decade of development, China-Russia relations have reached an unprecedented high level. The Treaty of Good-Neighborliness and Friendly Cooperation Between the People's Republic of China and the Russian Federation signed on July 16, 2001 is an important milestone in the development process of bilateral ties, as well as a programmatic document guiding the development of China-Russia ties. The two sides will abide by the principles and spirit defined in the Treaty and continue taking necessary measures to implement the Treaty and all other cooperation documents reached between the two sides in an all-round manner, so as to continuously enrich China-Russia strategic cooperative partnership with new content. The two sides stress that to strengthen political mutual trust, deepen economic cooperation, expand cooperation in humanities and social exchanges and conduct closer coordination and cooperation in international affairs is important content of China-Russia strategic cooperative partnership.

The two sides approve the Outline on Implementing the Treaty of Good-Neighborliness and Friendly Cooperation Between the People's Republic of China and the Russian Federation (2005-2008), holding that the Outline is of great realistic significance to implementing the above-mentioned Treaty by the two countries in the next few years, deepening and expanding cooperation in various fields and promoting continuous development of China-Russia strategic cooperative partnership.

The two sides reach consensus on setting the year 2006 as the "Russian Year" in China and 2007 the "Chinese Year" in Russia.

Both sides reaffirm that they will continue offering support to each other on significant issues involving the national unity, sovereignty and territorial integrity. Russia reiterates that it will as always adhere to the principled stance on the Taiwan and Tibet issues set forth in the Treaty of Good-Neighborliness and Friendly Cooperation Between the People's Republic of China and the Russian Federation signed on July 16, 2001 and all the other bilateral political documents signed previously, namely acknowledging there is but one China in the world, the government of the People's Republic of China is the sole legal government representing China and Taiwan is an inalienable part of China. Russia opposes "Taiwan independence" in any form, never accepts "two Chinas and one China, one Taiwan", opposes Taiwan's entry into the United Nations (UN) and other international organizations only sovereign states can participate in and refrains from selling weapons to Taiwan. Russia recognizes Tibet is an inseparable part of China. China supports all Russia's efforts in safeguarding national unity and combating the terrorist and separatist forces in Chechnya. The two sides indicate that exchanges of visits between heads of states, parliament speakers and prime ministers of the two countries and the meetings of sub-committees within the framework of the prime ministers' regular meeting mechanism have constituted the basic framework of bilateral cooperation. This is beneficial for the two sides to coordinate their stances on significant bilateral and international issues in time, conduct closer collaboration and respond to the challenges of the era. The two sides would like to continue efforts to improve and develop all the cooperation mechanisms, in a bid to ensure the continuous development of bilateral cooperation in politics, economy, science, technology, humanities and international affairs. The two sides hold that the launch of the high-level security consultation mechanism by the two countries as soon as possible is of great significance.

Both sides note that the agreement reached between the two countries on the trend of the boundary line in two sections of the China-Russia border area that were not agreed upon is a balanced and rational plan for the political win-win situation. The Complementary Agreement between the People's Republic of the China and the Russian Federation on the Eastern Section of the China-Russia Boundary signed this time and the two boundary agreements signed prior to that mark the complete identification of the trend of the over 4,300 km-long China-Russia border line. This result is worth cherishing and fully affirming. The resolution of the China-Russia boundary issue is a reliable guarantee for generations of friendship and good-neighborly cooperation between the two peoples, an important contribution to peace and stability of the Asia-Pacific region and the whole world and a successful model for all the countries in the world to address border disputes. The boundary agreement and other border-related agreements between the two countries provide new opportunities for the two sides to take joint actions in environmental protection, rational use of natural resources, shipping, economic cooperation, safeguarding security and stability in border areas and other specific areas, which will enrich the content of China-Russia strategic cooperative partnership. The experience of the two sides shows that peaceful dialogue, fairness, consultation on an equal basis, mutual understanding and accommodation and balance of interests are correct and effective approaches of addressing such complex and sensitive issues as the border one.

Both sides stress that to deepen China-Russia economic and trade cooperation including that in energy resources and investment in an all-round manner is an important factor of consolidating and developing China-Russia strategic cooperative partnership. China-Russia economic and trade cooperation enjoys the good momentum for development and it is fully possible to realize the goal of US$20 billion in bilateral trade volume by the end of this year. But the potentials of economic cooperation between the two countries are far from being fully tapped. The two sides will jointly take effective measures to formulate long and medium-term plans on comprehensive cooperation, improve the mix of bilateral trade, expand trade in mechanical and electrical products, improve the forms and approaches of economic, trade and investment cooperation, give priority to implementing large-scale cooperation programs in various fields, promote substantial progress of bilateral cooperation in energy resources, expand cooperation in the peaceful use of nuclear energy and strengthen scientific and technological cooperation in aerospace, nuclear energy and other energy resources, power, new materials, chemical industry, biology, communications, IT and other priority development areas.

Both sides hold that the establishment of China-Russia Entrepreneurs' Council is of great significance to promoting China-Russia economic and trade cooperation, and they express welcome to the convening of the first meeting of China-Russia Entrepreneurs' Council within the framework of the China-Russia Committee on Friendship, Peace and Development. China resolutely supports Russia to accede to the World Trade Organization (WTO) as soon as possible. With their joint efforts, the two sides have smoothly concluded the China-Russia bilateral market access negotiation on Russia's accession to the WTO, signed related documents and declared the mutual recognition of the other side's full market economy status. The two sides hold that this is an important expression of China-Russia strategic cooperative partnership and they would like to strengthen cooperation within the WTO based on the principle of mutual respect, equality and mutual benefit after Russia's accession to this organization.

II

The two sides earnestly review the UN's capacity and advantages in addressing significant international and regional issues, advocate they should stick to multilateralism and respect, give a play to and strengthen the roles of the UN and its Security Council, and hold that the UN's leading role is irreplaceable in safeguarding world peace and stability, effectively responding to the challenges and threats of the present era, promoting the establishment of a fair and rational world order and ensuring the development of all the countries on an equal basis. The two sides stress that the purposes and principles stipulated in the UN Charter still remain the basic norms that must be followed in dealing with international affairs.

Both sides hold that it is urgently needed to compose international disputes under the chairing of the UN and resolve crisis on the basis of universally recognized principles of international law. Any coercive action should only be taken with the approval of the UN Security Council and enforced under its supervision. The two sides acknowledge that to strengthen its capacity in responding to threats and challenges, enhance its representation and upgrade its working efficiency, it's necessary to properly reform the UN Security Council. The two sides indicate they stand ready to work along with other countries in making relentless efforts to establish a world of peace, development and harmony and realize a fair and rational international political and economic new order.

III

Both sides hold discussions on the status quo and prospects of combating international terrorism and note that terrorism, separatism and extremism pose grave threats to sovereign states' security as well as world peace and stability, indicating they will continue conducting cooperation in an all-round manner within the framework of related regional organizations and international institutions based on bilateral and multilateral collaboration. The two sides hold that the international community must unite to persistently and relentlessly fight against terrorism in all forms.

Both sides hold that they should strengthen global counter-terrorism cooperation with the UN as a platform and reformulate a whole set of strategies in response to terrorism. The two sides stress that only with the guidance of the UN, based on international law, in accordance with related resolutions of the UN and under close cooperation with the main coordinating center, the Counter-Terrorism Committee of the UN Security Council, can the above-mentioned objectives be comprehensively fulfilled. The two sides will push the Shanghai Cooperation Organization (SCO) and the Counter-Terrorism Committee of the UN Security Council to continue their constructive collaboration on the counter-terrorism issue.

Both sides insist that there be no double standard in counter terrorism. The elimination of terrorism requires full cooperation of all the countries in the world. None of those who create terrorist incidents, directly or indirectly refuge or sponsor terrorists can get away from responsibility for the crimes. Both sides point out that poverty, backwardness, social unfairness, extremist ideas, conflicts and wars are all hotbeds of terrorism.

Both sides reaffirm that as part of international terrorism, the terrorist and separatist forces in Chechnya and the "East Turkistan" should be the targets for the international fight against terrorism. The two sides will take targeted, necessary and pragmatic steps within bilateral and multilateral frameworks. China understands and firmly supports all measures taken by Russia to resume the constitutional order of the Republic of Chechnya and to fight against terrorism. Russia firmly supports all measures taken by China to fight against the terrorist and separatist forces in "East Turkistan" and to eliminate terrorist jeopardy.

IV

The strategic and cooperative partnership between China and Russia and the collaboration between the two countries in the United Nations (UN), Shanghai Cooperation Organization (SCO) and other international organizations have contributed significantly to safeguarding world peace and security. Such worldly ideas as fairness and rationality, equality and reciprocity as well as mutual respect have been embodied throughout the activities of the representative regional organization of SCO.

Both sides believe that the purposes and principles of the SCO are compliant with the development trend of the time and the actual situation of the region. The activities of the organization help consolidate regional security and stability and promote the common development of countries in the region. It is a priority for Chinese and Russian foreign policies to push forward the development of the SCO which both sides regard as an important means to build up peace, security and cooperation on the Eurasian Continent, especially in Central Asia as well as a basic factor to establish a multilateral world pattern based on the international law in the future.

V

Both sides reiterate that they will work together to prevent any form of space armament and call on all countries to support the initiative of China and Russia to covenant relevant international legal documents through negotiations.

Both sides stress that the proliferation of weapons of mass destruction and their carriers as well as relevant materials constitute a serious threat to international peace and security. The two sides believe that further coordination is needed to address the threat. To this end, the two sides welcome the adoption of Resolution 1540 by the UN Security Council that as they deem is a very important step to prevent the proliferation of weapons of mass destruction and their carriers. Both sides agree to strictly implement the resolution and to enhance UN's role in the non-proliferation area.

Both sides prioritize the strengthening of international nuclear non-proliferation mechanism, noting that the Treaty on the Non-proliferation of Nuclear Weapons signed on July 1, 1968 is an important pillar for this mechanism and also a significant factor to maintain world peace and security. The two sides believe that it is very important to hold the 2005 Review Conference to the Treaty on the Non-proliferation of Nuclear Weapons. Considering the significance of the Treaty on the Comprehensive Ban of Nuclear Testing signed on September 24, 1996 on nuclear disarmament and the enhancement of nuclear non-proliferation mechanism, both sides propose the early entry into force of the treaty. Both sides give top priority to the coordination of international efforts to eliminate terrorist hazards. Both sides think special attention should be given to the protection of nuclear materials and the prevention of illegitimate transfer of nuclear materials. Both sides will take measures to develop coordination within the framework of the multilateral mechanism on the control of nuclear export.

To establish a nuclear free area is one of the steps to ensure stability in Asia and the world at large. Both sides fully support the establishment of a nuclear free area, especially in Central Asia.

VI

Both sides support the denuclearization of the Korean Peninsula, deeming that the nuclear issue on the Korean Peninsula must be resolved through dialogue at an early date and that the six-party talks are an effective mechanism to realize the objective. Both sides positively appraise the achievements made during the third round of six-party talks which was held in June 2004.

Both sides reaffirm that they will continue to be committed to the six-party talks and trying to seek a solution acceptable to all parties involved. Both sides stress that the ultimate goal is to ensure the nuclear free status of the Korean Peninsula, maintain lasting peace, stability and security on the Korean Peninsula and in the whole region and boost common development.

Both sides are concerned about the continuous escalation of the violent incidents in Iraq, stressing that the local situation should be stabilized through internal dialogue with a particular focus on the national consensus over major issues, such as the future reconstruction of the country, which as they believe helps to build up a new and democratic Iraq. Both sides propose to carefully implement Resolution 1546 by the UN Security Council, especially the schedule for political process in the resolution. Both sides emphasize to hold international conferences on the Iraqi issue will inject new vitality to local reconstruction efforts. Both sides consider it necessary to minimize the damage of the Iraqi War to international relations through joint efforts in a bid to safeguard the interest of the whole international community.

Both sides support a lasting, fair and comprehensive solution to the conflicts between the Arabic states and Israel on the basis of relevant resolutions adopted by the UN Security Council. Both sides indicate the "roadmap" plan formulated by the four-party mechanism remains the best scheme to realize the co-existence of Israel and Palestine and to ensure both of them to maintain peace and security.

Both sides suggest that Afghanistan be built into a democratic and prosperous sovereign state with no terrorism, no drugs and in harmony with the whole international community. The first and foremost task is to ensure the reliable security of the region and the international community should provide broad assistance to the reconstruction of Afghanistan with the leadership of the UN. The work should be done in line with the resolution by the UN Security Council and under the consistent supervision of the UN Security Council. Both sides will continue to make efforts to respond to the threat of drug proliferation in Afghanistan, including the participation of international efforts to build a peripheral anti-drug security zone around the country.

Both sides welcome the move toward full dialogue between India and Pakistan, considering it conducive to the development of bilateral relations in various fields, the interests of both countries and the peace and stability in South Asia to settle differences through peaceful means, to take measures to enhance trust, to create new roads and to develop cooperation in sports, culture and other areas between India and Pakistan.

VII

Both sides will enhance dialogue, coordinate actions and safeguard peace, stability and prosperity in the Asia Pacific region. Both sides are willing to conduct close bilateral or multilateral collaboration with other countries and regional forums.

Both sides will be committed to the promotion of an integrated security cooperation system in the Asia Pacific region with all participants enjoying equal rights, which will help maintain global stability. Both sides emphasize that the SCO initiative on the gradual establishment of a partnership network with multi-party participation in the Asia Pacific region is of realistic significance. Both sides are willing to take joint and active actions to carry out the initiative.

Both sides consider the regional forum of Association of South East Asian Nations (ASEAN) the major official channel for multilateral security dialogue and cooperation in the Asia Pacific region at present. Over the past ten years or more, the forum has played an important role in promoting mutual understanding, enhancing mutual trust and boosting regional security dialogue and cooperation. Both sides would like to continue to enhance coordination and cooperation so as to contribute to the development of the ASEAN regional forum and regional stability and security.

The Chinese side reiterates its support for Russia's participation in multilateral dialogue and cooperation in the region. China understands and supports Russia to conduct regional dialogues with the Asia-Europe Meeting (ASEM), Asian Cooperation Dialogue, "10+3", China-Japan-Korea Cooperation as well as Russia's wishes to establish relations with these cooperation mechanisms.

President of the People's Republic of China
Hu Jinatao

President of the Russian Feduation
Vladimir V. Putin

‹67›

Joint Statement between the United States and the United Kingdom concerning the Middle East Peace Process (12.11.2004)

> Both sides recommitted themselves to the "Two-State Vision" and agreed to "support the Palestinians as they choose a new President" and mobilize support behind a plan to ensure that the Palestinians have a political, economic and security infrastructure they need to create a viable state.

The United States and the United Kingdom share a vision of freedom, peace, and democracy for the Broader Middle East. That vision must include a just and peaceful resolution of the Arab-Israeli conflict, based on two democratic states — Israel and Palestine — living side by side in peace and security. Now is the time to seize the opportunity of new circumstances in the region to redouble our efforts to achieve this goal. This will require a series of steps which we look forward to taking with our international partners and the parties.

First, we re-commit to the overarching two-state vision set out by President Bush in his statement of June 24, 2002 and repeated in the Roadmap.

Second, we will support the Palestinians as they choose a new President within the next sixty days and as they embark upon an electoral process that will lead to lasting democratic institutions.

Third, following that, the President and the Prime Minister have agreed to mobilize international support behind a plan to ensure that the Palestinians have the political, economic, and security infrastructure they need to create a viable state. There will be no lasting solution without a Palestinian state that is democratic and free, including free press, free speech, an open political process, and religious tolerance. Such a state will need a credible and unified security structure capable of providing security for the Palestinians and fighting terrorism. There must also be effective economic development and transparent financial structures which provide for the economic and social needs of the Palestinian people. The plan will be developed intensively over the coming period of time in concert with all the relevant partners.

Fourth, we endorse and support the disengagement plan of Prime Minister Sharon from Gaza and stipulated parts of the West Bank as part of this overall plan.

Fifth, these steps lay the basis for more rapid progress on the Roadmap as a reliable guide leading to final status negotiations.

❮68❯

IAEA Resolution on Iran (29.11.2004)

Noting that Iran had continued enrichment related activities, including the production of UF6 up to 22 November 2004, the Board of Governors welcomed the decision of Iran to continue its suspension of all enrichment and reprocessing activities as a "voluntary, non-legally-binding, confidence building measure".

The Board of Governors,

(a) Recalling the resolutions adopted by the Board on 18 September 2004 (GOV/2004/79), 18 June 2004 (GOV/2004/49), 13 March 2004 (GOV/2004/21), 26 November 2003 (GOV/2003/81) and on 12 September 2003 (GOV/2003/69) and the statement by the Board of 19 June 2003 (GOV/OR.1072),

(b) Noting with appreciation the Director General's report of 15 November 2004 (GOV/2004/83) on the implementation of Iran's NPT Safeguards Agreement (INFCIRC 214),

(c) Noting specifically the Director General's assessment that Iranian practices up to October 2003 resulted in many breaches of Iran's obligations to comply with its Safeguards Agreement, but that good progress has been made since that time in Iran's correction of those breaches and in the Agency's ability to confirm certain aspects of Iran's current declarations,

(d) Also noting specifically the Director General's assessment that all the declared nuclear material in Iran has been accounted for, and that such material is not diverted to prohibited activities, but that the Agency is not yet in a position to conclude that there are no undeclared nuclear materials or activities in Iran,

(e) Recalling the Board's previous requests to Iran to suspend all enrichment related and reprocessing activities as a voluntary confidence building measure,

(f) Noting with concern that Iran has continued enrichment related activities, including the production of UF6 up to 22 November 2004, in spite of the request made by the Board in September that Iran immediately suspend all such activities,

(g) Noting with interest the agreement between Iran, France, Germany and the UK with the support of the High Representative of the EU, made public on 15 November (INFCIRC 637), in which Iran states its decision to continue and extend its suspension of all enrichment related and reprocessing activities; and noting with satisfaction that, pursuant to this agreement, notification of this decision was sent by Iran to the Director General on 14 November with the Agency invited to verify the suspension with effect from 22 November 2004,

(h) Recognizing that this suspension is a voluntary confidence building measure, not a legal obligation,

(i) Recognizing the right of states to the development and practical application of atomic energy for peaceful purposes, including the production of electric power, consistent with their Treaty obligations, with due consideration for the needs of the developing countries,

(j) Stressing the need for effective safeguards to prevent nuclear material being used for prohibited purposes, in contravention of agreements, and underlining the vital importance of effective safeguards for facilitating cooperation in the field of nuclear energy, and

(k) Commending the Director General and the Secretariat for the work they have done to date to resolve all questions relevant to safeguards implementation in Iran,

1. Welcomes the fact that Iran has decided to continue and extend its suspension of all enrichment related and reprocessing activities, and underlines that the full and sustained implementation of this suspension, which is a voluntary, non-legally-binding, confidence building measure, to be verified by the Agency, is essential to addressing outstanding issues;

2. Welcomes the Director General's statements of 25 and 29 November 2004 that the above decision has been put into effect, and requests the Director General to continue verifying that the suspension remains in place and to inform Board members should the suspension not be fully sustained, or should the Agency be prevented from verifying all elements of the suspension, for as long as the suspension is in force;

3. Welcomes Iran's continuing voluntary commitment to act in accordance with the provisions of the Additional Protocol, as a confidence building measure that facilitates the resolution of the questions that have arisen, and calls on Iran once again to ratify its Protocol soon;

4. Reaffirms its strong concern that Iran's policy of concealment up to October 2003 has resulted in many breaches of Iran's obligations to

comply with its NPT Safeguards Agreement; at the same time acknowledges the corrective measures described in the Director General's report;

5. Welcomes the Director General's intention to pursue his investigations into the remaining outstanding issues, in particular the origin of contamination and the extent of Iran's centrifuge programme, as well as the full implementation of Iran's Safeguards Agreement and Additional Protocol, with a view to providing credible assurances regarding the absence of undeclared nuclear material and activities in Iran;

6. Underlines the continuing importance of Iran extending full and prompt cooperation to the Director General in the above pursuit, and requests Iran as a confidence building measure to provide any access deemed necessary by the Agency in accordance with the Additional Protocol; and

7. Requests the Director General to report to the Board on his findings, as appropriate.

❮69❯

Chairman's Statement on the 10th ASEAN Summit, Vientiane (29.11.2004)

> The ASEAN adopted the Vientiane Action Programme (VAP) to realize the establishment of the ASEAN Community comprising three pillars, namely the ASEAN Security Community (ASC), ASEAN Economic Community (AEC) and Socio-Cultural Community (ASCC). The members also agreed to hold the first East Asia Summit (EAS) in 2005 and expressed satisfaction with the deepening ASEAN-India Cooperation.

1. ASEAN Leaders today held a very productive meeting under the Theme "Advancing a Secure and Dynamic ASEAN Family through Greater Solidarity, Economic Integration and Social Progress".
2. We took note of the convening of this Summit at a time when our region is being confronted with fundamental changes in the regional and international scene such as the recent terrorist attacks, the hike in oil prices, the spread of avian flu, etc. In responding to those challenges, we stressed the importance of a higher degree of coherence of efforts to achieve the objectives of ASEAN Vision 2020.
3. During the ASEAN Summit, we discussed issues of common concern to all members, including political and economic developments, in particular the latest developments on terrorism, the Korean Peninsular, the situation in Iraq and the Middle East.

Vientiane Action Programme (VAP): A Vehicle to Building an ASEAN Community through realizing comprehensive Integration.

4. We adopted the ASEAN Security Community Plan of Action and the ASEAN Socio-Cultural Community Plan of Action to implement the Declaration of ASEAN Concord II to realize the establishment of the ASEAN Community comprising three pillars, namely the ASEAN Security Community (ASC), ASEAN Economic Community (AEC) and Socio-Cultural Community (ASCC) that are closely intertwined and mutually reinforcing for the purpose of ensuring durable peace, stability and shared prosperity in the region and beyond. In this connection, we reaffirmed our commitment to achieving an ASEAN

Community through initiatives and approaches to accelerate economic integration.

5. In furtherance of, and intensifying, our cooperation in the fight against transnational crimes, we also adopted the ASEAN Declaration against Trafficking in Persons, Particularly Women and Children.
6. We noted the Assessment Report on the Implementation of the Ha Noi Plan of Action (HPA) and agreed that the successful implementation of the HPA has significantly contributed to the realization of the end-goal of the ASEAN Vision 2020 and the Declaration of the ASEAN Concord II leading to the establishment of the ASEAN Community in 2020.
7. At the 10th ASEAN Summit, we signed the Vientiane Action Programme, a six-year plan, which is the successor of the HPA to realize the end goal of the ASEAN Vision and the Declaration of ASEAN Concord II. The VAP focuses on deepening regional integration and narrowing the development gap within ASEAN, particularly the least developed Member Countries. We agreed to establish an ASEAN Development Fund (ADF) to support the implementation of the VAP and future action programmes. In this connection, we called on our Dialogue Partners, other countries and regional and international organizations to support the implementation of the VAP.
8. To further deepen regional economic integration, we also signed the ASEAN Framework Agreement for the Integration of Priority Sectors and we tasked the Ministers responsible for ASEAN Economic Integration to continue coordination and monitoring of the implementation of all measures specified in the Roadmaps to ensure the successful integration of the priority economic sectors within the timeframe.
9. We noted with satisfaction that our respective economies have recovered with good prospect for further economic growth for the remaining year and in 2005.

Bridging the Development Gap

10. Bridging the development gap is extremely important for regional economic integration and is a crucial part of confidence-building efforts to assist members to cope with challenges. In this regard, we noted progress made in the implementation of the Initiative for ASEAN Integration (IAI) and Roadmap for Integration of ASEAN (RIA). We welcomed Singapore's additional contribution of S$28.9 million (US$17.6 million) to support the implementation of the IAI as an important symbol of its commitment to foster closer economic integration and enhance ASEAN's competitiveness as a region. Our

top priorities include developing human resources, infrastructure, information technology, and energy with the support and cooperation of the private sector, our Dialogue Partners, other countries, and regional and international financial institutions.

11. We reaffirmed the importance of sub-regional growth areas in ASEAN development and integration process such as the Mekong Basin Development Cooperation and the BIMP-EAGA. We discussed ways and means to accelerate the pace of development of these growth areas in ASEAN. We welcomed the contribution of other sub-regional development frameworks in the region such as the GMS, and ACMECS to help close the development gap within ASEAN. These frameworks should serve as building blocks for East Asia and Asia-wide cooperation. We also welcomed the Asia Cooperation Dialogue (ACD) and Asian Bond Market Development.

CLMV Summit

12. We listened with interest to the outcome of the CLMV Summit and we supported the Vientiane Declaration on Enhancing Economic Cooperation and Integration among Cambodia, Laos, Myanmar and Vietnam to convey, as a message, of our strong political will and determination of the Leaders of CLMV countries to accelerate the narrowing of their development gaps and ASEAN's economic integration.

Regional and International Political and Economic Issues

13. We discussed a wide range of issues related to ASEAN political and security cooperation.

14. We reaffirmed the importance of the Treaty of Amity and Cooperation in Southeast Asia as a code of conduct governing relations between countries in the region for the promotion of peace and stability in the region. We warmly welcomed the accession of the Republic of Korea and the Russian Federation to the TAC and encouraged other non-Southeast Asian countries to accede to the Treaty. We also welcomed the steps being taken by ASEAN and China to implement the Declaration on Conduct of Parties in the South China Sea.

15. We underlined the importance of strengthening relations and cooperation with other regions such as with Latin America and Europe through FEALAC and ASEM respectively. In this regard, we strongly supported Indonesia's initiative to build a bridge of cooperation between Asia and Africa through the convening of the Asia-Africa Summit on 21-22 April 2005 in Jakarta and the observance of Golden Jubilee of the 1955 Asia-Africa Conference on 23 April 2005 in Bandung, Indonesia.

16. We condemned in the strongest terms the recent terrorist acts and reaffirmed our determination to work together to mitigate the adverse impact of such attacks on ASEAN countries and urged the international community to assist us in this effort.
17. We reaffirmed our commitment to a peaceful and comprehensive solution to the nuclear issue on the Korean Peninsula. In this connection, we noted with encouragement the achievement by the three rounds of the Six-Party Talks. We shared the view that the Six-Party Talks should be reconvened at the earliest possibility to bring about the common goal of denuclearisation on the Korean Peninsula.
18. We noted that current developments in Iraq and the Middle East remained causes of great concern. With regard to the post-war Iraq, we reaffirmed our position that the United Nations must continue to play a central role in the reconstruction and rehabilitation of Iraq taking the responsibility for the maintenance of international peace and security.
19. While discussing current economic developments in the region and in the world, we expressed our determination to work together to minimize the adverse impact on our economies brought about by the hike in oil prices and avian flu. In this connection, we supported energy cooperation, in particular, in alternative energy, such as bio-fuels, and hydroelectric power, and the establishment of the Outbreak Response Teams.

Strengthening Cooperation with Dialogue Partners

20. We noted the progress made in the political and economic cooperation with our Dialogue Partners. In this regard, we expressed satisfaction with the overall progress of the ASEAN+3 cooperation. We reaffirmed our determination to continue to drive the ASEAN+3 cooperation and to work closely with China, Japan and the Republic of Korea in promoting East Asia cooperation.
21. We discussed the convening of an East Asia Summit (EAS). We agreed to hold the first EAS in Malaysia in 2005 and in this connection, tasked our Foreign Ministers to work out the details concerning its modality and participation.
22. We expressed our satisfaction with the deepening of ASEAN-India cooperation. We welcomed the enhancement of AFTA-CER linkages, which will lay the firm foundation for future cooperation. We were also pleased to upgrade the relations between ASEAN and the Russian Federation and looked forward to the ASEAN-Russia Summit in Malaysia next year.

Institutional Strengthening of ASEAN

23. We directed our Ministers, Senior Officials and the ASEAN Secretariat to continue the work of developing an ASEAN Charter and to review ASEAN's mechanism, including the frequency of ASEAN's meetings at all levels, with a view to rationalize them and make them more effective. We also agreed to further strengthen the ASEAN Secretariat, particularly in undertaking policy analysis and providing recommendations to ASEAN Member Countries in carrying out ASEAN cooperation. We agreed to consider the findings and recommendations of our Ministers and Officials on this matter at our next meeting.

Other Matters

24. We reaffirmed our commitment to the United Nations. We further underlined the importance of reform of the United Nations and the enhanced role of ASEAN and ASEAN Member States within the United Nations system. In this connection, we endorsed the candidature of H.E. Dr. Surakiart Sathirathai, Minister of Foreign Affairs of Thailand, for the post of United Nations Secretary-General and underscored the importance of Indonesia's intention to seek permanent membership in the United Nations Security Council.
25. In order to strengthen the cooperation between ASEAN and the United Nations we decided to convene the second ASEAN-UN Summit in New York during the 60th session of the UN General Assembly. In this regard, we tasked our Foreign Ministers to make the necessary preparations to ensure the success of the said Summit.
26. We expressed our appreciation to the ASEAN Business Advisory Council (ABAC) and agreed to continue our support for its role as an important component to the overall strategy of increasing the private sector's engagement in ASEAN economic policy deliberations. We once again underlined the need for closer coordination between the private sector and relevant government agencies in the implementation of ABAC's recommendations.

‹70›

Executive summary of the report of the UN High Level Panel on Threats Challenges and Change (30.11.2004)

Recognising that in today's world, "a threat to one is a threat to all", the High-level Panel identified six clusters of threats, namely, war between states; violence within states; poverty, disease and environmental degradation; NBC weapons; terrorism; and transnational organised crime. To meet these challenges, the Panel suggested inter alia, revitalizing the General Assembly and Economic and Social Council; restoring credibility to the Commission on Human Rights; and making the composition of the Security Council better reflect today's realities.

In his address to the General Assembly in September 2003, United Nations Secretary-General Kofi Annan warned Member States that the United Nations had reached a fork in the road. It could rise to the challenge of meeting new threats or it could risk erosion in the face of mounting discord between States and unilateral action by them. He created the High-level Panel on Threats, Challenges and Change to generate new ideas about the kinds of policies and institutions required for the UN to be effective in the 21st century.

In its report, the High-level Panel sets out a bold, new vision of collective security for the 21st century. We live in a world of new and evolving threats, threats that could not have been anticipated when the UN was founded in 1945 – threats like nuclear terrorism, and State collapse from the witch's brew of poverty, disease and civil war.

In today's world, a threat to one is a threat to all. Globalization means that a major terrorist attack anywhere in the industrial world would have devastating consequences for the well-being of millions in the developing world. Any one of 700 million international airline passengers every year can be an unwitting carrier of a deadly infectious disease. And the erosion of State capacity anywhere in the world weakens the protection of every State against transnational threats such as terrorism and organized crime. Every State requires international cooperation to make it secure.

There are six clusters of threats with which the world must be concerned now and in the decades ahead:

- war States;
- violence within States, including civil wars, large-scale human rights abuses and genocide;
- poverty, infectious disease and environmental degradation;
- nuclear, radiological, chemical and biological weapons;
- terrorism; and
- transnational organized crime.

The good news is that the United Nations and our collective security institutions have shown that they *can* work. More civil wars ended through negotiation in the past 15 years than the previous 200. In the 1960s, many believed that by now 15-25 States would possess nuclear weapons; the Nuclear Non-Proliferation Treaty has helped prevent this. The World Health Organization helped to stop the spread of SARS before it killed tens of thousands, perhaps more.

But these accomplishments can be reversed. There is a real danger that they will be, unless we act soon to strengthen the United Nations, so that in future it responds effectively to the full range of threats that confront us.

Policies for prevention

Meeting the challenge of today's threats means getting serious about prevention; the consequences of allowing latent threats to become manifest, or of allowing existing threats to spread, are simply too severe.

Development has to be the first line of defence for a collective security system that takes prevention seriously. Combating poverty will not only save millions of lives but also strengthen States' capacity to combat terrorism, organized crime and proliferation. Development makes everyone more secure. There is an agreed international framework for how to achieve these goals, set out in the Millennium Declaration and the Monterrey Consensus, but implementation lags.

Biological security must be at the forefront of prevention. International response to HIV/AIDS was shockingly late and shamefully ill-resourced. It is urgent that we halt and roll back this pandemic. But we will have to do more. Our global public health system has deteriorated and is ill-equipped to protect us against existing and emerging deadly infectious diseases. The report recommends a major initiative to build public health capacity throughout the developing world, at both local and national levels. This will not only yield direct benefits by preventing and treating disease in the developing world itself, but will also provide the basis for an effective global defence against bioterrorism and overwhelming natural outbreaks of infectious disease.

Preventing wars within States and between them is also in the collective interest of all. If we are to do better in future, the UN will need real improvements to its capacity for preventive diplomacy and mediation. We will have to build on the successes of regional organizations in developing strong norms to protect Governments from unconstitutional overthrow, and to protect minority rights. And we will have to work collectively to find new ways of regulating the management of natural resources, competition for which often fuels conflict.

Preventing the spread and use of nuclear, biological and chemical weapons is essential if we are to have a more secure world. This means doing better at reducing demand for these weapons, and curbing the supply of weapons materials. It means living up to existing treaty commitments, including for negotiations towards disarmament. And it means enforcing international agreements. The report puts forward specific recommendations for the creation of incentives for States to forego the development of domestic uranium enrichment and reprocessing capacity. It urges negotiations for a new arrangement which would enable the International Atomic Energy Agency to act as a guarantor for the supply of fissile material to civilian nuclear users at market rates, and it calls on Governments to establish a voluntary time-limited moratorium on the construction of new facilities for uranium enrichment and reprocessing, matched by a guarantee of the supply of fissile materials by present suppliers.

Terrorism is a threat to all States, and to the UN as a whole. New aspects of the threat – including the rise of a global terrorist network, and the potential for terrorist use of nuclear, biological or chemical weapons – require new responses. The UN has not done all that it can. The report urges the United Nations to forge a strategy of counterterrorism that is respectful of human rights and the rule of law. Such a strategy must encompass coercive measures when necessary, and create new tools to help States combat the threat domestically. The report provides a clear definition of terrorism, arguing that it can never be justified, and calls on the General Assembly of the UN to overcome its divisions and finally conclude a comprehensive convention on terrorism.

The spread of transnational organized crime increases the risk of all the other threats. Terrorists use organized criminal groups to move money, men and materials around the globe. Governments and rebels sell natural resources through criminal groups to finance wars. States' capacity to establish the rule of law is weakened by corruption. Combating organized crime is essential for helping States build the capacity to exercise their sovereign responsibilities and in combating the hideous traffic in human beings.

Response to threats

Of course, prevention sometimes fails. At times, threats will have to be met by military means.

The UN Charter provides a clear framework for the use of force. States have an inherent right to self-defence, enshrined in Article 51. Long-established customary international law makes it clear that States can take military action as long as the threatened attack is imminent, no other means would deflect it, and the action is proportionate. The Security Council has the authority to act preventively, but has rarely done so. The Security Council may well need to be prepared to be more proactive in the future, taking decisive action earlier. States that fear the emergence of distant threats have an obligation to bring these concerns to the Security Council.

The report endorses the emerging norm of a responsibility to protect civilians from large-scale violence – a responsibility that is held, first and foremost, by national authorities. When a State fails to protect its civilians, the international community then has a further responsibility to act, through humanitarian operations, monitoring missions and diplomatic pressure – and with force if necessary, though only as a last resort. And in the case of conflict or the use of force, this also implies a clear international commitment to rebuilding shattered societies.

Deploying military capacities—for peacekeeping as well as peace enforcement—has proved to be a valuable tool in ending wars and helping to secure States in their aftermath. But the total global supply of available peacekeepers is running dangerously low. Just to do an adequate job of keeping the peace in existing conflicts would require almost doubling the number of peacekeepers around the world. The developed States have particular responsibilities to do more to transform their armies into units suitable for deployment to peace operations. And if we are to meet the challenges ahead, more States will have to place contingents on stand-by for UN purposes, and keep air transport and other strategic lift capacities available to assist peace operations.

When wars have ended, post-conflict peacebuilding is vital. The UN has often devoted too little attention and too few resources to this critical challenge. Successful peacebuilding requires the deployment of peacekeepers with the right mandates and sufficient capacity to deter would-be spoilers; funds for demobilization and disarmament, built into peacekeeping budgets; a new trust fund to fill critical gaps in rehabilitation and reintegration of combatants, as well as other early reconstruction tasks; and a focus on building State institutions and capacity, especially in the rule of law sector. Doing this job successfully should be a core function of the United Nations.

A UN for the 21st century

To meet these challenges, the UN needs its existing institutions to work better. This means revitalizing the General Assembly and the Economic and Social Council, to make sure they play the role intended for them, and restoring credibility to the Commission on Human Rights.

It also means increasing the credibility and effectiveness of the Security Council by making its composition better reflect today's realities. The report provides principles for reform, and two models for how to achieve them – one involving new permanent members with no veto, the other involving new four-year, renewable seats. It argues that any reforms must be reviewed in 2020.

We also need new institutions to meet evolving challenges. The report recommends the creation of a Peacebuilding Commission – a new mechanism within the UN, drawing on the Security Council and the Economic and Social Council, donors, and national authorities. Working closely with regional organizations and the international financial institutions, such a commission could fill a crucial gap by giving the necessary attention to countries emerging from conflict. Outside the UN, a forum bringing together the heads of the 20 largest economies, developed and developing, would help the coherent management of international monetary, financial, trade and development policy.

Better collaboration with **regional organizations** is also crucial, and the report sets out a series of principles that govern a more structured partnership between them and the UN.

The report recommends strengthening the Secretary-General's critical role in peace and security. To be more effective, the Secretary-General should be given substantially more latitude to manage the Secretariat, and be held accountable. He also needs better support for his mediation role, and new capacities to develop effective peacebuilding strategy. He currently has one Deputy Secretary-General; with a second, responsible for peace and security, he would have the capacity to ensure oversight of both the social, economic and development functions of the UN, and its many peace and security functions.

The way forward

The report is the start, not the end, of a process. The year 2005 will be a crucial opportunity for Member States to discuss and build on the recommendations in the report, some of which will be considered by a summit of heads of State. But building a more secure world takes much more than a report or a summit. It will take resources commensurate with the scale of the challenges ahead; commitments that are long-term and sustained; and, most of all, it will take leadership – from within States, and between them.

❮71❯

Japan's National Defense Program Guideline for FY 2005 and After (10.12.2004)

While acknowledging the "close cooperative relationship" between Japan and the US the Guideline mentions that "unpredictability and uncertainty still remains in the situation on the Korean Peninsula as well as in the Taiwan Straits". The Guideline states that Japan will establish necessary defence force structure, "including the introduction of ballistic missile defence systems, to cope effectively with ballistic missile attacks".

I. Purpose

Based on the Security Council and Cabinet Decision "On Introduction of Ballistic Missile Defense System and Other Measures" of December 19, 2003, the Government of Japan hereby presents the "National Defense Program Guideline for FY 2005 and After" as a guideline for Japan's future security and defense capabilities designed to preserve peace and security of Japan as well as peace and stability of the international community in the new security environment surrounding Japan.

II. Security Environment Surrounding Japan

1. As demonstrated in the 9.11 terrorist attacks in the United States, non-state actors, such as international terrorist organizations, have emerged as a serious threat in today's security environment in addition to the traditional problems such as inter-state military confrontations. Against the backdrop of ever-deepening interdependence among states and globalization, new threats and other various situations that affect peace and security, including proliferation of weapons of mass destruction and ballistic missiles as well as international terrorist activities (hereinafter referred to as "the new threats and various situations"), pose an imminent challenge to today's international community. Moreover, we have to bear in mind that the traditional strategy of deterrence does not work as effectively as in the past vis-à-vis international terrorist organizations which do not have their own state or people to protect.

   In the meanwhile, more than ten years have passed since the end of the Cold War, and mutual cooperation and interdependence among major powers have deepened, exemplified by the growing trust between the United States and Russia. Under these circumstances, international coordination and cooperation on security issues have taken root in the international community as the stable international environment serves the interests of all nations, and nations of the world are making wide range of efforts including those under the framework of international organizations such as the United Nations.

In this context, the United States, as the sole superpower, continues to play an important role in international peace and stability by taking proactive measures to combat terrorism and prevent proliferation of weapons of mass destruction.

Besides, military force has begun to play broader roles and is actively used for various purposes, such as preventing conflict and reconstructing failed states in addition to deterring and/or responding to armed conflict.

2. In the vicinity of Japan, efforts are being made to promote and strengthen bilateral and multilateral coordination and cooperation, as a result of further expansion and deepening of interdependence among the nations in the region in recent years.

   In contrast, while Russian military power in the Far East has significantly decreased in quantitative terms after the end of the Cold War, large-scale military force, including nuclear capabilities, continues to exist in this region, and a number of countries have been modernizing their military forces. In addition, unpredictability and uncertainty still remain in the situation on the Korean Peninsula as well as in the Taiwan Straits. North Korea is developing, deploying, and proliferating weapons of mass destruction and ballistic missiles, and maintains a large number of special operations forces. North Korea's such military activities constitute a major destabilizing factor to the regional security and a serious challenge to the international efforts for non-proliferation. In addition, China, which has a strong influence on the security in this region, has been modernizing its nuclear and missile capabilities as well as naval and air forces, and expanding its area of operation at sea. We have to remain attentive to its future course.

   In this context, close cooperative relationship between Japan and the United States, based on the Japan-U.S. Security Arrangements, continues to play a key role for the security of Japan as well as peace and stability in the Asia-Pacific region.

3. In light of the security environment surrounding Japan as described above, while on the one hand a full-scale invasion against Japan has become less likely to occur, Japan has to deal with new threats and various situations in addition to the security problems in the region.

4. In considering Japan's security, we have to take the following factors into account: that the country has security vulnerabilities resulting from its narrow land, long coastal lines and numerous small islands, high population density, and the concentration of population and industry in urban areas and a large number of important facilities in coastal areas; that Japan is prone to disaster in geographical and geological terms; and that the security of sea lines of communication is indispensable to its prosperity and growth.

III. Basic Principles of the Security of Japan

1. Basic Principles

The first objective of Japan's security policy is to prevent any threat from directly reaching Japan and, in the event that it does, to repel the threat as well as to minimize the damage. The second objective is to reduce the chances of any threat arising in various parts of the world in order to prevent it from reaching Japan.

Japan will try to achieve these objectives by integrating its own efforts and cooperative efforts with the United States and the international community. To this end, Japan will, make diplomatic efforts to support United Nations activities for international peace and security, and to promote cooperative relationships with foreign countries, maintain close cooperative relationship with the United States based on the Japan-U.S. Security Arrangements, establish a basis for national security by preserving domestic political stability, and build up efficient defense force.

Under the Constitution of Japan, in accordance with fundamental principles of maintaining exclusively defense-oriented policy and of not becoming a major military power that might pose a threat to foreign countries, Japan will continue to uphold the basic policies of securing civilian control, adhering to the three non-nuclear principles, and building modest defense capability on its own initiative.

To cope with the threat of nuclear weapons, Japan continues to rely on the nuclear deterrent provided by the United States, while at the same time play an active role in taking realistic step-by-step measures for nuclear disarmament and non-proliferation. It will also play an active role in international disarmament and non-proliferation efforts regarding other weapons of mass destruction and delivery means such as missiles.

2. Japan's Own Efforts

(1) Basic Ideas

Based on the awareness that any country's security depends first and foremost on its own endeavors, Japan will make its utmost efforts, by utilizing all available means, to prevent any threat from reaching the country directly. In addition, it will engage in its own diplomatic activities to prevent the emergence of threats by improving international security environment, based on the principle of acting closely with the international community and its alliance partner.

(2) Japan's Integrated Response

In the event that these efforts failed to prevent the threat from reaching Japan, the Government of Japan would take an integrated response by swiftly making appropriate decisions through mechanisms such as the Security Council, bringing together all relevant organizations, and having them cooperate adequately. To achieve this, the Government will strive to improve its ability to collect and analyze information to facilitate decision-making. Through an appropriate role-sharing, relevant organizations, such as the Self-Defense Forces, the police, and the Japan Coast Guard, will ensure their close coordination through increased information sharing, joint exercises and other activities, and improve their overall performance. In addition, the Government will establish necessary civil defense systems, for example, to respond to different types of disasters and to quickly issue warning signals. For that purpose, the central and local governments will work closely together to establish adequate systems.

(3) Japan's Defense Capability

Defense capability is the ultimate guarantee for its national security, representing its will and ability to repel any threat in case it reaches Japan. Japan's defense capability has been built upon the "National Defense Program Outline for FY 1996 and After" (adopted by the Security Council and the Cabinet on November 28, 1995), which incorporated the key elements of the Basic Defense Force Concept espousing that rather than preparing to directly counter military threat, Japan, as an independent state, should maintain the minimum necessary basic defense capability lest it becomes a destabilizing factor in this region by creating a power vacuum. Combined with the Japan-U.S. Security Arrangements, this policy has been successful in preventing armed invasion from occurring.

Given the new security environment, the future defense force should be capable of effectively responding to the new threats and various situations while preserving valid elements of the Basic Defense Force Concept. In addition, based on the awareness that peace and security of Japan are inextricably linked to the peace and stability of the international community, Japan should be able to proactively and on its own initiative participate, in order to promote its own peace and security, in activities that nations of the world cooperatively undertake to improve international security environment (hereafter called "international peace cooperation activities").

We have to take it into account that while roles which the defense capability has to play are multiplying, the population of the youth in Japan keeps decreasing resulting from low birth rate, and the fiscal conditions continue deteriorating.

From this standpoint, Japan's future defense capability should be a multi-functional, flexible, and effective force with high level of readiness, mobility, adaptability and multi-purpose capability, and be equipped with advanced technologies and intelligence capabilities comparable to global military-technological level. In building such defense force without expanding its size, the Government of Japan should work to attain greater results with limited resources by rationalizing and streamlining personnel, equipment, and operations.

3. Japan-U.S. Security Arrangements

The Japan-U.S. Security Arrangements are indispensable for Japan's security. In addition, the U.S. military presence is critically important to peace and stability in the Asia-Pacific region, which continues to be stricken with unpredictability and uncertainty. Moreover, close cooperative relationship between Japan and the United States based on the Japan-U.S. Security Arrangements plays an important role in facilitating international efforts to prevent the new threats and various situations, such as terrorism and ballistic missile attacks, from emerging, and to cope with them if necessary.

From this point of view, the Government of Japan will on its own initiative engage in strategic dialogue with the United States on wide-ranging security issues such as role-sharing between the two countries and the military posture such as force structure of the U.S. forces in Japan, while trying to share common views on the new security environment and on strategic objectives in that context. In doing so, the Government of Japan will bear in mind the need to reduce the excessive burden that U.S. military bases and facilities place on local communities, while maintaining the deterrent that the U.S. military presence in Japan provides.

In addition, Japan will continue to strengthen the Japan-U.S. Security Arrangements by actively promoting intelligence exchange, operational cooperation including that in the "situations in areas surrounding Japan," cooperation on ballistic missile defense, equipment and technology exchange, and efforts to make the stationing of U.S. forces in Japan smooth and efficient.

4. Cooperation with the International Community

In order to improve international security environment and help maintain security and prosperity of Japan, the Government of Japan will proactively engage in various diplomatic efforts, including a strategic use of Official Development Assistance (ODA). Based on the recognition that threat to peace and stability of the international community by situations such as regional conflicts, proliferation of weapons of mass destruction and international terrorist attacks would in turn seriously affect its own peace and security, Japan will, on its own initiative, proactively participate in international peace cooperation activities as integral part of its diplomatic efforts.

In particular, stability in the region spreading from the Middle East to East Asia is critical to Japan given the fact that it traditionally has close economic ties with the region, that Japan's sea lines of communication run through the region, and that Japan depends heavily on foreign countries for energy and natural resources. In this context, Japan will strive to stabilize the region by promoting various cooperative efforts, in conjunction with other concerned countries, to deal with common security challenges in the region.

To enable the international community to effectively address new challenges in the twenty-first century, we will have to undertake the reform of the world's only global and comprehensive international organization—the United Nations—to make it more effective and reliable. Japan will actively pursue this goal.

In the Asia-Pacific region, multilateral regional frameworks for security such as the ASEAN Regional Forum (ARF) and multilateral efforts to cope with common agendas such as developing counter-terrorism and counter-piracy measures are taking root. By continuing to support these positive developments, Japan will continue to play an appropriate role, in addition to the combined efforts with the United States, to promote stable security environment in this region.

IV. Vision for the Future Defense Capability

1. Role of the Defense Capability

Based on the assessment as described above, Japan's future defense capability should be able to effectively carry out missions in the following areas. Japan will develop and maintain necessary Self-Defense Forces posture in an efficient manner to achieve this.

(1) Effective Response to the New Threats and Various Situations

Japan will try to cope effectively with the new threats and various situations by developing and deploying highly ready and mobile defense force units capable of responding properly to various different situations in accordance with the characteristic of the units and Japan's geographical characteristics. When such situations actually take place, the defense force will act quickly and appropriately to seamlessly respond to situations in smooth and close collaboration with the police and other relevant organizations in accordance with the circumstances and division of labor. Japan's response to and necessary Self-Defense Forces posture for the key elements of the new threats and various situations will be the following:

a. Response to Ballistic Missile Attacks

Japan will establish necessary defense force structure, including the introduction of ballistic missile defense systems, to cope effectively with ballistic missile attacks. With this effort and dependence on nuclear deterrent provided by the United States combined, we will adequately respond to the threat of nuclear weapons.

b. Response to Guerrillas and Special Operations Units Attacks

Japan will maintain necessary defense force structure to respond effectively to attacks carried out by guerrillas and special operations units, by enhancing readiness and mobility of the defense force units, and by coping with such attacks in a flexible manner.

c. Response to Invasion against Outlying Islands

Japan will maintain necessary defense force structure to respond effectively to invasion against outlying islands, by improving and strengthening capabilities to transport and deploy forces, and by coping with the invasion in a flexible manner.

d. Patrol and Surveillance in the Peripheral Sea and Air, and the Response to the Violation of Territorial Airspace and the Intrusion of Armed Special-Operations Vessels and Others

Japan will maintain necessary defense force structure, involving warships, aircraft and other necessary assets, to maintain around-the-clock patrol and surveillance in the peripheral sea and air. We will also maintain fighter aircraft units to respond instantly and adequately to the violation of territorial airspace. And we will also maintain destroyers and other assets to respond adequately to armed special-operations vessels in the peripheral sea and foreign submarines which navigate submerged in the territorial sea of Japan.

e. Response to Large-Scale and/or Unconventional Disaster (Nuclear, Biological, and Chemical Disasters)

Japan will cope effectively with various situations, such as large-scale and/or unconventional disaster(nuclear, biological and chemical disasters), where protection of life and property is needed, by maintaining the posture equipped with defense force units and specialized capabilities to conduct disaster relief operations in any part of Japan.

(2) Preparations to Deal with Full-Scale Invasion

Since the likelihood of full-scale invasion against Japan will remain small in the foreseeable future, we will modify our current defense force concept that emphasized Cold War type counter-armor warfare, anti-submarine warfare and anti-air warfare, and will make a sweeping review to reduce personnel and equipment earmarked for coping with full-scale invasion. At the same time, however, considering the fact that the indigenous purpose of defense capability is to cope with full-scale invasion, and that establishing such a force from scratch would take a long time, we will maintain the most basic part of the defense force, taking orientation of neighboring countries into account and making use of technological progress.

(3) Proactive Efforts on Its Own Decision to Improve International Security Environment

In order to engage adequately in international peace cooperation activities, Japan will take the following measures: develop education and training systems, highly ready force posture for relevant units, and transport and other required capabilities; establish necessary infrastructure to quickly dispatch and maintain defense force units overseas for an considerable period of time; and make necessary arrangements including the effort to properly embed international peace cooperation activities within the Self-Defense Forces mission priorities.

Japan will strongly promote activities for international peace and stability, such as security dialogue and defense exchanges including bilateral and multilateral training and exercises, and arms control and disarmament efforts engineered by international organizations such as the United Nations.

2. Fundamental Measures for Our Defense Capabilities

Following are fundamental measures for realizing defense capabilities that can carry out the missions described above:

(1) Enhancing Joint Operation Capabilities

To have three services of the Self-Defense Forces operate in an integrated manner and enable them to execute their missions swiftly and effectively, we will employ them jointly, and enhance necessary arrangements. We will create a central organization to facilitate joint operations, and establish infrastructure for jointness in training and education as well as intelligence and communications. In doing so, we will reexamine existing organizations to enhance their effectiveness.

(2) Strengthening Intelligence Capabilities

In order to respond effectively to the new threats and various situations and employ our defense capability successfully in any situations, it is imperative for the Government to be able to collect, analyze, and share intelligence promptly and adequately, and to identify indications of a situation at the earliest possible time. For this purpose, we will cultivate various intelligence collection capabilities taking consideration of security environment, technological progress and other relevant factors, and enhance our ability to analyze and evaluate intelligence in a comprehensive manner. We will also strengthen Japan's intelligence community, of which the Defense Intelligence Headquarters is a part, to attain first-class intelligence capabilities.

(3) Incorporating Advanced Technologies

We will incorporate fruits of advanced technological innovations such as development of information and communications technologies, into our defense capability. In particular, we will develop reliable command and control system as well as speedy intelligence sharing systems, which are indispensable for joint operations, in tune with advanced information and communication technologies available at home and overseas. In addition, we will construct advanced systems for command and communications and a network for information and communications with sufficient protection against possible cyber attacks.

(4) Efficient Use of Human Resources

The Government of Japan will take various means to maintain high morale and strict discipline in the Self-Defense Forces. Japan will also recruit, cultivate, train and educate human resources to adequately cope with diversification and internationalization of the Self-Defense Forces missions, and to properly operate rapidly advancing high-tech equipment.

It will also promote research and education on security issues and enhance human basis for security issue.

The posture of defense capability required to fulfill the missions described above is indicated in the attachment.

V. Additional Elements for Consideration

1. In developing, maintaining, and operating the defense force as described in section IV, we will take the following elements into consideration.

(1) Mindful of the markedly worsening fiscal conditions, we will curb defense expenditures by further rationalizing and streamlining our defense capability, and will try to make it successfully carry out its missions by harmonizing its operations with other measures taken by the Government.

(2) The Government of Japan will try to make the procurement and the research and development (R&D) process more effective and efficient by taking the following measures: curbing life-cycle cost, including purchase price, of the defense equipment; actively using cutting-edge technologies developed by private enterprises, universities, and governmental organizations; allocating R&D resource in a more focused manner; and appropriately and timely reviewing different R&D projects. At the same time, we will work to establish truly necessary defense production and technological base, especially that of core technological areas indispensable for our national security.

(3) In order to efficiently develop and maintain defense-related facilities, the Government of Japan will, in close cooperation with relevant local authorities, take various measures to harmonize these facilities with local communities.

2. This National Defense Program Guideline provides the vision for our defense force for approximately next ten years. However, we will

review and, if necessary, revise it after five years from now or in case there is a significant change in the security environment, taking consideration of the security environment, technological progress, and other relevant factors at the time.

Attachment

Ground Self-Defense Force

Authorized Number of SDF Personnel	155,000
Regular Personnel	148,000
Reserve Personnel who can be promptly mobilized	7,000
Major Units	
Regionally Deployed Units	8 divisions 6 brigades
Mobile Operation Units	1 armored division Central Readiness Group
Surface-to-air Guided Missile Units	8 anti-aircraft artillery groups
Major Equipment	
Battle Tanks vehicles	Approx. 600
Main Artillery	Approx. 600 guns per vehicle

Maritime Self-Defense Force

Major Units	
Destroyer Units (for mobile operations)	4 flotillas (8 divisions)
Destroyer Units (regional district units)	5 divisions
Submarine Units	4 divisions
Minesweeper Units	1 flotilla
Patrol Aircraft Units	9 squadrons
Major Equipment	
Destroyers	47
Submarines	16
Combat Aircraft	Approx. 150

⟨72⟩

Summary of US Intelligence Reforms and Terrorism Prevention Act 2004 (17.12.2004)

The Act creates a Director of National Intelligence (DNI) with broad, strategic authority over budgets and missions, and creates a National Counter-Terrorism Centre (NCTC) to deal specifically with terrorist threats. The Act also makes a number of recommendations on transportation security, border and immigration controls, and the role of diplomacy in the war on terrorism.

The salient recommendations of the US Intelligence Reform and Terrorism Prevention Act passed in December 2004 are:

1. Director of National Intelligence

There is established a Senate-confirmed Director of National Intelligence (DNI) who shall not also serve as the Director of the Central Intelligence Agency (CIA) or as the head of any other element of the intelligence community. The DNI shall not be located in the Executive Office of the President.

2. Authorities of the DNI

(a) Budget Build: The DNI shall "develop and determine" an annual budget for the National Intelligence Program (NIP) budget based on budget proposals provided by the heads of agencies and organizations of the intelligence community and their respective department heads. The heads of such agencies and organizations must also provide to the DNI such other information as the DNI requests for the purpose of determining the NIP budget.

(b) Budget Execution: The DNI shall "ensure the effective execution" of the annual budget for intelligence and intelligence-related activities. The Director of OMB must apportion NIP funds at the "exclusive direction" of the DNI for allocation to the elements of the intelligence community. The DNI is further responsible for managing NIP appropriations by "directing the allotment or allocation" of such appropriations through the heads of departments containing agencies or organizations of the intelligence community. Department comptrollers must allot, allocate, reprogram, or transfer NIP funds "in an expeditious manner."

The DNI "shall monitor the implementation and execution of the National Intelligence Program by the heads of elements of the intelligence community" that manage NIP programs or activities, including with audits and evaluations. The DNI shall report to the President and to Congress within 15 days of learning that a department comptroller has acted in a manner that is inconsistent with the direction of the DNI in carrying out the NIP.

(c) Transfer and Reprogramming of Funds: NIP funds may not be transferred or reprogrammed without approval of the DNI, except in accordance with procedures prescribed by the DNI. All transfers or reprogrammings by the DNI:

(1) must be for a higher priority intelligence activity;

(2) must support an emergent need, improve program effectiveness, or increase efficiency; and

(3) may not involve funds from the CIA Reserve for Contingencies or a DNI Reserve for Contingencies. With approval from OMB and after consulting with affected department heads, the DNI may transfer or reprogram NIP funds out of any department or agency as long as the amount in a single fiscal year is less than $150 million, is less than 5% of the department's or agency's NIP funds, and does not terminate an acquisition program. These limits would not apply if the DNI obtains the concurrence of the affected department head.

(d) Transfer of Personnel: In the fiscal year after the effective date of the Act, the DNI

(1) is authorized 500 new personnel billets within the Office of the DNI, and

(2) may, with the approval of the OMB director, transfer 150 personnel funded within the NIP to the Office of the DNI for not more than 2 years.

For the first 12 months after a national intelligence center is created, the DNI may transfer 100 personnel authorized for elements of the intelligence community to that center. The DNI must receive the approval of the director of OMB and notify appropriate Congressional committees of such transfers. In accordance with procedures developed between the DNI and the heads of departments and agencies concerned, and upon approval of the director of OMB, the DNI may also transfer unlimited numbers of personnel authorized for an element of the intelligence community to another such element for a period of not more than two years. The DNI may only make such transfer if the personnel are being transferred to an activity that is a higher priority intelligence activity, and the transfer supports an emergent need, improves program effectiveness, or increases efficiency. The DNI must notify appropriate Congressional committees of such transfers.

It is the Sense of the Congress that 21st Century national security threats continue to challenge the intelligence community to respond rapidly and flexibly to bring analytic resources to bear, that the Office of the DNI and any analytic centers should be fully supported with appropriate personnel levels, and the President should utilize all legal and administrative discretion to ensure that the DNI and the intelligence community have the necessary resources and procedures to meet emerging threats.

(e) Tasking and Analysis: The DNI establishes objectives and priorities for the intelligence community and manages and directs tasking of collection, analysis, production, and dissemination of national intelligence. The DNI approves requirements for collection and analysis, including requirements responding to the needs of consumers. The DNI also provides advisory tasking to intelligence elements outside of the NIP. The DNI may establish national intelligence centers as the DNI determines necessary. To ensure accurate all-source intelligence, the DNI must implement policies and procedures to, among other things, ensure competitive analysis and that alternative views are brought to the attention of policymakers.

(f) Personnel Management: The DNI, in consultation with the heads of other agencies or elements of the intelligence community, develops personnel policies and programs to enhance the capacity for joint operation and facilitate staffing of community management functions. An individual's service in more than one element of the intelligence community would be a condition of promotion to certain positions. The policies shall not be inconsistent with those applicable to uniformed services personnel.

In addition, the NID will prescribe regulations to provide incentives for service on the staff of the DNI, the national intelligence centers, NCTC, or other positions in support of the intelligence community management functions. It is the Sense of the Congress that policies to facilitate the rotation of personnel should seek to duplicate within the intelligence community the joint officer management policies established by the Goldwater-Nichols Department of Defense Reorganization Act of 1986 and the amendments on joint officer management made by that Act. Assignment of commissioned officers to the Office of the DNI will be considered joint-duty assignments for the purposes of the amendments on Department of Defense joint officer management made by the Goldwater-Nichols Department of Defense Reorganization Act of 1986.

The DNI has the same personnel authorities over employees of the Office of the DNI that the Director of Central Intelligence has under current law with respect to CIA employees. Employees and applicants for employment of the Office of the DNI have the same rights and protections as CIA employees under current law.

(g) Protection of Sources and Methods / Classification: The DNI shall protect sources and methods from unauthorized disclosure and, in order to maximize the dissemination of intelligence, establish and implement guidelines for classification under applicable law, Executive orders, or Presidential directives.

(h) Foreign Liaison: The DNI shall oversee the coordination of relationships with the intelligence or security services of foreign governments or international organizations.

(i) Acquisition / Milestone: The DNI has the same acquisition and appropriation authorities given to the CIA Director in the CIA Act of 1949 except for that Act's section 8(b), which allows the CIA Director to expend sums made available to the CIA without regard to any of the laws or regulations relating to the expenditure of government funds. The DNI also has the same authority as the CIA Director to waive provisions of the Federal Property and Administrative Services Act of 1949. The DNI has exclusive milestone milestone decision authority for NIP-funded major systems, except that with respect to Department of Defense programs the DNI has joint authority with the

Secretary of Defense. If the DNI and the Secretary of Defense are unable to reach agreement on a milestone decision, the President resolves the conflict.

(j) Common Services: The DNI shall, in consultation with department heads, coordinate the performance by elements of the intelligence community of services of common concern to the intelligence community that the DNI determines can be more efficiently accomplished in a consolidated manner.

(k) Appointments: The DNI shall recommend to the President nominees for Principal Deputy DNI and for CIA Director. The DNI has the right to concur in the appointment or the recommendation for nomination of the heads of NSA, NRO, and NGA; the Assistant Secretary of State for INR; the Directors of the Offices of Intelligence and Counterintelligence at DOE; the Assistant Secretary for Intelligence and Analysis at the Department of the Treasury; the Executive Assistant Director for Intelligence of the FBI; and the Assistant Secretary of Homeland Security for Information Analysis. The DNI must be consulted for appointments or recommendations for the Director of DIA and the Deputy Assistant Commandant of the Coast Guard for Intelligence.

3. Definition of National Intelligence

The bill defines national intelligence to include information gathered in the U.S. or abroad that pertains to more than one agency and involves threats to the U.S., its people, property, or interests; the development, proliferation, or use of weapons of mass destruction; or any other matter bearing on national or homeland security.

4. Information Sharing

The 9/11 Commission found that the biggest impediment to a greater likelihood of "connecting the dots" was the resistance to information sharing, and recommended a new, government-wide approach to information sharing. This section addresses this recommendation by requiring the President to establish an Information Sharing Environment (ISE) to facilitate the sharing of terrorism information among all appropriate Federal, State, local, tribal and private sector entities, through the use of policy guidelines and technologies.

5. National Counterterrorism Center

The National Counterterrorism Center (NCTC) is established in the Office of the DNI. The Director of the NCTC is Senate-confirmed and may not simultaneously serve in any other capacity in the executive branch. The Director of the NCTC reports to the DNI on budget and intelligence matters, but to the President on the planning and progress of joint counterterrorism operations (other than intelligence operations). The NCTC will conduct "strategic operational planning," which is defined to include the mission, the objectives to be achieved, the tasks to be performed, interagency coordination of operational activities, and the assignment of roles and responsibilities. The NCTC Director shall monitor the implementation of strategic operational plans and shall obtain relevant information from departments and agencies on the progress of such entities in implementing the plans.

6. National Counterproliferation Center

The President shall establish a National Counterproliferation Center (NCPC) not later than 18 months after the date of enactment. The President may waive this requirement if the President determines that it does not materially improve the government's ability to halt the proliferation of weapons of mass destruction. Such a waiver shall be made in writing and it must be submitted to Congress.

7. National Intelligence Centers

The DNI is authorized to establish national intelligence centers to address intelligence priorities, such as regional issues. These centers shall have primary responsibility, in their areas of intelligence responsibility, for providing all-source analysis and for identifying and proposing to the DNI intelligence collection and production requirements. The DNI shall ensure that the centers have sufficient personnel and that the intelligence community shares information in order to facilitate their mission. Each center shall have a separate budget account.

8. Joint Intelligence Community Council

There is established a Joint Intelligence Community Council (JICC), chaired by the DNI, which is composed of the Secretaries of State, Treasury,

Defense, Energy, and Homeland Security, as well as the Attorney General and such other officers as the President may designate. The JICC shall assist the DNI by advising on budget and other matters and by ensuring the timely execution of the programs, policies, and directives of the DNI.

9. Education and Training

The DNI develops a comprehensive education, recruitment, and training plan to meet the linguistic requirements for the intelligence community. The DNI is further responsible for establishing an integrated framework that brings together the educational components of the intelligence community to promote joint education and training. Finally, the DNI establishes an Intelligence Community Scholarship Program, to provide college scholarships for students in exchange for service within the intelligence community.

10. Open Source Intelligence

The DNI shall ensure that the intelligence community makes efficient and effective use of open source information and analysis. It is the sense of Congress that the DNI should establish an intelligence center for the purpose of coordinating the collection, analysis, production, and dissemination of open source intelligence, and the DNI must report to Congress on this matter.

11. Transportation Security

This section implements key 9/11 Commission recommendations with respect to transportation security by requiring that the Secretary of Homeland Security develop and implement a national strategy for transportation security.

(a) Aviation Security: These sections implement 9/11 Commission recommendations to improve passenger prescreening (including improved use of the "no fly" and "automatic selectee" lists), and to ensure that these watchlists do not violate privacy or civil liberties. It also implements a recommendation to give priority attention to screening passengers and their bags for explosives. This subtitle also directs the Transportation Security Administration to develop a plan for implementing improved explosives detection equipment. Other provisions help protect air marshals, improve performance of airport screeners and enhance in-line baggage screening. Additional provisions improve pilot licenses, general aviation security, biometric technology and technology to protect against shoulder fired missiles.

(b) Air Cargo Security: Pursuant to a general 9/11 Commission recommendation to improve air cargo security, this subtitle requires the Transportation Security Administration to develop better technologies for air cargo security, authorizes funding for equipment and research and development, requires the Department finalize its air cargo regulations within 8 months, and requires a pilot program to evaluate the use of currently available and next generation blast-resistant containers.

(c) Maritime Security: This subtitle directs the Transportation Security Administration to begin screening passengers and crew of cruise ships against comprehensive consolidated terrorist databases within 180 days. It also requires certain maritime-security plans, reports and assessments to be completed in a timely manner.

12. Border protection, immigration and visa matters

(a) Advanced Technology Northern Border Security Pilot Program: This subtitle permits the Secretary of Homeland Security to carry out a pilot program to test advanced technologies that will improve border security between ports of entry along the northern border of the U.S., requires a report to Congress, and authorizes appropriation of such sums as may be necessary to carry out the pilot program. Among the program's features would be the use of advanced technology for border surveillance, and operation in remote stretches along the border with long distances between 24-hour ports of entry and a relatively small presence of border patrol agents.

(b) Border and Immigration Enforcement:

Border Surveillance: This section requires the Secretary of Homeland Security to submit to the President and Congress a plan for the systematic surveillance of the southwest border of the U.S. by remotely piloted aircraft, and to implement such plan as a pilot program. Among the missions of this program would be the interdiction of the illegal movement of people, weapons, and other contraband across the border, and assisting in the dismantling of smuggling and criminal networks along the border. This section also authorizes the appropriation of such sums as may be necessary to carry out this provision.

Increase in Full-Time Border Patrol Agents: This section requires the Secretary of Homeland Security, in each of fiscal years 2006 through 2010, to increase the numbers of border patrol agents by not less than 2,000, subject to available appropriations. In addition, this provision would require a number of agents equaling at least 20% of each year's increase in agents to be assigned to the northern border.

Increase in Full-Time Immigration and Customs Enforcement Investigators: This section requires the Secretary of Homeland Security, in each of the fiscal years 2006 through 2010, to increase the numbers of Immigration and Customs Enforcement investigators by not less than 800, subject to available appropriations.

13. Immigration Reform

Bringing in and Harboring Certain Aliens: This section increases criminal penalties for alien smuggling and requires the Secretary of DHS to develop an outreach program in the U.S. and abroad to educate the public about the penalties for illegally bringing in and harboring aliens.

Deportation of Aliens Who Have Received Military-Type Training from Terrorist Organizations: This section renders deportable any alien who has received military training from or on behalf of an organization that, at the time of training, was a designated terrorist organization.

Study and Report on Terrorists in the Asylum System: This section requires the General Accounting Office to conduct a study evaluating the extent to which weaknesses in U.S. asylum system could be exploited by terrorists.

14. Terrorism prevention

(a) Individual Terrorists As Agents of Foreign Powers ("Lone Wolf" Provision): Sec. 6001 authorizes the issuance of warrants under the Foreign Intelligence Surveillance Act of 1978 (FISA) for individuals involved in international terrorism, but not affiliated with a known terrorist group. The authority is subject to a sunset at the end of 2005. Sec. 6002 requires semiannual reports by the Attorney General to the House and Senate Committees on Intelligence and Judiciary regarding the number of persons targeted for FISA orders allowing electronic surveillance, searches, and access to records; the frequency of use of information in criminal proceedings; and summaries of significant legal interpretations of the Act and copies of decisions of FISA courts. Such reports are to be submitted in a manner consistent with the protection of the national security.

(b) Money Laundering and Terrorist Financing: This section authorizes funding for a series of technology enhancements to improve the data maintained by the Department of Treasury's Financial Crimes Enforcement Network (FinCEN), while reducing compliance burdens on financial institutions. It also reauthorizes the National Money Laundering Strategy and the Financial Crime-Free Communities Support Program.

(c) Money Laundering Abatement and Financial Antiterrorism Technical Corrections: This subtitle makes a number of technical corrections to the USA PATRIOT Act. It also makes permanent the provisions of title III of the USA PATRIOT Act, which include only provisions related to money laundering and financial transactions, by repealing section 303 of the Act, which provides that the provisions of title III will terminate after September 30, 2004, if both Houses of Congress enact a joint resolution to that effect.

15. Weapons of Mass Destruction Prohibition Improvement Act

Sec. 6802 expands Federal jurisdiction over crimes involving weapons of massdestruction and re-establishes chemical weapons as weapons of mass destruction. Sec. 6803 provides that a person who participates in or provides material support to a nuclear weapons or weapons of mass destruction program of a foreign terrorist organization is subject to imprisonment for up to 20 years. Makes possession, attempt to possess or conspiracy to posses a radiological weapon subject to imprisonment for a period of a term of years, up to life.

16. The Role of Diplomacy, Foreign Aid, and the Military in the War on Terrorism:

This subtitle reflects and implements 9/11 Commission recommendations regarding the importance of using all elements of national power, including diplomacy, military action, intelligence, covert action, law enforcement, economic policy, foreign aid, public diplomacy, and homeland defense to win the war on terrorism. It includes findings and a Sense of Congress on the role of terrorist sanctuaries in providing support for terrorist operations and the need to identify terrorist sanctuaries and develop and implement a strategy to eliminate such sanctuaries. It includes a provision that would amend the Export Administration Act to include a government's actions to prevent and eliminate terrorist sanctuaries as a criterion for the licensing for export of sensitive dual-use technology to that country. It also amends current law to ensure that the State Department Patterns of Global Terrorism reports include assessments of the actions countries have taken to prevent their territories from being used as terrorist sanctuaries.

Pakistan: This subtitle includes findings regarding Pakistan's role in countering the growth of terrorism, and a Sense of Congress that the United States should make a long-term commitment to ensuring a stable and secure future in Pakistan, as long as its leaders remain committed to combating extremists, with a range of assistance to Pakistan. It includes language extending the ability of the President to waive foreign assistance restrictions on Pakistan for fiscal years 2005 and 2006.

Afghanistan: This subtitle includes a series of provisions entitled the "Afghanistan Freedom Support Act Amendments of 2004" designed to provide flexibility to United States assistance to Afghanistan. Among other things, these provisions amend the Afghanistan Freedom Support Act of 2002 to make permanent a Coordinator for Assistance for Afghanistan, authorize the Coordinator to support and develop education, the rule of law, democratic and cultural institutions in Afghanistan, and repeal the current law prohibiting assistance to Afghanistan. It authorizes such sums as may be necessary to the President for each fiscal year from FY2005-FY2009 to provide assistance to Afghanistan.

Saudi Arabia: The subtitle includes findings regarding the need to strengthen the relationship and dialogue between the United States and Saudi Arabia. It includes findings regarding the need to combat the stereotypes of the U.S. in the Muslim world and a Sense of Congress that the Government of the United States should offer an example of moral leadership in the world that includes a commitment to treat all people humanely and encourage reform, freedom, democracy, and moderation in the Islamic world.

Promoting engagement with countries with predominately Muslim populations: The subtitle authorizes the President to expand international exchange programs and calls for a long-term and sustainable investment in promoting engagement with countries with predominately Muslim populations. It also establishes a pilot program to provide grants to students from countries with predominantly Muslim populations to study in American-sponsored school in their countries. The subtitle includes findings regarding the need to improve education in the Middle East and authorizes the President to establish an International Youth Opportunity Fund to provide financial assistance for the improvement of public education in the Middle East.

Middle East Partnership Initiative: The subtitle includes findings regarding the importance of economic development in combating the breeding grounds for terrorism and declares it is a Sense of Congress that a comprehensive United States strategy to counter terrorism should include economic development policies. It authorizes to be appropriated such sums as may be necessary for each of fiscal years 2005 and 2006 for the Middle East Partnership Initiative, a program that is currently authorized in law, and expresses the Sense of Congress that a significant portion of those fund should be made available to promote the rule of law in the Middle East.

Designations of Foreign Terrorist Organizations: The subtitle recognizes the need to cut off funding for terrorists and emphasizes the importance of targeting terrorist financial facilitators It includes a provision that eliminates the current requirement that designations of Foreign Terrorist Organizations(FTOs) lapse after two years unless renewed by the Secretary of State and replaces this requirement with procedures allowing entities designated as FTOs to petition the Secretary every two years to have their designations revoked, and a mandatory review of designations after five years if they have not previously been reviewed as a result of a petition.

17. Improving Intelligence Analysis

Alternative Analysis Not later than 180 days after the effective date of the Act, the DNI shall establish a process and assign an individual or entity the responsibility of ensuring that elements of the intelligence community conduct alternative analysis as appropriate. Not later than 270 days after the effective date of the Act, the DNI must submit a report to the Congressional intelligence committees concerning implementation.

Safeguarding Objectivity in Intelligence Analysis: Not later than 180 days after the effective date of this Act, the DNI shall identify an individual within the Office of the DNI who shall be available to analysts within the Office of the Director of National Intelligence to counsel, conduct arbitration, offer recommendations, and, as appropriate, initiate inquiries into real or perceived problems of analytic tradecraft or politicization, biased reporting, or lack of objectivity in intelligence analysis. Not later than 270 days after the effective date of this Act, the DNI shall provide a report to the Congressional intelligence committees on implementation.

Analytic Integrity: Not later than 180 days after the date of the enactment of this Act, the DNI shall assign an individual or entity to be responsible for ensuring that finished intelligence products produced by any element or elements of the intelligence community are timely, objective, independent of political considerations, based upon all sources of available intelligence, and employ the standards of proper analytic tradecraft.

The individual or entity assigned responsibility shall perform, on a regular basis, detailed reviews of finished intelligence product or other analytic products by an element or elements of the intelligence community covering a particular topic or subject matter; and shall be responsible for identifying on an annual basis functional or topical areas of analysis for specific reviews. Each review should include, among other things, whether the product or products concerned were based on all sources of available intelligence, properly describe the quality and reliability of underlying sources, properly caveat and express uncertainties or confidence in analytic judgments, and properly distinguish between underlying intelligence and the assumptions and judgments of analysts. Not later than December 1 each year, the DNI shall submit to the Congressional intelligence committees and other entities a report containing a description and the associated findings of each review.

18. Other Matters

Amendments to Clinger-Cohen Act Provisions to Enhance Agency Planning for Information Security Needs: This provision amends the Clinger-Cohen Act to explicitly require federal agencies to emphasize information security from the earliest possible stages of a new system's IT capital planning and investment decision-making process.

Enterprise Architecture: This section requires the Federal Bureau of Investigation (FBI) to continually maintain and update an enterprise architecture; and maintain a state of the art and up to date information technology infrastructure that is in compliance with the enterprise architecture of the FBI. Specifically the FBI is required to develop a detailed outline or blueprint of its information technology that will satisfy the ongoing mission and goals of the FBI and that sets forth specific and identifiable benchmarks. The Director of the FBI shall report to the House and Senate Judiciary Committees on whether the major information technology investments of the FBI are in compliance with its enterprise architecture and identify any inability or expectation of inability to meet the terms set forth in the enterprise architecture.

❮73❯

Excerpts from White Paper on China's National Defense in 2004 (28.12.2004)

The new while paper lists four factors as having a major impact on China's security. They are the rise of the "Taiwan independence" forces, the technological gap resulting from the revolution in military affairs, the risks and challenges brought about by the development of the globalization trends, and the prolonged existence of both unipolarity and multipolarity. The paper states that, "Should the Taiwan authorities go so far as to make a reckless attempt that constitutes a major incident of 'Taiwan independence', the Chinese people and armed forces will resolutely and thoroughly crush it at any cost."

Foreword

A panoramic view of the present-day world displays the simultaneous existence of both opportunities for and challenges to peace and development, and of positive and negative factors bearing on security and stability. The opportunities cannot be shared and the challenges cannot be overcome unless diverse civilizations, social systems and development models live together harmoniously, trust each other and engage in cooperation. Hence, the pursuit of peace, development and cooperation has become an irresistible trend of history.

The development goal for China to strive for in the first two decades of this century is to build a moderately prosperous society in an all-round way. As a large developing country, China has before it an arduous task for modernization, which calls for prolonged and persistent hard work. China will mainly rely on its own strength for development, and therefore poses no obstacle or threat to any one. China needs a peaceful international environment for its own development, which in turn will enhance peace and development in the world. Holding high the banner of peace, development and cooperation, China adheres to an independent foreign policy of peace and a national defense policy of the defensive nature. China will never go for expansion, nor will it ever seek hegemony.

A major strategic task of the Communist Party of China (CPC) in exercising state power is to secure a coordinated development of national defense and the economy, and to build modernized, regularized and revolutionary armed forces to keep the country safe. The Fourth Plenary Session of the 16th CPC Central Committee and the Enlarged CPC Conference of the Central Military Commission(CMC), held successively in September 2004, paid a high tribute toJiang Zemin for his outstanding contributions to national defense and military modernization, and appointed Hu Jintao Chairman of the CPC Central Military Commission. Meanwhile, the CMC composition was also readjusted and expanded, and the developmental direction for national defense and military modernization clearly defined. In the new stage of the 21st century, China's national defense and army building shall be guided by Deng Xiaoping Theory and the important thought of the "Three Represents," in an all-round way implement Jiang Zemin's thought on national defense and army building, maintain the fundamental principle and system of absolute Party leadership over the armed forces, and take the military strategy of the new era as an overarching guideline to actively push for the national defense and military modernization.

This White Paper, China's National Defense in 2004, is published to illustrate China's national defense policies and the progress made in the past two years in its defense and army building.

Chapter I The Security Situation

The current international situation continues to undergo profound and complex changes. Peace and development remain the dominating themes of the times. Although the international situation as a whole tends to be stable, factors of uncertainty, instability and insecurity are on the increase.

The trends toward world multipolarization and economic globalization are deepening amid twists and turns. New changes are occurring in the balance of power among the major international players, with the process of their realignment and the redistribution of their interests accelerated. New and profound readjustments have taken place in the relations among the world's major countries. While cooperating with and seeking support from each other, they are checking on and competing with one another as well. With their overall strength continuing to rise, the developing countries have become important players in promoting a multipolar world and democratized international relations. The United Nations is playing an irreplaceable role in international affairs. Economic globalization and technological advancement have generated new opportunities for development. As a result of accelerated global industrial restructuring, and the continued development of regional economic cooperation, world economy has witnessed new growth, with interdependence among nations deepened and their common interests increased. However, a fair and rational new international political and economic order is yet to be established. Tendencies of hegemonism and unilateralism have gained new ground, as struggles for strategic points, strategic resources and strategic dominance crop up from time to time. The Iraqi War has exerted a far-reaching influence on the international and regional security situations. The imbalance in world economic development has worsened, with the North-South gap continuing to widen, and economic security confronting new challenges.

The military factor plays a greater role in international configuration and national security. Worldwide Revolution in Military Affairs (RMA) is gaining momentum. The forms of war are undergoing changes from mechanization to informationalization. Informationalization has become the key factor in enhancing the warfighting capability of the armed forces. Confrontation between systems has become the principal feature of confrontation on the battlefield. Asymmetrical, non-contiguous and non-linear operations have become important patterns of operations. The world's major countries are making readjustments in their security and military strategies and stepping up transformation of their armed forces by way of developing high-tech weaponry and military equipment and putting forth new military doctrines. As a result, the generation gap in military technology between informationalization on the one hand and mechanization and semi-mechanization on the other is still widening, and military imbalance worldwide has further increased. The role played by military power in safeguarding national security is assuming greater prominence.

Traditional and non-traditional security issues are intertwined with the latter posing a growing threat. Some regional hot-spots have cooled down. Security cooperation at the regional level has deepened. The worldwide campaign against terrorism has made progress. International cooperation in the fields of information security, energy security, finance security and environment security has been enhanced. And international efforts to crack down on transnational crimes, prevent epidemic diseases, and reduce the impact of disasters have been intensified. However, world peace remains elusive. Geopolitical, ethnic, religious and other conflicts interact with political and economic contradictions, resulting in frequent outbreak of local wars and armed conflicts. International terrorist forces remain rampant. It seems rather difficult to eliminate completely the root causes of terrorism, making the fight against terrorism a long and demanding task before the international community.

The Asia-Pacific region enjoys basic stability in its security situation. As the world's most dynamic region economically, most nations in the region have made development the centerpiece of their policy. Major country relations continue to improve and grow. Peaceful consultation has become the basic approach to the settlement of disputes. Security dialogue and cooperation of various forms have become more animated. Asia-Pacific Economic Cooperation (APEC) is playing an important role in promoting common development. The institutionalization of the Shanghai Cooperation Organization (SCO) has been basically accomplished. The SCO is incessantly expanding and deepening its cooperation in the political, security, economic, humanitarian and other fields. The SCO is playing a greater role in promoting peace, stability and development in the region. China has established a strategic partnership with the Association of Southeast Asian Nations (ASEAN) dedicated to peace and prosperity in the region, and engaged in comprehensive cooperation that has seen rapid expansion. Cooperation in East Asia, with the ASEAN and China, Japan and the ROK as the main players, keeps expanding, leading to greater economic development and political and security trust in the region. The ASEAN Regional Forum (ARF) as the most important official channel for multilateral security dialogue in the Asia-Pacific region, plays a positive role in promoting security cooperation in the region. The nuclear issue on the Korean Peninsula has been brought onto the track of peaceful settlement through dialogue, and the process of the Six-Party Talks has made progress in the discussion of substantive issues and the institutionalization of the process. Tensions between India and Pakistan have been eased, and the two countries have maintained the momentum of peaceful dialogues.

Meanwhile, complicated security factors in the Asia-Pacific region are on the increase. The United States is realigning and reinforcing its military presence in this region by buttressing military alliances and accelerating deployment of missile defense systems. Japan is stepping up its constitutional overhaul, adjusting its military and security policies and developing the missile defense system for future deployment. It has also markedly increased military activities abroad. The foundation for the Six-Party Talks is not solid enough as uncertain factors linger in the settlement of the nuclear issue on the Korean Peninsula. The threat posed by terrorism, separatism and extremism is still grave. Such transnational crimes as smuggling, piracy, drug trafficking and money laundering are rampant. Many countries are confronted with the formidable task of eliminating poverty, achieving sustainable development and enhancing security in the area of public health.

The situation in the relations between the two sides of the Taiwan Straits is grim. The Taiwan authorities under Chen Shui-bian have recklessly challenged the status quo that both sides of the Straits belong to one and the same China, and markedly escalated the "Taiwan independence" activities designed to split China. Incessantly trumpeting their separatist claim of "one country on each side," they use referendum to engage in the separatist activities aimed at "Taiwan independence," incite hostility among the people on the island toward the mainland, and purchase large amounts of offensive weapons and equipment. They have not given up their attempt at "Taiwan independence" through the formulation of a so-called "new constitution for Taiwan." They are still waiting for the opportune moment to engineer a major "Taiwan independence" incident through the so-called "constitutional reform." The separatist activities of the "Taiwan independence" forces have increasingly become the biggest immediate threat to China's sovereignty and territorial integrity as well as peace and stability on both sides of the Taiwan Straits and the Asia-Pacific region as a whole. The United States has on many occasions reaffirmed adherence to the one China policy, observance of the three joint communiques and opposition to "Taiwan independence." However, it continues to increase, quantitatively and qualitatively, its arms sales to Taiwan, sending a wrong signal to the Taiwan authorities. The US action does not serve a stable situation across the Taiwan Straits.

China's national security environment in this pluralistic, diversified and interdependent world has on the whole improved, but new challenges keep cropping up. The vicious rise of the "Taiwan independence" forces, the technological gap resulting from RMA, the risks and challenges caused by the development of the trends toward economic globalization, and the prolonged existence of unipolarity vis-a-vis multipolarity — all these will have a major impact on China's security. Nevertheless, China is determined to safeguard its national sovereignty and security, no matter how the international situation may evolve, and what difficulties it may encounter, so as to join hands with the people around the world in advancing the lofty cause of peace and development for mankind.

Chapter II National Defense Policy

China persists in taking the road of peaceful development and unswervingly pursues a national defense policy defensive in nature, China's national defense is the security guarantee for the survival and development of the nation. The main tasks of China's national defense are to step up modernization of its national defense and its armed forces, to safeguard national security and unity, and to ensure the smooth process of building a moderately prosperous society in an all-round way.

Proceeding from the fundamental interests of the country, China's national defense policy is both subordinated to and in service of the country's development and security strategies. Firmly seizing and taking full advantage of the important strategic opportunities presented in the first two decades of this century, China sticks to keeping its development in pace with its security and makes great efforts to enhance its national strategic capabilities by using multiple security means to cope with both traditional and non-traditional security threats so as to seek a comprehensive national security in the political, economic, military and social areas.

China's basic goals and tasks in maintaining national security are:

- To stop separation and promote reunification, guard against and resist aggression, and defend national sovereignty, territorial integrity and maritime rights and interests.

- To safeguard the interests of national development, promote economic and social development in an all-round, coordinated and sustainable way and steadily increase the overall national strength.
- To modernize China's national defense in line with both the national conditions of China and the trend of military development in the world by adhering to the policy of coordinating military and economic development, and improve the operational capabilities of self-defense under the conditions of informationalization.
- To safeguard the political, economic and cultural rights and interests of the Chinese people, crack down on criminal activities of all sorts and maintain public order and social stability.
- To pursue an independent foreign policy of peace and adhere to the new security concept featuring mutual trust, mutual benefit, equality and coordination with a view to securing a long-term and favorable international and surrounding environment.

It is the sacred responsibility of the Chinese armed forces to stop the "Taiwan independence" forces from splitting the country. The Chinese government continues to adhere to the basic principles of "peaceful reunification" and "one country, two systems" along with the eight-point proposal on developing cross-Straits relations and advancing the process of peaceful reunification of the motherland at the current stage. So long as the Taiwan authorities accept the one China principle and stop their separatist activities aimed at "Taiwan independence," cross-Straits talks can be held at any time on officially ending the state of hostility between the two sides, including on the establishment of a confidence-building mechanism in the military field. The Chinese people are resolutely opposed to all separatist activities in whatever manifestation aimed at "Taiwan independence," to foreign interference of any form, and to arms sales to Taiwan or entrance to military alliance of any form with Taiwan by any country in the world. We will never allow anyone to split Taiwan from China through whatever means. Should the Taiwan authorities go so far as to make a reckless attempt that constitutes a major incident of "Taiwan independence," the Chinese people and armed forces will resolutely and thoroughly crush it at any cost.

To adapt itself to the changes both in the international strategic situation and the national security environment and rise to the challenges presented by the RMA worldwide, China adheres to the military strategy of active defense and works to speed up the RMA with Chinese characteristics.

- To take the road of composite and leapfrog development. Going with the tide of the world's military development and moving along the direction of informationalization in the process of modernization, the People's Liberation Army (PLA) shall gradually achieve the transition from mechanization and semi-mechanization to informationalization. Based on China's national conditions and the PLA's own conditions, the PLA persists in taking mechanization as the foundation to promote informationalization, and informationalization as the driving force to bring forward mechanization. The PLA will promote coordinated development of firepower, mobility and information capability, enhance the development of its operational strength with priority given to the Navy, Air Force and Second Artillery Force, and strengthen its comprehensive deterrence and warfighting capabilities.

- To build a strong military by means of science and technology. The PLA works to improve its combat capabilities by taking advantage of scientific and technological advances and aims at building qualitative efficiency instead of a mere quantitative scale, and transforming the military from a manpower-intensive one to a technology-intensive one. Implementing the Strategic Project for Talented People, the PLA focuses on training a new type of high-caliber military personnel. It works to build up a complete system of weaponry and equipment by stepping up development of new-and high-tech weaponry and equipment while upgrading those in active service. In an innovative spirit, the PLA endeavors to improve its training system as well as the means and methods of training so as to raise its military training to a higher level. Relying on national economic, scientific and technological development, the PLA is devoted to improving the level of scientific management and achieving a higher overall cost-effectiveness in military expenditure so as to modernize the armed forces with less input and better results.
- To deepen the reform of the armed forces. Based on the transformation of modern warfare and the requirements of the socialist market economy, the PLA seeks to achieve development and breakthroughs in the process of reform and innovation. The PLA develops its military theories in an innovative spirit, and explores the laws of building the army and conducting operations under the condition of informationalization. In accordance with the principle of making the troops smaller and better, as well as more integrated and efficient, and with emphasis on adjusting the organizational structure and reforming the command system, the PLA works to build and further improve the military structure and organization to make them appropriate in size, optimal in structure, streamlined in institutional set-up and flexible and swift in command. The PLA also works to readjust and regulate the relationship within the military as well as that with the government and society so as to put in place policies and mechanisms which will help motivate officers and soldiers.
- To step up preparations for military struggle. The PLA takes as its objective to win local wars under the conditions of informationalization and gives priority to developing weaponry and equipment, to building

joint operational capabilities, and to making full preparations in the battlefields. Meanwhile, it adheres to the people's war concept and develops the strategies and tactics of the people's war. To meet the requirements of integrated and joint operations, the PLA endeavors to establish a modern operational system capable of giving fuil play to the overall efficiency of the armed forces as well as the national war potentials. The PLA conducts more training and exercises with specific objectives in order to raise its capabilities in coping with various crises and contingencies.

– To carry out military exchanges and cooperation. In line with the national foreign policy, the PLA conducts military cooperation that is non-aligned, non-confrontational and not directed against any third party. The PLA takes part in the UN peacekeeping operations and international counter-terrorism cooperation. While promoting military exchanges in various forms, the PLA works to establish security dialogue mechanisms in order to create a military security environment featuring mutual trust and mutual benefit. It takes part in bilateral or multilateral joint military exercises in non-traditional security fields so as to enhance the joint capabilities to cope with threats in those fields. The PLA learns from and draws on the valuable experience of foreign armed forces, and introduces, on a selective basis, technologically advanced equipment and better management expertise from abroad to advance the modernization of the Chinese armed forces.

Part 2 B

Speeches delivered by International leaders

Part II

‹74›

Proposals made by US President George Bush on WMD non-proliferation at National Defence University (11.02.2004)

President Bush warned that the greatest threat before humanity today is the possibility of secret and sudden attack with weapons of mass destruction as these weapons "would be a first resort, the preferred means" in the hands of terrorists. He spoke at length about A.Q. Khan's "international network for the proliferation of nuclear technology and know-how" and mentioned that President Musharraf had assured that "his country will never again be a source of proliferation". He then outlined "seven proposals" to meet the challenge of proliferation such as expanding the work of proliferation security initiative, strengthening the laws and international controls governing proliferation, plugging the loophole in the Non-Proliferation Treaty so that nuclear material cannot be produced to build bombs under the cover of certain nuclear programmes, etc.

The President,

Thanks for the warm welcome. I'm honored to visit the National Defense University. For nearly a century, the scholars and students here have helped to prepare America for the changing threats to our national security. Today the men and women of our National Defense University are helping to frame the strategies through which we are fighting and winning the war on terror. Your center for Counterproliferation Research and your other institution colleges are providing vital insight into the dangers of a new era. I want to thank each one of you for devoting your talents and your energy to the service of our great nation.

I want to thank General Michael Dunn for inviting me here. I used to jog by this facility on a regular basis. Then my age kicked in (Laughter). I appreciate Ambassador Wolfgang Ischinger from Germany. Mr. Ambassador, thank you for being here today. I see my friend, George Schultz, a distinguished public servant and true patriot with us. George, thank you for coming; and Charlotte, it's good to see you. I'm so honored that Dick Lugar is here with us today. Senator, I appreciate you taking time and thanks for bringing Senator Saxby Chambliss with you, as well. I appreciate the veterans who are here and those on active duty. Thanks for letting me come by.

On September the 11th, 2001, America a and the world witnessed a new kind of war. We saw the great harm that a stateless network could inflict upon our country — killers armed with box cutters, mace and 19 airline tickets. Those attacks also raised the prospect of even worse dangers of other weapons in the hands of other men. The greatest threat before humanity today is the possibility of secret and sudden attack with chemical or biological or radiological or nuclear weapons.

In the past, enemies of America required mass armies and great navies, powerful air forces to put our nation, our people, our friends at risk. In the Cold War, Americans lived under the threat of weapons of mass destruction, but believed that deterrents made those weapons a last resort. What has changed in the 21st century is that, in the hands of terrorists, weapons of mass destruction would be a first resort, the preferred means to further their ideology of suicide and random murder. These terrible weapons are becoming easier to acquire, build, hide and transport. Armed with a single vial of a biological agent or a single nuclear weapon, small groups of fanatics or failing states could gain the power to threaten great nations, threaten the world peace.

America and the entire civilized world will face this threat for decades to come. We must confront the danger with open eyes and unbending purpose. I made clear to all the policy of this nation: America will not permit terrorists and dangerous regimes to threaten us with the world's most deadly weapons. (Applause.)

Meeting this duty has required changes in thinking and strategy. Doctrines designed to contain empires, deter aggressive states and defeat massed armies, cannot fully protect us from this new threat. America faces the possibility of catastrophic attack from ballistic missiles armed with weapons of mass destruction. So that is why we are developing and deploying missile defenses to guard our people. The best intelligence is necessary to win the war on terror and to stop proliferation, so that is why I have established a commission that will examine our intelligence capabilities and recommend ways to improve and adapt them to detect new and emerging threats.

We're determined to confront those threats at the source. We will stop these weapons from being acquired or built. We'll block them from being transferred. We will prevent them from ever being used. One source of these weapons is dangerous and secretive regimes that build weapons of mass destruction to intimidate their neighbors and force their influence upon the world. These nations pose different challenges. They require different strategies.

The former dictator of Iraq possessed and used weapons of mass destruction against his own people. For twelve years, he defied the will of the international community. He refused to disarm or account for his illegal weapons and programs. He doubted our resolve to enforce our word. And now he sits in a prison cell while his country moves toward a democratic future. (Applause.)

To Iraq's east, the government of Iran is unwilling to abandon a uranium-enrichment program capable of producing material for nuclear weapons. The United States is working with our allies and the International Atomic Energy Agency to ensure that Iran meets its commitments and does not develop nuclear weapons. (Applause)

In the Pacific, North Korea has defied the world, has tested long-range ballistic missiles, admitted its possession of nuclear weapons and now threatens to build more. Together with our partners in Asia, America is insisting that North Korea completely, verifiably and irreversibly dismantle its nuclear programs.

America has consistently brought these threats to the attention of international organizations. We're using every means of diplomacy to answer them. As for my part, I will continue to speak clearly on these threats. I will continue to call upon the world to confront these dangers and to end them. (Appalause)

In recent years, another path of proliferation has become clear, as well. America and other nations are learning more about black market operatives who deal in equipment and expertise related to weapons of mass destruction. These dealers are motivated by greed, fanaticism or both. They find eager customers in outlaw regimes; paid millions for the parts and plans they need to speed up their weapons programs. And the deadly technology and expertise on the market, there's the terrible possibility that terrorist groups could obtain the ultimate weapons they desire most.

The extent and sophistication of such networks can be seen in the case of a man named Abdul Qadeer Khan. This is the story as we know it so far.

A.Q. Khan is known throughout the world as the father of Pakistan's nuclear weapons program. What was not publicly known until recently is that he also led an extensive international network for the proliferation of nuclear technology and know-how.

For decades, Mr. Khan remained on the Pakistani government payroll earning a modest salary. Yet he and his associates financed lavish lifestyles through the sale of nuclear technologies and equipment to outlaw regimes stretching from North Africa to the Korean peninsula.

A.Q. Khan himself operated mostly out of Pakistan. He served as director of the network, its leading scientific mind, as well as its primary salesman. Over the past decade, he made frequent trips to consult with his clients and to sell his expertise. He and his associates sold the blueprints for centrifuges to enrich uranium, as well as nuclear design stolen from the Pakistani government. The network sold uranium, hexafluoride, the gas that the centrifuge process can transform into enriched uranium for nuclear bombs. Khan and his associates provided Iran and Libya and North Korea with designs for Pakistan's older centrifuges, as well as designs for more advanced and efficient models. The network also provided these countries with components and, in some cases, with complete centrifuges.

To increase their profits, Khan and his associates used a factory in Malaysia to manufacture key parts for centrifuges. Other necessary parts were purchased through network operatives, based in Europe and the Middle East and Africa. These procurement agents saw the trade in nuclear technologies as a shortcut to personal wealth. And they set up front companies to deceive legitimate firms into selling them tightly controlled materials.

Khan's deputy, a man named BSA Tahir ran SMB Computers, a business in Dubai. Tahir used that computer company as a front for the proliferation activities A.Q. Khan network. Tahir acted as both the network's chief financial officer and money launderer. He was also its shipping agent, using his computer firm as cover for the movement of centrifuge parts to various clients.Tahir directed the Malaysia facility to produce these parts, based on Pakistani designs, and then ordered the facility to ship the components to Dubai. Tahir also arranged for parts acquired by other European procurement agents to transit through Dubai for shipment to other customers.

This picture of the Khan network was pieced together over several years by American and British intelligence officers. Our intelligence services gradually uncovered this network's reach and identified its key experts and agents and money men. Operatives followed its transactions, mapped the extent of its operations. They monitored the travel of A.Q. Khan and senior associates. They shadowed members of the network around the world. They recorded their conversations. They penetrated their operations. We've uncovered their secrets. This work involved high risk. And all Americans should be grateful for the hard work and the dedication of our fine intelligence professionals.

Governments around the world worked closely with us to unravel the Khan network and to put an end to its criminal enterprise. A.Q. Khan has confessed his crimes. And his top associates are out of business. The government of Pakistan is interrogating the network's members, learning critical details that will help them prevent it from ever operating again. President Musharraf has promised to share all the information he learns about the Khan network and has assured us that his country will never again be a source of proliferation.

Mr. Tahir is in Malaysia, where authorities are investigating his activities. The Malaysian authorities have assured us that the factory the network used is no longer producing centrifuge parts. Other members of the network remain at large. One by one, they will be found and their careers in the weapons trade will be ended.

As a result of our penetration of the network, American and the British intelligence identified a shipment of advanced centrifuge parts manufactured at the Malaysian facility. We followed the shipment of these parts to Dubai and watched as they were transferred to the BBC China, a German-owned ship. After the ship passed through the Suez Canal bound for Libya, it was stopped by German and Italian authorities. They found several containers, each 40 feet in length, listed on the ship's manifest as full of used machine parts. In fact, these containers were filled with parts of sophisticated centrifuges.

The interception of the BBC China came as Libyan and British and American officials were discussing the possibility of Libya ending its WMD programs. The United States and Britain confronted Libyan officials with this evidence of an active and illegal nuclear program. About two months ago, Libya's leader voluntarily agreed to end his nuclear and chemical weapons programs, not to pursue biological weapons, and to permit thorough inspections by the International Atomic Energy Agency and the Organization for the Prohibition of Chemical Weapons. We're now working in partnership with these organizations and with the United Kingdom to help the government of Libya dismantle those programs and eliminate all dangerous materials.

Colonel Gadhafi made the right decision, and the world will be safer once his commitment is fulfilled. We expect other regimes to follow his example. Abandoning the pursuit of illegal weapons can lead to better relations with the United States and other free nations. Continuing to seek those weapons will not bring security or international prestige, but only political isolation, economic hardship and other unwelcome consequences. (Applause)

We know that Libya was not the only customer of the Khan network. Other countries expressed great interest in their services. These regimes and other proliferators like Khan should know: We and our friends are determined to protect our people and the world from proliferation. (Applause)

Breaking this network is one major success in a broad-based effort to stop the spread of terrible weapons. We're adjusting our strategies to the threats of a new era. America and the nations of Australia, France and Germany, Italy and Japan, the Netherlands, Poland, Portugal, Spain and the United Kingdom have launched the Proliferation Security Initiative to interdict lethal materials in transit. Our nations are sharing intelligence information, tracking suspect international cargo, conducting joint military exercises. We're prepared to search planes and ships, to seize weapons and missiles and equipment that raise proliferation concerns, just as we did in stopping the dangerous cargo on the BBC China before it reached Libya. Three more governments – Canada and Singapore and Norway – will be participating in this initiative. We'll continue to expand the core group of PSI countries. And as PSI grows, proliferators will find it harder than ever to trade in illicit weapons.

There is a consensus among nations that proliferation cannot be tolerated. Yet this consensus means little unless it is translated into action. Every civilized nation has a stake in preventing the spread of weapons of mass destruction. These materials and technologies, and the people who traffic in them, cross many borders. To stop this trade, the nations of the world must be strong and determined. We must work together, we must act effectively. Today, I announce seven proposals to strengthen the world's efforts to stop the spread of deadly weapons.

First, I propose that the work of the Proliferation Security Initiative be expanded to address more than shipments and transfers. Building on the tools we've developed to fight terrorists, we can take direct action against proliferation networks. We need greater cooperation not just among intelligence and military services, but in law enforcement, as well. PSI participants and other willing nations should use the Interpol and all other means to bring to justice those who traffic in deadly weapons, to shut down their labs, to seize their materials, to freeze their assets. We must act on every lead. We will find the middlemen, the suppliers and the buyers. Our message to proliferators must be consistent and it must be clear: We will find you, and we're not going to rest until you are stopped. (Applause).

Second, I call on all nations to strengthen the laws and international controls that govern proliferation. At the U.N. last fall, I proposed a new Security Council resolution requiring all states to criminalize proliferation, enact strict export controls, and secure all sensitive materials within their borders. The Security Council should pass this proposal quickly. And when they do, America stands ready to help other governments to draft and enforce the new laws that will help us deal with proliferation.

Third, I propose to expand our efforts to keep weapons from the Cold War and other dangerous materials out of the wrong hands. In 1991, Congress passed the Nunn-Lugar legislation. Senator Lugar had a clear vision, along with Senator Nunn, about what to do with the old Soviet Union. Under this program, we're helping former Soviet states find productive employment for former weapons scientists. We're dismantling, destroying and securing weapons and materials left over from the Soviet WMD arsenal. We have more work to do there.

And as a result of the G-8 Summit in 2002, we agreed to provide $20 billion over 10 years – half of it from the United States – to support such programs. We should expand this cooperation elsewhere in the world. We will retain [sic] WMD scientists and technicians in countries like Iraq and Libya. We will help nations end the use of weapons-grade uranium in research reactors. I urge more nations to contribute to these efforts. The nations of the world must do all we can to secure and eliminate nuclear and chemical and biological and radiological materials.

As we track and destroy these networks, we must also prevent governments from developing nucelar weapons under false pretenses. The Nuclear Non-Proliferation Treaty was designed more than 30 years ago to prevent the spread of nuclear weapons beyond those states which already possessed them. Under this treaty, nuclear states agreed to help non-nuclear states develop peaceful atomic energy if they renounced the pursuit of nucelar weapons. But the treaty has a loophole which has been exploited by nations such as North Korea and Iran. These regimes are allowed to produce nuclear material that can be used to build bombs under the cover of civilian nuclear programs.

So today, as a fourth step, I propose a way to close the loophole. The world must create a safe, orderly system to field civilian nuclear plants without adding to the danger of weapons proliferation. The world's leading nuclear exporters should ensure that states have reliable access at reasonable cost to fuel for civilian reactors, so long as those states renounce enrichment and reprocessing. Enrichment and reprocessing are not necessary for nations seeking to harness nuclear energy for peaceful purposes.

The 40 nations of the Nuclear Suppliers Group should refuse to sell enrichment and reprocessing equipment and technologies to any state that does not already possess full-scale, functioning enrichment and reprocessing plants. (Applause.) This step will prevent new states from developing the means to produce fissile material for nuclear bombs. Proliferators must not be allowed to cynically manipulate the NPT to acquire the material and infrastructure necessary for manufacturing illegal weapons.

For international norms to be effective, they must be enforced. It is the charge of the International Atomic Energy Agency to uncover banned nuclear activity around the world and report those violations to the U.N. Security Council. We must ensure that the IAEA has all the tools it needs to fulfill its essential mandate. America and other nations support what is called the Additional Protocol, which requires states to declare a broad range of nuclear activities and facilities, and allow the IAEA to inspect those facilities.

As a fifth step, I propose that by next year, only states that have signed the Additional Protocol be allowed to import equipment for their civilian nuclear programs. Nations that are serious about fighting proliferation will approve and implement the Additional Protocol. I've submitted the Additional Protocol to the Senate. I urge the Senate to consent immediately to its ratification.

We must also ensure that IAEA is organized to take action when action is required. So, a sixth step, I propose the creation of a special committee of the IAEA Board which will focus intensively on safeguards and verification. This committee, made up of governments in good standing with the IAEA, will strengthen the capability of the IAEA to ensure that nations comply with their international obligations.

And, finally, countries under investigation for violating nuclear non-proliferation obligations are currently allowed to serve on the IAEA Board of Governors. For instance, Iran – a country suspected of maintaining an extensive nuclear weapons program – recently completed a two-year term on the Board. Allowing potential violators to serve on the Board creates an unacceptable barrier to effective action. No state under investigation for proliferation violations should be allowed to serve on the IAEA Board of Governors – or on the new special committee. And any state currently on the Board that comes under investigation should be suspended from the Board. The integrity and mission of the IAEA depends on this simple principle: Those actively breaking the rules should not be entrusted with enforcing the rules. (Applause)

As we move forward to address these challenges we will consult with our friends and allies on all these new measures. We will listen to their ideas. Together we will defend the safety of all nations and preserve the peace of the world.

Over the last two years, a great coalition has come together to defeat terrorism and to oppose the spread of weapons of mass destruction – the inseparable commitments of the war on terror. We've shown that proliferators can be discovered and can be stopped. We've shown that for regimes that choose defiance, there are serious consequences. The way ahead is not easy, but it is clear. We will proceed as if the lives of our citizens depend on our vigilance, because they do. Terrorists and terror states are in a race for weapons of mass murder, a race they must lose. (Applause) Terrorists are resourceful; we're more resourceful. They're determined; we must be more determined. We will never lose focus or resolve. We'll be unrelenting in the defence of free nations, and rise to the hard demands of dangerous times.

May God bless you all. (Applause)

❮75❯

Address by President of Pakistan, Gen Musharraf to The India Today Conclave (13.03.2004)

In his address, Gen. Musharraf said that the Kashmir issue was central to the Pakistan-India animosity. This issue must be resolved "in an equitable and honourable manner acceptable to India, Pakistan and the Kashmiris." He further mentioned that "there is simultaneity" between the CBMs and the dialogue process on all substantive issues including Kashmir and also that the leaders on both sides have to be sincere, to develop confidence and trust in each other.

Thank you again everyone. Thank you very much Mr. Arun Puri the Editor-in Chief of *India Today*. All the ladies and gentlemen, good evening and Aslamo Alaikum. It is indeed my very special privilege to be addressing India Today Conclave via satellite. I only wish I was sitting in front of you and seeing you in person. I thank all the organizers and the management of *India Today* for this invitation and for affording me to this very unique opportunity of speaking to all of you. First of all let me congratulate all of you, let me congratulate India for the first victory after fifteen years in the first one day international at Karachi. I am very glad indeed that the match was most interesting, most well contested and extremely exciting. I am also glad that the people of Pakistan in general and the people of Karachi in particular welcomed the Indian team with a very open and a warm heart. I only hope that series in the future, the other one day internationals and the test matches are played in the same good welcoming spirit that we saw today. So I again congratulate all of you for winning today a very exciting and thrilling match. Coming to the subject, ladies and gentlemen, the theme of this year's Conclave is "India: Tomorrow, building a South Asia Century." I have been tasked to speak on the Future of Pakistan-India relations, the opportunities, risks, benefits, my expectations from the Indian leadership, possible United States role and my own world vision. I commend the organizers first of all for selecting such an apt subject bearing immense relevance to the region, particularly at this time. I wish this conclave success in the deliberation and pray for a prosperous South Asia through bridging mutual differences. Ladies and Gentlemen, quite clearly as the theme and its elaboration imply, realization of a South Asia Century requires collective will and application. India cannot go it alone. The hurdle in the application of this collective will indeed comes from continued Indo-Pakistan confrontation. Before getting involved in regional emancipation and bilateral conflict identification and resolution, I would like to share my overall global vision as I am required to do. Ladies and gentlemen, the 21st century is a century of globalization. The outlines of a global village are visible in all fields. It is a century of geo-economics and of inter-dependence. While on one hand we witness the start of integration of the world for the sake of human uplift on the other hand there is manifestation of enhanced destructive power of implements of confrontation. I am referring to weapons of mass destruction, or even the increased lethality of conventional weapons, rendering war an extremely dangerous and a very costly undertaking. Within these opposing realities, we also see the world fragmented, torn in conflict. Short of war low intensity conflict has seen the introduction of suicide bombing phenomenon, which provides a new and a very lethal weapon in the hands of a terrorist or a freedom fighter, whichever side of the divide you look for compensating for military and political weakness. Looking at each conflict in the last two decades unfortunately, they all involved Muslim countries. All of whom happen to be at the receiving end. Muslims today suffer from a sense of deprivation, a sense of hopelessness and a sense of powerlessness. Combined with poverty and illiteracy, this becomes an explosive mix vulnerable to adoption of an extremist or a militant path. Thus the world as a whole has become a dangerous place to live in. Improvement can only come through addressing Muslim concerns with justice. Within these outlined parameters we need to look at the power equation in our region. War or military confrontation do not constitute a viable solution any more. We must understand that the issue is not a game of numbers' alone. The strategy of military coercion with numbers is inapplicable when an adversary , albeit weaker, is prepared to accept losses and inflict maximum retaliatory damage, which may be untenable to the other side. The question that arises is, how to deal with this conflict torn hatred infested world and meet our collective duty to bring peace to this world, our common heritage. I have proposed a strategy of enlightened moderation. This is a two-pronged strategy. One prong is to be exercised by the Muslims through rejection of extremism and militancy and opting for socio-economic development using a restructured OIC as the driving force. The other prong of this strategy of enlightened moderation is to be implemented by the West; resolve all political disputes involving Muslims with justice. Success of this strategy, the overall strategy, indeed lies in the simultaneous success of both the prongs. After this brief look at the world let us come closer home, to our region, South Asia. We see an upheaval, turmoil in Afghanistan and Kashmir. If we can resolve these two issues, we will strike at the root of extremism and militancy, I am very sure. Pakistan is actively fighting against Al- Qaida along our western borders in the tribal areas. We had the will and the capability to eradicate all foreigners from our country. We will not allow Al-Qaida to maintain sanctuaries in Pakistan and operate outside Pakistan. Ladies and gentlemen, the Kashmir issue lies at the heart of Indo-Pakistan confrontation and hence is also the source of disunity of South Asia as a whole. As a result SAARC has merely existed on the periphery of impotence. We saw a visible and a very pleasant change in the last SAARC summit held at Islamabad. This was momentous not only for the thaw in Indo-Pakistan relations but also for signing of SAPTA, which is a big leap towards free trade within our region. It is said the past belonged to Europe, the present to America and the future to Asia. Within Asia, we see North East Asia, East Asia, China and South East Asia cooperating fully for mutual economic progress. South Asia and Central Asia sadly remain out of this prosperity loop, may I say. Quite clearly, common wisdom dictates intra-regional cooperation within SAARC and also ECO, the Economic Cooperation Organization, first, followed by inter-regional integration with the rest of Asia for joint benefits to our region. Pakistan's geography provides a critical linkage between the three regions of South Asia, Central Asia and West Asia. Indo-Pakistan rapprochement unleashes the entire economic, commercial, trade potential of this whole region. Undoubtedly the whole scenario provides a strong case for resolving disputes, ushering in an era of peace by joining hands for socio-economic development of our people and of our region. India and Pakistan must bury the past and chart a new roadmap for peace. I believe people of both our countries desire peace and may I also add are fed up of confrontation. This is evident from the welcoming response to the CBMs of the past one or two months. Revival of sports ties with a tour of Indian cricket team, finally we say, it is better late than never and the forthcoming SAF games, indeed auger well for the promotion of people to people contacts and we are witnessing this good contact during the one day international today at Karachi. Ladies and gentlemen, Pakistan and India have lost half a century in mutual squabbles. Let us face it. We have fought wars, tested nuclear weapons and have remained engaged in very hot confrontation throughout. Today South Asia is nuclearized. It is brimming with lethal weaponry, huge accusations of arsenal and sophisticated weapon technology make our region one of the most dangerous flashpoints in the world and it is of greatest concern to the world. South Asia also constitutes one of the most impoverished regions of the world. Social indices are appalling, millions live in dire poverty, misery and disease. At the centre of this dismal scenario is the spiraling vortex of Pakistan-India animosity .Kashmir, we say a paradise on earth, is the core issue that has bedeviled our relations throughout this half a century. Kashmir is the central issue that awaits a just and durable settlement. If Pakistan and India could settle Kashmir in accordance with aspirations of the Kashmiris, a new chapter in our troubled history will begin. This is very much possible if all parties are sincere in their quest for a just and durable peace through a solution acceptable to all of us not to one single country. I have proposed a four-point process whereby talks commence, centrality of Kashmir dispute is accepted, all solutions not acceptable to either of the three parties are taken off the table and of the remaining options the one deemed most feasible and acceptable is chosen. I believe nothing could be fairer than this. A solution will emerge if all sides are mindful of the problem, if all parties, especially Kashmiris are given the opportunity to have their due say and are associated with a credible, sincere and serious quest for a final settlement between Pakistan and India. I do not want to speak about history. The political and legal history of Kashmir is well recorded and well documented in the archives and resolutions of the United Nations. All that I urge is let us be pragmatic. Let us learn to accept hard facts. The issue of Kashmir is at the centrestage, we cannot deny it. It must be resolved in an equitable and honourable manner acceptable to India, Pakistan and Kashmiris, and I repeat, to India, acceptable to India, Pakistan and the Kashmiris. We are not talking of a solution acceptable to Pakistan alone. I wish to assure you that we are determined to take two steps forward if India takes one step and chooses to embark on a realistic quest for a just and durable peace with Pakistan on the basis of sovereign equality. India will find Pakistan sincere and responsive if it desires genuine improvement in relations. We are mindful of the difficulties posed by very rigid mindsets in the past. We must know if there is no movement towards a solution, I am afraid, everything will slide back to square one. Let us look at the very broad benefits from peace accruing to both our countries. May be this serves as a motivation towards normalisation. On trade, our market size will expand to 1.2 billion, equal to China. Opening vistas of trading opportunities within the region, the foreign direct investment which presently stagnates at three billion dollars could increase manifold. China attracts forty billion dollars. Access to alternate energy, natural gas from Iran and Central Asia can become available to the region, bringing down energy cost by at least fifty per cent and may I say India may be the maximum beneficiary. Tourism can flourish. The region has vast treasures of tourist attractions, not only for the domestic but also for the international tourists. Combined regional tours could benefit us all. Reduction in defense expenditure could take place. This will lead to availability of funds for social sectors and poverty reduction and lastly sports activities could be enhanced. Through mutual sports India and Pakistan could regain their lost glory at least in cricket and hockey. We must be aware, however, ladies and gentlemen, there are extremists on both sides who try to derail the peace process. We must not be deterred from our path and be prepared to deal with them with an iron hand. In fact in our own supreme interest, we must negotiate peace boldly as if there are no detracting extremists. And we must also deal with all extremists boldly and firmly as if there is no peace initiative going on. The joint statement, ladies and gentlemen, reached at Islamabad between me and Prime Minister Vajpayee provides a good framework for relationship of harmony and mutual respect. The CBMs already been initiated have generated tremendous goodwill. The Foreign Secretary level talks have furthered this dialogue process forward. The composite dialogue scheduled for May and June this year should augur well for our future relationship. In this garden path that is very visible, I would be blemished if I did not strike some words of caution. Firstly, there is a simultaneity, a linkage between CBMs, the confidence building measures, and the composite dialogue. CBMs cannot outstrip dialogue process on all substantive issues including Kashmir. Secondly, Kashmir dispute can never be sidelined or ignored. No leader in Pakistan can do that. We must move forward towards its resolution in tandem with the CBMs. And lastly while talking of Kashmir, sooner or later Kashmiris must join the peace process to make the solution practicable. Ladies and gentlemen, progress on dialogue towards serious resolution of disputes should set us thinking on other more substantive confidence building measures. Why can't our defense expenditure be cut down? It certainly can. Pakistan is not in an arms race. We maintain a quantified force level based on a perceived threat and a strategy of minimum deterrence. We are already reducing our strength, the strength of our army by fifty thousand, may I tell you, may I inform you today. We have kept our defense budget frozen for the last four years knowing fully well that our deterrent strategy is in place. India has to review its own strategy because your defense force levels, may I say, are not based on threat, but on your own power projection. The latest multi-billion dollar acquisitions and your vastly enhanced budgetary allocations to defense take you in that direction of power projection. In any case Pakistan will remain amiable for mutual, proportional reduction of forces. Ladies and gentlemen, I honestly feel that the present time is ideal for resolution of all disputes and ushering in an era of peace, harmony and prosperity. The people of our country want it. The influential business community is eagerly looking' forward to it in both the countries. I have interacted with many business leaders of your country. Media also seems to favour it. Where lies the stumbling block then. I am afraid it lies in the leadership alone. Leaders on both sides have to be sincere, to develop confidence and trust in each other. They are to be flexible enough to reach mutually acceptable solutions to previously intractable disputes and bold enough, they are to be bold enough to bulldoze all opposition and risks en route to peace, we have to show enough maturity to be able to resolve disputes bilaterally, within reasonable time line. It is only our failure, which then invites third party mediation or facilitation, or involvement or encouragement. You can choose the word yourself because I know there is some kind of an allergy to the words to the terms' mediation probably in your country. The US being the sole super power in a unipolar world has a responsibility of bringing a just peace in the world on all disputes for our future generation. Their involvement to a resolution of thorny Kashmir dispute will be a value only if we get stuck ourselves. If we make bilateral progress there is no need of outside interference or involvement. As Responsible nuclear weapon state we must demonstrate to the world that we have the courage and conviction to settle our problems in a civilized manner. We must demonstrate the courage and wisdom to write a new chapter of peaceful co-existence and mutually beneficial co-operation. I find distinct warm sentiments in Pakistan and India to engage constructively with each other. May I add that the people of both countries and the media certainly play a very important role in improving the environment, paving the way for a settlement of all disputes including the Kashmir dispute. Respect for basic principles of inter state conduct develop relations of sovereign equality and provide safe and sound foundations within which Pakistan India relations can thrive and prosper. Ladies and Gentlemen we in Pakistan look forward to sustaining the present positive momentum in our relations with India. This is a moment of hope and movement of optimism, let us nurture it carefully and make the process of engagement irreversible. Let us draw balance between the vast opportunities that exist for mutual gain and the hazards of falling back to self generated hatred, despair and confrontation. Pakistan and India must lead South Asia to new horizons of economic development and the other South Asian countries .certainly look forward to that. The roadmap delineated for the composite talks must be filled with other pointers and timelines for joint endeavours to resolve differences and disputes. It should not take long to fashion together a roadmap to progress and prosperity, reinforcing and utilizing the talent and the genius of our peoples using our resources optimally. I wish the India Today Conclave every success. I would indeed be very happy to answer or to take any questions from your side. I thank you all, ladies and gentlemen.

Speech made by US President George W. Bush, on Iraq and the War on Terror, at the US Army War College (24.05.2004)

In his speech President Bush mentioned that the US Agenda in Iraq was to see "a free and self-governing Iraq." This he said, "will deny terrorists a base of operation" and will "give momentum to reforms across the region". This would also mean "a decisive blow to terrorism" and "a victory for the security of America and the civilized world". President Bush then outlined the five steps in the US plan to help Iraq achieve democracy and freedom – "hand over authority to a sovereign Iraqi government, help establish security, continue rebuilding Iraq's infrastructure, encourage more international support, and move toward a national election."

Thank you all. Thank you and good evening. I'm honored to visit the Army War College. Generations of officers have come here to study the strategies and history of warfare. I've come here tonight to report to all Americans, and to the Iraqi people, on the strategy our nation is pursuing in Iraq, and the specific steps were taking to achieve our goals.

The actions of our enemies over the last few weeks have been brutal, calculating, and instructive. We've seen a car bombing take the life of a 61-year-old Iraqi named Izzadine Saleem, who was serving as President of the Governing Council. This crime shows our enemy's intention to prevent Iraqi self-government, even if that means killing a lifelong Iraqi patriot and a faithful Muslim. Mr. Saleem was assassinated by terrorists seeking the return of tyranny and the death of democracy.

We've also seen images of a young American facing decapitation. This vile display shows a contempt for all the rules of warfare, and all the bounds of civilized behavior. It reveals a fanaticism that was not caused by any action of ours, and would not be appeased by any concession. We suspect that the man with the knife was an al Qaeda associate named Zarqawi. He and other terrorists know that Iraq is now the central front in the war on terror. And we must understand that, as well. The return of tyranny to Iraq would be an unprecedented terrorist victory, and a cause for killers to rejoice. It would also embolden the terrorists, leading to more bombings, more beheadings, and more murders of the innocent around the world.

The rise of a free and self-governing Iraq will deny terrorists a base of operation, discredit their narrow ideology, and give momentum to reformers across the region. This will be a decisive blow to terrorism at the heart of its power, and a victory for the security of America and the civilized world.

Our work in Iraq has been hard. Our coalition has faced changing conditions of war, and that has required perseverance, sacrifice, and an ability to adapt. The swift removal of Saddam Hussein's regime last spring had an unintended effect. Instead of being killed or captured on the battlefield, some of Saddam's elite guards shed their uniforms and melted into the civilian population. These elements of Saddam's repressive regime and secret police have reorganized, rearmed, and adopted sophisticated terrorist tactics. They've linked up with foreign fighters and terrorists. In a few cities, extremists have tried to sow chaos and seize regional power for themselves. These groups and individuals have conflicting ambitions, but they share a goal: They hope to wear out the patience of Americans, our coalition, and Iraqis before the arrival of effective self-government, and before Iraqis have the capability to defend their freedom.

Iraq now faces a critical moment. As the Iraqi people move closer to governing themselves, the terrorists are likely to become more active and more brutal. There are difficult days ahead, and the way forward may sometimes appear chaotic. Yet our coalition is strong, our efforts are focused and unrelenting, and no power of the enemy will stop Iraq's progress.

Helping construct a stable democracy after decades of dictatorship is a massive undertaking. Yet we have a great advantage. Whenever people are given a choice in the matter, they prefer lives of freedom to lives of fear. Our enemies in Iraq are good at filling hospitals, but they do not build any. They can incite men to murder and suicide, but they cannot inspire men to live, and hope, and add to the progress of their country. The terrorists' only influence is violence, and their only agenda is death.

Our agenda, in contrast, is freedom and independence, security and prosperity for the Iraqi people. And by removing a source of terrorist violence and instability in the Middle East, we also make our own country more secure.

Our coalition has a clear goal, understood by all — to see the Iraqi people in charge of Iraq for the first time in generations. America's task in Iraq is not only to defeat an enemy, it is to give strength to a friend—a free, representative government that serves its people and fights on their behalf. And the sooner this goal is achieved, the sooner our job will be done.

There are five steps in our plan to help Iraq achieve democracy and freedom. We will hand over authority to a sovereign Iraqi government, help establish security, continue rebuilding Iraq's infrastructure, encourage more international support, and move toward a national election that will bring forward new leaders empowered by the Iraqi people.

The first of these steps will occur next month, when our coalition will transfer full sovereignty to a government of Iraqi citizens who will prepare the way for national elections. On June 30th, the Coalition Provisional Authority will cease to exist, and will not be replaced. The occupation will end, and Iraqis will govern their own affairs. America's ambassador to Iraq, John Negroponte, will present his credentials to the new president of Iraq. Our embassy in Baghdad will have the same purpose as any other American embassy, to assure good relations with a sovereign nation. America and other countries will continue to provide technical experts to help Iraq's ministries of government, but these ministries will report to Iraq's new prime minister.

The United Nations Special Envoy, Lakhdar Brahimi, is now consulting with a broad spectrum of Iraqis to determine the composition of this interim government. The special envoy intends to put forward the names of interim government officials this week. In addition to a president, two vice presidents, and a prime minister, 26 Iraqi ministers will oversee government departments, from health to justice to defense. This new government will be advised by a national council, which will be chosen in July by Iraqis representing their country's diversity. This interim government will exercise full sovereignty until national elections are held. America fully supports Mr. Brahimi's efforts, and I have instructed the Coalition Provisional Authority to assist him in every way possible.

In preparation for sovereignty, many functions of government have already been transferred. Twelve government ministries are currently under the direct control of Iraqis. The Ministry of Education, for example, is out of the propaganda business, and is now concerned with educating Iraqi children. Under the direction of Dr. Ala'din al-Alwan, the Ministry has trained more than 30,000 teachers and supervisors for the schools of a new Iraq.

All along, some have questioned whether the Iraqi people are ready for self-government, or even want it. And all along, the Iraqi people have given their answer. In settings where Iraqis have met to discuss their country's future, they have endorsed representative government. And they are practicing representative government. Many of Iraq's cities and towns now have elected town councils or city governments—and beyond the violence, a civil society is emerging.

The June 30th transfer of sovereignty is an essential commitment of our strategy. Iraqis are proud people who resent foreign control of their affairs, just as we would. After decades under the tyrant, they are also reluctant to trust authority. By keeping our promise on June 30th, the coalition will demonstrate that we have no interest in occupation. And full sovereignty will give Iraqis a direct interest in the success of their own government. Iraqis will know that when they build a school or repair a bridge, they're not working for the Coalition Provisional Authority, they are working for themselves. And when they patrol the streets of Baghdad, or engage radical militias, they will be fighting for their own country.

The second step in the plan for Iraqi democracy is to help establish the stability and security that democracy requires. Coalition forces and the Iraqi people have the same enemies — the terrorists, illegal militia, and Saddam loyalists who stand between the Iraqi people and their future as a free nation. Working as allies, we will defend Iraq and defeat these enemies.

America will provide forces and support necessary for achieving these goals. Our commanders had estimated that a troop level below 115,000 would be sufficient at this point in the conflict. Given the recent increase in violence, we'll maintain our troop level at the current 138,000 as long as necessary. This has required extended duty for the 1st Armored Division and the 2nd Light Cavalry Regiment — 20,000 men and women who were scheduled to leave Iraq in April. Our nation appreciates their hard work and sacrifice, and they can know that they will be heading home soon. General Abizaid and other commanders in Iraq are constantly assessing the level of troops they need to fulfill the mission. If they need more troops, I will send them. The mission of our forces in Iraq is demanding and dangerous. Our troops are showing exceptional skill and courage. I thank them for their sacrifices and their duty.

In the city of Fallujah, there's been considerable violence by Saddam loyalists and foreign fighters, including the murder of four American contractors. American soldiers and Marines could have used overwhelming force. Our commanders, however, consulted with Iraq's Governing Council and local officials, and determined that massive strikes against the enemy would alienate the local population, and increase support for the insurgency. So we have pursued a different approach. We're making security a shared responsibility in Fallujah. Coalition commanders have worked with local leaders to create an all-Iraqi security force, which is now patrolling the city. Our soldiers and Marines will continue to disrupt enemy attacks on our supply routes, conduct joint patrols with Iraqis to destroy bomb factories and safe houses, and kill or capture any enemy.

We want Iraqi forces to gain experience and confidence in dealing with their country's enemies. We want the Iraqi people to know that we trust their growing capabilities, even as we help build them. At the same time, Fallujah must cease to be a sanctuary for the enemy, and those responsible for terrorism will be held to account.

In the cities of Najaf and Karbala and Kufa, most of the violence has been incited by a young, radical cleric who commands an illegal militia. These enemies have been hiding behind an innocent civilian population, storing arms and ammunition in mosques, and launching attacks from holy shrines. Our soldiers have treated religious sites with respect, while systematically dismantling the illegal militia. We're also seeing Iraqis, themselves, take more responsibility for restoring order. In recent weeks, Iraqi forces have ejected elements of this militia from the governor's office in Najaf. Yesterday, an elite Iraqi unit cleared out a weapons cache from a large mosque in Kufa. Respected Shia leaders have called on the militia to withdraw from these towns. Ordinary Iraqis have marched in protest against the militants.

As challenges rise in Fallujah, Najaf, and elsewhere, the tactics of our military will be flexible. Commanders on the ground will pay close attention to local conditions. And we will do all that is necessary — by measured force or overwhelming force — to achieve a stable Iraq.

Iraq's military, police, and border forces have begun to take on broader responsibilities. Eventually, they must be the primary defenders of Iraqi security, as American and coalition forces are withdrawn. And we're helping them to prepare for this role. In some cases, the early performance of Iraqi forces fell short. Some refused orders to engage the enemy. We've learned from these failures, and we've taken steps to correct them. Successful fighting units need a sense of cohesion, so we've lengthened and intensified their training. Successful units need to know they are fighting for the future of their own country, not for any occupying power, so we are ensuring that Iraqi forces serve under an Iraqi chain of command. Successful fighting units need the best possible leadership, so we improved the vetting and training of Iraqi officers and senior enlisted men.

At my direction, and with the support of Iraqi authorities, we are accelerating our program to help train Iraqis to defend their country. A new team of senior military officers is now assessing every unit in Iraq's security forces. I've asked this team to oversee the training of a force of 260,000 Iraqi soldiers, police, and other security personnel. Five Iraqi army battalions are in the field now, with another eight battalions to join them by July the 1st. The eventual goal is an Iraqi army of 35,000 soldiers in 27 battalions, fully prepared to defend their country.

After June 30th, American and other forces will still have important duties. American military forces in Iraq will operate under American command as a part of a multinational force authorized by the United Nations. Iraq's new sovereign government will still face enormous security challenges, and our forces will be there to help.

The third step in the plan for Iraqi democracy is to continue rebuilding that nation's infrastructure, so that a free Iraq can quickly gain economic independence and a better quality of life. Our coalition has already helped Iraqis to rebuild schools and refurbish hospitals and health clinics, repair bridges, upgrade the electrical grid, and modernize the communications system. And now a growing private economy is taking shape. A new currency has been introduced. Iraq's Governing Council approved a new law that opens the country to foreign investment for the first time in decades. Iraq has liberalized its trade policy, and today an Iraqi observer attends meetings of the World Trade Organization. Iraqi oil production has reached more than two million barrels per day, bringing revenues of nearly $6 billion so far this year, which is being used to help the people of Iraq. And thanks in part to our efforts — to the efforts of former Secretary of State James Baker, many of Iraq's largest creditors have pledged to forgive or substantially reduce Iraqi debt incurred by the former regime.

We're making progress. Yet there still is much work to do. Over the decades of Saddam's rule, Iraq's infrastructure was allowed to crumble, while money was diverted to palaces, and to wars, and to weapons programs. We're urging other nations to contribute to Iraqi reconstruction — and 37 countries and the IMF and the World Bank have so far pledged $13.5 billion in aid. America has dedicated more than $20 billion to reconstruction and development projects in Iraq. To ensure our money is spent wisely and effectively, our new embassy in Iraq will have regional offices in several key cities. These offices will work closely with Iraqis at all levels of government to help make sure projects are completed on time and on budget.

A new Iraq will also need a humane, well-supervised prison system. Under the dictator, prisons like Abu Ghraib were symbols of death and torture. That same prison became a symbol of disgraceful conduct by a few American troops who dishonored our country and disregarded our values. America will fund the construction of a modern, maximum security prison. When that prison is completed, detainees at Abu Ghraib will be relocated. Then, with the approval of the Iraqi government, we will demolish the Abu Ghraib prison, as a fitting symbol of Iraq's new beginning.

The fourth step in our plan is to enlist additional international support for Iraq's transition. At every stage, the United States has gone to the United Nations — to confront Saddam Hussein, to promise serious consequences for his actions, and to begin Iraqi reconstruction. Today, the United States and Great Britain presented a new resolution in the Security Council to help move Iraq toward self-government. I've directed Secretary Powell to work with fellow members of the Council to endorse the timetable the Iraqis have adopted, to express international support for Iraq's interim government, to reaffirm the world's security commitment to the Iraqi people, and to encourage other U.N. members to join in the effort. Despite past disagreements, most nations have indicated strong support for the success of a free Iraq. And I'm confident they will share in the responsibility of assuring that success.

Next month, at the NATO summit in Istanbul, I will thank our 15 NATO allies who together have more than 17,000 troops on the ground in Iraq.

Great Britain and Poland are each leading a multinational division that is securing important parts of the country. And NATO, itself, is giving helpful intelligence, communications, and logistical support to the Polish-led division. At the summit, we will discuss NATO's role in helping Iraq build and secure its democracy.

The fifth and most important step is free, national elections, to be held no later than next January. A United Nations team, headed by Carina Perelli, is now in Iraq, helping form an independent election commission that will oversee an orderly, accurate national election. In that election, the Iraqi people will choose a transitional national assembly, the first freely-elected, truly representative national governing body in Iraq's history. This assembly will serve as Iraq's legislature, and it will choose a transitional government with executive powers. The transitional national assembly will also draft a new constitution, which will be presented to the Iraqi people in a referendum scheduled for the fall of 2005. Under this new constitution, Iraq will elect a permanent government by the end of next year.

In this time of war and liberation and rebuilding, American soldiers and civilians on the ground have come to know and respect the citizens of Iraq. They're a proud people who hold strong and diverse opinions. Yet Iraqis are united in a broad and deep conviction: They're determined never again to live at the mercy of a dictator. And they believe that a national election will put that dark time behind them. A representative government that protects basic rights, elected by Iraqis, is the best defense against the return of tyranny — and that election is coming.

Completing the five steps to Iraqi elected self-government will not be easy. There's likely to be more violence before the transfer of sovereignty, and after the transfer of sovereignty. The terrorists and Saddam loyalists would rather see many Iraqis die than have any live in freedom. But terrorists will not determine the future of Iraq.

That nation is moving every week toward free elections and a permanent place among free nations. Like every nation that has made the journey to democracy, Iraqis will raise up a government that reflects their own culture and values. I sent American troops to Iraq to defend our security, not to stay as an occupying power. I sent American troops to Iraq to make its people free, not to make them American. Iraqis will write their own history, and find their own way. As they do, Iraqis can be certain, a free Iraq will always have a friend in the United States of America.

In the last 32 months, history has placed great demands on our country, and events have come quickly. Americans have seen the flames of September the 11th, followed battles in the mountains of Afghanistan, and learned new terms like "orange alert" and "ricin" and "dirty bomb." We've seen killers at work on trains in Madrid, in a bank in Istanbul, at a synagogue in Tunis, and at a nightclub in Bali. And now the families of our soldiers and civilian workers pray for their sons and daughters in Mosul and Karbala and Baghdad.

We did not seek this war on terror, but this is the world as we find it. We must keep our focus. We must do our duty. History is moving, and it will tend toward hope, or tend toward tragedy. Our terrorist enemies have a vision that guides and explains all their varied acts of murder. They seek to impose Taliban-like rule, country by country, across the greater Middle East. They seek the total control of every person, and mind, and soul, a harsh society in which women are voiceless and brutalized. They seek bases of operation to train more killers and export more violence. They commit dramatic acts of murder to shock, frighten and demoralize civilized nations, hoping we will retreat from the world and give them free rein. They seek weapons of mass destruction, to impose their will through blackmail and catastrophic attacks. None of this is the expression of a religion. It is a totalitarian political ideology, pursued with consuming zeal, and without conscience.

Our actions, too, are guided by a vision. We believe that freedom can advance and change lives in the greater Middle East, as it has advanced and changed lives in Asia, and Latin America, and Eastern Europe, and Africa. We believe it is a tragedy of history that in the Middle East — which gave the world great gifts of law and science and faith — so many have been held back by lawless tyranny and fanaticism. We believe that when all Middle Eastern peoples are finally allowed to live and think and work and worship as free men and women, they will reclaim the greatness of their own heritage. And when that day comes, the bitterness and burning hatreds that feed terrorism will fade and die away. America and all the world will be safer when hope has returned to the Middle East.

These two visions — one of tyranny and murder, the other of liberty and life — clashed in Afghanistan. And thanks to brave U.S. and coalition forces and to Afghan patriots, the nightmare of the Taliban is over, and that nation is coming to life again. These two visions have now met in Iraq, and are contending for the future of that country. The failure of freedom would only mark the beginning of peril and violence. But, my fellow Americans, we will not fail. We will persevere, and defeat this enemy, and hold this hard-won ground for the realm of liberty.

May God bless our country

‹77›

Address by the President of the Russian Federation Mr. Vladimir Putin to the Federal Assembly of the Russian Federation (26.05.2004)

Listing out the "priority national goals," Mr. Putin stated that these were doubling the gross domestic product over the next decade, reducing poverty, increasing people's prosperity and modernizing the armed forces. Among the priorities in the foreign policy he listed deepening integration in the Commonwealth of Independent States, integration of the Russian economy into the international economy, increasing Russian export and developing political and economic dialogue with the USA, China, India and Japan.

Good afternoon, esteemed members of the Federation Council and the State Duma,

Dear citizens of Russia,

I think that, as in past years, there is no need in this audience to talk about recent results. We have all worked hard together to achieve them.

I would like to note simply that over these last four years, we have traversed a difficult but very important path. Now, for the first time in a long time, Russia is politically and economically stable. It is also independent, both financially and in international affairs, and this is a good result in itself.

Our goals are very clear. We want high living standards and a safe, free and comfortable life for the country. We want a mature democracy and a developed civil society. We want to strengthen Russia's place in the world. But our main goal, I repeat, is to bring about a noticeable rise in our people's prosperity.

We have better knowledge today of our own potential and we know what resources we have at our disposal. We understand the obstacles we could face in reaching the goals we have set and we are actively modernising the state in order to make sure that its functions correspond to the present stage of Russia's development – that of achieving a real rise in living standards.

I would like to recall that over the last decade of the twentieth century, with its economy in a state of collapse and its positions on world markets weakened,

Russia found itself having to simultaneously restore its statehood and create what for us was a new kind of economy, a market economy. Furthermore, it also had to defend its territorial integrity in the fight against international terrorism and stand up for the democratic achievements of its people.

Russia could be said to have passed through several stages since the beginning of the 1990s. The first stage involved dismantling the old economic system. It brought with it hardships and upheavals to the familiar way of life, acute political and social conflicts and was a very difficult time for our society

The second stage was the time of clearing the debris resulting from demolishing the old edifice. At the same time, we managed to check the most dangerous tendencies in economic and political life. Not all the decisions taken over those years were long-term in nature. In many cases, the federal authorities were more than anything else reacting to the serious threats we faced.

In fact, we have only recently reached the third stage in modern Russia's development, the possibility to achieve more rapid development and resolve more ambitious national tasks. We now have the necessary experience and tools to set ourselves genuinely long-term objectives.

Our economy has grown at a good rate overall over the last four years. People's living standards have risen a little. There has been a 1.5-fold increase in real incomes, and I emphasise that we are talking about real incomes. The number of people with less than subsistence-level incomes has dropped by a third. The economic growth rate was 7.3 percent last year and was 8 percent over the first four months of this year.

But even so, we must ask ourselves the question, have we done all we could and have we made use of every opportunity for economic growth and social development? And are we happy with the current state of affairs?

No, and above all, we are not happy with living standards in the country.

I would remind you that during its lengthy economic crisis, Russia lost almost half of its economic potential. Over the last four years we have managed to compensate for around 40 percent of this drop. But despite our efforts, we have still not caught up to where we were in 1989. Only by maintaining high growth rates of the kind we have now will Russia avoid being relegated to the backwaters of the world economy.

We must grow faster than the rest of the world if we want to take the lead within today's complex rules of global competition. We must be ahead of other countries in our growth rate, in the quality of our goods and services and level of our education, science and culture. This is a question of our economic survival. It is a question of ensuring that Russia takes its deserved place in these changing international conditions.

I realise that this is a far from easy task, but we are up to it and we can resolve it only through our own efforts.

Whether or not we can become a society of truly free people – free both economically and politically—depends only on us. Reaching our priority national goals depends only on us. These goals are well-known: doubling our gross domestic product over the next decade, reducing poverty, increasing people's prosperity and modernising the armed forces.

Again I would like to say that today, for the first time in many years, we can make forecasts not just for a few months or even a year ahead, but for a decade ahead. Our achievements over recent years now give us the base we need to finally tackle those problems that can be resolved, but only so long as we have certain economic potential, political stability and an active civil society.

It is far from everyone in the world that wants to have to deal with an independent, strong and self-reliant Russia. Political, economic and information pressure have become weapons in the global competitive battle today. Our efforts to strengthen our state are sometimes deliberately interpreted as authoritarianism.

In this respect I want to say that there will be no going back on the fundamental principles of our politics. Commitment to democratic values is dictated by the will of our people and by the strategic interests of Russia itself. Russia's greatest competitive asset and the main source of its development is its people. Making our country strong and prosperous requires ensuring a normal life for all our people, those people who are producing quality goods and services, are enriching our national culture and building a new country.

In order to open up this potential, we must create the conditions for a safe life and reduce the crime rate in the country. We must improve the nation's health, prevent increase in drug use and resolve the problem of homeless children.

We must bring down the mortality rate, increase people's life expectancy and overcome the population decline. We could find ourselves already in the near future facing labour shortages and an increased social burden placed on the younger generation of the workforce.

As you know, previous addresses tended to focus on the general social and economic objectives facing us. Today I think I should, and can, break with this tradition and focus on the objectives that concern practically every citizen and every Russian family.

Our task now is to resolve the most pressing problems for our citizens. These are, above all, accessible and good-quality housing, education and healthcare. We now have the capacities we need to find effective solutions to these problems and I would like to look at them in more detail.

Dear colleagues,

One of the most pressing problems we face today is providing people with affordable housing. This remains a real problem for the majority of people in Russia.

People need decent housing for rest, for work and for starting a normal family. But even the current rise in incomes does not always allow people to buy housing and improve its quality. This is one of the causes of the low mobility that prevents people from moving around the country in search of suitable work.

It must be admitted that very many people still live in dilapidated and unsafe buildings and apartments. Not enough housing is being built and what is built often does not measure up to modern safety and quality standards. Only people with high incomes can afford to buy new housing. The fact that young families are unable to afford housing of their own affects their plans to have children, and it is still quite common to find several generations all having to share the same apartment.

The conclusion is clear. The old methods and approaches, which did not solve the problem earlier, simply do not work today. We should stop deceiving people, forcing them to wait for years and even decades in line for housing. We need to create the possibilities for the bulk of the working population to buy housing on the market, while at the same time ensuring that low-income groups have access to social housing.

The government, regional and local authorities should work towards having at least a third of the population (and not a tenth, as is currently the case) able to buy housing that meets modern standards by 2010. They will buy housing through their own savings and with the help of mortgage schemes.

This means that mortgage schemes must become long-term and affordable for people. In order to prevent the situation when increased demand for housing pushes up prices competitive conditions for housing construction need to be ensured.

What are the steps we need to take here? They are basically well-known. I will name them now.

First, we need to put in place financial mechanisms that will enable people to improve their housing conditions not just through their current earnings and their savings, but also through their future earnings. We need to develop clear legal conditions for long-term mortgage schemes, conditions that will apply to citizens and to the construction companies.

Mortgages should become an affordable solution for people in the middle income group. Of course, we should also develop other forms of financing such as having future homeowners buy a stake in a building's construction or take part in housing savings programmes. For all this to work, we also must ensure that we have an effectively functioning state system for registration of real estate rights, a credit history bureau and a developed market for mortgage securities. These are the things to be done.

Second, we need to put an end to the monopolies on the construction markets. Russia's people are not obliged to pay the cost of the administrative barriers created in the construction sector or to ensure the excess profits of monopolist construction companies. What is needed are measures to reduce construction time and the expenses involved – clear-cut rules of municipal land use and construction, simplified procedures for getting all the approvals needed for construction and preparation of the necessary engineering and utilities infrastructure.

Third, guaranteed ownership rights for honest buyers of real estate is a question of principle importance. Real estate deals should be handled through transparent, comprehensible and, also important, inexpensive procedures.

Finally, we must bring order to provision of social housing. Contracts of social renting must become available to those who really need it. Furthermore, we should come up with additional measures to provide targeted support to individual categories of people, in particular young families. Some steps have already been taken in this direction but it is far from sufficient so far. We must increase our efforts in this area.

Now, a few words about healthcare modernisation. This is not the first time we have discussed this subject, but transformations in this area are taking place at a sluggish rate and have not brought any significant results so far.

Russia lags behind many countries today in its basic healthcare situation. Life expectancy in Russia is 12 years lower than in the United States, eight years lower than in Poland and five years lower than in China. This is due above all to a high mortality rate among working-age people. Child mortality is decreasing but is still 1.5-2 times higher than in the developed countries.

One of the main reasons for this situation is the country's ineffective healthcare system. Throughout the entire system, the quality and accessibility of medical services continue to drop today, while costs keep rising.

Guarantees of free healthcare assistance are often declarative. People still do not know what they are entitled to for free and what they must pay for themselves. The people with the lowest incomes have found themselves in the most difficult situation of all. They are forced to spend a large share of their already modest incomes on medical treatment and even end up unable to afford basic medicines, which is absolutely unacceptable.

The main aim of modernising the Russian healthcare system is to ensure affordable and good-quality healthcare for broad sections of the population. This means above all that guaranteed free healthcare services should be clear and known to all. Medical treatment standards should be drawn up and approved for each type of illness, along with an obligatory list of treatment and diagnostic procedures and the minimum requirements for healthcare provision. These standards should be applied in every city, town and village in the Russian Federation, and patients should have to pay only for additional medical services and for extra comfort.

Having an itemised list of standards will make it possible to calculate the real cost of these services and move away from the system of funding medical establishments based on estimates of their demands, to funding based on the amount and quality of healthcare services they actually provide. Healthcare services should be paid for in accordance with the principles of compulsory medical insurance. At the same time, incentives should be created to encourage the development of voluntary medical insurance.

The government and the parliament must ensure the legal framework for compulsory medical insurance, state-guaranteed medical services, private medical practice and for provision of fee-paying services.

The next priority is to develop the Russian education system.

I want to emphasise that Russian education, with its fundamental approach to learning, held and still holds a leading place in the world. It would be absolutely unacceptable to lose this advantage. The global competitive environment demands of us that we strengthen the practical component of our higher education system. This means, above all, placing higher demands on professional education, professional in the broad sense of the word.

Professional education today is not firmly bound to the situation on the labour market and more than half of higher education graduates do not find work in the professions in which they got their degrees. More and more people are going into higher education, but at the same time the level of teaching is falling.

Compared to the Soviet period the number of people entering higher education has tripled and is now practically the same as the number of secondary school graduates. Who benefits from this situation? And even with this number of university graduates, we still face a shortage of desperately needed qualified specialists.

One of the most serious problems is the lack of access to quality education for low-income groups. College studies involve additional costs that not all people can afford. The drop in the number of student residences and the small student allowances mean that children from low-income families, especially from remote towns and villages, are cut off from getting quality education.

But the results of reforms in this sector should be evaluated by the quality of education, its accessibility and its relevance to the labour market's demands. In this respect I want to name the following target criteria.

First, secondary-school graduates, no matter what the financial situation of their families, should have the opportunity to enter higher education in accordance with their level of knowledge.

This will require an absolutely transparent and objective system of evaluating knowledge to enter college, reviving on large-scale preparatory departments at the universities, and targeted provision of student allowances.

Young people who live far away from prestigious universities should have the opportunity to take these universities' entrance exams.

Second, we should aim at having the majority of graduates working in the professions for which they got degrees. Of course, this does not mean a return to the old system of allocating jobs from above to graduates. Rather, it is about forecasting the country's demand for the specialists it needs.

I think we could also consider a system where students can sign a contract under which they receive free education and then have to either work a certain amount of time in the professions for which they got degrees or else reimburse the money the state spent on their education. This system should begin with the professions in short supply today. I also think that it is in the interests of Russian business to take part in training the specialists the economy needs through making use of education loans. This practice already exists and we should make more active use of it.

Third, we need to introduce education standards that meet today's demands. Furthermore, the content of our education should measure up to the highest world standards. At the same time we must not forget about the areas in which we have built up our own achievements and we should ensure maximum development of these areas in which Russian education meets or even surpasses world requirements, and we do have such areas.

We must also go further in integrating education and research activities. Advancing research in universities and major academic centres should be a priority objective.

Dear colleagues,

Ensuring affordable and accessible healthcare and education and giving people the possibility of buying housing will help alleviate the problem of poverty. We currently have around 30 million people who earn less than the subsistence level. That is a huge figure, it being known that most of the poor people in this country are people of working age.

It is evident, that the state and the business community should direct their efforts at continuing to create jobs, especially in regions with persistent unemployment. They should also focus on developing small and medium-sized business and on effective use of targeted social assistance.

But only economic growth can provide a genuinely reliable foundation for long-term solutions to social problems, including the struggle against poverty.

As was said last year, we are entirely capable of doubling our economic potential over ten years. We can achieve this if we maintain average growth rates at least at the level we had over the first quarter of this year. Furthermore, if we maintain this kind of growth, we can hope to double our per capita GDP not in ten years time, but by 2010. The members of the government are also applauding – this means they agree.

An essential condition for ensuring a rapid rate of development is to complete the transformations currently taking place in many sectors of the economy and the social sphere.

Now I would like to say a few words on budget reform. The main principle of reform is to move from managing budget expenses to managing results. Overall, the government must develop a system for evaluating the plans and results of work of all the executive power bodies and only on this basis should it then sum up results, draw conclusions and make policy adjustments in each area.

Clearly set policy objectives and expected results should form the basis for the budget and its long-term planning. The independence the recipients of budget funds have in how they dispose of the allocated money should go hand in hand with responsibility for the results of their work.

I particularly want to emphasise that achieving an optimum level of state spending should be a basic principle of our economic policy. We do not have such a lot of money to spend. The government must above all carry out restructuring of the huge network of budget-funded institutions that sprout up all around the country and change procedures for their financing and in many cases even change their status.

This brings me to another very important issue. There are currently more than 35,000 federal state institutions in the country, many of which exercise control and supervision functions. These institutions often force their "services" – expert examinations, consultations and other – on business and individuals. This year, the government should revoke the powers of those institutions that are not part of the state management system. Moreover, state functions that have been declared superfluous should not be revived at regional and municipal level.

Steps also must be taken to bring order to state and municipal property. I have already said that each level of state power should only have the property that it needs to exercise its designated public functions, and no more than that. This should be kept in mind as ministries' functions are cut back further.

We should also be ready to introduce a new distribution of revenue collection powers and spending commitments between the different levels of the country's budget system. The regions and the municipalities should know exactly which functions they are supposed to exercise and which public services they are responsible for. And also, they need to know where the funding for these services will come from.

Finally, we need to clearly set and delimit each level of power's responsibilities for providing social assistance to the population. All the country's regions are directly concerned by the problems of ensuring affordable housing, education and healthcare. It would be only right then to actively involve them in drawing up the legal framework and the measures for practical implementation of the social programmes package, taking into account the division of powers between the different levels of state power.

All of these measures should result in a renewed system of inter-budget relations and increased independence and responsibility for the regions and the municipalities. I am aware of the regions' and municipalities' concerns regarding these questions. I hope that the government and the members of both houses of parliament will listen to these concerns, weigh up all the pros and cons and find solutions that are in keeping with the demands of the times and the economy.

Carrying out budget reform will in its turn make it possible to continue changes in the tax sphere. Over the last four years, serious steps have been made here. They have already begun to bring results – tax collection has increased, tax evasion has decreased, and the tax burden on the economy has dropped. But, of course, far from everything has been done.

And to move to an effective tax system, we need in the next two years to pass and implement a series of additional decrees.

How should the tax system look after reform is completed?

First, it should not be burdensome for business, neither by the level of tax rates, nor in the procedures of calculation and payment of taxes, regulation of tax checks and tax accounts.

Second, it should be fair for all economic agents. Taxation conditions should be equal for enterprises that work in the same sphere. Tax structure must exclude opportunities for tax evasion. Third, the tax system in Russia remains excessively oriented toward the fiscal function, to the detriment of other functions, above all the function of stimulating the growth of competitiveness. And here, the Russian tax system should become more favourable for investment and the development of business – more favourable than in competing countries. It should have itself sustainable competitive advantages.

To continue. The government has on several occasions raised the issue about the necessity to reduce the single social tax. We should bring a considerable percentage of work salaries out of the "shadows", protect the social rights of employees and stimulate citizens' concern for their own retirement pensions, thus reducing the burden on business.

Another problematic issue is value-added tax. Besides changing the procedure for levy of value-added tax, we need to further reduce tax rates, solve the issue of timely compensation of value-added tax on export operations, and in making capital investments, and also to finally put a stop to taxation of advance payments.

Finally, it is important to distinguish the lawful practice of tax optimization from cases of criminal tax avoidance.

I would like to stress that stability of budget and tax policy is a very important factor in the development of the economy. This stability, however, is not able to solve all the uncertainty of economic conditions in doing business. A balanced macroeconomic policy is needed. We need to continue what has been formed in the economy in recent years, namely a policy of gradually reducing inflation to 3% a year. And to create the necessary conditions to ensure full convertibility of the ruble over the next two years. We know about the laws passed in this sphere. We know that the Government and the Central Bank have set themselves this task. But they have made easier conditions for themselves – by 2007. It is quite possible to work faster now.

We should also create an effective system of using natural resources. We need transparent, non-corrupt conditions of access to them, for example, with the use of auctions. We need to move from administrative permits to full agreements – with a clear determination of the rights and responsibility of both the state and entrepreneurs. We need to ensure predictability and stability in these relations.

The system of resource payments also requires changes. It should provide equal conditions of competition both within the extractive sector, and between the extractive and processing industries. And it should also ensure rational use of natural resources.

I expect that the new Forestry codex and the Law on mining will answer all these questions.

Dear Assembly,

Among the most important tasks that the country faces, I would like to single out another one especially – the development of transport infrastructure. When we take into account the size of Russia and the geographic remoteness of certain territories from the political and economic centres of the country, I would say that the development of infrastructure is more than an economic task. Solving it will not just directly affect the state of affairs in the economy, but ensure the unity of the country as a whole – whether people feel they are citizens of a united, large nation, and whether they can make use of its advantages.

Today, the poor condition and low density of the road network, oil pipelines, the gas-transport system and the infrastructure of the power industry puts serious restrictions on the development of the Russian economy.

Factories cannot function normally if it is impossible to supply goods quickly and inexpensively. The undeveloped road and port infrastructure has already become an obstacle for export, as it is unable to cope with the growing volume of goods. And it is quite clear that with Russia's climatic conditions and extensive territory, infrastructural expenses make up a significant portion of the cost of many kinds of goods and services.

At the same time, a modern, well-developed transport infrastructure is capable of turning Russia's geographical features into a real competitive advantage for the country.

What needs to be done to achieve this? Above all, we need to unite the economic centres of the country, to provide economic subjects with unhindered access to regional and international markets, and at the same time to provide infrastructure services of a world standard.

The Government should find effective mechanisms of controlling quality and expenses in building new objects. In order to radically change the situation we need to create a competitive environment.

At the same time, the state must control the development of the country's infrastructure for a long time to come – I am convinced of this. Still, private investment will also make an important contribution to creating a branched transport infrastructure of high quality and reliability. However, for private capital, it is very important that the state have definite plans. From this viewpoint, the Government must announce its plans and projects, and the conditions to implement them. Such projects exist, and they need to be completed quickly. I will mention several of them.

For example, there are plans in the oil sector to diversify delivery of Russian oil. These plans are well-known. They involve expanding the capacity of the Baltic pipe system, opening the Western Siberia – Barents Sea pipelines, determining routes from oilfields in Eastern Siberia, bypassing the Bosporus and Dardanelle Straits, and integrating the Druzhba and Adriya oil pipelines.

However, this is not the first year that the Government has been unable to sort out its priorities. And a solution to this issue is, quite frankly, long overdue. I would note that the guidelines for passing the necessary decisions should be the realization of national tasks, and not the interests of individual companies.

As for the gas transport system, here we need first of all to develop the gas distribution network within the country – including expansion of the system to the east of Russia. In export, construction of the North European gas pipeline is most important. It will make it possible to diversify export flows, directly linking the networks of Russia and countries of the Baltic region with the total European gas network.

For Russia, modernization of roads is also important – not just roads that link the country's main economic centres, but also those used for transit. The basic network of roads needs to be gradually directed towards integration into the total European road network, and—through the Trans-Siberian corridor—into the road network of the Far East region. Another project is construction and reconstruction of highways in the North-South corridor. Something is already being done here, and this work needs to be continued.

These projects will make it possible to ensure inter-regional and transit flows on the main international transport routes. And, what is also important, to develop the territories which are next to these routes.

And finally, we have been talking about toll roads for a long time. I think that we need to begin realizing these projects on the main routes – of course, along with the existing free roads. The Government should determine a list of them very soon.

Undoubtedly, modernization of the army is a task of national importance. We need effective, well-equipped and modern Armed Forces for reliable protection of the country. So that we can easily solve internal socio-economic tasks.

We should secure our country from any forms of military and political pressure and potential foreign aggression. And thus modernizing the Russian Armed Forces remains a very important task, including equipping strategic nuclear forces with the most modern systems of strategic armaments. We have everything needed for this. And also, we need to equip other types of the Armed Forces with the appropriate tactical and operational weapons. I would like to note once more: an adequate quality of weapons is the characteristic that directly determines the degree of battle readiness of a modern army.

We are also beginning reform of social support guarantees for soldiers. A mortgage programme will be created for them. Three years after joining this programme, a soldier will be able to receive housing on mortgage conditions.

I also think that military education for training specialists in unique professions that are required by a modern army can also be provided at civil institutes of higher education.

I would like to stress: for successful modernization of the entire military system of the state, we need to know precisely how considerable sums of money – including those for housing, military medicine and education – are spent. Furthermore, the army and other law-enforcement institutions have an enormous amount of property. And this also needs to be accounted for and managed effectively. A transparent military economy is the necessary condition for reform.

All these steps should be targeted at increasing the prestige and attractiveness of military service.

I would like to remind the Defence Ministry and the Government as a whole: the volumes of funds spent, the interests of the country's defensive capacity, and also the important social parameters of reform make civil control over the effectiveness of changes in the army essential.

Dear colleagues,

The growth of the economy, political stability and the strengthening of the state have had a beneficial effect on Russia's international position. We have been able to a significant degree to make our foreign policy both dynamic and pragmatic.

It is clear that the scale of the tasks that the country faces has now changed substantially. And we need to make our foreign policy adequate to the goals and scope of the new stage of development. In other words, we need to use the tools of foreign policy for a more appreciable practical return in the economy, and in the realization of important national tasks.

Work on deepening integration in the Commonwealth of Independent States remains our priority, especially within the framework of the Common economic space, and the Eurasian economic community. This, without exaggeration, is one of the conditions of regional and international stability.

I am certain that the CIS should work effectively for the benefit of citizens of our countries. It should work by ensuring maximum openness of economies, and by removing barriers to mutual trade and information flows, business and social initiatives, and direct contact between people.

We are interested in further integration of the Russian economy into the international economy, including joining the WTO on conditions that are beneficial for us. Increasing competitiveness on international markets stimulates developed countries to increase support of their manufacturers and exports. The Russian Interior Ministry and the Government as a whole need to find more effective ways to increase Russian export, and to provide reliable protection of the interests of Russian companies abroad.

This approach is particularly important now, when the Russia and the EU are already immediate neighbours. The expansion of the European Union should not just bring us closer geographically, but also economically and spiritually. I am certain that this is a prerequisite of success, not just for Russian, but for all European business. This means new markets and new investment. Generally, it means new possibilities for the future of Greater Europe.

We will continue to develop political and economic dialogue with the U.S.A. and with such major partners as China, India and Japan, and we will work with other countries. Border and interregional cooperation are also a significant reserve of development of trade and economic, cultural and humanitarian ties.

It is clear that a necessary condition for solving these tasks is the effective security of Russia, and the inviolability of its borders. And an adequate response to the most serious threats of the 21st century – international terrorism, proliferation of weapons of mass destruction, regional conflicts – can only be provided by the united efforts of the international community, relying on the tools of the UN and international law.

Terrorism threatens the human rights and lives, destabilizes nations and entire regions of the world, and stands in the way of economic and social progress. And today, international terrorists continue to commit acts of violence and murder of peaceful citizens. They attempt to provoke chaos and destabilize the situation in various regions of the world. And Russia, unfortunately, is no exception here.

Despite such acts of provocation – including the recent political murder of the leader of Chechnya and the attempt to disrupt the work of legally elected bodies of power in the republic – our policy in fighting terror remains unchanged and consistent. No one and nothing will stop Russia on the path to consolidating democracy, and ensuring human rights and freedoms.

We will continue to work on developing internationally recognized instruments of law and collective mechanisms of neutralizing global threats. I consider the task of strengthening the anti-terrorist coalition to be one of the most important.

At the same time, I would like to note that no excuses about the necessity of fighting terrorism can be an argument for restricting human rights, or for creating unjustified difficulties in contact between people on the international stage.

To conclude the topic of foreign policy, I would like to stress: Russian society should see the practical results of our work in the international sphere. They are ensuring safety of the individual, increasing possibilities for enterprise, and effective protection of the rights of Russian nationals abroad. I expect that in cooperation with the Federal Assembly, we will be able to work even more productively in all the areas mentioned.

Dear deputies of the State Duma, members of the Federation Council,

Keeping to the strategic policy, continuing changes – those that have already been tested by the practice of the last four years – is the basis of our further stable development. At the same time, the only source and bearer of power in the Russian Federation is its multiethnic people. And only the people – through the institutions of the democratic state and civil society – have the right and are able to guarantee the stability of the moral and political foundations of the country's development for many years to come.

At the same time, we must make a critical assessment of the state of our democracy.

Is the political system in its present state a tool of real sovereignty of the people? And how productive is dialogue between the authorities and society?

It is clear that young Russian democracy has had considerable success in establishing itself. And those people who do not notice this success, or who do not want to notice it, are not quite honest. But our social system is still far from perfection. And it must be admitted: we are at the very beginning of the path.

Without a mature civil society, an effective solution to peoples' daily problems is impossible. The quality of their daily life directly depends on the quality of the social and political system. And here, of course, we still have many questions.

I would like to remind you: any power above all means great responsibility. It is unacceptable when civilised political competition is replaced with a self-interested fight for status revenue. When the financial side of the activity of political groups is still hidden from society. When election technologies and lobbyist services is primarily oriented towards the shadow sector. And all this takes place against the background of the dreary monotony of most party programmes.

I would like to say a few words about the role of non-political public organisations. In our country, there are thousands of public associations and unions that work constructively. But not all of the organisations are oriented towards standing up for people's real interests. For some of them, the priority is to receive financing from influential foreign foundations. Others serve dubious group and commercial interests. And the most serious problems of the country and its citizens remain unnoticed.

I must say that when violations of fundamental and basic human rights are concerned, when people's real interests are infringed upon, the voice of such organisations is often not even heard. And this is not surprising: they simply cannot bite the hand that feeds them. Of course, such examples cannot be grounds for us to make accusations against civil groups as a whole. I think that these problems are unavoidable, and of a temporary nature.

To reduce these problems and stimulate the further growth of institutions of civil society, we do not need to invent anything new. Our own experience and international experience has already proved the productiveness of an entire range of approaches. It is necessary to gradually transfer to the non-governmental sector functions which the state should not or is unable to perform effectively.

It is also worth using the experience of public boards that has been gained in a number of Russian regions. These permanent non-governmental organisations can provide independent examination of important normative documents. Documents that directly concern citizens' interests.

Political parties should also work more closely with public structures. Direct contact with people and society will help to improve the quality of people's representation at all levels. And parties should be interested in expanding their ranks, consolidating the material base, and the intellectual and staff potential. They should actively create groups in regional parliaments, and participate in the work of bodies of local self-administration.

Parties should increase their level of political culture, and learn the skills of inter-party dialogue and coalition activities. They should learn to come to power and leave it by the will of the people.

I will stress once more: any radical re-examination of economic policy, any restrictions on the rights and freedoms of citizens, a cardinal change in foreign policy guidelines – any divergence from the historic path chosen by Russia, a path that I even would say has been gained by suffering – may lead to irreversible consequences. And they must be absolutely ruled out.

Dear friends,

Today I have talked about the most important national tasks. I believe that creating a free society of free people in Russia is our most important task. But it is also the most difficult.

It is the most important task because people who are not free or independent are incapable of looking after themselves, their families, or their countries. It is the most difficult because freedom is not always valued and even more rarely used properly. Creative energy, enterprise, a sense of proportion and a will to victory cannot be introduced by decree, cannot be imported, and cannot be borrowed.

In aiming for a growth in citizens' prosperity, we will continue to maintain and stand up for the democratic achievements of the Russian people. We will consolidate the security of the state and strive for civilised solutions to key issues of world politics, founded on international law.

In this I count on the constructive cooperation of all branches and all levels of power.

I count on the support and solidarity of all citizens of Russia.

I count on their faith in themselves. In their abilities. In the success of our country.

Thank you for your attention.

‹78›

Keynote Address by IAEA Director General, Dr. Mohamed ElBaradei at Carnegie International Non-Proliferation Conference (21.06.2004)

> Mr. Baradei stated that from verifying the undeclared nuclear programmes of Iraq, Iran, Libya and North Korea, the IAEA came to the conclusion that "verification and diplomacy, used in conjunction", can be effective against proliferation. He also noted that the present system of nuclear export controls is deficient, and that the control of technology, in and of itself, is not an adequate barrier against further proliferation. Hence, the need for strengthening the controls of the nuclear non-proliferation regime, and plugging existing gaps; reaffirming and in some ways expanding the commitments of all parties to this regime; and reforming the existing system of collective security.

It has been nearly a year and a half since I spoke at the Carnegie International Non-Proliferation Conference. Already at that time — November 2002 — it seemed clear to me that we needed to revisit some of the basic assumptions and features of the current nuclear non-proliferation regime, and equally to consider new approaches to international security.

Since that time, the need for substantive change — to the international security system in general and to the nuclear non-proliferation regime in particular — has become even more obvious and urgent.

Today, I will outline for you my views on what we face, what we have learned, and the nature of the required reforms.

Non-Proliferation: changes in the security landscape

The Treaty on the Non-Proliferation of Nuclear Weapons (NPT) remains the global anchor for nuclear non-proliferation and nuclear disarmament. Despite flaws in the system, implementation of the NPT continues to provide important security benefits — by providing assurance that, in the great majority of non-nuclear-weapon States, nuclear energy is not being misused for weapon purposes. Although the NPT is sometimes perceived as a Western project, its benefits extend across any North-South or East-West geopolitical divide. The NPT is also the only binding agreement in which all five of the nuclear-weapon States have committed themselves to move forward on disarmament.

During the Cold War, security and non-proliferation were linked through two broad alliances (the North Atlantic Treaty Organization and the Warsaw Treaty Organization) in a nuclear standoff — a balance of terror, if you will — based on the rather morbid doctrine of mutually assured destruction, aptly referred to as MAD. As alliance leaders, both the Soviet Union and the United States protected and managed their respective spheres of influence and were able to minimize the number of States acquiring or trying to acquire nuclear weapons. India, Pakistan, Israel and South Africa, for a variety of geopolitical reasons, were exceptions.

However ill-conceived, this bipolar standoff had the effect of producing a modicum of stability within the alliances' spheres of influence, and President Kennedy's prediction of 15–25 nuclear-weapon States by 1975 did not materialize.

In the past decade and a half, the international security landscape has changed. With the dissolution of the Soviet Union, the Cold War rivalry disappeared. But the failure to establish the once much vaunted 'new world order' — by effectively addressing security concerns that persisted after the disappearance of the bipolar world or emerged in its aftermath — has resulted instead in a sort of 'new world instability'. Many ethnic and religious tensions, held in check during the Cold War, have erupted to the fore — and in many cases have turned into civil wars, further complicated by multiple protagonists from the outside. Yugoslavia is but one stark example.

Longstanding conflicts have also continued to fester, most notably on the Korean Peninsula, in the Middle East and in South Asia, with escalating tensions and in some cases increasing hostilities. Violence by sub-State actors has also risen to appalling new levels, as we have witnessed recently in Chechnya, Spain and elsewhere, and has resulted in the emergence of new types of conflicts that cannot easily be deterred by traditional means. An increasing polarization between the Western and Muslim cultures has emerged in the wake of September 2001. And while more than 30 States continue to be party to NATO or other alliances that contribute to their security and explicitly depend upon nuclear weapons, many other countries continue to face a sense of insecurity because of these and other new security threats.

Rather than trying to understand these changes in the international security landscape and adapting to the new threats and challenges — and harnessing the opportunities afforded by an increasingly globalized world to build an equally global security system — the trend has been towards inaction or late action on the part of the international community, selective invocation of norms and treaties, and unilateral and 'self-help' solutions on the part of individual States or groups of States. Against this backdrop of insecurity and instability, it should not come as a surprise to witness a continued interest, particularly in regions of tension, in the acquisition of nuclear weapons or other weapons of mass destruction. Four undeclared nuclear programmes have come to the fore since the early 1990s.

Lessons from Recent experience

Before I discuss specific proposals for moving forward, I would like to focus briefly on some of the lessons we at the IAEA have learned from our recent experience in verifying these undeclared nuclear programmes — in Iraq, Iran, Libya and North Korea.

Perhaps the most important lesson is the confirmation that verification and diplomacy, used in conjunction, can be effective. When inspections are given adequate authority, aided by all available information, backed by a credible compliance mechanism, and supported by international consensus, the system works. The Iraq experience demonstrated that inspections — while requiring time and patience — can be effective even when the country under inspection was providing less than active cooperation. All evidence to date indicates that Iraq's nuclear weapons programme had been effectively dismantled in the 1990s through IAEA inspection — as we were nearly ready to conclude before the war. Inspections in Iran over the past year have also been key in uncovering a nuclear programme that had remained hidden since the 1980s — and in enabling the international community to have a far more comprehensive picture of Iran's nuclear programme than at any time before.

But our experience in Iraq before the first Gulf War, and our recent experience in Iran and Libya, have also highlighted the importance to verification of the 'additional protocol' — that is, the supplement to a safeguards agreement with the IAEA that provides the Agency with significant additional authority with regard to both information and physical access. Without the authority provided by the protocol, our ability to draw conclusions is mostly limited to the non-diversion of material already declared, with little authority to verify the absence of undeclared nuclear material or activities.

Perhaps the most disturbing lesson to emerge from our work in Iran and Libya is the existence of an extensive illicit market for the supply of nuclear items, which clearly thrived on demand. The relative ease with which A.Q. Khan and associates were able to set up and operate a multinational illicit network demonstrates clearly the inadequacy of the present export control system. Nuclear components designed in one country could be manufactured in another, shipped through a third (which may have appeared to be a legitimate user), assembled in a fourth, and designated for eventual turnkey use in a fifth.

The fact that so many companies and individuals could be involved is extremely worrying. And the fact that, in most cases, this could occur apparently without the knowledge of their own governments, clearly points to the inadequacy of national systems of oversight for sensitive equipment and technology.

The present system of nuclear export controls is clearly deficient. The system relies on informal arrangements that are not only non-binding, but also limited in membership, and many countries with growing industrial capacity are not included. Moreover, at present there is no linkage between the export control system and the verification system. Export control information is not systematically shared with the IAEA, nor even fully among the members of the Nuclear Suppliers Group.

Let me be clear: even a verification system making use of the authority under the additional protocol may not reliably detect low levels of clandestine nuclear activity, such as that conducted in Iran and Libya for many years, unless at the very least supported and supplemented by the sharing of actionable information from an effective system of export controls — as well as by intelligence information, where applicable.

Our recent experience has also taught us a clear lesson regarding the accessibility of nuclear technology. The technical barriers to mastering the essential steps of uranium enrichment — and to designing weapons — have eroded over time, which inevitably leads to the conclusion that the control of technology, in and of itself, is not an adequate barrier against further proliferation.

Some estimates indicate that 40 countries or more now have the know-how to produce nuclear weapons, which means that if they have the required fissile material — high enriched uranium or plutonium — we are relying primarily on the continued good intentions of these countries, intentions which are in turn based on their sense of security or insecurity, and could therefore be subject to rapid change. Clearly, the margin of security this affords is thin, and worrisome.

Finally, the evolution of the North Korean situation over the past 18 months carries an equally disturbing lesson. For 12 years, the Democratic People's Republic of Korea (DPRK) has been in non-compliance with its NPT obligations. In January 2003, the DPRK capped its non-compliance by declaring its withdrawal from the NPT. Naturally, the Agency reported the situation to the United Nations Security Council. But now, more than a year later, the Security Council has not even reacted. This lack of response, this inaction, may be setting the worst precedent of all, if it conveys the message that acquiring a nuclear deterrent, by whatever means, will neutralize any compliance mechanism and guarantee preferred treatment.

On the other hand, I would note that verification and diplomacy have been an important part of the success so far in Iran and Libya, and in that sense I can only hope that the continuation of the six-party talks on the DPRK nuclear programme will yield results'.

The need for New Non-Proliferation and security Initiatives: Control, Commitment and collective security

With what I have covered so far as a backdrop, it should be clear that we are well beyond the point where a few quick fixes will adequately address the new and emerging threats. It is true that the international community comes at these issues from a wide range of perspectives, as evidenced by the failure of the Preparatory Committee of the 2005 NPT Review Conference to agree even on an Agenda for the conference.

But I find it encouraging that both governments and civil society are beginning to come forward with proposals on how to address these challenges — including the draft report recently released by the Carnegie Endowment. We are seeing some degree of overlap and complementarity in these proposals. In my view, this could be the beginning of a much needed discussion on non-proliferation and security — and we should do all we can to stimulate this dialogue, move it forward, and keep it in public focus.

In my view, these proposals fall into three categories: control, commitment and collective security — that is, strengthening the controls of the nuclear non-proliferation regime, and plugging existing gaps; re-affirming and in some ways expanding the commitments of all parties to this regime; and reforming the existing system of collective security in a manner that addresses the concerns of all.

Better Control

The first set of proposals should ensure that peaceful uses of nuclear technology are controlled in such a way that they do not lend themselves to further weapons proliferation. There are five aspects to this improved control.

First, we must tighten controls over the export of sensitive nuclear material and technology. The nuclear export control system should be binding rather than voluntary, and should be made more widely applicable, to include all countries with the capability of manufacturing sensitive nuclear related items. It should strike a balance between ensuring effective control and preserving the rights of States to peaceful nuclear technology. And as prescribed in April by Security Council resolution 1540, it should ensure effective national control over sensitive items, and criminalize the actions of individuals and companies involved in efforts to acquire nuclear weapons.

The aim should be easier access to non-sensitive technology and stronger control over the most sensitive parts. Practical arrangements should be put in place to ensure that relevant nuclear export information is shared with the IAEA, in a timely manner, to assist the Agency in carrying out its verification responsibilities.

Second, it is time that we revisit the availability and adequacy of controls provided over sensitive portions of the nuclear fuel cycle under the current non-proliferation regime. We should consider limitations on the production of new nuclear material through reprocessing and enrichment, possibly by agreeing to restrict these operations to being exclusively under multinational controls. These limitations would need to be accompanied by proper rules of transparency and, above all, by a reliable assurance of supply to legitimate would-be users.

This approach should also be extended to the end of the nuclear fuel cycle, by developing multinational approaches to the management and disposal of spent nuclear fuel. More than 50 countries have spent nuclear fuel stored in temporary sites, awaiting disposal or reprocessing. Not all countries have the right geology to store waste underground and, for many countries with small nuclear programmes, the costs of such a facility would be prohibitive. I am encouraged that the Russian Federation is considering one such collective disposal initiative. I hope to discuss this effort further when I travel to Russia later this week.

Considerable advantages — in safety, security and non-proliferation — would be gained from international cooperation in the front and the back end of the nuclear fuel cycle. I have recently established a group of international experts to explore the feasibility of such measures.

Third, we should work to help countries stop using weapon-usable material (separated plutonium and high enriched uranium — HEU) in their civilian nuclear programmes. Approximately 100 facilities in 40 countries, primarily research reactors, still use HEU for peaceful purposes — for example, to produce radioisotopes for medicine. Research reactors and critical assemblies in use worldwide should be converted to use only low enriched uranium.

Fourth, we should eliminate the weapon-usable nuclear material now in existence. Around the globe, stocks of HEU — which could be converted for weapons use by State or sub-State actors — should be eliminated, by 'down-blending' these stocks to low enriched uranium for use in civilian reactors to generate electricity — a 'megatons to megawatts' approach that builds on the successful Russia-US model.

The manner in which to eliminate plutonium stocks is still an open question — whether to burn the plutonium in mixed-oxide (MOX) fuel to generate electricity, or to mix it with high level radioactive waste for disposal in a vitrified form — but this too is a matter that should be resolved and acted upon with urgency.

Fifth, until these HEU and plutonium stocks have been eliminated, we should take steps to better protect the existing sensitive nuclear material around the world, with physical security measures that will ensure that such material does not fall into the wrong hands. Despite our best efforts, adequate physical protection is still lacking in many such facilities in various parts of the world. As Sam Nunn stated last November, "the most effective, least expensive way to prevent nuclear terrorism is to lock down and secure weapons and fissile materials in every country and in every facility that has them."

Just last month in Vienna, US Secretary of Energy Spencer Abraham announced an expanded 'Global Threat Reduction Initiative', with objectives very much in line with some aspects of these proposals, and the IAEA is in dialogue with the US Department of Energy to see how we can contribute to, support and broaden this initiative.

Renewed and Expanded Commitment

My second set of proposals involves guaranteeing and strengthening the commitment of all parties — nuclear-weapon States, non-nuclear-weapon States, and those currently outside the regime — to the basic tenets of nuclear arms control and disarmament. There are four essential aspects to this commitment.

First, a concrete roadmap for verified, irreversible nuclear disarmament, complete with a timetable, should be put in place. Thirty years after the enactment of the NPT, with the Cold War ended and over 30 000 nuclear weapons still available for use, it should be understandable that many non-nuclear-weapon States are no longer willing to accept as credible the commitment of nuclear-weapon States to their NPT disarmament obligations.

It is regrettable that two measures that have been seen as essential steps towards nuclear disarmament, and have been the focus of the nuclear disarmament community for many years, have been either aborted after considerable progress or failed to move forward at all. I refer, of course, to the failure to ratify and bring into force the Comprehensive Nuclear-Test-Ban Treaty and the lack of negotiations on an internationally verifiable Fissile Material (Cut-off) Treaty. With a disarmament roadmap in place, both of these measures should be revived.

In July 1996, the International Court of Justice (ICJ) declared unanimously that the obligation of nuclear-weapon States, under Article VI of the NPT, to "pursue [disarmament] negotiations in good faith", is a dual obligation that also includes the obligation "to bring to a conclusion" these negotiations. "The obligation involved here is an obligation to achieve a precise result — nuclear disarmament in all its aspects."

By contrast, a report recently presented to the US Congress by the US Departments of State, Defense and Energy advocated research on the development of advanced nuclear weapons, declaring that such a move was needed to increase the "credibility" of nuclear deterrence for the US and its allies. The report states that "to minimize any misperceptions about US capabilities or resolve, it is prudent ... at least to explore whether there are ways to provide the nuclear weapon stockpile with capabilities more appropriate for deterring 21st century threats in such areas as precision delivery, reduced collateral damage [and] earth penetration."

To my mind, it is hard to reconcile the opinion of the ICJ, underscoring the obligation to "bring to a conclusion" negotiations on disarmament, with these statements supporting the exploration of new types of nuclear weapons more than 30 years after entry into force of the Treaty establishing this obligation. But more importantly, if such efforts proceed, it is hard to understand how we can continue to ask the nuclear 'have-nots' to accept additional non-proliferation obligations — and to renounce any sensitive nuclear capability as being adverse to their security. As I have often stated, the continuing pursuit of asymmetric and divisive policies — such as 'the early bird gets the nukes'; pitting the interests of so-called 'civilized' nations against 'uncivilized'; failing to bridge the gap between those inside and outside the regime; and promoting policies that do not take into account the security of all — is unsustainable and counterproductive.

Clearly, the development of a security system that does not depend on nuclear deterrence or nuclear weapons will be a prerequisite to a roadmap for effective disarmament. Until the international community fully engages on the development of such a system, achieving complete nuclear disarmament will remain in the realm of rhetoric.

The difficulty of achieving this ultimate goal — the elimination of all nuclear weapons — should not be used, however, as a pretext for failing to achieve the intermediate step of drastic reductions in existing nuclear arsenals. In that regard, the announcement earlier this month by Linton Brooks — that the US would reduce its nuclear weapons stockpile by nearly half over the next eight years — is encouraging, if the intention is to eliminate the warheads in question in a verifiable and irreversible manner.

Second, any new adjustment to the regime must include India, Pakistan and Israel at the negotiating table. Without their inclusion in and commitment to this broad non-proliferation and security reform, our efforts will fail. None of the three States has joined the NPT, and their development of nuclear weapons or nuclear weapon capability has been outside of the current nuclear non-proliferation regime. Yet their status as known or presumed holders of nuclear weapons has clearly contributed to tensions in their respective regions.

In my view, the logical point for bringing India and Pakistan into the arms control process would be as part of this global 'disarmament roadmap'. In the case of Israel, this could also be achieved as part of a new security and disarmament structure in the Middle East that would go hand-in-hand with the peace process in that region.

Third, the integrity of the NPT should be ensured. The Treaty now allows any member to withdraw with three months notice. Any nation invoking this escape clause is almost certainly signaling its intent to develop nuclear weapons, which inevitably has serious implications for international peace and security. This provision of the Treaty should be curtailed. At a minimum, notice of NPT withdrawal should prompt an automatic review by the Security Council. And France has recently advanced a number of proposals for the development of a set of pre-agreed actions that would automatically be taken by the Security Council in such a case.

Fourth, the IAEA's additional protocol should be made the verification standard. Much effort was recently expended — and rightly so — to persuade Iran and Libya to give the IAEA broader rights of inspection, by accepting the authority provided to the Agency by the additional protocol. But the Agency should have the right to conduct these broader inspections in all countries. As I mentioned before, experience has shown that verification of the NPT's safeguards obligations in a credible manner requires the authority provided by the additional protocol. However, to date, only 56 States, out of the 184 non-nuclear-weapon States party to the NPT, have accepted the protocol.

Collective Security: Reforming the System

My third set of proposals relates to reforming the system for international security. It has four aspects.

First, we can only hope to make meaningful progress if we continue to keep our eyes focused on the security picture — seeking a comprehensive solution that addresses the security concerns of all. As a starting point, we must recognize that the current crisis of international insecurity will not be resolved by anything short of a functional system of collective security, as clearly hoped for in the United Nations Charter.

The Security Council must be able and ready to engage effectively in both preventive diplomacy and enforcement measures, with the tools and methods in place necessary to cope with existing and emerging threats to international peace and security. These should include: mechanisms for preventive diplomacy to settle emerging disputes; 'smart' sanctions that can target a government without adding misery to its citizens; and adequate forces to deal with the foreseeable range of situations — from maintaining law and order, to monitoring borders, to combating aggression.

In that context, I believe the Security Council should under certain circumstances authorize pre-emptive measures — collective pre-emptive measures — to address extreme threats to international peace and security, such as to prevent genocide, or to counter an imminent threat to use weapons of mass destruction in an act of aggression.

Second, once these non-proliferation and security measures are in place, we should aim for our legal regime related to nuclear weapons to emerge into a 'peremptory norm' of international law — a norm that is part of our collective conscience — not dependent on any particular treaty. In short, as with the ban on slavery or genocide, the renunciation of such weapons should be universal and permanent. This legal norm, however, cannot be contemplated without an agreed disarmament roadmap, and clear subscription to that roadmap by all States possessing nuclear weapons.

Third, we must work collectively to address not only the symptoms but also the root causes of insecurity and instability, including: the regional rivalries and conflicts I have already mentioned; the widening divide between rich and poor, in which two-fifths of the world's population lives on less than two dollars per day; the chronic lack of good governance and respect for human rights; and the increasing schisms between cultures and civilizations. We should not forget that nearly all efforts to acquire nuclear weapons are to be found in the Middle East and other areas of instability. Effective amelioration of these causes of global insecurity will require political resolve and more balanced 'North–South' relations.

Consider the current imbalance: as a global community, we spend $900 billion every year on armaments, $300 billion on subsidies to farmers in wealthy nations, and only $60 billion on development assistance to the developing world. Improving our performance in this 'global distributive justice' will go a long way towards pre-empting many of the security threats — let alone the social ills — that affect our planet.

Finally, our work to achieve consensus on these proposals should proceed with the initiation of an expanded public dialogue. Organizations like your own, the Carnegie Endowment for International Peace, should work to refine these proposals and ideas, and to bring them to the attention of governments and opinion leaders. As I indicated earlier, we should work to further stimulate public discourse on these ideas, at all levels of civil society, to make the global community understand that our survival is at stake — but that we can, in fact, solve the international security dilemma, including the nuclear dilemma, within our generation and within our own time.

In my view, the proposals I have outlined today — as well as those that have been developed by others — should be the focus of a summit on non-proliferation and global security, possibly in connection with the NPT Review Conference next year. The outcome of such a summit would be an agreed package of 'non-proliferation and security measures' that would build on existing arms control and security regimes but adapt them to present day realities.

Conclusion

As I see it, we have before us two possible courses of action. We can wait for the unthinkable to happen; or we can take notice of the writing on the wall and begin to act today.

With the continuing erosion of the effectiveness and even the legitimacy of the present arms control and security structure, we must have the wisdom and the foresight to understand — as has been aptly stated — that "as we are collectively menaced, so we must collectively act." I repeat that it is time to abandon the unworkable notion that it is morally reprehensible for some countries to pursue nuclear weapons, but morally acceptable for others to rely on them. Our aim must be clear: a security structure that is based on our shared humanity and not on the ability of some to destroy us all.

❮79❯

Speech by Minister of Defence of Russian Federation Sergei Ivanov on "Russia-NATO: Strategic Partners in Response to Emergent Threats" (13.07.2004)

According to Mr. Ivanov today we are living in "a complex and interdependent world". This world is endangered by common challenges arising out of instability, terrorism and a threat originating from "failed" States. Russia sees its future relations with NATO as "cooperation of professionals" to overcome the "Cold War" thinking inertia and to jointly confront these common challenges.

I'm glad to have the opportunity to address such a representative audience and to share with you some ideas that have occurred to me in this calm and reasonable city of which I have always had the most tender memories.

I'm ready to tell you how I regard or, rather, how we in Russia regard the state of present-day relations between Russia and NATO, the way we picture them in the near future and what relations we are striving for in the long-lasting perspective.

The widely circulating opinion that relations between our country and the North Atlantic Alliance have never been an easy issue in the foreign-policy and military-policy dialogue between Russia and the NATO member countries has already become the talk of the town.

Only ten years ago partnership with NATO seemed to be a sort of "mission impossible". No wonder—we started the dialogue after the "late frosts of Cold War," that didn't favor any conversation and were burdened down by mutual distrust and suspicion. Our dialogue followed forty years of strict silence, when security was a zero sum game because winning safety by one of the parties was regarded as a proportionate loss by the other one. We were all learning a new kind of mathematics, the mathematics of civilized survival and a so-called new "chemistry of relations", providing for equal rights and confidence. We were all learning to talk to each other, to listen to and to hear each other under new circumstances, after the world political landscape had undergone drastic changes.

Time has changed. We have become different. The world has become different. The age of the "cold war" has become a thing of the past, rubbing off, long and painful though the process may be, the stereotypes of confrontation ideology. All this has already become history. The reality of our day is a world where decisions are taken on the basis of compromise and consensus.

Now we realize better than before that we all live in a complex and interdependent world endangered by common challenges of the new generation. The understanding has come that global risks have an apocalyptic nature and call for adequate response, first of all by means of a joint effort by the world community. A "coalition of the willing" has to be transformed into a "coalition of the winning", as happened during World War II.

The end of the Cold War period has opened a Pandora's box: alongside with sober aspiration towards flexible cooperation, we witness centrifugal disorder, aggravation of tension and enhanced instability—after disintegration, or rather break-up, of Yugoslavia, after destabilization of the situation in the Caucasus, in South and Central Asia, in the Middle East. We readily and in a spirit of goodwill render assistance to our Western partners in operations in Afghanistan, share intelligence, grant the right of overflight and overland transit through our territory. We clearly realize that in modern global conditions an area of instability cannot be limited to the place of its origin. We realize that Afghanistan under Taliban was exporting instability to adjoining countries, drugs—to Europe, terrorism and refugees—all over the world. We have confronted a new kind of terrorism, one that is not politically motivated but is inspired by fanatic extremism and a brutal desire to kill. And finally, I keep on repeating that we see a threat originating from "failed" states that exist in Africa, Asia, and even in Europe. Such states act as sources of illegal migration, transit zones for trafficking drugs and weapons, permit slave markets and shelter terrorists.

Ladies and gentlemen, we are all facing the danger, it is knocking on everyone's door. A terrorist with ricin in London—what better reason is there for setting up a victory coalition? Nowadays one must take into consideration the fact that weapons of mass destruction are possessed not only by democratic governments but also by, to put it mildly, not the most stable regimes. That is why we not only have to rebuff the new global challenges with the help of new methods and technologies, but also have to act in agreement, as we did before.

I don't want to tire you with a long list of sources of "guaranteed delivery" of instability. Each separate link of such terrorist logistics is an earnest of our common vulnerability in the face of the threat menacing us all the time, everywhere, without prior notice and with the help of all means available—from a tube to a missile.

We ourselves must manage the changes, not vice versa. We ourselves must set up tasks and goals, act as their coordinators and bring them into life.

Failure is easily seen. Success is less visible. Victory does not have only one parent. Our common success is one of victory coalition.

Ladies and gentlemen, the world has changed. Yet, the new age must not necessarily be accompanied by dismantlement of the military and political legacy of the past. I have already said this and I want to say it again: Russia regards nuclear weapons and nuclear deterrence as the basis for global stability. Nuclear deterrence is a burden that the great powers have to keep on carrying. Nuclear deterrence gives birth to a higher responsibility of politicians for the decisions they make. Those politicians who have gone through a course in nuclear deterrence are, as a rule, more realistic. Please, believe me: if such a phenomenon as nuclear deterrence did not exist today, the number of armed conflicts would be much higher.

We are gradually moving towards nuclear deterrence of a new type: deterrence for the sake of securing strategic stability.

Russian leaders regard the maintenance of high fighting ability and combat readiness of strategic nuclear forces as their top priority task. The Russian Federation Defense Ministry does not make a secret out of its military planning. The aims and tasks of the Armed Forces, and their nuclear component, are clearly stated in our "white book"—"The Priority Tasks of the Development of the Armed Forces of the Russian Federation." We clearly and democratically declare the aims and tasks of Russia's military organization. The main aim of Russia's policy in the sphere of strategic deterrence is the guaranteed protection of sovereignty, territorial integrity and other vital national interests of Russia and its allies.

We closely follow what is being done in the sphere of strategic nuclear forces in the USA. Particularly, we take a considerable interest in the state of the US programs of the development of ultra small nuclear charges because each new type of armaments modifies the overall picture of global stability and we must take these modifications into consideration in our military planning.

I assure you that Russia is ready to take part in securing global strategic stability whatever the military-political situation in the world might be, given that strategic threats are the most dominant.

In essence, the gateway to a fair system of international relations lies through a full and innovative analysis of past experience. In this sense, we must constructively and with responsibility look at the interaction between Russia and NATO as an interaction between components of civilized strategic security.

How do we assess the North Atlantic alliance at present in our country?

First of all it is the most important geopolitical factor affecting the security of Russia's western borders. At the same time, it is one of the main institutions of the Euro-Atlantic community of states, providing for transatlantic communication for the allies. Russia is trying to establish normal working relations with each of the states of this community. Hence, it is our desire to set up working links with the key bodies of such a community, including the new NATO.

At the same time we in Russia feel that the North Atlantic Alliance shares our desire.

Having signed a declaration "Russia-NATO Relations: A New Quality" in Rome more than two years ago we have stepped up the NATO-Russia relations to the level of greater responsibility for the security and stable development of our common civilized space.

It can be stated today with some certainty, that we really managed to fill the ideas proclaimed in the Rome declaration with practical content. This practical content is concrete joint ventures. Theoretical discussions of problem issues more and more often give way to practical action. It is very important that such practical actions should not be reduced to tactical actions undertaken for action's sake only, but be made part and parcel of strategic relations within the framework of the victory coalition.

Cooperation between the Navies is at present the most dynamic of all the spheres of common activities.

I'll give you only a few examples. Several working groups on naval problems have been set up under the aegis of Russia-NATO Council. The agenda of the Council for the current year includes more than 100 items, 20 of which deal with naval problems.

Russia regularly takes part in sessions of the Conference of National Armaments Directors (CNAD) and the NATO Standardization Agency.

We regard as positive the mutual desire of Russia and NATO to cooperate in the sphere of research on compatibility of the systems of search for and rescue of submarine crews within the framework of the Industrial Consultative Group.

Russian Navy plans to take part in NATO exercise "Sorbet Royal - 2005" relating to the search for and rescue of the disabled submarine crews.

In the sphere of naval cooperation, we have managed to attain an unprecedented level of transparency of the military activity that is an important factor of all-European stability.

In recent years we have witnessed an effective development of Russia-NATO cooperation in such an important sphere as peacemaking.

We regard as extremely important the document "Political Aspects of Basic Concept for Russia-NATO Joint Peacekeeping Operations", fixing the principles of joint peacekeeping activity on an equitable basis.

To activate joint peacekeeping activity, preparations are being made for the so-called "procedure exercise", during which Russian and NATO experts are going to specify military aspects of joint operations more exactly. Without such work it would be absolutely impossible to even speak of anything practical.

It took very little time to set up a new constructive component of liaison between Russia's Ministry of Defense and NATO military structures.

Regardless of their introductory nature, all these measures made a significant contribution mainly to such priority areas as interaction between bodies of operative control, interoperability of means of communications and information, exchange of experience in personnel training, compatibility of national Armed Forces components (Air Force, the Navy).

Under the aegis of the Russia-NATO Council Working Group on Peacekeeping, practical recommendations were worked out to develop cooperation within the framework of the Russia-NATO Council on crisis regulation. Possibilities are being examined to cooperate with NATO in the sphere of logistical support of peacekeeping operations.

Cooperation between Russia and NATO in the sphere of military transport aviation is aimed at drawing up a joint program of maneuvers, comprising training tasks for military transport aviation during peacekeeping operations.

On the whole we managed to start a practical dialogue between the Ministry of Defense of the Russian Federation and NATO, obtain a considerable amount of information on the state of things in the sphere of operative compatibility, draw up priority directions for further cooperation.

In other words we reached a better understanding of each other, now we know in what direction we are moving.

It is understood that not all the differences in our relations have been solved.

You are all well aware of our calmly negative attitude towards expansion of the North Atlantic alliance, including the problem "NATO - Baltics - CFE". What alarms us the most, from the point of view of our own security, is the NATO deployment of means and forces on the territory of its new members. It may become an obstacle in the way of development of further cooperation between Russia and NATO if in the near future these sensitive issues are not solved on the basis of mutual benefit and equality. We all need practical deeds—clear-cut and understandable steps towards the interests of each other. We all need a new level of military and political transparency of functioning of the Alliance; we all need specific actions to remove a new gray zone in European arms control.

I think I should speak out on the last issue in more detail.

Our anxiety over the state of arms control in Europe is based on the fact that the "gray zone" in this sphere has evolved in Europe for the first time in the last fifteen years. We wouldn't like Europe to return to the principles of balance of power, but there may be no vacuum in the military-political situation. Especially if this vacuum is filled with irresponsible statements of nationalistic character. Frankly speaking, the existence of European states that do not observe standard norms of democracy and human rights is interpreted by Russia as a threat. And this is logical: Russia is a democratic country that is able to protect its democratic achievements. The states deviating from norms of democracy and human rights, as a rule, become a source of threat to their neighbors, because they tend to provoke military and political tension. That is why the Defense Minister is now talking about the state of democracy and human rights in Latvia, Estonia and some other countries—members of the Alliance.

In any case, the ball is now in the court of our European partners, who ought to prove to Russia their devotion to the principles of stability and joint action in European security by their effort to teach some of the new member-countries the elementary foundations of democracy and military-political transparency. We are not satisfied with the situation, when everything comes down to promises and statements. The well-known principle "trust but verify" is ever so actual, mainly as a result of such ambiguities.

The Russian side hopes that the positive experience of naval and peacekeeping cooperation may be extended to other spheres of joint action. In other words, we all need a new, more profound and practical agenda, in Russia-NATO relations.

For example, in the sphere of the struggle against terrorism.

We welcome the fact that the antiterrorist sphere has become an integral part of cooperation between Russia and the North Atlantic Alliance. We have come to share, which is important, a common understanding that any attempt to negotiate with terrorists contradicts the very idea of democracy.

Though even here there is a place for blatant inconsistency: on the one hand European countries at the EU summit issue a declaration on cooperation in fighting terrorism; on the other hand they are pushing Russia to start negotiations with terrorists in Chechnya.

I want everyone to hear this: Russia has never negotiated and will never negotiate with terrorists and bandits. All attempts to impose on us a kind of "reconciliation" with terrorists are doomed to failure. What is more, they show us the insincerity of some of our partners.

Another issue that stirs our anxiety is that some ruling political elites keep tolerating the existence on their own territories some structures supporting extremists and don't express clear-cut condemnation of terrorism. It is well known, that international terrorists, wanted by authorities but escaping justice, may find refuge in some of the European countries. Terrorists will do their best to undermine the global antiterrorist coalition, which is the base of today's world order.

Unfortunately, in some of the NATO countries, as well as in Europe as a whole, some politicians are still thinking in terms of the "cold war", when each of Russia's failures was interpreted as their personal victory and when each of Russia's foes automatically became their friend. Beware: such friends tend to bite the giving hand. This is being proved by the new history in Afghanistan and in the Balkans.

I hope that here I don't have to try to convince you of the extreme danger of the terrorist threat, which is the result of the process of globalization that has become a reality of the modern world.

Our common task is to draw up an efficient system of measures to prevent and nip in the bud any act of terrorism, as well as to secure the inevitable punishment of terrorists and their accomplices.

You must agree that this is one of those absolutely new tasks, which call for greater NATO unity than the "policy of deterrence" towards the no longer existent Russian threat to NATO. You know, the aims and priorities of the Alliance, at least as declared openly, have changed de facto. Wouldn't it be logical to give a new sense to the acronym NATO and decipher it as "New Anti Terrorist Organization"?

Russia and its military organization including the Armed Forces play not the last role in the sphere of antiterrorism. In this connection I cannot avoid one question, which, I know, interests many of you.

The question is about the changes, which are underway in the Russian Armed Forces. The Army and the Navy of our country have returned to the normal life of a military organism.

Russia's leaders are well aware of the existing problems and know how to solve them.

Problems are being solved. Permanent personnel cuts and structural reshuffles of different kinds gave way to a full-scale military construction. As a result, we witness a considerable increase in the fighting capacity of the Armed Forces due, among other reasons, to setting up troops of permanent fighting readiness. Military alignments have been set up, which are capable of executing tasks at any theatre of war on the perimeter of Russia's territory.

We managed to reveal in time a complex of modern threats that predetermined the arrangement of a system of priorities in military policy and military planning.

The practical realization of a contract service system has begun. This process implies a large number of difficulties, but the main steps have already been taken—the system is working and only needs fine-tuning.

At present, the number of contract servicemen, including officers, makes up virtually half of the total number of personnel. By the year 2008 we expect this number to go up to as high as nearly 70%. Nearly every second sergeant is going to be a contract serviceman.

On our way towards reforming the Armed Forces, we do not regard the contract principle as an end in itself, but as a way of finding better solutions to the problems of increasing the fighting ability of the Armed Forces.

We managed to significantly raise the level of fighting training, step up the number and widen the scale of military exercises.

This was proved by the latest exercise "Mobility-2004", unique in its aims and tasks, during which the troops were trained in strategic mobility.

I can say that we never had such training before. During it we checked the level of liaison between civil and military air controller services, tested the readiness of various services to solve questions of mobilization readiness. The main goal of the exercise - improvement of the Armed Forces mobility —was successfully achieved.

We clearly realize that apart from an improvement of fighting skills the Armed Forces need modern weapons and military equipment. The most important of the latest achievements in this field is the optimization of the arms and equipment delivery system.

Among the main directions in the sphere of military reform is improvement of military science and the system of military education, as well as the social component of the Armed Forces. We have started the practical solution of the acute problem of housing of servicemen by means of a mortgage & savings system and by setting up a fund for official lodging. A new moment, I want to draw your attention to, is the process of overall reorganization of the central bodies of military control with the aim of improving their operative ability to make strategic decisions and to attain a new quality of troop control.

This work is being done on the basis of an analysis of the results of the latest local military conflicts, including the war in Iraq, as well as in the framework of the administrative reform, which is underway in our country.

The Russian Armed Forces have not only got out of the system crisis of the 90s. We have learned serious lessons from the poor situation that the military organization of our country used to be in.

Nowadays nobody in Russia has illusions as to whether or not a modern country is able to exist without strong power structures.

On the other hand, now we understand better the specific features of the relations between the Armed Forces and civil society, more clearly realize their place in the political structure of Russia, which is following the road towards creation of a strong democratic state.

It is this understanding that provides the basis for further constructive dialogue with all subjects of international politics, including NATO.

At the end I want to emphasize that Russia sees its future relations with NATO as cooperation of professionals, strategic cooperation in the framework of a professional "coalition of the victorious", the members of which are able to overcome the "cold war" thinking inertia and to jointly confront the titanic global challenge to modern civilization.

Ladies and gentlemen!

I think that today we are in a position to set up such an effective system, such a professional coalition, which would fully protect us all against unilateral uncoordinated decisions in the military sphere and in the framework of which we could confront common global challenges and threats.

Everybody is going to benefit from this—Russia, the NATO countries and the world as a whole.

Thank you.

<80>

Speech at the UNGA by UN Secretary General Kofi Annan (21.09.2004)

> Citing the examples of Iraq, Darfur, Uganda, Beslan, the Israel-Palestine conflict, etc., the UN Secretary General said that today "the rule of law is at risk around the world" and "we see fundamental laws shamelessly disregarded". He then called upon the present generation "to strengthen the rule of law for all – which alone can guarantee freedom for all".

Mr. President, Excellencies, Ladies and Gentlemen,

It is good to see so many countries represented here at such a high level. I know this reflects your understanding that, in these difficult times, the United Nations is – as you stated four years ago in the Millennium Declaration – "the indispensable common house of the entire human family".

Indeed today, more than ever, the world needs an effective mechanism through which to seek common solutions to common problems. That is what this Organization was created for. Let's not imagine that, if we fail to make good use of it, we will find any more effective instrument.

This time next year you will be meeting to review progress in the implementation of the Millennium Declaration. By then I hope you will be ready to take bold decisions together on the full range of issues covered in the Millennium Declaration, helped by the report of the eminent Panel on Threats, Challenges and Change, which will be available before the end of this year.

As I said a year ago, we have reached a fork in the road. If you, the political leaders of the world, cannot agree or reach agreement on the way forward, history will take the decisions for you, and the interests of your peoples may go by default.

Today I will not seek to pre-judge those decisions, but to remind you of the all-important framework in which they should be taken – namely, the rule of law, at home and in the world.

The vision of "a government of laws and not of men" is almost as old as civilisation itself. In a hallway not far from this podium is a replica of the code of laws promulgated by Hammurabi more than three thousand years ago, in the land we now call Iraq.

Much of Hammurabi's code now seems impossibly harsh. But etched into its tablets are principles of justice that have been recognised, if seldom fully implemented, by almost every human society since his time:

Legal protection for the poor.

Restraints on the strong, so that they cannot oppress the weak.

Laws publicly enacted, and known to all.

That code was a landmark in mankind's struggle to build an order where, instead of might making right, right would make might. Many nations represented in this chamber can proudly point to founding documents of their own that embody that simple concept. And this Organization – your United Nations – is founded on the same simple principle.

Yet today the rule of law is at risk around the world. Again and again, we see fundamental laws shamelessly disregarded – those that ordain respect for innocent life, for civilians, for the vulnerable – especially children.

To mention only a few flagrant and topical examples:

In Iraq, we see civilians massacred in cold blood, while relief workers, journalists and other non-combatants are taken hostage and put to death in the most barbarous fashion. At the same time, we have seen Iraqi prisoners disgracefully abused.

In Darfur, we see whole populations displaced, and their homes destroyed, while rape is used as a deliberate strategy.

In northern Uganda, we have seen children mutilated, and forced to take part in acts of unspeakable cruelty.

In Beslan, we have seen children taken hostage and brutally massacred.

In Israel we see civilians, including children, deliberately targeted by Palestinian suicide bombers. And in Palestine we see homes destroyed, lands seized, and needless civilian casualties caused by Israel's excessive use of force.

And all over the world we see people being prepared for further such acts, through hate propaganda directed at Jews, Muslims, against anyone who can be identified as different from one's own group.

Excellencies,

No cause, no grievance, however legitimate in itself, can begin to justify such acts. They put all of us to shame. Their prevalence reflects our collective failure to uphold the rule of law, and instil respect for it in our fellow men and women. We all have a duty to do whatever we can to restore that respect.

To do so, we must start from the principle that no one is above the law, and no one should be denied its protection. Every nation that proclaims the rule of law at home must respect it abroad; and every nation that insists on it abroad must enforce it at home.

Yes, the rule of law starts at home. But in too many places it remains elusive. Hatred, corruption, violence and exclusion go without redress. The vulnerable lack effective recourse, and the powerful manipulate laws to retain power and accumulate wealth. At times even the necessary fight against terrorism is allowed to encroach unnecessarily on civil liberties.

At the international level, all states – strong and weak, big and small – need a framework of fair rules, which each can be confident that others will obey. Fortunately, such a framework exists. From trade to terrorism, from the law of the sea to weapons of mass destruction, States have created an impressive body of norms and laws. This is one of our Organization's proudest achievements.

And yet this framework is riddled with gaps and weaknesses. Too often it is applied selectively, and enforced arbitrarily. It lacks the teeth that turn a body of laws into an effective legal system.

Where enforcement capacity does exist, as in the Security Council, many feel it is not always used fairly or effectively. Where the rule of law is most earnestly invoked, as in the Commission on Human Rights, those invoking it do not always practise what they preach.

Those who seek to bestow legitimacy must themselves embody it; and those who invoke international law must themselves submit to it.

Just as, within a country, respect for the law depends on the sense that all have a say in making and implementing it, so it is in our global community. No nation must feel excluded. All must feel that international law belongs to them, and protects their legitimate interests.

Rule of law as a mere concept is not enough. Laws must be put into practice, and permeate the fabric of our lives.

It is by strengthening and implementing disarmament treaties, including their verification provisions, that we can best defend ourselves against the proliferation – and potential use – of weapons of mass destruction.

It is by applying the law that we can deny financial resources and safe havens to terrorists – an essential element in any strategy for defeating terrorism.

It is by reintroducing the rule of law, and confidence in its impartial application, that we can hope to resuscitate societies shattered by conflict.

It is the law, including Security Council resolutions, which offers the best foundation for resolving prolonged conflicts – in the Middle East, in Iraq, and around the world.

And it is by rigorously upholding international law that we can, and must, fulfil our responsibility to protect innocent civilians from genocide, crimes against humanity and war crimes. As I warned this Assembly five years ago, history will judge us very harshly if we let ourselves be deflected from this task, or think we are excused from it, by invocations of national sovereignty.

The Security Council has just requested me to appoint an international commission to investigate reports of human rights violations in Darfur and determine whether acts of genocide have been committed. I shall do so with all speed. But let no one treat this as a respite, during which events in that devastated region continue to take their course. Regardless of their legal definition, things are happening there which must shock the conscience of every human being.

The African Union has nobly taken the lead and the responsibility in providing monitors and a protective force in Darfur – as well as seeking a political settlement, which alone can bring lasting peace and security to that society. But we all know the present limitations of this new-born Union. We must give it every possible support. Let no one imagine that this affair concerns Africans alone. The victims are human beings, whose human rights must be sacred to all of us. We all have a duty to do whatever we can to rescue them, and do it now.

Excellencies,

Last month, I promised the Security Council that I would make the Organization's work to strengthen the rule of law and transitional justice in conflict and post-conflict societies a priority for the remainder of my tenure.

By the same token, I urge you to do more to foster the rule of law at home and abroad. I ask all of you here today to take advantage of the arrangements we have made for you to sign treaties on the protection of civilians – treaties that you yourselves negotiated – and then, go back home, and implement them fully and in good faith. And I implore you to give your full support to the measures I shall bring before you, during this session, to improve the security of United Nations staff. Those non-combatants, who voluntarily put themselves in harm's way to assist their fellow men and women, surely deserve your protection, as well as your respect.

Throughout the world, Excellencies, the victims of violence and injustice are waiting. They are waiting for us to keep our word. They notice when we use words to mask inaction. They notice when laws that should protect them are not applied.

I believe we can restore and extend the rule of law throughout the world. But ultimately, that will depend on the hold that the law has on our consciences. This Organization was founded in the ashes of a war that brought untold sorrow to mankind. Today we must look again into our collective conscience, and ask ourselves whether we are doing enough.

Excellencies,

Each generation has its part to play in the age-old struggle to strengthen the rule of law for all – which alone can guarantee freedom for all.

Let our generation not be found wanting.

Thank you very much.

<81>

Speech by US President George W. Bush to United Nations General Assembly (21.09.2004)

President Bush said that human dignity is dishonoured by oppression, corruption, tyranny, bigotry, terrorism and violence against the innocent. He called upon the international community to unite for "the defeat of terror, the protection of human rights, the spread of prosperity, the advance of democracy".

Mr. Secretary General, Mr. President, distinguished delegates, ladies and gentlemen: Thank you for the honor of addressing this General Assembly. The American people respect the idealism that gave life to this organization. And we respect the men and women of the U.N., who stand for peace and human rights in every part of the world. Welcome to New York City, and welcome to the United States of America.

During the past three years, I've addressed this General Assembly in a time of tragedy for my country, and in times of decision for all of us. Now we gather at a time of tremendous opportunity for the U.N. and for all peaceful nations. For decades, the circle of liberty and security and development has been expanding in our world. This progress has brought unity to Europe, self-government to Latin America and Asia, and new hope to Africa. Now we have the historic chance to widen the circle even further, to fight radicalism and terror with justice and dignity, to achieve a true peace, founded on human freedom.

The United Nations and my country share the deepest commitments. Both the American Declaration of Independence and the Universal Declaration of Human Rights proclaim the equal value and dignity of every human life. That dignity is honored by the rule of law, limits on the power of the state, respect for women, protection of private property, free speech, equal justice, and religious tolerance. That dignity is dishonored by oppression, corruption, tyranny, bigotry, terrorism and all violence against the innocent. And both of our founding documents affirm that this bright line between justice and injustice — between right and wrong — is the same in every age, and every culture, and every nation.

Wise governments also stand for these principles for very practical and realistic reasons. We know that dictators are quick to choose aggression, while free nations strive to resolve differences in peace. We know that oppressive governments support terror, while free governments fight the terrorists in their midst. We know that free peoples embrace progress and life, instead of becoming the recruits for murderous ideologies.

Every nation that wants peace will share the benefits of a freer world. And every nation that seeks peace has an obligation to help build that world. Eventually, there is no safe isolation from terror networks, or failed states that shelter them, or outlaw regimes, or weapons of mass destruction. Eventually, there is no safety in looking away, seeking the quiet life by ignoring the struggles and oppression of others.

In this young century, our world needs a new definition of security. Our security is not merely found in spheres of influence, or some balance of power. The security of our world is found in the advancing rights of mankind.

These rights are advancing across the world — and across the world, the enemies of human rights are responding with violence. Terrorists and their allies believe the Universal Declaration of Human Rights and the American Bill of Rights, and every charter of liberty ever written, are lies, to be burned and destroyed and forgotten. They believe that dictators should control every mind and tongue in the Middle East and beyond. They believe that suicide and torture and murder are fully justified to serve any goal they declare. And they act on their beliefs.

In the last year alone, terrorists have attacked police stations, and banks, and commuter trains, and synagogues — and a school filled with children. This month in Beslan we saw, once again, how the terrorists measure their success — in the death of the innocent, and in the pain of grieving families. Svetlana Dzebisov was held hostage, along with her son and her nephew — her nephew did not survive. She recently visited the cemetery, and saw what she called the "little graves." She said, "I understand that there is evil in the world. But what have these little creatures done?"

Members of the United Nations, the Russian children did nothing to deserve such awful suffering, and fright, and death. The people of Madrid and Jerusalem and Istanbul and Baghdad have done nothing to deserve sudden and random murder. These acts violate the standards of justice in all cultures, and the principles of all religions. All civilized nations are in this struggle together, and all must fight the murderers.

We're determined to destroy terror networks wherever they operate, and the United States is grateful to every nation that is helping to seize terrorist assets, track down their operatives, and disrupt their plans. We're determined to end the state sponsorship of terror — and my nation is grateful to all that participated in the liberation of Afghanistan. We're determined to prevent proliferation, and to enforce the demands of the world — and my nation is grateful to the soldiers of many nations who have helped to deliver the Iraqi people from an outlaw dictator.

The dictator agreed in 1991, as a condition of a cease-fire, to fully comply with all Security Council resolutions — then ignored more than a decade of those resolutions. Finally, the Security Council promised serious consequences for his defiance. And the commitments we make must have meaning. When we say "serious consequences," for the sake of peace, there must be serious consequences. And so a coalition of nations enforced the just demands of the world.

Defending our ideals is vital, but it is not enough. Our broader mission as U.N. members is to apply these ideals to the great issues of our time. Our wider goal is to promote hope and progress as the alternatives to hatred and violence. Our great purpose is to build a better world beyond the war on terror.

Because we believe in human dignity, America and many nations have established a global fund to fight AIDS, tuberculosis, and malaria. In three years the contributing countries have funded projects in more than 90 countries, and pledged a total of $5.6 billion to these efforts. America has undertaken a $15 billion effort to provide prevention and treatment and humane care in nations afflicted by AIDS, placing a special focus on 15 countries where the need is most urgent. AIDS is the greatest health crisis of our time, and our unprecedented commitment will bring new hope to those who have walked too long in the shadow of death.

Because we believe in human dignity, America and many nations have joined together to confront the evil of trafficking in human beings. We're supporting organizations that rescue the victims, passing stronger anti-trafficking laws, and warning travelers that they will be held to account for supporting this modern form of slavery. Women and children should never be exploited for pleasure or greed, anywhere on earth.

Because we believe in human dignity, we should take seriously the protection of life from exploitation under any pretext. In this session, the U.N. will consider a resolution sponsored by Costa Rica calling for a comprehensive ban on human cloning. I support that resolution and urge all governments to affirm a basic ethical principle: No human life should ever be produced or destroyed for the benefit of another.

Because we believe in human dignity, America and many nations have changed the way we fight poverty, curb corruption, and provide aid. In 2002 we created the Monterrey Consensus, a bold approach that links new aid from developed nations to real reform in developing ones. And through the Millennium Challenge Account, my nation is increasing our aid to developing nations that expand economic freedom and invest in the education and health of their own people.

Because we believe in human dignity, America and many nations have acted to lift the crushing burden of debt that limits the growth of developing economies, and holds millions of people in poverty. Since these efforts began in 1996, poor countries with the heaviest debt burdens have received more than $30 billion of relief. And to prevent the build-up of future debt, my country and other nations have agreed that international financial institutions should increasingly provide new aid in the form of grants, rather than loans.

Because we believe in human dignity, the world must have more effective means to stabilize regions in turmoil, and to halt religious violence and ethnic cleansing. We must create permanent capabilities to respond to future crises. The United States and Italy have proposed a Global Peace Operations Initiative. G-8 countries will train 75,000 peacekeepers, initially from Africa, so they can conduct operations on that continent and elsewhere. The countries of the G-8 will help this peacekeeping force with deployment and logistical needs.

At this hour, the world is witnessing terrible suffering and horrible crimes in the Darfur region of Sudan, crimes my government has concluded are genocide. The United States played a key role in efforts to broker a cease-fire, and we're providing humanitarian assistance to the Sudanese people. Rwanda and Nigeria have deployed forces in Sudan to help improve security so aid can be delivered. The Security Council adopted a new resolution that supports an expanded African Union force to help prevent further bloodshed, and urges the government of Sudan to stop flights by military aircraft in Darfur. We congratulate the members of the Council on this timely and necessary action. I call on the government of Sudan to honor the cease-fire it signed, and to stop the killing in Darfur.

Because we believe in human dignity, peaceful nations must stand for the advance of democracy. No other system of government has done more to protect minorities, to secure the rights of labor, to raise the status of women, or to channel human energy to the pursuits of peace. We've witnessed the rise of democratic governments in predominantly Hindu and Muslim, Buddhist, Jewish and Christian cultures. Democratic institutions have taken root in modern societies, and in traditional societies. When it comes to the desire for liberty and justice, there is no clash of civilizations. People everywhere are capable of freedom, and worthy of freedom.

Finding the full promise of representative government takes time, as America has found in two centuries of debate and struggle. Nor is there any — only one form of representative government — because democracies, by definition, take on the unique character of the peoples that create them. Yet this much we know with certainty: The desire for freedom resides in every human heart. And that desire cannot be contained forever by prison walls, or martial laws, or secret police. Over time, and across the earth, freedom will find a way.

Freedom is finding a way in Iraq and Afghanistan — and we must continue to show our commitment to democracies in those nations. The liberty that many have won at a cost must be secured. As members of the United Nations, we all have a stake in the success of the world's newest democracies.

Not long ago, outlaw regimes in Baghdad and Kabul threatened the peace and sponsored terrorists. These regimes destabilized one of the world's most vital — and most volatile — regions. They brutalized their peoples, in defiance of all civilized norms. Today, the Iraqi and Afghan people are on the path to democracy and freedom. The governments that are rising will pose no threat to others. Instead of harboring terrorists, they're fighting terrorist groups. And this progress is good for the long-term security of us all.

The Afghan people are showing extraordinary courage under difficult conditions. They're fighting to defend their nation from Taliban holdouts, and helping to strike against the terrorist killers. They're reviving their economy. They've adopted a constitution that protects the rights of all, while honoring their nation's most cherished traditions. More than 10 million Afghan citizens — over 4 million of them women — are now registered to vote in next month's presidential election. To any who still would question whether Muslim societies can be democratic societies, the Afghan people are giving their answer.

Since the last meeting of this General Assembly, the people of Iraq have regained sovereignty. Today, in this hall, the Prime Minister of Iraq and his delegation represent a country that has rejoined the community of nations. The government of Prime Minister Allawi has earned the support of every nation that believes in self-determination and desires peace. And under Security Council resolutions 1511 and 1546, the world is providing that support. The U.N., and its member nations, must respond to Prime Minister Allawi's request, and do more to help build an Iraq that is secure, democratic, federal, and free.

A democratic Iraq has ruthless enemies, because terrorists know the stakes in that country. They know that a free Iraq in the heart of the Middle East will be a decisive blow against their ambitions for that region. So a terrorists group associated with al Qaeda is now one of the main groups killing the innocent in Iraq today — conducting a campaign of bombings against civilians, and the beheadings of bound men. Coalition forces now serving in Iraq are confronting the terrorists and foreign fighters, so peaceful nations around the world will never have to face them within our own borders.

Our coalition is standing beside a growing Iraqi security force. The NATO Alliance is providing vital training to that force. More than 35 nations have contributed money and expertise to help rebuild Iraq's infrastructure.

And as the Iraqi interim government moves toward national elections, officials from the United Nations are helping Iraqis build the infrastructure of democracy. These selfless people are doing heroic work, and are carrying on the great legacy of Sergio de Mello.

As we have seen in other countries, one of the main terrorist goals is to undermine, disrupt, and influence election outcomes. We can expect terrorist attacks to escalate as Afghanistan and Iraq approach national elections. The work ahead is demanding. But these difficulties will not shake our conviction that the future of Afghanistan and Iraq is a future of liberty. The proper response to difficulty is not to retreat, it is to prevail.

The advance of freedom always carries a cost, paid by the bravest among us. America mourns the losses to our nation, and to many others. And today, I assure every friend of Afghanistan and Iraq, and every enemy of liberty: We will stand with the people of Afghanistan and Iraq until their hopes of freedom and security are fulfilled.

These two nations will be a model for the broader Middle East, a region where millions have been denied basic human rights and simple justice. For too long, many nations, including my own, tolerated, even excused, oppression in the Middle East in the name of stability. Oppression became common, but stability never arrived. We must take a different approach. We must help the reformers of the Middle East as they work for freedom, and strive to build a community of peaceful, democratic nations.

This commitment to democratic reform is essential to resolving the Arab-Israeli conflict. Peace will not be achieved by Palestinian rulers who intimidate opposition, tolerate corruption, and maintain ties to terrorist groups. The long suffering Palestinian people deserve better. They deserve true leaders capable of creating and governing a free and peaceful Palestinian state.

Even after the setbacks and frustrations of recent months, goodwill and hard effort can achieve the promise of the roadmap to peace. Those who would lead a new Palestinian state should adopt peaceful means to achieve the rights of their people. and create the reformed institutions of a stable democracy. Arab states should end incitement in their own media, cut off public and private funding for terrorism, and establish normal relations with Israel. Israel should impose a settlement freeze, dismantle unauthorized outposts, end the daily humiliation of the Palestinian people, and avoid any actions that prejudice final negotiations. And world leaders should withdraw all favor and support from any Palestinian ruler who fails his people and betrays their cause.

The democratic hopes we see growing in the Middle East are growing everywhere. In the words of the Burmese democracy advocate, Aung San Suu Kyi: "We do not accept the notion that democracy is a Western value. To the contrary; democracy simply means good government rooted in responsibility, transparency, and accountability." Here at the United Nations, you know this to be true. In recent years, this organization has helped create a new democracy in East Timor, and the U.N. has aided other nations in making the transition to self-rule.

Because I believe the advance of liberty is the path to both a safer and better world, today I propose establishing a Democracy Fund within the United Nations. This is a great calling for this great organization. The fund would help countries lay the foundations of democracy by instituting the rule of law and independent courts, a free press, political parties and trade unions. Money from the fund would also help set up voter precincts and polling places, and support the work of election monitors. To show our commitment to the new Democracy Fund, the United States will make an initial contribution. I urge other nations to contribute, as well.

Today, I've outlined a broad agenda to advance human dignity, and enhance the security of all of us. The defeat of terror, the protection of human rights, the spread of prosperity, the advance of democracy — these causes, these ideals, call us to great work in the world. Each of us alone can only do so much. Together, we can accomplish so much more.

History will honor the high ideals of this organization. The charter states them with clarity: "to save succeeding generations from the scourge of war," "to reaffirm faith in fundamental human rights," "to promote social progress and better standards of life in larger freedom."

Let history also record that our generation of leaders followed through on these ideals, even in adversity. Let history show that in a decisive decade, members of the United Nations did not grow weary in our duties, or waver in meeting them. I'm confident that this young century will be liberty's century. I believe we will rise to this moment, because I know the character of so many nations and leaders represented here today. And I have faith in the transforming power of freedom.

May God bless you.

‹82›

Address by Pakistan President General Pervez Musharraf, to the UNGA (22.09.2004)

General Musharraf called upon the industrialized world to support an "Islamic renaissance through adequate financial and technical assistance and larger trade opportunities". He also called for the resolution of all outstanding international disputes which affect Muslims. He also mentioned that Pakistan was "firmly committed to resolving all disputes with India peacefully including the Kashmir dispute".

Mr. President,

Excellencies,

Distinguished Delegates,

Allow me to extend our warm felicitations on your election as the President of the General Assembly. We congratulate H.E. Mr. Julian Hunte for his successful stewardship of the 58th Session of the Assembly.

I also reaffirm our deep appreciation for the wise leadership of the Secretary General, H.E. Mr. Kofi Annan, and his services for the cause of peace and progress in the world.

Mr. President,

A profound transformation is underway in international relations. The dangerous balances of the Cold War have been replaced by the complex and equally dangerous realities of our world today. It is a world marked by intensifying globalization – of economies, production, trade and information, on one side, and terrorist violence, poverty and disease, on the other.

The growing asymmetries in power among States, discrimination in the dispensation of international justice, repression of peoples' legitimate aspirations, and growing socioeconomic disparities, have precipitated "new threats" to international peace and security: The threat of terrorism, proliferation of weapons of mass destruction, and imploding States. The world today sees turmoil and upheaval everywhere – especially in the Third World and more specifically in the Muslim World. Too many fronts have been opened, too many battle lines drawn. The time for closing fronts has come. The world today is crying for peace, reconciliation and reform. Our objective today has to be harmony through reconciliation and accommodation, globally and regionally.

Mr. President,

Terrorism poses the most urgent threat to many countries, including the most powerful States. For many of us, the terrorist threat is close and personal. Terrorism threatens Pakistan's vital national interests and objectives. We have thus participated actively in the unprecedented global campaign against it. Pakistan has led the way in this campaign. Our counter-terrorist campaign is ongoing. The global cooperation against Terrorism has been highly successful. Determined and collective action has contained and disrupted the violent agendas of the terrorists. We are winning the battle against terrorists. However, what we are doing is insufficient to win the ultimate war against them. The immediate anti-terrorist response has to be accompanied by a clear, long-term strategy striking at the root of the problem if we are to ensure final success against this scourge.

Mr. President,

I had proposed the two pronged strategy of Enlightened Moderation to overcome terrorism and prevent a clash of civilizations. The last Islamic Summit in Malaysia endorsed this plan which involves, on the one hand, internal socio-economic reform in the Muslim world and, on the other, active support from the major powers to ensure political justice and socio-economic revival for all Islamic peoples. While the Islamic World has taken its first step in the form of nominating a Commission of Eminent Persons to propose measures for a Renaissance in the Muslim World, the major powers of the West have yet to show movement, by seriously trying, to resolve internationally recognized disputes affecting the Muslim world.

The industrialized world must support the endeavour for an Islamic renaissance especially through adequate financial and technical assistance and larger trade opportunities. Most importantly, justice must be offered to Islamic peoples in the form of resolution of all outstanding international disputes which affect Muslims. There is no time to lose. Action has to be taken before an iron curtain finally descends between the West and the Islamic World.

Mr. President,

The tragedy of Palestine is an open wound inflicted on the psyche of every Muslim. It generates anger and resentment across the Islamic World. Continued Israeli violence and erection of the illegal separation wall by them, usurping more Palestinian land, as well as suicide attacks by misguided Palestinians, are frustrating the prospects of peace and prolonging the agony of the Palestinian people. While Pakistan stands for peace – recognizing the right of Israel to exist, as also the right of the Palestinians to have their own homeland, we can never accept the usurpation of additional Palestinian land. Israel has no right to erect its separation wall beyond its 1967 boundaries. Pakistan calls on Israel to withdraw the wall from all occupied Palestinian lands, taking it back to the pre-1967 boundaries. We also call on Israel to stop the daily atrocities against Palestinians. Pakistan also call on President Yasser Arafat to use his influence to reciprocally halt the Intifada and give peace a chance. A major responsibility rests with the Quartet, and in particular with the world's greatest power, to secure a fair and peaceful solution of the problem, realizing the vision of two states – Israel and Palestine – living side by side in peace and security. The US can and must play the role of a just broker of peace. Peace must succeed in the Middle East; failure, Mr. President, is no more an option.

Mr. President,

It has always been my conviction that Pakistan and India can resolve all their differences, including over Jammu and Kashmir, through a sincere dialogue. The dangerous confrontation of 2002 and the three wars prior to that between our two countries have demonstrated that there is no military solution to our problems. The aspiration for peace enjoys popular support in Pakistan and, I also believe, in India. Neither country can achieve its ambition for social and economic progress in the absence of peace. We must achieve peace for the sake of the impoverished people of South Asia – for their development and prosperity.

After several aborted attempts, Pakistan and India have been able to initiate Confidence Building Measures (CBMs) and a composite dialogue this year to address all outstanding issues. Pakistan has pursued this process with complete sincerity, giving bilateralism a final chance. We feel that the dual channels of CBMs and the Dialogue Process must proceed in tandem. We also are firmly committed to resolving all disputes with India peacefully including the Kashmir dispute. This cannot be ignored. Its resolution cannot be delayed. We desire a resolution of Kashmir which is just and acceptable to India, Pakistan and the people of Kashmir. We also seek strategic stability with India. I am glad to say, Mr. President, that uptill now the normalization process has progressed well, in a cordial atmosphere. Now that the negotiations are entering the difficult stage of grappling with solutions to previously irreconcilable disputes, Pakistan hopes that India shows the same sincerity, flexibility and boldness that Pakistan will demonstrate. I look forward to my meeting day after tomorrow with Prime Minister Manmohan Singh. I would like to convey to him that this is the moment for peace – we must not allow it to slip away.

Mr. President,

Iraq has taken a serious turn, to the anguish of the entire world community. It is imperative that together with closing the Palestine and Kashmir fronts, we also wind down the Iraq confrontation. Pakistan stands for restoration of peace and stability in Iraq, ensuring its unity and territorial integrity. This can only be achieved through handing over governance authority to the people of Iraq and allowing them full control over their natural resources. Internal law and order and security can be best promoted by local Iraqi Police or Militia, which needs to be built up expeditiously. At an opportune time, and, on request of people and Government of Iraq, the Muslim World could play a role in bringing peace and harmony to this conflict torn Nation.

Mr. President,

The forthcoming elections in Afghanistan will be an important landmark in the country's progress towards democracy and stability. Pakistan will do all it can to prevent terrorists from using our territory to disrupt the Afghan election process. The subsequent Parliamentary elections in April 2005 would also augur well for self governance in Afghanistan. While the political channel is progressing well and we wish President Karzai all success, the process of building the Afghan National Army and reconstruction effort in Afghanistan needs to be accelerated to install durable peace in Afghanistan.

Mr. President,

In our globalized world, peace and development are interdependent – now more than ever. Despite dynamic growth in some parts of the developing world, economic and social disparities are increasing. The rich are richer; the poor are poorer. Over two billion people on our planet — a quarter of the world's population — live in abject poverty, afflicted by hunger, disease and conflict. Islands of peace and prosperity cannot coexist for long within oceans of instability and poverty.

A bold and innovative global strategy is required to redress the growing inequalities. Good governance is a precondition for development. But, it is equally essential to rectify the glaring inequities and imbalances in the international financial and trade systems. Official Development Assistance can and must be doubled. Innovative ways can and must be adopted to generate the financial resources required for development. The billions transferred abroad by corrupt leaders should be returned to the looted countries to finance poverty alleviation, education and health. International investment flows should be consciously directed to the poorer developing countries. It can unleash the latent power of the poor for consumption and production. We also know by now that trade, and not just aid, is the way to promote growth and to benefit from globalization. However, it has to be made more equitable. It should eliminate unfair agricultural subsidies, remove high and escalating tariffs that discriminate against the products of the poor and offer special and differential treatment to disadvantaged developing countries. In my view, we need more than a level playing field; we need a field tilted in favour of the developing countries.

Unless the world's leaders generate the political will required to agree and implement these measures urgently, the Millennium Development Goals, proclaimed by the United Nations, will remain a mirage.

Mr. President,

In Pakistan, we are well on the way to transforming our country into a modem, progressive, tolerant, democratic, Islamic state, reflecting the vision of our founding father, the Qaid-e-Azam. Democracy has been restored in Pakistan. The people have been empowered through a revolutionary Local Government System. Our women have been empowered. However, like other developing countries, Pakistan confronts several challenges. But, we are confident of success. Our governance is good. Our national priorities are clear.

Mr. President,

Today, there is welcome resurgence of support for multilateralism. This must be a multilateralism based on the principles of the UN Charter, a cooperative and democratic multilateralism. It must seek just, peaceful and durable solutions to conflicts and disputes. It must promote a programme for nuclear disarmament and non-proliferation. It must foster global development and prosperity.

All our collective aspirations can be best pursued within this World Organization.The United Nations must be strengthened and revitalized to respond to the challenges of Twenty-first Century. The UN Security Council should become more effective, democratic and representative. There is no agreement on the aspiration of a few States to acquire permanent membership of the Security Council. The overwhelming majority of states are against the creation of new centres of privilege. The Council should be enlarged to ensure the representation of the mostly small and medium states which have joined the United Nations over the last three decades. We have to consider new ideas to craft a consensus on the enlargement of elected members on the Security Council.

Mr. President,

Pakistan believes that a new consensus on peace, security and development, can and should be achieved on the occasion of the 60 th Anniversary of the United Nations next year.

The summit meeting .suggested by the Secretary General for next year must lead to a negotiated Final Document adopted by consensus. This historic Summit will, I hope, create a new paradigm to achieve universal peace and prosperity.

‹83›

Statement by Jack Straw, 'Global Security is our shared responsibility at the United Nations General Assembly (23.09.2004)

Mr. Jack Straw said that to make collective action work the UN should focus on three important areas. It should have a broader approach to tackle threats such as poverty, disease and environmental degradation; the "principle of non-interference" should be qualified "by a duty to protect"; and thirdly, there is an "urgent need to combat global terrorism".

Mr President,

Congratulations on your election.

Eighteen months ago, the United Nations faced divisions more serious than any since the Cuban Missile Crisis of October 1962. We all worried whether the strength and unity which we had built up since the end of the Cold War could survive.

Then last year we saw Kofi Annan standing at his now famous fork in the road. But in the year since, almost instinctively, we have decided to follow our Secretary-General's directions. This Organisation has not been plunged, as some predicated, into paralysis: instead, I have felt a powerful if unspoken determination to make the United Nations work, and work more effectively, to fulfil its central task: to secure peace around the world.

Over the last 12 months we have dealt with new crises like that in Darfur in Sudan, where we have set clear tasks for the Sudanese Government and the rebel groups. We have tackled the situation in the Democratic Republic of the Congo and the Great Lakes; mobilised international support for the new Iraq; and addressed a long list of hugely-important subjects which rarely receive the coverage they should in the media – Haiti, Georgia, Timor-Leste, Bougainville, Western Sahara.

We have shown in these actions the unity of purpose which is one of the strongest weapons in our hands to defeat the evils which today afflict the globe. And the search for consensus has not been confined to the Security Council. I am proud that just a few months after the difficult times of early last year, France, Germany and the United Kingdom came together to work, as we continue to do, on the Iran dossier before the International Atomic Energy Agency.

I recognise, of course, the frustrations before all of us, not least over the Israel-Palestine conflict – where the clear path to peace set out in the Roadmap and endorsed by the Security Council remains elusive. But all in all we have shown the will to make collective action work – though we know, too, that we need to go further. In particular, we need to get better at tackling threats which have changed dramatically since the UN's foundation. Today the greatest threats to our security often come not from other functioning sovereign states, but from terrorist organisations, from failing states, and from man-made shocks to our environment like climate change, which can exacerbate state failure and breed internal instability.

The High-Level Panel appointed by the Secretary-General is preparing its recommendations for how we can address these challenges. We should remember that we have one great advantage. Though its institutions and the founding text of the Charter has hardly changed in 60 years, the United Nations is not an Organisation set in stone – but a set of living institutions based on a shared will to make collective security work. It has adapted in the past – with the development of peacekeeping, a greater focus on individual rights, or the setting of global targets for development. I am confident that it can adapt in the future.

Of course, institutional change is part of that. At the UN's foundation, one-eighth of its members could expect to be elected members of the Security Council at any one time. Today it is less than one-eighteenth. The United Kingdom has long supported the case for expanding the Security Council to say 24 members, including amongst the permanent membership Germany and Japan – two countries which between them contribute 28 per cent of the UN's budget –; India, which represents one sixth of the world's population; and Brazil, which just missed permanent membership in 1945.

But we should not see an expansion of the Security Council, or other institutional change, as a panacea. The bigger need is to adapt our common understanding, the UN's jurisprudence if you like, and its operational effectiveness – so that we can respond more quickly and more thoroughly to today's new threats.

Let me highlight three areas which to me seem particularly important. First, our approach must be broader, tackling threats to the most vulnerable, such as poverty, disease and environmental degradation. Second, we must build a new consensus by expanding the scope of collective action. And third, we must deal with the threat of terrorism which menaces us all and everything for which we stand.

A Broader Approach

Mr President,

So, first – the need for a broader approach which addresses the complex and interdependent nature of security today.

Here, we have to do more to meet the Millennium Development Goals and promote sustainable development, especially in Africa. And we must do so not just because of our concern for justice and our common humanity; but also to reduce the stresses on states and peoples which affect our collective security. We can't have security without development, or development without security.

As the Secretary-General highlighted in his speech on Tuesday, we have to do more to entrench the rule of law and justice, especially in states recovering from conflict. The UK will pursue work on the Secretary-General's report during our Security Council Presidency next month.

We could also use the UN to agree, to monitor and to help to implement globally-accepted norms of good governance.

And we need to act together, quickly, on climate change – perhaps the greatest long-term threat to our world in terms of stability and security, not just the environment. We must begin by implementing Kyoto; and we must also agree emissions reductions beyond 2012.

A New Consensus

Mr President,

Second is the need to build a new consensus on the scope of collective action.

We all represent independent, sovereign states. But even as we founded the UN we recognised that sovereignty was a trust in the hands of a nation's government: there to be respected, not abused, either from without or within. An abuse from without could be dealt with through the inherent right of self defence recognised in Article 51 of the Charter. But an abuse from within which threatens the peace could and should be dealt with by the Security Council under the powers enshrined in the other articles of Chapter VII of the Charter, and by the many Conventions within the UN framework, including, for example, the 1948 Genocide Convention. No longer could or should the world turn away from unspeakable barbarities like the Holocaust.

We have not however always lived up to these high expectations – as the tragedies of Rwanda and Bosnia ten years ago remind us. But today we must resolve to do so and to engage – both in situations of humanitarian catastrophe or grave violations of international humanitarian law, and in the face of other threats to international peace and security. The principle of non-interference has to be qualified by a duty to protect, especially where governments are failing in that duty.

So we need for example to be ready to support greater use by the Secretary-General of his powers under Article 99 to bring threats to the peace to the Security Council's attention; and we must act quickly and effectively in response, because prevention is better than cure. We should look to work more closely with regional organisations, as we are doing with the African Union in Darfur. We need more discussion on the criteria for when the international community might have to intervene with military force in the most extreme circumstances. And we must get better at engaging for the long term in countries recovering from conflict, co-ordinating our efforts in response to locally-agreed priorities.

Global Terrorism

Mr President,

My third point is the urgent need to combat global terrorism – a menace directed at all of us.

If we have learnt anything in the three years since 11 September 2001 it is that international terrorism is indiscriminate in its targets, and merciless in its hatred. Christian, Jew, Hindu, Buddhist, Sikh, Muslim, people of no religion or any religion, and of every or no shade of political opinion – all have died through the terrorists' bullet or bomb.

My friend, Sergei Lavrov, spoke eloquently a moment ago of the tears still wet from the horrific massacre at Beslan. Sergei, your tears are my tears, and Russia's tears are the world's tears. And we resolve to fight terrorism together.

Today, in Iraq, we are seeing again the depths which the terrorists plumb. Of course, the vast majority of the victims of terrorism in Iraq are Iraqis – and our thoughts and condolences are with the Government and people of Iraq, and with their families. But some are foreigners who are helping Iraqis to build a more stable and prosperous country. One is Ken Bigley, a British engineer, held hostage by terrorists who have barbarically murdered his two American comrades. Our thoughts and prayers are with their families; and we continue to do all we can to secure Mr Bigley's release.

Yes, I know – how could I forget – that opinions have differed over the rightness of the military action taken in Iraq 18 months ago. But I warrant that no nation is in favour of the terrorist insurgency now occurring there. For we all recognise that what is being attempted by the terrorists in Iraq is an attack both on the Iraqi people and on everything for which this organisation stands: safety, security, human rights. We must come together to defeat the terrorists and their despicable aims.

Mr President,

The threat of terrorism confronts democratic, properly-functioning states with an acute dilemma: to fight those who recognise none of the values for which we stand, while remaining true to those values.

Our commitments under international conventions express many of those values and the importance which we attach to them. But equally, those

Conventions cannot be allowed to shelter those involved in terrorism. They were designed to protect citizens from abuse by states, not by terrorists. The 1951 Convention on Refugees protects those with a well-founded fear of persecution. I am proud that Britain and so many other nations have offered that protection where it was required. But as the 1951 Convention itself sets out, asylum is not an unqualified right: it does not apply to anyone who has committed a war crime, a crime against humanity, or other serious crime, or who is guilty of acts contrary to the purposes and principles of the United Nations.

We must never stoop to the level of the terrorist: to torture, mistreatment, unjustified incarceration, and nor will any country in the EU be party to the return of suspects to such conditions or to face the death penalty. But we cannot let terrorists exploit a protection designed for the persecuted, not the persecutors. We shall therefore be working closely with Russia on its important draft Security Council Resolution, to see how best we can prevent those who commit, support and finance terrorism from sheltering behind a refugee status to which they are not entitled, and to look at ways to ensure the speedier extradition of such individuals.

Mr President,

We, the United Nations, have over the last year begun to show a new determination to come together and make collective action work.

A year from now, we will meet again here to review the High-Level Panel's recommendations and the Millennium Development Goals, and to set the UN's agenda for the next decade. The coming year, as we prepare for that Summit, will be vital for building consensus, understanding, and resolve.

The UK's Chairmanship of the G8 next year will focus on tackling climate change; and on Africa, on which the independent Commission for Africa will be producing recommendations for how best we can support the radical agenda for change and development designed by Africa itself through NEPAD and the African Union. And our Presidency of the European Union will help us to lead efforts for a successful outcome in the Doha Development Round, and for building the EU's crisis-management capabilities.

Mr President,

More than ever, global security is our shared responsibility. In the year ahead, as we continue to adapt to today's threats and challenges, we must find renewed determination and political will to make collective security work. The United Kingdom is determined to play its full part in that.

⟨84⟩

Address by Israeli Prime Minister Ariel Sharon at the opening of the Knesset Session (11.10.2004)

While stating that "the Roadmap" was the only plan to enable progress toward a viable political agreement with the Palestinians, Mr. Sharon said that the Palestinians had done nothing to abide by their commitments under that plan. Israel, while adhering to the Roadmap was forced "to take steps of its own to consolidate its political and international standing" and for this reason the government had initiated the plan "to disengage from the Gaza Strip".

Honorable President and Mrs. Katzav,

Mr. Speaker,

Distinguished Knesset members,

I am honored to address the Knesset today, as the law requires, to report on the major government activities during the recent period, primarily those which are expected to take place during the upcoming Knesset session.

At the conclusion of our recent holiday we were all awakened, in shock and dismay, to a new height of horror which occurred in the Sinai terror attacks. Again we had to grit our teeth and brace ourselves in the face of the inferno. Again we had to make a terrible sacrifice to the "Molech" of terror, hatred and murder.

We were attacked twice: once because we are Israelis and because of the hatred towards us for insisting on preserving our right to live a normal life in a Jewish state of our own – to live in it, work in it and rest on our holidays. And twice because we are part of the enlightened world, a world of free nations which champions liberty, tolerance and democracy as supreme values in contrast with the barbarity, tyranny and fanaticism which every terrorist all over the world worships.

The torch of liberty which we carry alone in the darkness of the Middle East is the one which the murderers seek to extinguish. But it will not be extinguished, as we refuse to capitulate to violence. We refuse – and we will always refuse – to abandon our lives as Jews, Israelis and free people, and we will never let go of the sword which defends the torch of our independence.

By standing in this house, which symbolizes more than anything the sovereignty of the Jewish people in the land of Israel and the liberty of our citizens in a democratic regime, we are defeating the ongoing onslaught against us.

In the coming weeks, this house will be forced to make difficult decisions, which are vital to the security, prosperity and future of the State of Israel. The Government will submit for democratic decision the difficult issues which will determine the character of the State and the nature of our lives here in the coming years.

Such decisions are not easy. We must also take into account those who oppose them and those who will be adversely affected by our decisions, and it is incumbent upon us to make an effort to understand them and relieve their suffering through substantial aid.

However, the duty of a national leadership, which is embodied here, in this house, is to make decisions using a broad national vision.

The Knesset is the supreme institute of Israeli democracy. As long as it has not made a decision, we are facing contention! Once it has made its decision – unity!

A democratic decision by the majority of the members of this house is the key to creating a wide national consensus, which is the fundamental basis for the existence and success of the state.

Members of Knesset,

The IDF forces are currently operating deep inside the Gaza Strip, to foil and sabotage the shooting against the Jewish communities inside and surrounding the Gaza Strip. Thousands of soldiers, together with members of other security forces, are risking their lives with courage and skill to enable the residents of Sderot, the communities around it and the communities of the Gaza Strip to maintain normal lives. The area of civil confrontation in Israel has been shifting from one sector to the next, from north to south, from the city centers to the border settlements. Every time it is a different population which is forced to shoulder the heavy burden.

The situation in Gaza has taught us that we cannot settle for active defense, assistance to the areas in confrontation or even IDF offensive activity. It will be difficult for us to pursue them if Israel finds itself in a political stalemate, isolated in the international community.

The readiness of many members of the Security Council to denounce Israel for its defensive activities has taught us that the world is no longer interested in the question of who started and who is to blame.

The world is not too concerned by the firing of rockets and missiles at Jewish communities or by the murder of women and children. Furthermore, it condemns us for our actions to protect ourselves and our children.

This is the international reality.

Therefore it is important to guarantee that our friends in the world, primarily the United States, will stand by us and help us thwart the diplomatic campaign, while the IDF thwarts the terror campaign. This understanding found expression last week in the American veto at the Security Council. It exists only due to the fact that the United States knows that Israel has been acting, at its own initiative and with the widest possible international coordination, to produce a positive change.

The policy of my government has always been that there could be no political progress before the elimination of terrorism. This principle was fully recognized in President Bush's vision and in the Roadmap, and we are committed to it.

Israel adheres to its support of the Roadmap, which is the only plan to enable progress toward a viable political agreement. This plan compels the Palestinians to take a series of practical steps towards the eradication of terrorism and a fundamental governmental reform, before progress can be achieved toward political negotiations.

To date, the Palestinians have done nothing to abide by their commitments under the Roadmap. On the contrary – they have increased the terror attacks, the violence and incitement in every sector, and have refrained from promoting reforms. The blame for the political deadlock and their inability to progress toward a realization of their national aspirations rests solely on their shoulders.

Israel is interested in renewing the political negotiations under the Roadmap. However, as long as the Palestinians continue to evade all the commitments made to us, the United States and the international community, regarding the fight against terrorism and comprehensive reform, there can be no progress on the political negotiations.

As long as there is no genuine partner for peace and until such time as there is a Palestinian partner who will fulfil all the commitments under the Roadmap and with whom we can enter into political negotiations and make progress toward peace, Israel is forced to take steps of its own to consolidate its political and international standing, improve its ability to provide security for its citizens and fight terrorism, and improve the humanitarian condition of the civilian population.

I reiterate and emphasize, the Roadmap was and is the only political plan accepted by the State of Israel, and we adhere to it. The negotiations in accordance with the Roadmap will be renewed only once the Palestinians fulfil all those prior conditions which I detailed.

It is for this reason that the Government initiated the plan to disengage from the Gaza Strip. It is no secret that this plan is a source of great controversy among the public. As I have promised in the past, I intend to submit this plan for Knesset debate and approval in two weeks time, on October 25.

The Knesset will hold an open discussion on the Government's plan, at which I will present in full all the considerations which motivated the Government to initiate the plan.

Each member will have the opportunity to review the documents, study the subject at length, express their opinion and vote.

This is how a democratic regime operates.

And it will be the first in a series of difficult decisions which the Government will submit to the Knesset during the upcoming session.

Mr. President, Members of Knesset,

After the Knesset approves the plan – as I believe it will – we can start implementing it in accordance with a practical and detailed timetable.

This way we can carry out the decisions of the Government and Knesset during 2005, strictly monitoring the developments on the ground.

We must preserve our ability to constantly examine the political and security situations and adjust our actions to the reality, in order to best serve Israel's interests, primarily the ability to defend ourselves and confront terrorism.

The second decision which the Knesset will be required to make concerns the Relocation and Compensation Bill.

This Bill will be submitted to the Knesset during the first week of November, detailing all the arrangements for compensation to residents who will be forced to relocate their homes and their communities.

I know, and we must all realize, how difficult it is for a family to abandon its lifestyle. After all, these are people who were sent to the Gaza Strip by Israeli governments. Some of them have been living there for thirty years, some even more. Each one built a home, raised a family. Children were born there and people are buried there.

I know and understand their pain. I know how difficult it is to leave a home which you built with your bare hands, a field you ploughed, a greenhouse you nurtured, a tree you planted, a garden you tended. The land, the landscape, the memories.

I feel sorry for all those who refuse to understand it, those who rejoice at the uprooting, whose sole desire is to witness the images of Jewish settlers torn from their land.

I, on the other hand, feel their pain, which is more real and more deep than anyone can imagine.

And I say to our brethren the settlers – despite all the harsh words and the stormy emotions – my hand will always be extended to them and my heart will always be open to them, to understand them and help them bear the changes which they will be forced to experience.

This is the reason I have chosen Yonatan Basi to head the administration – a man of the land, a devout man, a resident of the borderland, who knows and understands what I know and understand. I have instructed him, and all those engaged in this matter, to act with the maximum sensitivity and generosity towards the settlers, and this is what we will do.

From this podium I thank him for agreeing to take on this heart-rending mission, a mission which has torn his own heart too.

Ladies and Gentlemen, distinguished Knesset,

In the coming period, the Knesset will be forced to address not only political and security decisions.

I stated, even before I was elected Prime Minister, that Israel does not have the ability or the privilege to choose between the political-security banner and the socio-economic one. It must wave both banners at the same time.

My Government inherited an economy which was on the verge of complete financial collapse, as a result of the global and local crisis of the year 2000.

Not many are aware of just how close the economic waves were to drowning the entire economic ship in the vortex.

We were compelled to take harsh emergency steps, which adversely affected many sectors of society. We were forced to make cuts and were not always able to assist those among us who needed assistance, as they needed air to breathe.

We did not hesitate to tackle a series of subjects, which I can say – as one who has served as Minister in many governments in numerous capacities – have not been tackled since the establishment of the State.

I am convinced that this Government will be remembered as the most revolutionary government in the economic sphere in many years.

The reforms which we have carried out – and those we are expected to carry out in the coming year – curbed the deterioration and placed the market on a solid basis for growth renewal.

- We acted in the capital market to rescue the pension funds and protect the members' savings from huge deficits.
- We carried out a comprehensive reform in the work market, including extricating 40% of the foreign workers, and produced some 90,000 new jobs for Israelis in the past year.
- We reduced the tax burden on the middle class, and will continue tax reductions to reach every working citizen. By this we have encouraged entrepreneurship and work in the marketplace.
- We renewed the momentum of foreign investment which is expected to reach $5 billion this year, while we are preparing for a comprehensive reform in encouraging capital investment and

transforming Israel into a competitive factor in the global arena in this field.

- We privatized *El Al* and *Zim* and will continue with the privatization of the banks and *Bezek* this year.
- We have carried out a series of projects in the field of infrastructures, primarily the entry of natural gas into the electricity market and water desalination plants, some of which will become operative this year.
- We formulated a five-year plan, with an overall investment of 20 billion NIS, to develop the railway system in Israel. The train connecting Tel Aviv and Ben-Gurion airport was inaugurated this week, a segment part of the train that will travel to Modiin, and from there to Jerusalem.

Mr. President, Members of Knesset,

We are currently at a crucial moment socially and economically.

The economic stabilization is complete with a steady interest of some 4%; the exchange rate is stable; inflation is negligible; there is increased foreign investment simultaneously with the guarantees which we have received from the United States Government; and there is growing confidence on the part of the international markets, as was manifested, inter alia, (and I suggest that everyone look into it) in the *Economist* rating, which placed Israel third among the rising markets.

The coming year could mark the turning point in the difficult transformation process from stagnation to growth, from recession and slump to a new period of growth and prosperity.

These trends find expression in the state budget which will be submitted for Knesset approval, during the first week of November.

Approval of the budget and the reforms accompanying this budget is vital in order to achieve the required transformation.

At this point I declare the supreme national goal to be – after we have succeeded in stabilizing the market – the creation of new jobs, to alleviate the plight caused by unemployment. In the second quarter of the year there were some 288,000 unemployed in the State of Israel, which constitutes 10.7 percent of the work force. This rate is too high.

All the government economic activities in the coming year are slated to begin reducing this rate to a tolerable level.

Creating work places in a modern market cannot simply be dictated by the Government. What is required is an overall economic policy which will create for the market, primarily the private sector, the ability and incentive to produce more, sell more, export more, and thus create new work places for Israelis.

Therefore we will continue to direct resources to the productive market by continuing cuts in the public sector; increasing competition which results in business growth, privatizing and encouraging external investment, primarily in the field in which we enjoy a relative edge – the technological field.

We will continue the large structural reform, mainly a comprehensive reform in the capital market and the banking system, to reduce centralization. We will also initiate a comprehensive reform in the Real Estate market, the main purpose of which is to best utilize Israel's land reserves for growth, without unnecessary bureaucracy.

We have reached agreements with the leadership of the local authorities, which include the allocation of hundreds of millions of Shekels for a joint process of recovery and efficiency in local authorities.

Simultaneously with the economic reforms, in 2005 we will start the most important reform of all – education reform.

Our hearts were filled with pride last week over the extraordinary scientific achievement by the Israeli scientists who won the Nobel Chemistry Prize, Prof. Avraham Hershko and Prof. Aharon Chechanover.

They prove to the world – but first of all to ourselves – the glorious achievements towards which the Jewish mind can lead us.

The Dovrat Reform, for the implementation of which we allocated 1.7 billion NIS this year alone, is the key to guaranteeing our moral future, concurrently with being a vital step towards closing social gaps.

Our goal is to provide every child in Israel with the best possible basis and equal opportunities to support themselves, contribute to society, but mainly – to realize all their talents and abilities.

Mr. President, Mr. Speaker, distinguished Knesset,

Just as in the political and security fields there are no difficult decisions which are not painful, the same applies to the socio-economic field. The structural reforms constitute a fundamental change, and many workers feel, understandably, that they might be adversely affected. I understand these concerns.

I am aware – perhaps more than some of the Government critics – of the difficulties and hardships that some of the citizens, certainly the weaker ones, experience daily.

I sympathize with the feelings of despair of those who have no employment and the anxiety of those who could lose their jobs and livelihood.

Therefore, all these reforms must be carried out through dialogue with the workers, but they also require their understanding that the reforms will be carried out – all of them, in full.

The attempt to paralyze the market by wild strikes will not succeed.

These strikes, primarily in the essential services, hurt the employees, mainly those from the private sector whose businesses are paralyzed as a result of strikes in the public sector.

It is therefore my intention to initiate a proposal to establish a system of dialogue and agreement between the Government, the employers and the employees, in order that we may carry out the necessary reforms and at the same time avoid any damage to the vital sectors of Israel's economy.

I call upon you, Knesset members, to take an unequivocal stand: in the political sphere, as in the economic one, argument is allowed, protest is allowed, even cries are allowed, but what cannot be allowed is a devastating blow to our lives and our ability to act together to promote national interests.

Members of Knesset,

We are facing difficult decisions. You are the national leadership of the citizens of Israel and therefore you will be required to make decisions and lead the public towards the implementation of those decisions.

As I said at the beginning of my address – this is the essence of democratic life: we part in contention until the decision is made, and once it is made, we unite in its implementation.

The Knesset is the elected institute and it alone will discuss and decide. We will all accept its verdict and act together, with true unity, to implement the decisions.

We have a mandate to decide,

We have a mandate to rule,

We have a mandate to act together, in full agreement, for the entire people of Israel.

Thank you.

‹85›

Address by Secretary General of ASEAN H.E. Ong Keng Yong (18.10.2004)

Mr. Yong said that ASEAN and India need to work closely in maintaining peace and stability, expanding economic linkages and in areas such as science and technology, energy security, health and ICT. He also emphasized that ASEAN and India "should develop extensive people-to-people interactions".

Defining Moments in ASEAN-India Relations

1. I am honoured to be invited to deliver this lecture under the India-ASEAN Eminent Persons Lecture Series. I would like to thank the organiser, the Research and Information System for the Non-Aligned and Other Developing Countries (RIS) of India, for providing me the opportunity to speak to such a gathering of distinguished persons.
2. Southeast Asia and India are no strangers. The civilisational links go back thousand of years. These linkages manifest themselves in the many historical monuments, the rich cultural heritage, the religious affiliations, the diverse culinary delights and the linguistic influences in Southeast Asia. I remember a quote describing India from the famous American author, Mark Twain, who said *"India is the cradle of the human race, the birthplace of human speech, the mother of history, grandmother of legend and great grandmother of tradition."*
3. The contemporary relationship between Southeast Asia and India was shaped by events of the time. After independence, India acted as an inspiration for many newly independent nations in Southeast Asia being the largest democracy in the world. At the same time, these countries in Southeast Asia and India recognised the strategic importance of developing relations with one another. In fact, the Indian navy held its first-ever naval exercise outside the Commonwealth with Indonesian navy and India and Indonesia signed a bilateral cultural agreement, both in 1960.
4. Unfortunately, the relationship remained lukewarm for the next three decades due to the divergence in ideological outlook and security relationships during the Cold War. Relations were put back on track

with the adoption of the "Look East Policy" by India in 1991 and ASEAN's strong desire to forge closer ties with India.

5. India became a Sectoral Dialogue Partner of ASEAN in 1992, focusing cooperation in economic and development cooperation. This was the first defining moment in ASEAN-India dialogue relations. The second defining moment in ASEAN and India relations came about three years later in December 1995 when India became a full Dialogue Partner of ASEAN. This elevated the interactions between ASEAN and India from the senior official to the ministerial level and enabled cooperation in the political and security field, including India's participation in the ASEAN Regional Forum (ARF), the only such security forum in the Asia-Pacific. The third defining moment occurred when ASEAN and Indian leaders agreed to their annual summit.

6. This transformation did not come easily. The financial crisis of 1997 and the developments in South Asia also affected the dialogue relations between ASEAN and India. However, ASEAN-India dialogue relations endured these challenges and are now on the upswing. This paved the way for both sides to enter into a new level of a strategic partnership, which will see the signing of a Joint Declaration and the adoption of a Plan of Action for a forward-looking relationship at the forthcoming ASEAN-India Summit in November 2004 in Vientiane, Laos. That will be the next defining moment in the relationship. These defining moments in ASEAN-India relations remind me of the words of the great soul, Mahatma Gandhi who said, *"Strength does not come from physical capacity. It comes from an indomitable will."*

ASEAN and India in the Big Picture

7. Globalisation, widely defined as the rapid increase in cross-border economic, social, technological exchange under conditions of capitalism, and its challenges have brought ASEAN and India closer compared with the Cold War years when both had divergent worldviews and domestic policies. At the same time, many other developments are exerting pressure on our relationship.

8. The September 11, 2001 attacks on the United States and the subsequent terrorists attacks that we are seeing in many parts of the world have become a new threat to global and regional security. Southeast Asia and India are not spared this menace as shown by recent terrorist attacks in the region. This non-conducive circumstance is against the desire of ASEAN and India to create an environment of peace and stability, which is essential to propel and spur the positive economic growth being enjoyed by both regions.

9. Proliferation of nuclear technology and materials is another concern of the international community, including ASEAN and India. The

spread of nuclear technology and materials could have far-reachin implications, especially when it falls into the hands of unscrupulou individuals or terrorists. ASEAN welcomes India's support for th Southeast Asia Nuclear Weapon Free Zone (SEANWFZ) Treaty, whic aims at making ASEAN a nuclear-free zone, for the purposes c promoting world peace and security.

10. Regional security and stability also hinges on other threats an challenges, especially the non-traditional issues such as maritim security, trafficking in drugs, arms smuggling and human trafficking These problems cannot be tackled by any single country or a grou of nation-states. They must be handled and managed collective because of their transnational nature.

11. The insufficiency of confidence-building measures, polic predictability, transparency and mutual understanding in the realm regional security cooperation is a troubling thought. As we work c the immediate economic concerns and socio-cultural development agenda, the governments of ASEAN and India must also act togeth to improve regional conditions to promote security and stability.

12. Unilateralism and disregard for international law require the attenti of ASEAN and India since they have far-reaching effects on t future of inter-state relations. Unilateralist approach and selective u of international laws will victimise the small, poor and vulnerat countries. Secretary-General of the United Nations, Kofi Annan, his recent address to the 59th UN General Assembly has emphasis the importance of the rule of law and that *"it must be put to practi and permeate the fabric of our lives"*.

Competitiveness is survival

13. We in ASEAN have made it a priority to remain competitive in t globalisation era. The ten economies of ASEAN are working toget to enhance their collective competitiveness through various ma initiatives such as the implementation of the ASEAN Free Trade A (AFTA), ASEAN Investment Area (AIA) and the fast tracking of priority sectors. Greater economic integration is not only for industr located in the region but also for investors and consumers as w Freer trade eases the burden of procuring raw materials a intermediate goods elsewhere and this, for one, would dr manufacturing companies in ASEAN to be more cost competit and likewise enjoy economies of scale. There is no denying that a competitive manufacturing sector attracts foreign direct investme (FDI), the growth of supporting industries in the region would stimulated as well. The ultimate beneficiaries would be the consum in ASEAN with wider choice of quality goods and services an competitive prices.

14. As AFTA reduces the tariff on goods and promotes more intra-ASEAN trade, AIA was created to ensure that investments flow freely within the region and that the principle of non-discrimination is applied. The AIA arrangement allows investors to harness the various complementary advantages of ASEAN Member Countries in order to maximize business and production efficiency at lower costs. As for accelerating regional integration through the 11 priority sectors in which the region enjoys competitive advantage, ASEAN is drafting the roadmap for each priority sector to chart out clear milestones for further integration. The 11 priority sectors are automotives, wood-based products, rubber-based products, textile/apparels, agro-based products, fisheries, electronics, healthcare, information and communications technology (ICT), air travel and tourism.

15. There is no choice for ASEAN but to constantly review its strategies and policies to make ASEAN more business-friendly and competitive. The end-in-mind is to offer unparalleled opportunities to the business community to leverage upon. Such opportunities are not confined to the traditional sectors but extended to those in the "New Economy" as well. In other words, we are not neglecting the knowledge-based sectors. Economic integration in ASEAN is not an option but a survival imperative. Regions across the globe are also integrating, opening up their markets and making available bigger markets in order to be more attractive to business people and investors. ASEAN Member Countries cannot afford to be complacent. To make itself even more attractive, ASEAN has embarked on economic integration beyond the borders of ASEAN through the various proposed FTAs with China, Japan, India, the Republic of Korea, Australia and New Zealand. Thus, ASEAN is adding more breadth and depth to its collective size.

ASEAN and India Weaving a Regional Fabric

16. ASEAN and India are natural partners. Geographically, India shares maritime borders with Indonesia and Thailand and a land border of 1,600 kilometres with Myanmar. History-wise, I have talked about Indian legacy in ASEAN.

17. On the economic front, India is an emerging economy of the world with a Gross Domestic Product of more than US$500 billion and a consumer market of more than 1.2 billion people. India will grow steadily by 6 per cent in the next few years. India is also committed to implementing its free trade agreement with ASEAN covering trade, investment and services. India's trade with ASEAN is already US$13 billion. In comparison, trade with South Asian Association for Regional Cooperation (SAARC) countries is only US$7 billion. India expects

to achieve a trade figure of about US$30 billion by 2007 with ASEAN in the light of the increasing services transactions, investments, projec executions and labour flows as well as a diversifying trade baske with manufacturing goods playing an increasing role.

18. It is in India's interest to forge a closer partnership with ASEAN fo a number of reasons. The per capita income of ASEAN is twice tha of India and ASEAN is rapidly opening up market opportunities ASEAN has a rich natural resource base. India eyes the possibilitie of integrating into the value chain of multi-national companies thrivin in ASEAN. Besides, countries like Malaysia, Singapore and Thailan are becoming major investors in India, especially in infrastructur development and venture capital activities.

19. India is also interested in plugging itself to the East Asia econom due to its latent potential. The Indian economy is increasingly integrate with East Asian economies. The East Asian countries account fo nearly 25% of India's total trade. India has a web of cooperatio with East Asian countries, especially ASEAN through the ASEAN India dialogue process, the bilateral free trade agreements wit Singapore and Thailand and sub-regional initiatives such as th Mekong-Ganga Cooperation and the Bangladesh-India-Myanmar-Sr Lanka-Thailand Economic Cooperation (BIMST-EC). India believe that its dynamic economy of over US$500 billion and its capabilitie in software and services that complements with East Asia's hardwar and manufacturing will be attractive reasons for a Pan Asian economi integration. The former Indian Prime Minister Atal Bihari Vajpaye had already mooted the idea of an Asian economic communit comprising the ten ASEAN economies and economies of Chin Japan and the Republic of Korea, in October 2003 at the ASEAN India Summit in Bali, Indonesia.

Advancing the Viable Partnership

20. ASEAN and India need to focus on developing a partnership that ha the dual objectives of addressing the challenges of globalisation an working closely to reap the opportunities of the same univers phenomena. There are enough opportunities and challenges to comp ASEAN and India to work closely in maintaining peace and stabilit expanding economic linkages and improving the critical huma capacities.

21. With its dynamic economic growth and superiority in comput software, engineering and sciences, India will play an important ro in maintaining the peace, stability and prosperity of the region. Ind has acceded to ASEAN's Treaty of Amity and Cooperation i Southeast Asia in 2003 signalling its desire to contribute to the peac

and security of Southeast Asia. India is an active member of the ASEAN Regional Forum (ARF), and it has worked together with ASEAN in several areas, including search and rescue, and counter sea piracy to help advance the ARF process.

22. The ARF should be utilised vigorously to promote peace and stability by allowing participants to become more familiar with the dynamics and realities of the security environment and created awareness of each other's strategic preoccupations. Like-minded countries of the Asia-Pacific and beyond can be encouraged to cooperate more extensively with the ARF agenda.

23. ASEAN and India, through the ARF and other multilateral fora, should also address non-traditional security threats or transnational concerns such as maritime security, trafficking in drugs, arms smuggling and human trafficking. ASEAN and India could also work together to curb the proliferation of nuclear technology and materials.

24. ASEAN and India could work together with other like-minded countries to strengthen the United Nations to demonstrate their commitment towards multilateralism and ensure that the world body remains the sole guardian of international laws, and the protector of the weak and vulnerable.

25. With increasing competition and the need to remain ahead in this era of knowledge-based globalised economy, ASEAN and India must expand and deepen their economic linkages. ASEAN and India should work closely under the Framework Agreement on Comprehensive Economic Cooperation to realise their economic potentials in trade in goods and services and investment as soon as possible. By doing so, ASEAN and India could enhance their respective attractiveness as FDI destinations and increase their competitiveness as a producer, exporter and service provider in the global market place.

26. ASEAN and India could work closely together with other developing countries under the auspices of the World Trade Organisation (WTO) to ensure greater equity in global trade and that globalisation benefits all countries. We should not allow global trade to be manipulated for the benefit of a handful of rich countries and large multinationals.

27. ASEAN and India should also look at expanding air, sea and land transport linkages to promote trade, tourism, and other economic activities. Trade fairs and business summits should be held on a regular basis to assist each other's business communities to find right partners for joint ventures and business deals. Improving travel-related regulation will also help to spur tourism and boost the travel business industry.

28. Cooperation in science and technology should be expanded to include commercialisation of new technologies such as biotech and pharmaceuticals. Constant innovation and cutting-edge research are indispensable if ASEAN and India want to move up the value chain to reduce cost and to reap returns. Combining the talents of 1.2 billion people of India and 500 million citizens of ASEAN will certainly make a huge market base for our industries and enhance our competitive position in the global economy.
29. Energy security in another area of common concern to both of us. ASEAN and India could look into promoting sustainable and optimal utilisation of energy, and alternative source of energy. In addition, both sides should consider measures to enhance trade and investment in the energy sector. The rising oil prices have made this a very pressing issue. Yet, for the longer term, energy security is an imperative for continued economic growth and prosperity.
30. In order to build and enhance the capacities of our peoples, ASEAN and India could share their expertise, experience and comparative advantages in critical sectors of the economy and other areas such as health and ICT. While both ASEAN and India are developing countries, we have amongst us some of the finest and talented people, and leading institutions.
31. ASEAN and India should develop extensive people-to-people interactions involving exchange programmes among youth, media personnel, academics, business people, government officials and artists and literati. We need to give more attention to the people's component in our partnership and to narrow the perception gaps among our people. More exchange of visits at the grassroots level can take place. The more they meet, the better they value each other. I have attached a 10-point wish list. As the great Indian statesman Jawaharlal Nehru eloquently said, *"We live in a wonderful world that is full of beauty, charm and adventure. There is no end to the adventures that we can have if only we seek them with open eyes."*

Conclusion

32. While ASEAN and India are busy engaging themselves to build a long lasting and durable partnership, both sides need to be vigilant or mindful of drawbacks that could momentarily cause irritation in the relations. Greater dialogue, interactions and channels of communications are needed to ensure we are constantly developing our mutual understanding to avoid any misapprehension. It is important to ensure decisions are swiftly implemented so that we could progress speedily in the many areas of cooperation. The momentum to enhance cooperation should not be held back by clouded lens and red tape.

33. The challenges and opportunities are aplenty for the partnership that ASEAN and India is forging. The partnership is what people in the business called "a work in progress". It is continuous and evolving. The partnership is not an end to itself. We in ASEAN and India need to nurture it carefully so that the partnership could withstand the knocks and challenges of globalisation and other concerns that might arise from time to time. We need to also provide new impetus to the partnership by expanding and deepening cooperation. ASEAN and India can be the catalyst for the region's peace and prosperity and deliver the change we all want to see.

Thank you.

Ten Points for Advancing ASEAN-India People-to-People Partnership

- Introduce more segments of people's sector into ASEAN-India dialogue partnership to broaden and deepen the foundation of this relationship
- Increase knowledge of ASEAN and India at all levels of society through more information exposure in mass media
- Identify 10 Indian cities for twinning with 10 ASEAN cities ('sister cities' concept)
- Intensify efforts to connect relevant non-governmental bodies in ASEAN and India dealing with development and welfare of women
- Innovate cultural exchange programmes/projects to extend coverage and reach to target audience
- Initiate dialogue among civil society organisations on promoting public health, environment protection and inter-civilisation relations
- Improve e-linkages among the national organisations responsible for youth affairs in ASEAN and India
- Institute exchange programmes for 10 Indian universities and 10 counterpart universities in ASEAN
- Inspire more intellectual interactions between ASEAN and India through more conferences, lectures and seminars
- Implement agreed plan of actions for grassroots cooperation between ASEAN and India

❮86❯

Address by the Prime Minister of Israel Ariel Sharon at the opening of the Discussions on the Disengagement Plan in the Knesset (25.10.2004)

Defending the decision to disengage in the Gaza Strip, Mr. Sharon said that he was firmly convinced that "this disengagement will strengthen Isreal's hold over territory which is essential to our existence...". He further mentioned that this was an essential and necessary step in the current situation and was "not meant to permanently freeze the situation which will be created."

Mr. Speaker, Members of Knesset,

This is a fateful hour for Israel. We are on threshold of a difficult decision, the likes of which we have seldom faced, the significance of which for the future of our country in this region is consistent with the difficulty, pain and dispute it arouses within us. You know that I do not say these things with a light heart to the representatives of the nation and to the entire nation watching and listening to every word uttered here in the Knesset today. This is a people who has courageously faced, and still faces the burden and terror of the ongoing war, which has continued from generation to generation; in which, as in a relay race, fathers pass the guns to their sons; in which the boundary between the frontline and the home front has long been erased; in which schools and hotels, restaurants and marketplaces, cafes and buses have also become targets for cruel terror and premeditated murder.

Today, this nation wants to know what decision this house will make at the end of this stormy discussion. What will we say to them, and what message will we convey to them? For me, this decision is unbearably difficult. During my years as a fighter and commander, as a politician, Member of Knesset, as a minister in Israel's governments and as Prime Minister, I have never faced so difficult a decision.

I know the implications and impact of the Knesset's decision on the lives of thousands of Israelis who have lived in the Gaza Strip for many years, who were sent there on behalf of the Governments of Israel, and who built homes there, planted trees and grew flowers, and who gave birth to sons and daughters, who have not known any other home. I am well aware of the fact that I sent them and took part in this enterprise, and many of these people are my personal friends. I am well aware of their pain, rage and despair. However, as much as I understand everything they are going through during these days and everything they will face as a result of the necessary decision to be made in the Knesset today, I also believe in the necessity of taking the step of disengagement in these areas, with all the pain it entails, and I am determined to complete this mission. I am firmly convinced and truly believe that this disengagement will strengthen Israel's hold over territory which is essential to our existence, and will be welcomed and appreciated by those near and far, reduce animosity, break through boycotts and sieges and advance us along the path of peace with the Palestinians and our other neighbors.

I am accused of deceiving the people and the voters because I am taking steps which are in total opposition to past things I have said and deeds I have done. This is a false accusation. Both during the elections and as Prime Minister, I have repeatedly and publicly said that I support the establishment of a Palestinian state alongside the State of Israel. I have repeatedly and openly said that I am willing to make painful compromises in order to put an end to this ongoing and malignant conflict between those who struggle over this land, and that I would do my utmost in order to bring peace.

And I wish, Mr. Chairman, to say that many years before, in 1988, in a meeting with Prime Minister Yitzchak Shamir and with the Ministers of the Likud, I said there that I believe that if we do not want to be pushed back to the 1967 lines, the territory should be divided.

As one who fought in all of Israel's wars, and learned from personal experience that without proper force, we do not have a chance of surviving in this region, which does not show mercy towards the weak, I have also have learned from experience that the sword alone cannot decide this bitter dispute in this land.

I have been told that the disengagement will be interpreted as a shameful withdrawal under pressure, and will increase the terror campaign, present Israel as weak, and will show our people as a nation unwilling to fight and to stand up for itself. I reject that statement outright. We have the strength to defend this country, and to strike at the enemy which seeks to destroy us.

And there are those who tell me that, in exchange for a genuine signed peace agreement, they too would be willing to make these painful compromises. However, regrettably, we do not have a partner on the other side with whom to conduct genuine dialogue, in order to achieve a peace agreement. Even prime ministers of Israel who declared their willingness to relinquish the maximum territory of our homeland were answered with fire and hostility. Recently, the chairman of the Palestinian Authority declared that "a million shaheeds will break through to Jerusalem". In the choice between a responsible and wise action in history, which may lead to painful compromise and a "holy war" to destroy Israel, Yasser Arafat chose the latter – the path of blood, fire and shaheeds. He seeks to turn a national conflict which can be terminated through mutual understanding into a religious war between Islam and Jews, and even to spill the blood of Jews who live far away.

Israel has many hopes, and faces extreme dangers. The most prominent danger is Iran, which is making every effort to acquire nuclear weapons and ballistic missiles, and establishing an enormous terror network together with Syria in Lebanon.

And I ask you: what are we doing and what are we struggling over in the face of these terrible dangers? Are we not capable of uniting to meet this threat? This is the true question.

The Disengagement Plan does not replace negotiations and is not meant to permanently freeze the situation which will be created. It is an essential and necessary step in a situation which currently does not enable genuine negotiations for peace. However, everything remains open for a future agreement, which will hopefully be achieved when this murderous terror ends, and our neighbors will realize that they cannot triumph over us in this land.

Mr. Chairman, with your permission, I will read several lines from a famous essay which was published in the midst of the Arab Revolt of 1936 – and we must bear in mind that the Jewish community in Israel numbered less than 400,000. This essay by Moshe Beilinson was published in "Davar", as I mentioned, during the murderous Arab Revolt of 1936 (and I quote): "How much longer? People ask. How much longer? Until the strength of Israel in its land will condemn and defeat in advance any enemy attack; until the most enthusiastic and bold in any enemy camp will know; there are no means to break the strength of Israel in its land, because the necessity of life is with it, and the truth of life is with it, and there is no other way but to accept it. This is the essence of this campaign."

I am convinced that everything we have done since then confirms these emphatic words.

We have no desire to permanently rule over millions of Palestinians, who double their numbers every generation. Israel, which wishes to be an exemplary democracy, will not be able to bear such a reality over time. The Disengagement Plan presents the possibility of opening a gate to a different reality.

Today, I wish to address our Arab neighbors. Already in our Declaration of Independence, in the midst of a cruel war, Israel, which was born in blood, extended its hand in peace to those who fought against it and sought to destroy it by force (and I quote): "We appeal – in the very midst of the onslaught launched against us now for months – to the Arab inhabitants of the State of Israel to preserve peace and participate in the upbuilding of the State on the basis of full and equal citizenship and due representation in all its provisional and permanent institutions."

A long time has passed since then. This land and this region have known more wars, and have known all the wars between the wars, terror and the difficult counter-actions undertaken by Israel, with the sole purpose of defending the lives of its citizens. In this ongoing war, many among the civilian population, among the innocent, were killed. And tears met tears. I would like you to know that we did not seek to build our lives in this homeland on your ruins. Many years ago, Zeev Jabotinsky wrote in a poem his vision for partnership and peace among the peoples of this land (and I quote): "There he will be saturated with plenty and joy, the son of the Arab, the son of Nazareth and my son."

We were attacked and stood firm, with our backs to the sea. Many fell in the battle, and many lost their homes and fields and orchards, and became refugees. This is the way of war. However, war is not inevitable and predestined. Even today, we regret the loss of innocent lives in your midst. Our way is not one of intentional killing.

Forty-eight yeas ago, on the eve of our Independence Day in 1956, against the background of the return of the bodies of ten terrorists who committed crimes in Israel, murderous acts in Israel, and who were delivered in wooden coffins to the Egyptians at a border crossing in the Gaza Strip. On this, the Hebrew poet, Natan Alterman wrote the following:

"Arabia, enemy unknown to you, you will awake when you rise against me,

My life serves as witness with my back against the wall and to my history and my G-d,

Enemy, the power of whose rage in the face of those who rise to destroy him until the day,

Will be similar only to the force of his brotherhood in a fraternal covenant between one nation and another."

This was during the time of the terrorist killings and our retaliatory raids.

Members of Knesset,

With your permission, I wish to end with a quotation from Prime Minister Menahem Begin, who at the end of December 1977, said on this podium (and I quote):

"Where does this irresponsible language come from, in addition to other things which were said? I once said, during an argument with people from Gush Emunim, that I love them today, and will continue to like them tomorrow. I told them: you are wonderful pioneers, builders of the land, settlers on barren soil, in rain and through winter, through all difficulties.

However, you have one weakness – you have developed among yourselves a messianic complex.

You must remember that there were days, before you were born or were only small children, when other people risked their lives day and night, worked and toiled, made sacrifices and performed their tasks without a hint of a messianic complex. And I call on you today, my good friends from Gush Emunim, to perform your tasks with no less modesty than your predecessors, on other days and nights.

We do not require anyone to supervise the Kashrut of our commitment to the Land of Israel!

We have dedicated our lives to the land of Israel and to the struggle for its liberation, and will continue to do so."

I call on the people of Israel to unite at this decisive hour. We must find a common denominator for some form of "necessary unity" which will enable us to cope with these fateful days with understanding, and through our common destiny, and which will allow us to construct a dam against brotherly hatred which pushes many over the edge. We have already paid an unbearably high price for murderous fanaticism. We must find the root which brings us all together, and must carry out our actions with the wisdom and responsibility which allow us to lead our lives here as a mature and experienced nation. I call on you to support me at this decisive time.

Thank you.

<87>

LTTE leader Mr. V. Pirapaharan (Prabhakaran) Hero's Day Speech (27.11.2004)

Mr. Prabhakaran called upon the government of Sri Lanka to resume peace talks, without conditions, on the basis of the Interim Self-Governing Authority as proposed by his organization. He cautioned the Sri Lankan government that if peace talks were further delayed he would be compelled to launch the freedom struggle of the Tamil nation.

'Today we are faced with a critical and complex situation, unprecedented in the history of our liberation struggle. We are living in a political void, without war, without a stable peace, without the conditions of normalcy, without an interim or permanent solution to the ethnic conflict. Our liberation struggle will be seriously undermined if this political vacuum continues indefinitely.

'Three years have lapsed since we entered into a ceasefire agreement with the Government of Sri Lanka, after three decades of protracted armed struggle. You are fully aware that during this period of ceasefire we have been making every endeavour, with sincerity and commitment, to seek a negotiated settlement to the Tamil national question through peaceful means. In various capitals of foreign nations, with Norway as facilitators, we engaged in peace talks with the government. The six sessions of negotiations held over the duration of six months, turned out to be futile and meaningless. Sub-committees that were set up for the de-escalation of the conflict, for the restoration of normalcy, for the rehabilitation and resettlement of the displaced and for the reconstruction of the war damaged infrastructure, became non-functional. In the meantime, the Sri Lanka government, having excluded our liberation organization, participated in the donor conference held in Washington, thereby undermining our status as equal partners in the peace process. It was in these objective conditions that our organization decided to express our displeasure and disappointment by temporarily suspending the talks. Our intention was not to terminate the talks and put an end to the peace process. During the period of suspension we urged the government of Mr Ranil Wickremesinghe to formulate and submit a draft proposal for an interim administrative structure. We emphasized that the envisaged interim administrative mechanism should be invested with adequate authority to deal with the rehabilitation of the war affected people and to reconstruct the war devastated Tamil nation.

'We were not satisfied with the three successive draft proposals on an interim set-up submitted by Ranil's government. The draft frameworks lacked adequate administrative authority and they were unacceptable to us. Ultimately, we decided to formulate our own set of proposals. We discussed with our people at different levels and consulted political experts, legal specialists and constitutional scholars in the Tamil Diapsora and finalized our proposals for an Interim Self-Governing Authority. This is an original and pragmatic framework embodying necessary structures and mechanisms to address the urgent existential problems of our people. The proposed framework is invested with substantial authority to effectively and expeditiously undertake all tasks of resettlement, rehabilitation, reconstruction and development in the Tamil homeland. We submitted this proposal to establish an Interim Self-Governing Authority to Ranil Wickremesinghe's government on the 1 November last year and also released it to the media for public debate.

'Some international governments welcomed our proposal, because it was the first time the Liberation Tigers had clearly and explicitly spelt out their political ideas in writing. Ranil Wickremesinghe's government did not reject our proposal for an Interim Self-Governing Authority to deal with the rehabilitation of the war affected people and to reconstruct the war devastated Tamil nation. His government viewed our proposals as different from their drafts, yet it agreed to resume peace talks on that basis, whereas the Sri Lankan Freedom Party outrightly condemned our interim administrative framework as the foundation for a separate Tamil state. As the leader of the Sri Lanka Freedom Party and as the President, Chandrika Kumaratunga went a step further by taking punitive action that plunged the southern polity into a crisis. Ranil Wickremesinghe's regime was suddenly and seriously destabilised when President Kumaratunga took over three key Ministries, including Defence. Eventually, following the dissolution of Parliament by the President, Ranil's government collapsed.

'The ethnic contradiction between the Sinhala and Tamil nations became acute as a consequence of the general elections held at the beginning of the year. The elections paved the way for the hegemonic dominance of Sinhala-Buddhist chauvinistic forces in the southern political arena. The Janatha Vimukthi Peramuna (JVP), an anti-Tamil political party steeped in a muddled ideology of racism, religious fanaticism and orthodox communism, won a substantial number of seats and became the third largest Sinhala political organisation. President Chandrika has embraced this racist political party as the most important ally and partner in her coalition government. This government is constituted by an unholy alliance of incompatible parties articulating antagonistic and mutually contradictory views and policies on the Tamil national question.

'While the verdict of the general election helped to reinforce Sinhala-Buddhist hegemonism in the Sinhala south, Tamil nationalism arose as a unified collective force in the northeastern Tamil homeland. The political ideals of our liberation organisation received the overwhelming support of the Tamil people. Our organisation received the popular endorsement as the sole representative of our people. Our proposals to establish an Interim Self-Governing Authority received a mandate from our people. The Tamil National Alliance gained a sweeping victory by winning twenty-two seats, thereby becoming the political voice and the democratic force representing our liberation organisation. As never before, this general election has polarized the Sinhala and Tamil ethnic formations into two distinct nations, as two separate peoples with divergent and mutually incompatible ideologies, consciousness and political goals.

'Though there was a change of government in southern Sri Lanka and chauvinistic forces were able to gain political power, we continued to observe ceasefire and wanted to promote the peace process. We informed the Freedom Alliance government of Chandrika Kumaratunga, through the Norwegian facilitators, that we were prepared to resume peace talks based on our proposal to set-up an Interim Self-Governing Authority. It was at that time confusion and policy differences emerged within the ruling coalition.

'Politically, the most powerful partner in the Alliance, the JVP, vehemently opposed granting political rights or devolution of power to the Tamil people. It has severely criticised the Norwegian government, which plays the role of facilitator. It has also outrightly rejected our proposal for an Interim Self-Governing Authority. The JVP has warned that it would break away from the ruling coalition if peace talks resumed on the basis of our proposal. The extremist, hard-line attitude of the JVP towards peace and ethnic reconciliation has become a major challenge to Chandrika Kumaratunga.

'The government of Kumaratunga is facing a multi-dimensional crisis. On one side, the international community is exerting pressure on the government to resolve the ethnic conflict through peaceful means. On the other, the donor countries continue to insist that granting of the pledged aid package is conditional upon progress in the peace talks. Furthermore, the economy of the country is sliding into an abyss. With these multiple problems, the government is compelled to engage the LTTE in peace negotiations. But the internal contradictions and the fundamental policy differences in the ruling alliance have become a stumbling block to the resumption of peace negotiations. There is no clear, coherent policy orientation, or a consensus approach within the political parties of the coalition government. Since she has aligned herself with political parties drenched in anti-Tamil racism, militarism and Sinhala-Buddhist hegemonism, the President cannot advance the peace process based on a coherent, consistent strategy and policy. This is the authentic political reality prevailing in southern Sri Lanka. This political reality of the lack of consensus is skilfully covered up and concealed to the international community.

'We submitted our proposals for an interim administration at the final stage of our negotiations with Ranil Wickremesinghe's government. The leadership of the United National Party continues to insist that peace talks can be resumed based on our set of proposals, but the Kumaratunga government is imposing a condition for the resumption of talks. The government says that any form of interim administration should be an integral part of a permanent settlement. While we are demanding an interim administrative set-up, the Kumaratunga government is insisting on talks for a permanent settlement to the ethnic conflict.

'There are important reasons as to why we are insisting on the formation of an interim administrative set-up as early as possible. As a consequence of a brutal and protracted war our people are facing urgent existential needs and immense humanitarian problems. Hundreds of thousands of displaced Tamils continue to languish in refugee camps in appalling conditions. In the meantime, the donor governments have pledged a massive aid package for the relief and rehabilitation of the war affected people. Therefore, it is of critical necessity that an interim administrative mechanism should be instituted with adequate powers to undertake the task of providing relief and rehabilitation to the suffering Tamil population and to reconstruct the war devastated Tamil homeland.

'Though we have entered into a ceasefire agreement and observed peace for three years and participated in the peace talks for six months, our people have not yet received any peace dividends. The intolerable burden of the day-to-day life problems is suffocating our people. Our people are desperately anticipating relief and resolutions to their urgent existential problems. For these reasons we want the immediate resumption of peace talks, based on our proposal, so that an interim administrative authority can be established as early as possible to address the grievances of our people. If some elements of our proposals are deemed problematic or controversial, these issues can be resolved through discussions at the negotiating table. Once the interim administrative authority is institutionalised and becomes functional we are prepared to engage in negotiations for a permanent settlement to the ethnic problem. That is our position.

Our position is reasonable. We are advocating this position in relation to the actuality of the concrete conditions prevailing in the Tamil homeland. Nevertheless, President Kumaratunga is inviting us for talks on a permanent solution, advancing a position that even an interim administrative set-up should be worked out within the contours of a final settlement. We can point out different reasons as to why she gives primacy to talks on a permanent solution. One reason could be her strategy to satisfy extremist racist elements, particularly to placate the JVP, who are deadly opposed to our proposal for an interim administration. The second reason could be to impress upon the international community that she is genuinely committed to resolving the Tamil national question. The third reason could be to prolong the peace negotiations indefinitely by opting to talk on a most intractable and complex issue. We can come up with several other reasons. Whatever the real reason, we can clearly and confidently say one thing; it is apparent from the inconsistent and contradictory statements made by President Kumaratunga that her government is not going to offer the Tamil people either an interim administration or a permanent solution.

'I do not wish to elaborate here the bitter historical experience of political negotiations we have engaged in with the Sinhala political leadership for more than fifty years to resolve the ethnic problem of the Tamil people. This is a political truth deeply buried in the collective psyche of the Tamil nation. Over a long period of time, we had talks on linguistic rights, on equal rights, on regional autonomy, on federal self-rule and entered into pacts and agreements, which were later torn apart and abrogated. Our liberation organisation is not prepared to walk the path of treachery and deception once again.

'The Sinhala political organizations and their leadership, which are deeply buried in the mud of Sinhala-Buddhist chauvinism, will never be able to comprehend the political aspirations of the people of Tamil Eelam. None of the major Sinhala political parties are prepared to recognize the fundamentals underlying the Tamil national question. None of the Sinhala political organizations is prepared to accept the northeastern region as the historical homeland of the Tamil-speaking people, that the Tamils constitute themselves as a distinct nationality and that they are entitled to the right to self-determination, including the right to secede.

The southern political movements do not have the maturity and magnanimity or the political sagacity to understand and accept the fundamentals of the Tamil national question, nor do they possess a consensus or a collective vision on the Tamil issue. What we can observe in the southern political spectrum is division, disunity and mutually divergent, contradictory notions and policies. We are surprised to note that President Kumaratunga is showing concern and interest in resolving the ethnic conflict when political parties aligned to her coalition government are advocating incoherent and irrational policies and articulating brazen forms of racism. We wish to make an open request to all the political parties constituting the governing Freedom Alliance, as well as to the opposition United National

Party, to declare publicly their official policy on the fundamentals of the Tamil national question, particularly on the core demands of the Tamil's concerning homeland, nationality and the right to self-determination.

'It will be meaningful to talk about a permanent settlement if the Sinhala political organisations have a clear, coherent policy, a proper insight and a consensus approach towards the Tamil national question. If not, there is no meaning in engaging in talks about a permanent solution. There is division, discord, confusion and contradiction within the Sinhala political leadership on the Tamil issue. Having realized the truth that the Sinhala political leadership will not be able to offer a reasonable permanent solution to our people, we submitted an interim solution. We expressed our desire to resume negotiations, based on our proposals for an interim mechanism, to provide relief to our people's urgent existential needs. But the government of Kumaratunga is deliberately impeding the peace efforts by insisting that talks should be about a permanent settlement. Having covered up the serious policy differences and internal contradictions behind the curtain of a loose political alliance, President Kumaratunga is accusing the Tamil Tigers of intransigence. We are confident that the international community will soon be able to see the real face of Chandrika, who is acting with a deceptive mask of peace.

'We cannot continue to be entrapped in a political vacuum without an interim solution or a permanent settlement, without a stable peace and without peace of mind. The Sinhala nation neither assimilates and integrates our people to live in co-existence nor does it allow our people to secede and lead a separate existence. We cannot continue to live in the darkness of political uncertainty, without freedom, without emancipation, without any prospects for the future. There are borderlines to patience and expectations. We have now reached the borderline. At this critical moment we wish to make an urgent appeal to the Sri Lanka government. We urge the government to resume the peace negotiations without conditions, based on our proposal for an Interim Self-Governing Authority. If the Government of Sri Lanka rejects our urgent appeal and adopts delaying tactics, perpetuating the suffering of our people, we have no alternative other than to advance the freedom struggle of our nation. We call upon the concerned international governments to understand our predicament and prevail upon the Sri Lanka government to resume peace talks based on our fair and reasonable stand.'

Speech by Uzbekistan President Islam Karimov in the 16th Session of Oliy Majlis (02.12.2004)

President Karimov said that Oliy Majlis (Parliament) had adopted 94 laws and 307 decrees during a five year period (since 2000). This has led inter alia to consolidation of political and economic sovereignty, international recognition, revival of cultural heritage and Islamic legacy and the establishment of democratic principles and civic institutions in Uzbekistan.

Assalomu-Alaykum, dear fellow countrymen!

Distinguished deputies!

First of all, it is with a great pleasure that I express my sincere greetings to you here today on the concluding session of Oliy Majlis.

Together we have almost passed a five-year period of time.

I believe it is our duty and obligation to express the deepest gratitude to the Almighty for helping us, those on the state's service, to protect our population from hardships and disasters, at the difficult, unstable and challenging time, and conclude our work that we started in the last century, today on the threshold of the new fifth year of the 21st century.

I may take it for granted that the legislative work of the Parliament and of you, esteemed deputies, not only helps us to deal with our today's issues, but also it serves as foundation for our prosperous and successful future.

By historic reckoning last five years is not a long period, but it will give us a great pleasure to recall its very special place in the development of our country and milestones of our political, social and economic life.

No doubt, the following historic efforts were realized in Uzbekistan during that period:

- consolidating of political, economic sovereignty and national statehood;
- boosting of recognition on international arena;
- reviving of cultural heritage, Islamic legacy, national customs and traditions;
- establishing of democratic principles and civic institutions;

Without bias it was defined in the reports, you having now in your hands, and in the preceding speech on the activity of the Parliament during this term by the Chairman of Oliy Majlis Mr. Erkin Khalilov that your multifaceted work in adopting of 94 laws and 307 decrees will promote positive transformations in our country, broaden its opportunities and potential and serve as a legal foundation for the benefit of the present and future generations.

It is not an exaggeration to say that we can witness an influence, impact and effect of the Parliament in every field of our life.

It is worth to point out particularly Uzbekistan's fast-growing economy, macroeconomic stability, positive changes in a variety of industries, growing exports, consolidated banking and financial system, implemented large-scale construction projects, and most importantly, rise in peoples real income and life standards.

I think there will be no mistake if we assess all these achievements as the practical outcomes and direct effects in our life of the laws and resolutions adopted by Oliy Majlis since 2000.

While speaking about the activity of the Parliament during this period, it is impossible to neglect the significant role and importance of our laws in providing the peace and security of our country, fighting against such challenges as religious extremism and international terrorism, and protecting the peaceful life of our people.

I believe, today it's necessary and timely to remember again the calls and statements expressed many times from the high rostrum of Oliy Majlis appealing to not only our people, but also the international community at large for vigilance and awareness, struggling for peace, along with the activity of the Parliament against the international terrorism, organized crime, nonproliferation of weapons of mass destruction and drug trafficking.

It is necessary to particularly underscore that the laws adopted in the sphere of economy, namely, on the issues of property ownership, private companies, small businesses and entrepreneurship, liberalization of manufacturing industries, reducing the responsibilities of the state in management and control, limiting its interference into the economic activity of companies, and first of all, into the activity of private companies are serving for the creation of the strong legal foundation and boosting our development.

Taking this opportunity, I would like to put a special emphasis on another issue. It is necessary to stress in particular that regardless of the importance and significance of the issues considered and discussed by our deputies during their deliberations, all adopted laws and resolutions are in line with today's requirements, meet the international legal standards, are adopted with the vision to our long and continuous future.

Special importance was paid to the protection of human rights and freedoms, ensuring the freedom of speech, in general, making the interests of a person a priority, enrooting democratic values into the minds of our people and, I think, that these dimensions should remain in the center of our attention in the future as well.

It is worth to note that in the process of building a new society, the principle of separation of powers among independent branches, which is the most important prerequisite and symbol of democracy, i.e. the issues of establishing legislative, executive and judicial authorities acting on these standards, became the foundation of the activity of the Parliament.

It is necessary to particularly mention the fact that you, esteemed deputies, have adopted the Laws on courts and public prosecutor aimed at reforming the judiciary system that were supported by our people and the international community. The same is true for a number of legal documents dealing with specialization of criminal and civil litigation, and especially, reviewing the laws and codes and making necessary amendments mitigating the criminal punishments, with consideration of principles of justice in protecting a person, his rights and interests.

Moreover, I feel obliged to mention that the laws and resolutions aimed at profoundly reforming of the agriculture, which is nowadays one of the crucial branches of economy, have served to raise the agriculture to a qualitatively new level, to meet modern standards, to increase its efficiency, and thus to improve the living standards of our population that predominantly lives in rural areas.

In brief, today there are all grounds to state with satisfaction the fact of substantial contribution of our Parliament, I repeat it, of you, dear people's deputies, into the process of further developing our country, protecting the peace and stability of our Homeland, realizing dreams and hopes of our people during this short time span.

Dear friends!

Today we are all living up with the breath and mood of the elections into the bicameral parliament and local councils to be held on 26th December for the first time in the history of our country.

We all should view this important political event as a process, which puts to test Uzbekistan's image and prestige in the international arena and before the world community, the extent of compliance of democratic reforms pursued in our country with international standards and requirements.

It is necessary to reiterate that the forthcoming elections, first of all, should be conducted in accordance with constitutional norms and principles, laws and norms on elections, freely, openly and transparently, without any external influence and pressure. They should be unbiased and fair, in other word, manifest voters' free will and aspirations. We all bear responsibility for that.

Seven international conferences and seminars on this issue were held over the last three months with the participation of 29 representatives, prominent scientists and political analysts from democratic countries and international organizations, including the UN, the OSCE, the EU, as well as authoritative American and Asian organizations. This once again proves that we have prepared for the elections in an open, transparent atmosphere.

It must be clear to everyone that we consider the experience of the international community and developed countries to be suitable in our intention to hold truly democratic elections that would meet international standards. In the process of preparing and conducting the elections we would like to accept their critical and at the same time fair remarks and recommendations.

We should demonstrate to the international community that we are not inclined to retire in our shell, complacently pretend that we know everything ourselves, applying a disparaging approach and neglecting others' experience and advice.

In a word, our hopes and aspirations are directed at one goal. It is to conduct in collaboration with international observers the elections on the highest level that would be second to none.

We are all well aware that not only elections are an opportunity for everyone to express his or her free will by voting for an appropriate candidate, but are also above all a fight.

It is natural that representatives of political parties and initiative groups taking part in this political process are to engage in debates and ardent disputes among themselves.

The nature and very essence of democracy demands such a fight and we all well understand this. However, I wish that at the same time those parties coming to the political arena, their leaders and supporters of candidates from initiative groups always remember that our people's and society's common interest, national unity and accord are above all.

In this regard, we have the right to expect that such notions as the peace and prosperity of the country, well being of the people that stand at the core of our national idea will become a common aim to all political forces participating in the elections.

Naturally, the political culture and activity of representatives from parties and initiative groups, voters and deputies their respect for and observance of our Constitution and laws should set an example to others and, especially, to the youth.

I believe that someone among you will be blessed to gain electorate's confidence and become the winner in this fight. Meanwhile, I hope that the Oliy Majlis within its power will continue its extensive work until the formation of the new parliament.

Standing at this highest rostrum, on my own behalf and on behalf of our people I would like to express a deep gratitude to you, dear deputies, for your fruitful work on the course of our homeland's prosperity and defense, social and economic development of our country. I wish you all sound health, happiness, success and luck in your future activity.

‹89›

Excerpts from Afghan President Hamid Karzai's inauguration speech (07.12.2004)

President Karzai said that the elections stood for "the reconstruction and development" of Afghanistan. He thanked the world community for its cooperation in rescuing Afghanistan "from the grip of terrorism" and urged Afghanistan's neighbours to support the country.

The attendance of representatives of various countries at this historic gathering is clear proof of Afghanistan's good relations and cooperation with the international community.

All the votes cast at the presidential election were for Afghanistan, whether they were cast for me or for any other candidate. All these votes were cast for the reconstruction and development of Afghanistan.

During the election campaign we told the people of Afghanistan about the future government's policy. It included the following main items: strengthening the security forces; ensuring full security and stability throughout the country; eradicating poppy cultivation; combating narcotics production and trafficking; disarmament and reintegration; tackling poverty; creating wealth and making efforts towards public welfare, particularly in rural areas.

Our fight against terrorism is not over, although, God willing, terrorism as a devastating phenomenon is no longer a serious threat to our country's stability. Its destructive activities, its involvement in narcotics production and trafficking and its activities in the region and throughout the world are cause for concern. To fight terrorism, there is still a serious need for regional and international cooperation. The continuation of this cooperation will help tackle the evil of terrorism in the world.

Afghanistan was rescued from the grip of terrorism as a result of the vital cooperation of the international community. The country has taken important steps towards building a system and bringing about peace, stability and security ever since and has successfully put a difficult era behind it.

The country is starting another phase in its life today as a legitimate colleague of the international community. The helpful and timely assistance of the USA and the efforts of the UN in the fight against terrorism and the reconstruction of the country's devastated institutions are worthy of special mention.

We also express our great appreciation to the European Union, Japan, Canada and a number of our neighbours in the region and other donor countries.

We hope to see the international community's cooperation with Afghanistan continuing. Afghans greatly appreciate the international community's moral and material support and will never forget it.

A stable, secure and strong Afghanistan is in the interests of our neighbours, the region and the world.

Afghanistan assures its neighbours that it will always remain their friend and colleague and expects similar treatment from them.

Dear compatriots, I congratulate you all on the beginning of this new phase in Afghanistan's modern history and pray for the success of the Afghan nation from God, the Almighty.

Index